INDIFFERENCE

INDIFFERENCE

On the Praxis of
Interspecies Being

NAISARGI N. DAVÉ

DUKE UNIVERSITY PRESS
Durham and London   2023

All rights reserved Printed in the United States of America on
acid-free paper ∞ Project Editor: Ihsan Taylor
Designed by Courtney Leigh Richardson
Typeset in Portrait Text by Westchester Publishing Services

Library of Congress Cataloging-in-Publication Data
Names: Davé, Naisargi N. (Naisargi Nitin), [date] author.
Title: Indifference : on the praxis of interspecies being /
Naisargi N. Davé.
Description: Durham : Duke University Press, 2023. |
Includes bibliographical references and index.
Identifiers: LCCN 2022054309 (print)
LCCN 2022054310 (ebook)
ISBN 9781478025139 (paperback)
ISBN 9781478020158 (hardcover)
ISBN 9781478027133 (ebook)
Subjects: LCSH: Human-animal relationships—Moral and ethical
aspects—India. | Animals and civilization—India. | Animal rights—
Moral and ethical aspects—India. | Indifferentism (Ethics) |
BISAC: SOCIAL SCIENCE / Anthropology / Cultural & Social | SOCIAL
SCIENCE / Ethnic Studies / Asian Studies
Classification: LCC QL85 .D385 2023 (print) | LCC QL85 (ebook) |
DDC 591.50954—dc23/eng/20230412
LC record available at https://lccn.loc.gov/2022054309
LC ebook record available at https://lccn.loc.gov/2022054310

Cover art: *6 April 2020, lockdown day 13*, 18 × 24 in. © dhruvi acharya.
Courtesy of the artist.

For Wendy

CONTENTS

INTRODUCTION. What Is Indifference?

I am not, I like to think, an indifferent person, and nor is this an indifferent book. By *indifference* I mean living with others in their otherness such that human and nonhuman animals might flourish in immanent encounters. Indifference to difference is an indifference to the thatness of others: not acquiring, not desiring, not in thrall, not hankering, not assimilating, not repairing, not consuming, not anthropologizing, not staring.[1] Indifference is the posture of immersion, side by side, rather than the face to face.[2]

Indifference is not normally thought of highly. As Madhavi Menon says, it conjures images of slouchy shrugs among other signs of self-centered apathy.[3] Yet these impressions are often tinged with a revealing envy for the insouciance of youth or, worse, racist, elitist, and ableist disdain for people going about their own business. In both my understanding of indifference and in Menon's, as she argues it in *Indifference to Difference: On Queer Universalism*, indifference is not a lack but a stance, a cultivated demeanor, that is born of the queer desire and the queer belief in an otherwise way of being.[4]

Let's be honest. There is no shortage of the opposite of indifference in our world, which is the desire for difference—finding, wrangling, and utilizing it. And where has this gotten us? Anthropology? Heterosexuality? Capitalism? Empire? Friends, I think we can do better.

---

1 Lauren Berlant is on the side of "beloved thatness," which they argue is a social principle different from love normatively constituted, if love too often seeks to hold, to have, and to forge. Thatness, Berlant says, makes space for a vision of the "impersonal world." Berlant, "A Properly Political Concept of Love," 690.

2 Tonkiss, "The Ethics of Indifference," 298.

3 Menon, *Indifference to Difference*, 14.

4 "Indifference," Menon writes, "argues for a radical break with the identity that undergirds liberal and conservative politics alike": Menon, *Indifference to Difference*, 2.

For Opacity

Curiosity is a trait often held in high regard, particularly among intellectuals, with its opposite—being incurious—viewed as a sign of dereliction. It must be twenty years now since I read an essay about Vladimir Nabokov's *Lolita*, which argued that we know Humbert Humbert is a sociopath when he comes upon a glass cabinet of mounted butterflies and fails to examine it.[5] I was troubled by this claim. Besides having to now wonder whether I might be a sociopath—an always unwelcome interpellation—I wondered at this premise that one's goodness is demonstrated by an interest in pinned butterfly carcasses. It is not Humbert I am trying to redeem (I confess I've never managed to appreciate *Lolita*) but it is incuriosity.

Curiosity is the foundation of anthropology, so fundamental that it is our common sense—normalized, not subject to much comment. But it has been a more explicitly valued disposition in multispecies anthropology, attributable, I think, to the field-defining work of Donna Haraway. Like any thinker to whom one is indebted, Haraway provides both departure points and homes in which one would like to dwell. This matter, regarding curiosity, is for me one of the points of divergence.

Haraway begins *When Species Meet* (2008) on a walk in the forest with her canine friend, Cayenne Pepper, and the anthropologist James (Jim) Clifford. There the threesome come upon an organic mass of moss and wood they call "Jim's dog." Haraway writes, "Jim's dog is a provocation to curiosity, which I regard as one of the first obligations and deepest pleasures of worldly companion species."[6] This commitment to curiosity leads Haraway to a vigorous undressing of the already naked Jacques Derrida, on the grounds that his unrobed shame before his cat spurs him into a philosophical reflection on the misogynistic, homophobic, carnivorous, ableist, and anthropocentric essence of Man rather than a curiosity about what this specific cat was thinking and whether she might want to play.[7] "Shame," Haraway writes, "trumped curiosity."[8] I find this either/or hierarchizing curious from the author of "A Cyborg Manifesto,"

---

5 Nafisi, *Reading Lolita in Tehran*, 25; Nabokov, *Lolita*.

6 Haraway, *When Species Meet*, 7.

7 Derrida, *The Animal That Therefore I Am*, 1–51. The central situation of this foundational text in animal studies is Derrida's "little cat" following him into the bathroom, believing this a momentary stop on the way to the kitchen, only to find him fully, frontally naked for his morning ablutions. The philosopher "follows" this experience, this mutual embarrassment, to the end(s) of anthropocentrism.

8 Haraway, *When Species Meet*, 22.

which professed, "One is too few, but two are too many."[9] Curiosity about the specific One is more vital than being stopped short in the face of one's unearned and illegitimate power? Are these states of being really at odds?

One answer to the last question is *yes*, but maybe not in the way Haraway intended. I think curiosity often functions to stop short the stopping short that *should* be the lot of those who look, stare, take in, pillage, acquire, ingest, dissect, admire, anthropologize, steal, exhibit, repair, voice, recoil, sell, and possess. Haraway suggests that, rather than stopping short, we do better by going forth, forming "knots, with actual animals and people looking back at each other."[10] A central precept of multispecies ethnography is this: that we be curious, that we look, and that we accept that being a being in this entangled world means being eaten by one another. Eyes and mouth, fist and heart.

When I read this text most recently—it is one of those books always on or near my desk—I had just that morning listened to a talk by Fred Moten. Moten describes how, in his childhood neighborhood, there were no fighting words quite like "What are you looking at? Are you looking at me?"[11] And I was reminded of Milan Kundera, who writes in *Immortality* that "looks were like weights that pressed her down to the ground. . . . [E]very day we are stabbed by thousands of looks."[12] This is not unrelated to John Berger's thesis in *Ways of Seeing* that these stabs that are looks are why women are nude, rarely naked, as was Derrida's privilege as he toweled and philosophized.[13] I think, too, of a moment Audre Lorde relates in *Sister Outsider*, in which she is stared at, in her inexpensive winter coat, by a white woman on a train and Lorde feels the recoil, the otherness, the whiteness of curiosity.[14] I can say for myself that, as a dyke, the curious gaze of normal people is rarely a pleasure. *Are you looking at me?* Shouldn't we at least have a say in who eats us?

An alternative to the curiosity ethos is provided by the Martinican French poet and philosopher Édouard Glissant. In *Poetics of Relation*, Glissant issues a demand for opacity: *We clamor for the right to opacity for everyone.*[15] Glissant contrasts opacity with the driver of Western thought: the requirement for

---

9 Haraway, "A Cyborg Manifesto," 143.

10 Haraway, *When Species Meet*, 42.

11 Fred Moten, *Poetry Reading, University of Toronto* (video, University of Toronto, posted April 5, 2017), https://www.youtube.com/watch?v=Ka37oU3O2Us.

12 Kundera, *Immortality*, 30.

13 John Berger, "Episode 2," *Ways of Seeing*, television series, BBC Two, 1972.

14 Lorde, "Eye to Eye," 147–48.

15 Glissant, *Poetics of Relation*, 194.

transparency, an epistemological and moral motivation that manifests through grasping and reduction, conquest and ingestion (I'm reminded of that glass case in Nabokov).[16] Glissant refuses this requirement for transparency, refuses to be on the side of the knower or the known, knowing both to be relations of taking rather than "giving on and with" (*donner-avec*).[17] He feels it so violently that he says it twice in the span of a few pages: "As for my identity, I'll take care of that myself."[18] Autological thought might read this autologically, which is to say, as an insistence on an essential molar lonesomeness. But that would be to misread Glissant. "The right to opacity," he writes, "would not establish [autology]: it would be the real foundation of Relation, in freedom."[19] The foundation of Relation lies not in the dubious right to gaze-available difference but in the exercise and respect of singular opacities.

I think it's telling that Glissant ends this brief section of *Poetics of Relation*, "For Opacity," with the opaque story of the fin de siècle French ethnographer Victor Segalen, who died mysteriously in the Breton woods with an open copy of *Hamlet* lying next to his body. Glissant's thesis is that the ethnographer died of curiosity—or, to put it differently, "died of the opacity of the Other, of coming face to face with the impossibility of accomplishing the transmutation that he dreamed of."[20] If only Segalen had known that "respect for mutual forms of opacity"—not the ethnological desire for difference—would have been the true realization of his ethical generosity![21] But now we see this Glissantian respect for mutual forms of opacity, this clamor for the right to it, increasingly in the turn of this latest century in anthropology and the arts. Perhaps fewer of us are dying of—or more to the point, being picked off by—curiosity.[22]

The clamor for opacity sounds in the work of the abstract expressionist, Julie Mehretu, a queer Ethiopian-born artist whose refusals of figuration are

16 Glissant, *Poetics of Relation*, 190.
17 Glissant, *Poetics of Relation*, 191–92.
18 Glissant, *Poetics of Relation*, 191–92. In the second instance Glissant phrases it, "As far as my identity is concerned, I will take care of it myself."
19 Glissant, *Poetics of Relation*, 190.
20 Glissant, *Poetics of Relation*, 193.
21 Glissant, *Poetics of Relation*, 194.
22 There is curiosity, and there is what we do with curiosity, the ends to which we pursue ours and the rights we believe it bestows. I thank Celeste Pang, who put the curiosity I am arguing against this way: "Lest I extinguish the other, I am extinguished." Segalen, whose extinguishing (transmutation) of the other was thwarted, was himself extinguished.

a direct homage to Glissant.[23] The clamor animates Audra Simpson's ethnographic refusals.[24] It is in Savannah Shange's Black girl methodology in which "you can follow me but I'm not gonna talk to you."[25] It is in Julietta Singh's unthinking mastery.[26] It is in John Jackson's thin and not thick description.[27] It is in Eva Giraud's rejoinder to Haraway, an ethic not of entanglement, but of exclusion or nonrelation—of at least *sometimes* just leaving folks alone.[28] It is in Denise Riles's right to be lonely; in Fran Tonkiss's right to the "precarious freedom . . . of the fragile trust in the indifference of others"; in Georg Simmel's mutual strangeness; in Paul B. Preciado's ephemeral brush in his trans man's body with universality, a "peaceful and anonymous place where everyone leaves you the fuck alone."[29] *As for my identity, I'll take care of that myself.* It is in Matei Candea's inter-patience, "an active cultivation of inaction."[30] Imagining life from the perspective of a lab-bound meerkat, Candea suggests, "ignoring another living being . . . emerges as a positive achievement in a world of predation."[31] It hums, too, in Audre Lorde's love poem "For Judith":

Hanging out
means being
together
upon the earth
boulders
crape myrtle trees
fox and deer
at the watering hole
not quite together
but learning
each other's ways.[32]

23 See Patterson-West, "Julie Mehretu."
24 Simpson, "On Ethnographic Refusal."
25 Shange, "Black Girl Ordinary," 15.
26 Singh, *Unthinking Mastery.*
27 Jackson, *Thin Description,* 158.
28 Giraud, *What Comes after Entanglement?*
29 Preciado, *Can the Monster Speak?*, 36; Riley, "The Right to Be Lonely"; Simmel, "The Stranger"; Tonkiss, "The Ethics of Indifference."
30 Candea, "I Fell in Love with Carlos the Meerkat," 249.
31 Candea, "I Fell in Love with Carlos the Meerkat," 249.
32 "For Judith," in Lorde, *Our Dead behind Us,* 42.

There is a curiosity here, yes, an awareness of other others who pose risk and promise, or maybe simply beauty. We might call this being together not quite together in our beloved thatnesses a relation of unfolding immanence.

Indifference is not, as Glissant says for opacity, the antithesis of relationality or the antithesis to relations of care. In fact, it is among the central beliefs of this book that care is born first of indifference, out of respect for the opaque thatness of the object other. The ethos of indifference—a not desiring *to do anything* with, for, and via the difference of others—is, for me, a response to what I think of as "compulsory intimacy," or the will toward ontological slippage, which makes a (post)humanist virtue of mixing when folks might rather be let alone and, in that being let alone, thrive in relations of regard.[33] My understanding of indifference is Relational: of mutually existing *in difference* rather than being different beings seeking to grasp, gaze, admire, and master the difference of others.[34] This book is about the praxis of being that exists

33 I am thinking here with Zakiyyah Iman Jackson's *Becoming Human*. Jackson analyzes the raciality that is at the heart of the human-animal distinction, a plastic raciality whose object is the abjection of all that is counter to whiteness. Jackson diagnoses in this will to plasticity what she calls an "ontological slippage," which operates not only, in the case of white supremacy, as a negating slippage among Blackness, femaleness, and animality *but now, too*, in the case of multispecies and posthumanist scholarship, as a celebratory slippage between human and animal that finds ethical promise in entanglement, analogy, and mixture: see Jackson, *Becoming Human*. See also Emily K. Crandall, "Interview: Zakiyyah Iman Jackson on *Becoming Human*," *Always Already Podcast* (July 20, 2020), in which Jackson says: "I wanted to push back against post-humanist notions that ontological slippage was . . . somehow ethical, in and of itself, because in looking at the history of Blackness, ontological slippage was less an ethical promise and something more like a racial nightmare" (https://alwaysalreadypodcast.wordpress.com/2020/07/02/jackson/). I'm reminded here of something Aniket Jaaware writes in his anti-caste literary manifesto: "We are not seeking 'humanity.' We are seeking an animality that lets be": Jaaware and Rao, *Practicing Caste*, 200.

34 This formulation of indifference as a *residing in difference* is indebted to Madhavi Menon, as well as to Gilles Deleuze. Menon writes, "Indifference . . . names an anti-ontological state of being that would acknowledge and embody difference without becoming that difference": Menon, *Indifference to Difference*, 2. Indifference as *being in difference* comes, too, from Deleuze's ontology of difference in *Difference and Repetition*. Deleuze makes a conceptual distinction between vernacular difference (difference in the everyday parlance of identity society) and *difference*. The former understands identity as primary and difference as secondary, manifesting as particular qualities that depart from the Same. *Difference*, according to his ontology of difference, is immersive. We live in difference, *are* difference, and this difference

there at the watering hole, one of awareness of, and response to, the presences of opaque others. In that, *Indifference* argues for an interspecies relational ethic premised on mutual regard rather than curiosity, love, or animus.

For Janine

I was born and raised in Atlanta, Georgia, the elder child of Gujarati parents of the Nagar Brahmin caste. My father's father, Jaymukh, was a customs officer of stern disposition who, with his wife, Nalini, and three youngest children, moved around the country as his posts were assigned. My father was left back in Ahmedabad, raised by aunts and uncles in the caste *pol* where he was born. My mother's father, Rustom Munshi, was a liberal judge, and her mother, Suvarna (née Majmudar), a poet. They, too, moved often for Rustombhai's postings, including a long residence in Bhopal, but lived primarily in the Nava-rangpura area of Ahmedabad in a bungalow called Nisarg.

Left largely to his own devices, my father hatched a plan to go to Amer-ica. He was accepted at Ohio State and informed his parents weeks before he departed. An uncle lent him money, and with the proverbial ten dollars in his pocket he set sail. He worked nights as a bellhop at the Columbus Sheraton and went on to earn an MBA at the University of Missouri. Toward the end of his program, he returned to Ahmedabad to be engaged to my mother, an ar-ranged marriage, though she had been permitted by her doting father to refuse twenty-four suitors prior. By the time she joined my father, he was employed in Atlanta. He worked as a suit salesman at the mall. My mom, despite her be-ginner's English, sold cosmetics door to door for Avon. I was born in 1975; my brother, Prerak, four years later.

What my household was doctrinaire about was patriarchy; less so religion. My paternal grandmother was observant. We converted the modest wet bar off the kitchen of our suburban home into a *mandir* for her, and her early morn-ing ritual self-flagellations served as my alarm clock. As for my father, when he was in the Ozarks he had gotten in with some Christians who took him to a Billy Graham rally. Something changed in him that day. In his briefcase he carried no images of us, nor of Krishna, but of a blue-eyed Jesus. Every night before sleeping, after completing our academic competence quizzes, he had

constitutes the Spinozan univocality of existence. Indifference to difference, or *being in difference*, is being indifferent to vernacular difference (the one premised on the primacy of the Same) and immersed instead in a difference that is in perpetual expression. This difference cannot be desired, for it simply *is*.

my brother and me recite the Lord's Prayer: Our Father, who art in heaven, hallowed be thy name.[35]

We ate dairy-rich vegetarian, a diet shaped by caste distinction rather than ethics, until I was around ten. My father, by now an executive at Fannie Mae, I think felt emasculated at dinners with southern businessmen and began to eat meat, particularly steak, and to enjoy wine, beer, and whiskey. At first this liberal attitude toward meat was delimited by the threshold of the home: we could eat Chicken McNuggets and Burger King burgers so long as we didn't require my mother to prepare meat for us. But soon this edifice crumbled and my brother and I ate as many hotdogs as we could handle, my mom serving them up quite tastily and—because complaint was not an option in my father's house—without complaint.

I was destined to be a medical doctor from utero and, since I had no say in this, took aggressively little interest in my education. I enrolled at the University of Georgia, as many of the AP kids in my high school did, and rented an apartment with my best friend and her boyfriend. By October I was a lesbian, taking women's studies classes and developing tastes for everything foreign to my closeted upbringing, including, in no small measure, pork chops and bacon. In my third year in Athens, I moved into a rental house off Prince Avenue. One Saturday morning I looked out the living room window to see a sinewy, gorgeous androgyne in jeans and a tank top, a carabiner of keys clipped to her belt loop, mowing our front grass. Never in all my days had I seen a vision like this. I asked my roommate, Kate, and her poet friend, K. C., if they knew who she was. "Janine," K. C. said. And then, in that way of hers that made everything sound sexually suggestive: "She's a vegan." That evening, at our usual Huddle House hangout, I ordered dry toast and black coffee for dinner and have been vegan ever since.

I still am not certain whether I became vegan to be desired by Janine or to be Janine, but either way she never gave me the time of day. I don't believe we ever so much as had a conversation—maybe I managed a shy hello from my

35 A Hindu reverence for Jesus and Christianity is also not unusual. The Lord's Prayer was taught in English and in translation in many Indian schools as a vocation of imperial rule: see Viswanathan, *Masks of Conquest*, 57–59. The titular character in V. S. Naipaul's *A House for Mr. Biswas*, for example, is taught the prayer through the *King George V Hindi Reader*. My father's family were also staunch Gandhians (my grandmother refused tea all her life), and Gandhi, as Parama Roy puts it, had a "heartfelt reverence for Christ and the New Testament": Roy, "Meat-Eating, Masculinity, and Renunciation in India," 66.

porch as she mowed the grass for my landlord. But the unreasoned decision that night at the Huddle House took. I read Carol J. Adams in a gender studies course; allowed myself to listen to ethical arguments for veganism in a way I wouldn't, or couldn't, when I ate meat; enjoyed the self-expressions that made me alien to my family; and came to speak, feel, and deeply identify with an ethics that rejects the use and abuse of animals, human and nonhuman all.

For a long time, I was too embarrassed to share this story about Janine, particularly with students who would ask in the context of animal studies courses how and when I became vegan. I felt it demonstrated a deficit of integrity, an excess of impressionability. But surely there are worse things than being impressed upon in this life! Particularly by an opaque object other who is minding her own business and asking nothing of you—sadly, nothing at all. But the reason I grew comfortable with this story is for its ability to demonstrate a central axiom in feminist, queer, Marxist, and antiracist traditions: that theory emerges from action. As with my dykeness I dove on in, chasing a feeling, an impression, a clamor: from affect, a world; from a hunch, a new way to see that world. Though Janine is a story about desire, Janine is also a story about indifference. Desire rendered me indifferent to what ordering dry toast and black coffee would mean for my identity, my future, my politics. So I suppose another thing I mean by *indifference* is getting out of our own way so that we are more free to respond to what moves us.[36] Indifference is, in this sense, an expansion and intensification of the capacity to affect and to be affected.[37] (A reader might rightly point out that I then proceed to narrow my own way by adopting an ideology. An excellent point. For what it's worth, I advocate inconsistency—indifference to sameness and difference—in most matters, the subject of chapter 3.)

But here is *not* why I'm telling the story of Janine: to suggest that my pan-species ethic of eating and not eating was born only of something queer and antipatriarchal, and not embedded in a caste inheritance. My ability to eat and experiment with meat and to capitalize on such practices rather than be punished, or worse, is an expression of Brahminism, as was my childhood vegetarianism and the distinctions it was thought to confer.[38] Tiffany Lethabo

36 I thank Jaya Sharma for this formulation.
37 I am grateful to Lisa Stevenson, who summarized one theme of this book as "I am indifferent to the call, therefore I answer the call."
38 For readers less familiar with India and the ways in which caste and other minority oppression is grounded in the purity politics of vegetarianism and cow protection, I describe this landscape in chapter 1.

King writes in *The Black Shoals* that she and most of us scholars and artists and others "write to live with [ourselves]," not to *reconcile* but to voice our hauntings and make of them an inheritance that cares for the survival and thriving of those who live under relations of conquest in which we too are embedded, complicit.[39] This book cares for the survival and thriving of animal others and cares for the survival and thriving of those human persons, Dalits and Muslims and others, whose freedoms and lives have been stolen in the name of animal ethics, or casteist anti-meat movements, in India—the most vile kind of cynical politics that destroys everything it nears, including its own vacant soul. For King, the inheritance of care is bestowed on her by Black radical struggle. My inheritance is not radical. But I want for what I make to be.

This Book

This book is the result of years of research, writing, thinking, reading, and feeling about human-animal relations in India and elsewhere. I began fieldwork for this project in 2008, but funded and in earnest in 2011 for the next many years. I am methodical in most things, but in ethnography my method resonates more with the historian Susan Buck-Morss, who wrote in *Dreamworld and Catastrophe* that "the idiosyncratic intuitions of the author provided the search engine" for her study.[40] I followed my intuitions; went where I was invited; and, in general, said yes to who and what turned up.[41] The ethnographic material for this book draws from time in Banaras (Varanasi), Bangalore (Bengaluru), Bhopal, Bombay (Mumbai), Madras (Chennai), Dimapur, Goa, Haryana, Hyderabad, Jaipur, New Delhi, Pune, and Udaipur.[42]

Each chapter presents an attempt to answer an ethical question about how humans and animals live and die in a shared world. Anthropology's relationship to ethics has tended toward description of the ethical lives and moral systems of "others," but I attempt here to treat ethnography, like literature, as insight into ethical questions that resonate beyond culture, species, or

---

39 King, *The Black Shoals*, xiii.

40 Buck-Morss, *Dreamworld and Catastrophe*, 10.

41 "Say yes to who and what turns up" is taken, with radical nongratitude, from Derrida, *Of Hospitality*, 77.

42 In this book I tend to use the colonial names such as Bombay and Banaras, but not always consistently. Between the two hard places of Anglicization (or Portuguesization) and saffronization, I suppose I truck with the former, which has the slight advantage of longer familiarity.

periodization—even if their relevance and resonance surely have limits.[43] In both methodological and everyday praxis, I'm drawn toward actions that generate their own queer contexts rather than being shaped first by their frame. I say more about what I mean by this in chapter 3.

Each chapter deals with, and in, indifference—but differently, and with the case for indifference developing over the course of the book. Chapter 1, in which I spend time, in part, with past and present volunteers in animal shelters, demonstrates an intimate indifference to the species boundary of skin. The biographical chapter 2, which traces the lives of three women welfarists in India during the Second World War, pivots on an indifference to soap, which is also an indifference to the belonging-in-sameness that the attachment to difference ultimately produces. The indulgently argumentative chapter 3, sparked by one ethnographic scene and its many interpretations, argues for an indifference to consistency, resulting in a readiness to live *in difference*. Chapter 4, on a working cow and a working goat who each refuse, calls for an indifference to the difference between listening and saying. Chapter 5, a narrative interlude in which I go on a walk with an animal healer in Bombay, represents a love indifferent to the differentiations love so often demands. Chapter 6, on creaturely hands, interspecies touch, and how to conjure a lucky break, takes the theme of indifference on more centrally through the matter of indifference to dirt. The coauthored chapter 7, on interspecies touch of the bestial kind in India's dairy farms and animal sterilization clinics, argues in part for an indifference to innocence. Chapter 8, in which I visit poultry farms to explore the industrial cultivation of carnal appetite, revolves around a chosen indifference to the far future, which means attention to all that we can bear. The chapters differ, too, in their degrees of abstraction versus ethnographic immersion, and where the latter is concerned, I do my best (and surely fail sometimes) to not be overly nosy—curious—toward anyone, human and animal alike. This is my offering for an anthropology after the fire, an anthropology at the watering hole,

not quite together
but learning
each other's ways.[44]

---

43 For an excellent review of the anthropology of ethics from the queer perspective of an affect alien, see Yo-Ling, "After Knowledge."
44 "After the fire" refers to Jobson, "The Case for Letting Anthropology Burn." The italicized lines are from "For Judith," in Lorde, *Our Dead behind Us*, 42.

WITNESS. How Do We Come to Occupy a Different Skin?

Maneka Gandhi, of the Nehru-Gandhi political dynasty, is India's most notorious animal activist. In the introduction to one of her books, *Heads and Tails*, she explains what brought her to this work. She references the memoir of one of India's first animal welfarists, Crystal Rogers, an Englishwoman born in 1906 who found herself called by the sight of a dying animal to stay and work in India. The passage Gandhi cites from Rogers reads:

> I was on my way to New Zealand when I saw a horse which caused me to remain in India. It was standing at the side of a very busy road, with the crows tearing the flesh off its back. As I ran towards it, it turned its head towards me and to my horror I saw that it had bleeding sockets from which the crows had already pecked out its eyes. I rang up the SPCA [Society for the Prevention of Cruelty to Animals] but there was little that could be done and the horse had to be shot. If any passerby had done something earlier the horse might have been saved.

I cancelled my journey to New Zealand and stayed in India to see what I could do for animal suffering. We need to fight on every front. If we run away and hide our heads to avoid seeing the sight which horrifies us, we are unworthy of the compassion that has been granted us by the Almighty.[1]

Gandhi then writes: "Crystal is one of the people who opened my eyes twenty years ago and showed me how to work for what I believed in instead of merely showing concern."[2]

I want to think about the variety of ways both Rogers and Gandhi invoke sight and the eyes. Rogers sees a horse which compels her to stay; Rogers sees, but the horse, its eyes pecked out by crows, cannot; we are told to see the sight that horrifies us; Gandhi's eyes are opened by a story about sight, its willful absence, and its pitiable loss. This centrality of sight and of the human witnessing of acts of violence against animals in animalist narratives is not unusual.[3] Similar to a coming-out story, animal activists in India and perhaps elsewhere stake their commitment to a way of life based on one critical moment after which nothing can ever be the same. This chapter traces those processes— optic, haptic, psychic, and epistemic—through which lives "act up," toward becoming, but not quite *being*, other.[4]

1 It's not clear where in Rogers's writings this passage is pulled from, as the quoted section does not correspond to the published version of the story in Rogers's memoir, *Mad Dogs and an Englishwoman*. That said, Rogers died before completing her memoir, and there are differences between her personal papers and the final book form, the latter of which was posthumously collated by animal welfarists, including Maneka Gandhi. This passage appears in Gandhi, *Heads and Tails*, 5.
2 Gandhi, *Heads and Tails*, 5.
3 *Animalist* is a term in use in India and elsewhere to refer to people who act politically alongside and on behalf of animals. Those who self-identify as animalists in India usually differentiate themselves from cow protectionists and others whose actions are motivated in part or whole by casteism and communalism. In general, I avoid the term *activist* in this book, as it conveys both too much and too little. I leave it, instead, to the span of this book to settle impressions.
4 I'm inspired here by Joshua Bennett, who writes about a Black literary tradition of "interspecies empathy" in which "nonhuman—and thus also, ostensibly, nonthinking—life forms are acting up and out in ways we might not expect or yet have a language for": Bennett, *Being Property Once Myself*, 5.

Moral Biographies, Affective Histories

Animalism in India is inseparable from a larger affective history of liberalism, a history that, in turn, is entwined with the history and politics of empire.[5] If we were to replace "horse" or "animal" in Rogers's recollections with the phrase "the female child" or "the Hindu woman," her memoir would hardly read differently from, say, Katherine Mayo's anti-India polemic *Mother India* (1927), a book that, in its portrayal of everyday acts of violence against women and girls, was a tool of empire, arguing for the need to stay fast in India to protect its most vulnerable from barbarity and neglect.[6] Indeed, animal welfare in India—like pro-women reform in colonial India—is significantly shaped by foreign hands. Some of the largest animal shelters and NGOs are founded or funded by foreigners who came to India on holiday or for work and found themselves, like Rogers, compelled to stay.

Two British women helped catalyze the first High Court judgment in India prohibiting the killing of street dogs. Vets by training, they had taken it upon themselves to sterilize strays, seeing that the consequence of their overpopulation on Goan beaches was to be killed by dog shooters who would exchange a tail at the municipal office for a sum of rupees. When the women found out that the city had committed a mass culling of dogs they had already sterilized, they set in motion a series of events that would lead to the founding of People for Animals, Goa, and the building of a landmark court case.[7]

Then there is that other Englishwoman, Ingrid Newkirk of People for the Ethical Treatment of Animals (PETA), renegade and murder fantasy of carnivores and vivisectionists everywhere.[8] There is a special place in Newkirk's heart for the Indian animal, in part because she spent some of her childhood in Delhi, the daughter of a government-worker father and a mother who worked in a leper colony with Mother Theresa. As an adult, Newkirk returned to India to walk the trail that many cattle are made to walk, the thousand miles from Gujarat—one of the highest dairy-producing states, but one in which Hindutva *gaurakshaks* have secured the illegality of slaughter—to West Bengal, one

5   Though, as Leela Gandhi shows, animal activism in India is also inseparable from an affective history of radicalism in which vegetarianism was part of a broader fin de siècle anticolonialism that grew affective bonds between queers in metropole and colony: Gandhi, *Affective Communities*.

6   Mayo, *Mother India*.

7   *Viniyog Parivar Trust v. Municipal Corporation of Greater Mumbai*, writ petition no. 1596 of 1998. I thank Norma Alvarez for first telling me this story.

8   Specter, "The Extremist."

of ten states in which cow slaughter is legal.[9] Newkirk's journey was the basis for a film on India's leather industry and is the reason she won't quit India. In 2000, she set up a PETA office in Bombay with which she is involved daily.

In some regards, the involvement of foreigners is a boon for animal welfare; culturally and socially, however, it is a liability. Critics of animal welfare have every reason to paint the movement as a product of neocolonial meddling and elite interests and as working against the free exercise of India's food and labor cultures. Making matters worse where reputational liabilities are concerned is cow protectionism, or *gauraksha*, which posits itself as an indigenous animal welfare politics in India but is only a means for fascistic violence against Dalit and Muslim minorities.[10]

Cow protectionism, anyway, is not animal welfare: it is exclusively about the cow, and the cow as a weaponized symbol that separates those who eat or slaughter cows (Muslims, Dalits, tribal people, and Christian minorities) from those who, by doctrine, do not (caste Hindus, or *savarnas*). Because of this cloaking of caste terror and fascism in the guise of "animal protection," many on the left, including queer activists I've worked with, express their progressivism in part by eating beef and other meat. In their eyes, animal activists are, at best, elite and out of touch with important human issues, and at worst, casteist and anti-Muslim. This perspective is supported by the demographics of animal welfare groups, which are predominantly *savarna*.

Animalists, in turn, tend to respond to these perceptions in unproductive ways. For instance, PETA asked a Muslim vegan to pose for a poster holding a dog.[11] If that was too subtle, they also insisted he wear a *topi*, or skullcap.[12] The Indian Vegetarian Congress, founded in the 1950s, boasts about the rare occasions

---

9 The others are Arunachal, Goa, Kerala, Tamil Nadu, Mizoram, Meghalaya, Manipur, Nagaland, and Tripura. On cattle smuggling across the West Bengal and Bangladesh border and its relation to Hindutvite cow protectionism, see Ghosh, "*Chor*, Police, and Cattle"; Sur, "Time at Its Margins."

10 As Gyan Pandey shows, modern *gauraksha* not only is not welfarist; it is not even homegrown. Cattle protection was conceived as an anticolonial endeavor and thus emerged in an unequal encounter with the foreign: Pandey, "Rallying round the Cow."

11 Muslims are widely regarded as thinking of dogs as "unclean," a notion I discuss in chapter 5. For nuanced readings on the relation between Islam and dogs, see Bhan and Bose, "Canine Counterinsurgency in Indian-Occupied Kashmir"; Kavesh, *Animal Enthusiasms*; Khan, "Dogs and Humans and What Earth Can Be"; Subaşi, *Dogs in Islam*.

12 I thank Faizan Jaleel for this conversation.

it has given its college paper prize to Muslims.[13] Try as some animalists might, however, to distance themselves from Hindu, dominant-caste, anti-minority politics, communal and casteist positions continue to sound from within animal rights forums.

Animal activism finds challenges in India's changing economy, as well. The conspicuous consumption of animal products, from leather to meat, increased among elite and upwardly mobile groups during India's years of economic growth. That rise itself has been accomplished through the trade in animals, with India becoming the biggest exporter of leather in Asia and the biggest producer of milk in the world.[14] But under whose watch did India become such a renowned specialist in the mass exploitation of cows? Well, of course, under the party of cow protectionists and anti-slaughter campaigners: the right-wing Bharatiya Janata Party (BJP).[15] And who but India's foremost animal activist and former *bahu* of the Indian National Congress Party is a star politician of the BJP?[16] Of course: Maneka Gandhi.

Gandhi's moral biography is as mercurial as she is. She was not yet sixteen when, at a cousin's party, she was approached by a man in a white kurta and red scarf. The line at the buffet was long and he wasn't accustomed to waiting, so he asked whether she would share her mutton with him. She declined.[17] And so did Maneka Anand first meet Sanjay Gandhi, son of Prime Minister Indira Gandhi and grandson of India's first prime minister, Jawaharlal Nehru: over a plate of lamb. Maneka, who was so apolitical that she didn't know who

13 E. Giridhar, interview by the author, Chennai, India, July 8, 2011.

14 Narayanan, "Cow Protection and Bovine Frozen-Semen Farms in India," 8.

15 Alok Gupta and I do a deep dive into the hypocrisy of the BJP's "cow protection" in chapter 7. For other work that exposes the interspecies violence of Hindutva, see everything by Yamini Narayanan, including "Cow Is a Mother," "Cow Protection as 'Casteised Speciesism,'" and "Sperm to Slaughter."

16 *Bahu* means daughter-in-law. Maneka Gandhi joined the BJP after being cast out of the Congress Party. At one point, this was mostly a functional arrangement—the BJP gave her a political stage for her animal activism, and she gave it celebrity and a minor victory over its archenemy, Sonia Gandhi—rather than one based on ideological synergy. But over the years, Maneka Gandhi has adopted in speech and policy the virulence of the BJP, and regardless of whether the arrangement was functional or substantive, she bears responsibility for the consequences of Hindutva hate speech against Muslim and Dalit minorities.

17 This is how Gandhi tells it to me, anyway: Maneka Gandhi, interview by the author, New Delhi, June 11, 2011. Khushwant Singh says that the two were inseparable all night. He also does not mention the mutton: Singh, *Truth, Love, and a Little Malice.*

Sanjay was—she was but a young towel model—married into one of the world's great political dynasties—and, as it happened, into a family of animal and environment protectionists.

Jawaharlal Nehru made it his personal mission as prime minister to pass the Prevention of Cruelty against Animals Act (PCA) in 1960. His daughter, Indira Gandhi, sponsored environmental legislation, most famously the conservation initiative Project Tiger.[18] Her politics appear to have been deeply felt. A visiting dignitary had given Indira a tiger skin rug, and likely under an adviser's suggestion she displayed that rug in her drawing room. Writing a letter to her elder son, Rajiv, who was studying at Cambridge, Indira mourned the life of that tiger over two handwritten pages now on display at the Indira Gandhi Memorial Museum on Safdarjung Road. "Someday," she wrote, "I hope people will shoot only cameras, and not guns, in the jungle."

Animal lovers perhaps, but they were meat eaters all, the Nehru-Gandhis, until one night at dinner when Maneka was pontificating about the treatment of animals. She was putting a spoonful of meaty soup to her mouth when Sanjay said, "How can you go on about animal cruelty while eating meat? Either stop eating it or shut up." And just like that, an epiphany. So obvious to her was her hypocrisy that she dropped the spoon that instant, the soup scalding her wrist. "See?" she said to me as she pulled up the sleeve of her kurta. "The scar is still there."[19]

That same year, she asked her husband for some property under an overpass in South Delhi, which he gave to her as a birthday gift. Gandhi, in turn, gave the property to a friend who started an animal shelter called Friendicoes. "So that was the beginning?" I asked. She laughed. "Yes! What a stupid beginning! My husband was the boss of this city. My mother-in-law was the prime minister of India. And I asked for a shop under a flyover. This is one of my problems. And it was one of my husband's problems, too. Everybody talks about how wicked he was, but the truth is that he was just young. He had no idea what power he had. Neither of us did."[20] Well, people *do* talk about how wicked he was. It is some sort of brutal irony—yet another—that he conducted a mass sterilization program of India's poor during his mother's autocratic Emergency regime in

18 For a critique of the conservationism that Project Tiger and other such initiatives have wrought on those who live among big cats in the Himalayas, see Mathur, *Paper Tiger*.

19 On the wound as trace, the scar as birthmark, see Ahmed, *The Cultural Politics of Emotion*, 27.

20 Maneka Gandhi, interview by the author, New Delhi, May 29, 2008.

1975–77, anecdotally aided by Maneka Gandhi, who now claims responsibility for instituting the Animal Birth Control (ABC) Program to sterilize stray dogs.[21] Since her husband's death in a plane crash in 1980, and her banishment from home and party shortly after, she has devoted herself to animals, founding India's largest animal rights organization, People for Animals (PFA). She exploits her name for all it is worth. "I thank god every day," she told me, "for making me a Gandhi."

I have spent a lot of time at the Gandhi compound on Ashoka Road over the years. Her home is a government-appointed bungalow that doubles as PFA's central office and an unofficial home for unwanted animals. She by turns loved and hated me. Her beleaguered chef made tasty meals. If I sat longer than she at the table for lunch, she would call me a "fat cow" with startling, genuine rage. After one such outburst, as an unspoken apology, she placed an airline ticket to Rajasthan on my desk and asked me to join her on a business trip. So it is with some hard-earned experience that I know she works seven days a week, from morning to night, usually sitting behind a cluttered desk, wearing plain cotton *salwar kameez* (never silk, never wool!), thin from years of wear. She advocates for cows, pigs, dogs, cats, frogs, elephants, donkeys, rats, camels, and chickens by writing weekly newspaper columns; lobbying fellow Parliament members; and threatening over the phone to have people beaten, hanged upside down in their underwear, killed, maimed, and disappeared. Given her history, nobody takes these as idle threats. She is, her terrorizing included, tireless in her efforts. The heavy bags under her eyes and frequent bouts of illness are testament to a compulsion that doesn't let her go.

"Why do you work so much?" I asked her once while accompanying her on a doctor-mandated walk. "Aren't you worried about the consequences, the enemies you make, the stress?" She told me I had asked the wrong question; *she* has nothing to do with it. She said she is "a machine that is designed to do this, exactly this, only this. It is a machine so sensitive," she continued, "that its skin literally prickles with another's pain. But there is no inside to the machine. There is just this skin." *There is no inside. There is just this skin.* What Gandhi wanted me to see was the limitation of my perspective, of the assumption that she is a subject with volition, one who stops and starts at will. Perhaps she was once such a subject, but the day the soup scalded her skin she became something new: subject to the world rather than being a subject in it.

21 On the Emergency, see Prakash, *Emergency Chronicles*; Tarlo, *Unsettling Memories*. On Sanjay Gandhi, see Mehta, *The Sanjay Story*. I say more about the ABC program, and its actual origins, in later chapters.

At the heart of this transformation was what she considers her guiding princi-ple: surrender. The activists she takes on as protégés are few and far between for they must be hardy sorts with thick skin and must share with Gandhi one thing above all: that "in the face of that which is bigger than you, stronger than you, you give yourself over to it, you surrender."

The universe is such a thing—bigger, stronger—and what Gandhi wanted me to see is that the readiness to be transformed is not an act of courage but the only thing that makes any sense. We are all bound to lose, standing up to the world. The only way to survive is to give yourself over, to trust that you will be alternately battered and buoyed. And survive she feels she must. So labor, terrify, and beleaguer she does.

The Perpetual Witness

This is why I was surprised when she said to me one day, from behind her desk, wearing a world-weary expression: "I only wish there were a slaughterhouse next door. To witness that violence, to hear those screams. . . . I would never be able to rest."[22] As far as I could tell, she never really rested anyway, just like so many others I know: Abodh, the director of Welfare for Stray Dogs (WSD), whose personal cell phone is the default animal emergency line for all of Bombay and who has not had an uninterrupted night of sleep in twenty years; Abodh's fieldworker, Dipesh, who treats animals on the streets six days a week, voluntarily treats his own neighborhood animals on Sundays, and in his spare time—such as it is—works another job to keep his ailing parents alive; Maya and Anamika, who each finally got engaged to marry but had no time for love, and so lost it. All these people have witnessed something that allows them no respite; all who, once transformed, are now forever compelled by something that appears to usurp their very being.

To *witness*, as Rogers and Gandhi each invoked the term, is to see in a man-ner that is present, to root themselves when they might rather run or turn away. Voyeurism of horror is characterized by the same stubborn presence but is distinct from witnessing in two crucial ways. One, in witnessing and being

22 This is a sentiment similar to that expressed by Western activists and writers such as Paul McCartney, Michael Pollan, and Timothy Pachirat, one that imagines "glass-walled" slaughterhouses that would transform our treatment of animals through horror and repugnance. Pachirat, for example, calls for a "politics of sight" in which activists work to render transparent the violence society systematically conceals, creating a kind of reverse panopticon: Pachirat, *Every Twelve Seconds*, 242–43.

present to pain, as some describe it, they seek to place themselves in a situation in which they could—if brave enough—change the events that they are framed and marked by.[23] To witness is to be *implicated and culpable in an event that is not at all inexorable*. Two, to be a voyeur is to heighten the affective experience of being alive in your own skin ("I have survived this moment and now *I* feel euphoric"); in witnessing, by contrast, that skin is shed, something in you seeks to exist no longer after the event is over. The fiction of the self is blown apart.

Or is it? Perhaps the better question is: Must it be?

Witnessing can be as much about creating truth as exploding it, as much about the safely encased human self as the radically exfoliated one. Consider *witness* not as the thing one does but as the imperative. "Witness," Descartes says, "the fact that the beasts have less reason than men . . . that they have no reason at all."[24] This is the other meaning of *witness*: witnessing as "behold" or "we see that," as an appeal to evidence that is presumed to be commonly shared, that—because of the privileged linking of ocularity to reason—demands that each be in lockstep with all others who see.[25] In witnessing, vision is not always singularly intimate; it is its opposite: *common sense*. And what is less world-transformative than appeals to (a) common sense? That seems reason enough to be skeptical of the privileging of sight and of the ethics of witnessing.[26]

Derrida reminds us of another reason to be wary. Witnessing, he says, is autobiographical; it is proof that I am, that we are.[27] The animal is objectively staged for this purpose: it is seen but does not itself see, like the animal in Descartes who is rendered an automaton, appealing to a man who witnesses an animal that does not see him in turn. This is the animal that exists as theoretical spectacle, an object for the human who says, "I am, because I see that." (*See that* here has two meanings: I see that thing and I see that this is true.) Derrida

23 See also Das, *Life and Words*.

24 Descartes, *The Philosophical Writings of Descartes*, cited in Derrida, *The Animal That Therefore I Am*, 77.

25 In pointing out specific examples of the ocularity-reason nexus, I do not wish to replicate what Jonathan Sterne has called the "audiovisual litany," which overstates this privileging of ocularity to then valorize sound and resonance—a reverse privileging that helps constitute what Robin James calls the "sonic episteme" of neoliberalism: James, *The Sonic Episteme*; Sterne, *The Audible Past*.

26 For further reflections on the ambivalent nature of witnessing's promise for politics and ethics, see "Witnessing: Truths, Technologies, Transformations," a special issue of the *Cambridge Journal of Anthropology* (39, no. 1 [2021]) edited by Liana Chua and Omri Grinberg.

27 Derrida, *The Animal That Therefore I Am*.

calls the witnessed animal the "spectacle for a specular subject."[28] That specular subject becomes the subject he is in the act of seeing, but not through the act of being reflected back to himself in the animal's gaze. This is the Levinasian animal, the one that does not have a face capable of compelling a relationship of ethical obligation.[29]

That is the Levinasian animal, but what kind of animal is Crystal Rogers's horse—the one with crows tearing the flesh off its meatless back and with bleeding sockets from which those crows pecked out its eyes? Does this animal have a face? Is this animal a theoretical spectacle, objectively staged for Rogers's memoir of "I am?" I don't know. That animal senses Rogers running toward it, and it in turn turns to "face" Rogers. The animal, in other words, responds. Rogers is transformed, recognizing in herself an ethical responsibility in the moment of seeing the animal other. I have a hard time seeing her as only a specular subject. The specular subject only sees himself reflected in his own gaze; the animal's gaze cannot reflect to him his soul.[30]

Rogers is not that specular subject because she, I think, does see her soul reflected in the gaze of the animal, but that soul, like the sockets of the animal's eyes, is empty. The witnessing subject, I want to say, is stripped away: revealed to be, and becoming, *cipher*, becoming emptiness—the emptiness that, Giorgio Agamben argues, is the nothing-space between human and animal, the space of ontological vulnerability.[31] Yet we cannot take this emptiness, this nothingness, too far. As Veena Das reminds us, the witness of violence is only a witness because she survives it—because she has witnessed, she has an obligation to live.[32]

28 Derrida, *The Animal That Therefore I Am*, 82.
29 Emmanuel Levinas argued that the animal face, unlike the human one, cannot compel ethical obligation, though he was unable to specify why this is beyond a retreat to metaphysics: see Levinas, "The Paradox of Morality." See also Calarco, *Zoographies*, 55–78. That said, Levinas's beautiful and strange short essay "The Name of a Dog" suggests a more capacious orientation. For more on Levinas's errant dog, Bobby, see Bunch, "Posthuman Ethics and the Becoming Animal of Emmanuel Levinas"; Burgat, "Facing the Animal in Sartre and Levinas"; Herzog, "Dogs and Fire"; Kendall, "The Face of a Dog"; Kendall-Morwick, "Dogging the Subject: Samuel Beckett, Emmanuel Levinas, and Posthumanist Ethics"; Plant, "Welcoming Dogs."
30 Derrida, *The Animal That Therefore I Am*, 82.
31 Agamben, *The Open*, 92. On ciphering as an ethical act, see Skaria, *Unconditional Equality*.
32 Das, *Life and Words*.

To witness, then, might best be understood as a radical interpenetration of life and death: to exercise a disciplined presence to violence, which opens up a death, which then compels a new kind of life in a previously unimaginable skin. In the case of some, this is a skin inhabited by the animal.

Camellia Satija, a Hindu animal activist in Delhi in her sixties, does not appear, on the face of it, to wear a skin unusual for a person of her social position. I first met her a decade ago as I was trying to track down an animal rights organization called Kindness to Animals and Respect for Environment (KARE). The address I had found through a website took me not to an NGO or animal shelter but to Rio Grande, an upscale shop in the M Block marketplace of GK I in South Delhi. I learned from the salesclerk that Satija was the owner of the shop and the founding trustee of the defunct KARE. The clerk called Satija and, curious to meet me, she drove over in her SUV. She led me through the store to her second-floor office and offered me a seat.

"So," she began, "does this really interest you, this work of mine?" I answered that it did, and she began a slow reveal, bringing out reports, pamphlets, court filings, and photographs, all filed away behind store financials and inventories. There was much more in the basement of her house, entire shelving units worth. "Thirty years of my life," she said. I asked her to tell me about those years, and she began with images.

The slaughterhouse footage she had in her possession, she said, was "more valuable to me than gold. Those images reminded me. Of how the world is. Of the pain we cause. Even without watching the videos, just knowing that they were in the cabinet served a purpose. They would never let me stop." She told me about her illicit visits to the Idgah abattoir in New Delhi, where the footage she shot was later shown on the state-owned broadcast service, Doordarshan—an effort by the government, doubtless, to generate anti-Muslim sentiment.[33] (Satija says she "disagrees" with the opportunism of the right, which exploits animal ethics—and, she says, "an ancient Hindu spiritualism"—in its

33 The Idgah slaughterhouse, which stood for nearly two centuries, was relocated in 2009 after numerous court filings. For a detailed history of Idgah and the community of Qureshi Muslims who work across New Delhi's "meatscapes," see Ahmad, *Delhi's Meatscapes*. Idgah's functions were relocated to Ghazipur, a site I discuss in chapter 8.

Interestingly, Doordarshan combines two words—*door* and *darshan*—to mean, put simply, "to see from afar." But *darshan* means more than "to see." It is a religious practice in Hinduism that involves both seeing the sacred and being beheld by it in turn, combining, we might say, the visual with the haptic. On *darshan*, see Eck, *Darsan*; Jain, *Gods in the Bazaar*, 90. For more on the state-run broadcast service Doordarshan,

bid for false power and that she regrets her labor and that of others being used for those purposes.)[34]

Telling me about her visits to Idgah, Satija continued: "It's not just the sights that you always remember. Worse even than the looks in the animals' eyes, worse than the screams, was the stench of death. Even now, I wake up in the middle of the night with that stench in my nostrils."[35] For Satija, the value of witnessing slaughter is that it forces her always to move, to stave off complacency and the pretenses that enable it. The social action, then, that is compelled by witnessing—which is also defined by a disciplined staying put in the face of horror—is also a kind of *running*: fervent movement away from the bounded self that only impotently remembers and toward that which suffers on account of your life. This is the defining dynamic of witnessing: a staying put in the face of death, only to then move away from one's own impotence and toward the Other in a relation of being that thins the human skin and thickens—at least some forms of—relationality.

Satija's witnessing of the suffering of animals did more for her than force her to work. It also forced her—as she believed it would compel all of us who saw—to become the animal in pain. "To realize the suffering of animals," she said to me, "requires you to become an animal that talks. Because they cannot [talk], that becomes my responsibility." I meditate on this notion of the speechless animal in chapter 4 but want to think now, through the rubrics of humanism and its others, about what it means for Satija to "become an animal" that talks. Is this an act of anthropomorphic assimilation, of ontological slippage, or of something (in)different?

Becoming Animal

Elizabeth Povinelli elaborates a history of the concept of intimacy in post-Enlightenment Western thought.[36] Intimacy is the freely chosen bond between sovereign subjects, a foundational fiction of autological society that sets itself apart from the genealogical—those who are incapable of intimacy because

including its role in stoking communal violence, see Mankekar, *Screening Culture, Viewing Politics.*

34 I interviewed Satija again after an earlier version of this chapter was published: Camellia Satija, interview by the author, New Delhi, July 14, 2014.

35 The phrase "stench of death" is loaded in India with caste violence, as communities of leatherworkers would be shunned on the basis of "stench."

36 Povinelli, *The Empire of Love.*

their bonds are already chosen for them in advance along such lines as caste, custom, and kin. What interests me about these stories of animals and witnessing is, in part, how they contribute to destabilizing that autological fiction by showing how an act of intimacy—intimate because singular, because it exfoliates the social skin, because it expands the boundaries of possible relationality—both exceeds and resists sovereignty.

First, the animal subject of the intimate relation is brought into its intimacy with a human through its unfreedom. Second, by entering into intimacy with an animal in pain, the woman seeks not to be free or even to exercise freedom but to render herself more deeply subject to unequal relations of obligation and responsibility: in fact, to surrender.[37] But the intimacy of human and animal, by showing that intimacy is other than a freely chosen bond between two sovereign, and thus presumably human, subjects does not only explode the species divide. Intimacy also reintroduces and stabilizes the species chasm.

As Satija describes it, what realizing the suffering of animals makes imperative is a simultaneous sublimation and deployment of the self as human subject to and for the needs of the unfree other. The human actor simultaneously becomes the animal—her own skin shed in sublimation—and *hyper*embodies herself as human by doing precisely that which defines what it is (for her) to be human: to speak; to "give voice" for that unfree other who cannot speak, the witness still safely encased in her human self. Satija exemplifies how voice itself emerges in what Das calls the "zone between two deaths"—here, the death of the animal and the death of the man the witness was in the moment before he witnessed.[38] But the voice that emerges in the zone between two deaths not only cries against injustice; it also calls forth the very cleavage between human and animal that enables that injustice to thrive at all.

Or does it? Perhaps the better question is: Must it?

An obvious and eminently reasonable analysis of Satija's vision of "becoming an animal" is the one I've offered: that despite its aim to break from violence, action on behalf of animals only reproduces liberal anthropocentric humanism.[39] But then again, that is just one interpretation, and perhaps its flaw is precisely that it is eminently reasonable—a kind of approach to the world that, too, finds its foundation and value in the tradition of metaphysics. What if it is my very assumption of anthropocentric humanism in Satija's

---

37 Elaborating on ethical cultivation that involves submission to unfreedom, see Mahmood, *The Politics of Piety*.

38 Das, *Life and Words*, 61–62.

39 Ticktin, "Non-human Suffering."

desire to "become an animal that talks" that is the problem here: that my assumption of anthropocentrism results from *my* being locked in a closed, binary logic of representation in which (1) I know what human and animal "are"; and (2) I know that they are either different or the same. Instead of hearing in her claim, "I = it" or "it = me," why am I not hearing "I + it + z = something we have never thought before"?[40]

Satija did not say she wanted to *be* an animal but that she wanted to *become* one. The difference between being and becoming is like that between witnessing and specular subjects, a difference that is, to use Brian Massumi's words, between rendering the self molar and dissolving the self into supermolecularity. We are all capable of becoming, Massumi says; all we have to do is want it.[41] We have to want to escape our limitations, a desire that may be sparked by philosophy, by touch, or by witnessing. But that desire may also be conflicted: oscillating between the desire for molarity (which manifests in "being" something other) and the desire for supermolecularity (which does not ever manifest: it is only becoming). I do not know the nature of Satija's desires, but I am willing to say that my unwillingness to accept that she becomes an animal in a way that is disruptive rather than productive of anthropocentric humanism is a case of excess reason, and that the reason of reason is to hobble.[42]

I never saw Satija at work—never saw her becoming animal with my own eyes—and so I cannot say I beheld her becoming to be true, so let me move for a moment to something I did witness. In the summer of 2013, I spent a week with an American family, the Abrams-Meyers, who had moved from Seattle to a hilly village outside Udaipur, in the northwestern Indian state of Rajasthan. They were Jim, Erika, and Claire, and when I stepped out of the Udaipur train station and gave the name of the village I wanted to get to, the rickshaw driver said, "Erika *ka ghar?*," which Erika told me might happen. The driver delivered me to their gate, and the sound of the engine brought Claire to the door, followed closely by Erika, who was quite literally flapping with excitement. They were all very tall, these Americans. Jim had once been a literature professor; Claire, then twenty-two, was twelve when the family left Seattle

40 Or, as Deleuze and Guattari put it, playing off Virginia Woolf, "Five o'clock is this animal! This animal is this place! That is how we need to feel": Deleuze and Guattari, *A Thousand Plateaus*, 263.

41 Massumi, *A User's Guide to Capitalism and Schizophrenia*, 94.

42 The Urdu word for reason, also used in Hindi and Gujarati, is *aqal*, which has roots in the Arabic *uqul*, "to hobble a camel": Adonis, *Sufism and Surrealism*, 80.

and hadn't been formally schooled since, which might account for her insight about the world.

Erika. Well, Erika, I have to say, is a lot like Big Bird. And I can say that because I know she doesn't mind, for she has nothing against either birds or Muppets and is quite aware that she is tall, wild, and gangly. While I was there, the family was moving their animal shelter to a larger site, and this involved carrying animals in their arms, one by one, from a van into large outdoor enclosures. So I usually saw her in house pants and a kurta, sometimes with her glasses on her head; sometimes with her head covered with a bandana that she otherwise wore around her neck. I think I will always remember the sight of her, slightly disheveled, slightly mad-looking, but somehow calm, and everything revolving around her in a steady, necessary orbit, and she is carrying a bucket full of water even though it has been a very long and hot day, and the dogs trail behind her and she is harried but full of love. I can see why an animalist named Jaivardan says Erika "is like a god" to him, and another named Rohit calls her "the mother of animals," and why Timmie Kumar, who directs Jaipur's Help in Suffering and has a cult following herself, told me she "fell to the ground and wept when I first saw Erika with the animals." I know that sounds overly dramatic, but somehow it is not when you see a woman rolling in the dirt with salivating, joyous, romping three-legged dogs. I wish I had fallen to the ground in tears myself.

One of the things about Erika, as with any witness, is her mix of movement and stillness. She walked me to the large-animals section of the shelter, populated mostly by donkeys, goats, and cows, with a couple of paralyzed pigs. We came upon a large lump on the ground, covered by burlap but for hooves and a tail. I saw the body rising and falling with laborious breath: it was a dying cow, her neck unnaturally bent. Because of Rajasthan's anti-cow slaughter legislation Erika couldn't euthanize her. She had been dying for days. Erika had hoped that the previous day would be the cow's last, and she told me what they do at times like those: Erika calls the workers over, one by one or perhaps two at a time, and she asks them to stop whatever they are doing and just be there with the animal.[43] She got down on the ground, next to this burlap

---

43 In *Decolonizing Extinction*, Juno Salazar Parreñas reveals the difficult working conditions—physically and in terms of respect for dignity—faced by human laborers at animal rehabilitation centers in Borneo. Parreñas's descriptions resonate with my observations, as well, though I hope it is out of a sense of truth and not naivete that I feel the Abrams-Meyers operated their workplaces with respect for human and animal dignity. Some of the examples, even if the earnestness may cause some

and flesh, and demonstrated to me: "Just be silent next to its dying body, stroking its head if they feel they can, cradling it, kissing it, or just sitting there, body to body, life to life, death to death. Say you're sorry that it's leaving this world, if you feel moved to say that, say you're sorry that it lived in a world like this, if that's what you want to say. Whatever you do, just be there." It is in these moments of being-with, she added, that the social boundaries between humans, too, fall apart when they are together, all from their varying backgrounds with their butts equally on the shit- and piss-strewn ground and their hands on the body of an animal in pain, sometimes crying, sometimes stoic, sometimes calm, but all the time, and all of them, *there*, facing the boundary between life and death that will someday hunt us all down, regardless of the skin we wear.

These Are Becomings, All

I turned to Erika to answer a question Satija provoked: Can we become animal, become other, in a way that is disruptive rather than productive of liberal anthropocentric humanism? Or, to put it differently: Can we become something other than the safely encased, safely critical human self? I have no doubt that I watched something of Erika die in that moment, that I witnessed her becoming other through her surrender to becoming death. I wouldn't feel right reducing that moment to a reproduction of anthropocentrism, though surely one could make that argument if they wanted to. But more important, I want to suggest that it doesn't matter *what* she became. She affected me, forever, just as she affects all those who enter her orbit.

The effect of becoming—in the Deleuzian sense, anyway—is not to go from one thing to another, but to be a phenomenon, an event, an act of bordering in which both original categories are revealed to be other than what they are. Becoming is pure effectuation, pure *indifference*, only the effect of affectively redefining the places we started from. In this particular case, it was "woman" and "animal." In another case it was "man" and "rat." This is from Gilles Deleuze and Félix Guattari's *A Thousand Plateaus*:

to cringe: the expectation that all (human) food plates are to be shared from; Jim's *jugaad* fashioning of upright mops and brooms; strict limitations on the work hours of non–Abrams-Meyers; and a Gandhian or Guattarian radical equality in which everyone, regardless of role, cleans stalls and toilets.

When Hofmannsthal contemplates the death throes of a rat, it is in him that the animal "bares his teeth at his monstrous fate." This is not a feeling of pity . . . still less an identification. It is a composition of speeds and affects. . . . [I]t makes the rat become a thought, a feverish thought in the man, at the same time that the man becomes a rat gnashing its teeth in its death throes. The rat and the man are in no way the same thing . . . but are expressed . . . in an affectability that is no longer that of subjects. Unnatural participation.[44]

Becoming; unnatural participation; turning the self not into another *kind* of self but only into a question machine. Movements for justice are full of becomings. They are defined and made by them.

In 1998, the film *Fire*, about the love affair between two sisters-in-law in a middle-class home in New Delhi, was released across India. What followed were violent public clashes instigated by fascistic goons who claimed that the film was an abomination. There are no lesbians in India, they said. Lesbians responded with three simple words: "Indian and Lesbian."[45]

Is this so unlike Satija's claim that she becomes an animal? Wasn't "Indian and Lesbian" an act of becoming, too? Those words were certainly, when first uttered, as improbable as a wealthy, middle-aged Hindu woman saying, "I am an animal." The very identity of India, after all, was its exclusion of queer, and the very identity of queer was its exclusion from citizenship, mirroring the mutual exclusions of human subject and animal abject.[46] "Indian and Lesbian," over the riotous weeks that followed that utterance, was indeed a becoming, an effectuation, a question machine, affectively redefining dominant categories of social understanding, birthing inbred monstrosities where there was once, so we thought, a simple abyss between this and that. Lesbians became Indian, as did Black men become citizen in another radical becoming in Memphis, in 1968, as the sanitation workers' strike gave rise to a mass of signs

---

44 Deleuze and Guattari, *A Thousand Plateaus*, 259. Hugo Hofmannsthal was an Austrian writer who published at the turn of the twentieth century. In this section of their text, Deleuze and Guattari discuss a number of writers who, through their "unnatural participation" beyond the human, act as "sorcerers," able to throw the self, and an openhearted reader, into upheaval.

45 Davé, "Indian and Lesbian and What Came Next." For more on the film and controversy, see Ghosh, *Fire*; Gopinath, *Impossible Desires*.

46 On queer exclusion from Hindu citizenship, see Bacchetta, "When the (Hindu) Nation Exiles Its Queers."

that was also a singular becoming—this time with four words instead of three: "I Am a Man."

These are becomings, all: a lesbian becoming human, a Black man becoming man, a woman becoming animal. But putting it this way, there are at least two differences between the first two becomings and the last one. The first two begin with a movement from the particular to the general, while the last one begins with a movement from the general-particular (human but still *only* woman) to the particular. This first difference might explain the second, which is that the first two becomings we believe (for who would not want to ascend to what they already are?), while the last one most of us don't believe (for who, really, would want to become an animal in pain?).

But what do I know? What do I know of her heart other than what she tells me of it, and she tells me that she becomes an animal because she has witnessed an animal in pain. But then I think, *Can it really be so?* A lesbian can be an Indian because she already is; a Black man can be a man because he already is; but Satija cannot be an animal because I know what an animal is and an animal is not this perfumed and bejeweled woman with a daughter in the Ivy League. Throughout all of this, I know. But what if we were to surrender to the spirit of becoming, to carnally enact a critique of anthropatriarchy by allowing other facets of the sensorium to reign? What if we were to become Satija, to see what she sees, to experience what inspires her to shed her skin and become the animal that writhes at night—to make her, and what she sees, a feverish thought coursing through our flesh? Could we feel, then, that she is not becoming or failing to become a subject, but becoming an event, an operation on the categories of thought and action that we hold on to, demanding that we not *be* something new but become something immanent? It might be to be like Timmie Kumar, to come apart in the face of something extraordinary. Or to place arms around the body of an other, ear to its flesh, and be filled with the pulse of its enormous, failing heart.

BIOGRAPHY. Why Is Moral Attention to the Animal so Repulsive?

The short answer to this question is fascism, on the one hand, and the affective history of European liberalism, on the other. In fact, I could probably leave it there, this chapter consisting of that response followed by a list of references to a host of important work across the anthropology of South Asia illustrating the intersections between animal welfare and Hindu fascist neo/imperialism.[1]

---

[1] Adcock, "Preserving and Improving the Breeds"; Adcock and Govindrajan, "Bovine Politics in South Asia"; Chatterjee, "Beefing Yoga"; Chigateri, "Glory to the Cow"; De, "Cows and Constitutionalism"; Ghassem-Fachandi, "Ahimsa, Identification, and Sacrifice in the Gujarat Pogrom"; Ghassem-Fachandi, "The Hyperbolic Vegetarian"; Ghosh, "*Chor*, Police and Cattle"; Govindrajan, *Animal Intimacies*; Hansen, *The Saffron Wave*; Hardy, "Provincializing the Cow"; Narayanan, "Animating Caste"; Narayanan, "Cow Protection as 'Casteised Speciesism'"; Staples, *Sacred Cows and Chicken Manchurian*; Subramaniam, "The Ethical Impurative"; Sur, "Time at Its Margins"; Yang, "Sacred Symbol and Sacred Space in Rural India."

But what I offer in this chapter are sketches of three moral biographies that further develop the answer to why moral attention to the animal in India is so repulsive, through and beyond those two axes. I argue that both fascism and the affective history of European liberalism are represented in strange, coincidental, and also profoundly dissimilar ways by a pair of *devis* and an Englishwoman, all contemporaries and all central to the early history of animal welfare in India: the Nazi Aryosophist Savitri Devi Mukherji (1905–82); the genial Englishwoman Crystal Rogers (1906–96); and the legendary dancer, parliamentarian, and theosophist Rukmini Devi Arundale (1904–86). It does pain me to conjoin these so-called *devis* (goddesses) in this chapter because one (Savitri) was an odious creature and the other (Rukmini), a luminous one. But in telling these three stories together I seek to stage a conversation about the moral and theoretical problems surrounding care for animals in India, for which contemporary Hindu fascism provides one key but not exclusive explanatory force. I show that the explanation lies, too, in the fear of a queer (non)future, or the rise of Aunty Nation.

The Odious: Savitri Devi Mukherji

Savitri Devi advocated for the rights of animals and nature as part of her advancement of the Hindu-Aryan myth. The homepage of her archive, hosted by the American extreme-right activist Greg Johnson, displays an image of her—pale-skinned, tight-lipped, sari-clad—with the caption "Woman against Time."[2] (Another page on the site features a photograph of a cat bearing a startling resemblance to Adolf Hitler—a "Kitler," as such cats are known on the internet.) In recent years, Savitri Devi became an iconic figure for the American and European New Right, including for the likes of the American neo-Nazi Richard Spencer, the former Trump strategist Steve Bannon, and the Greek Golden Dawn Party.[3]

Savitri Devi was born Maximiani Portas in 1905 in Lyons, France, to an English mother and Greek Italian father.[4] Despite this mixed heritage, her allegiances

---

2 *Woman against Time: The Savitri Devi Archive*, Counter-Currents Publishing, San Francisco, 2022, https://www.savitridevi.org.

3 Margaronis, "Savitri Devi."

4 I have drawn most of the biographical details of Savitri Devi's life, except where noted, from Goodrick-Clarke, *Hitler's Priestess*. I thank Gayle Rubin for introducing me to Savitri Devi and Goodrick-Clarke and for sharing her archive of Savitri Devi's work with me. For those interested in reading yet more about Savitri Devi, I recom-

from early childhood were fixed on the side of cats and Aryans. In *And Time Rolls On*, a transcript of late interviews she conducted for Ernst Zundel, she describes being upset as a child by supposedly rural French practices of torturing cats by fire. "I heard of all that when I was a child," she said. "It put me absolutely against mankind. And when I started hearing of some movement in Germany, the National Socialist movement, [people saying] 'It's inhuman!' 'Inhuman?' I said, 'Well, goodness me. I'm going to go into it. If it's inhuman, I like it. I wouldn't have touched [Nazism] if it were human. But inhuman? All right."[5] Her rejection of what she calls, in *The Impeachment of Man*, the "man-centered" traditions of Judeo-Christianity was in part what drove her allegiance to Greece, which she saw as a once- mighty font of a vitalist Aryan paganism.[6] The aftermath of World War I, and what appeared to be the desertion of Greece by the British and French, stoked her lifelong animosity toward Britain—an animosity that would be welcomed in India when she joined forces with elite nationalists such as Subhas Chandra Bose, who rejected Gandhi's pacifism toward England in favor of Hitler's militant aggression.

Savitri Devi's biographer, the late Nicholas Goodrick-Clarke, speculates in *Hitler's Priestess* that it was in Greece, and in light of its postwar disappointments, that Savitri Devi became compelled to travel to India, seeing daily the swastikas that adorned Heinrich Schliemann's Palace of Ilion in Athens and familiarizing herself with his theories on the Aryan relationship between Homeric myths and the Vedas.[7] Motivated by mythology, poetry, and rumors of a nature-worshiping land in which a caste system honored both blood and order, Maximiani Portis went to India in 1932. She immersed herself in reading and was influenced most of all by Bal Gangadhar Tilak's *The Arctic Home in the Vedas* (1903), in which Tilak argued for a long Aryan march from the North

mend Greg Johnson's "Savitri Devi's Communist Nephews." Despite the fact that this biographer is nearly as odious as his subject, it is an attentive piece, exemplified in an extraordinarily lengthy footnote regarding whether Savitri Devi's late-life apartment in Delhi smelled bad or not. Johnson wrote the essay after reading Sumanta Banerjee's article "Memories of My Nazi Maami [Aunt]" in the *Times of India* in April 1999, which, in turn, was written after the *Times of India* ran a review of Goodrick-Clarke's *Hitler's Priestess*.

5 Devi, *And Time Rolls On*, 148

6 Devi, *The Impeachment of Man*.

7 The swastika, originally a Hindu and Buddhist symbol representing equilibrium, was adopted separately in Italy and Germany in 1920. In Fiume, Italy, it was adopted by a group called Yoga, founded by Guido Keller; in Germany, of course, it was adopted by the Nazi Party: Buscemi, "The Sin of Eating Meat," 139.

Pole to India at the dawn of the Ice Age.[8] As Romila Thapar explains, Tilak presented a challenge for other supporters of Hindutva who espoused what Thomas Trautmann calls the "alternative view" in the Aryan debate: that the Aryans did not immigrate to or invade the Indus Valley but were indigenous to it.[9] Tilak's theory was later reconciled by Hindutvite nationalists such as V. D. Savarkar and M. S. Golwalkar, chief of the right-wing Rashtriya Swayamsevak Sangh (RSS), both of whom derived their anti-Muslim Hindutva philosophy from German ethnic nationalism.[10] They, through Tilak, acknowledged the Aryans' Arctic origins but by placing the North Pole, back in the Ice Age, in what is present-day Odisha.[11] What was key to Savitri Devi through her Hindutvite readings was that Hitlerism was the resurgence of an Aryan tradition that was not European but archaically *Indo*-European. And that India, because of both the prevalence of caste and resistance to the Abrahamic religions, had done more to preserve that racial and spiritual tradition than any place in Europe or the wider world.

These were among the learnings that Savitri Devi (still Maximiani Portas) brought with her to Rabindranath Tagore's Shantiniketan in 1935. Little did she know that Tagore's ashram was a haven for liberals, homos, ex-pats, and Jews, among them Tagore's secretary, Margaret Spiegel, who pronounced Savitri, with her Indo-Aryan fantasies, "worse than an entire pack of Nazis rolled into one."[12] Undeterred by how repugnant she was already known to be, she would teach English and history across the country; adopt the Hindu name Savitri Devi in 1936; take pilgrimages to Ayodhya and Brindaban; and, in 1938, marry a Bengali Brahmin, Asit Krishna Mukherji, who was the editor of the pro-German Hindu nationalist magazine *New Mercury*.[13] It was a match made in Aryan heathendom, except, of course, for the matter of caste. They were

8 Devi, *And Time Rolls On*, 133.

9 Thapar, "The Theory of Aryan Race and India"; Trautmann, *The Aryan Debate*.

10 Cowan, *The Indo-German Identification*, 182; Goodrick-Clarke, *Hitler's Priestess*, 50. See also Jha, "Guruji's Life."

11 Thapar, "Some Appropriations of the Theory of Aryan Race Relating to the Beginnings of Indian History," 116.

12 Devi, *And Time Rolls On*, 26. On the other hand, Tagore was also viewed as an inspiration to some Italian proto-fascists who saw in both the poet and in Mahatma Gandhi the embodiments of an Oriental, mystical vegetarian purity. Buscemi, "The Sin of Eating Meat," 145.

13 For more on Mukherji from the perspective of his extended kin, see Johnson, "Savitri Devi's Communist Nephews." Johnson suggests that Mukherji persuaded Nehru to request his wife's release from a German prison in 1949.

married in 1940 but were and remained celibate. As Savitri puts it in her interviews, one does not *found* a family in India. One *continues* a family that has existed for centuries, and you cannot continue a family unless you are of the same caste. "So we became friends. It was perfectly all right. . . . Our link between us was the Führer."[14]

In 1937, she requested an audience with Swami Satyananda, president of the Hindu Mission in Calcutta. Satyananda welcomed the self-proclaimed Aryan devotee of Hitler and invited her to give lectures on behalf of the mission across Bengal, Bihar, and Assam. She requested permission to talk about Hitler and National Socialism. Satyananda was more than willing and, in expressing his enthusiasm, espoused a theory that would influence Savitri Devi and far-right activists for nearly three-quarters of a century: that Hitler is an avatar of Vishnu—specifically, the tenth and final incarnation of Vishnu, Kalki the Destroyer, who would end the Kaliyūga and begin again the Golden Age of righteousness.[15]

After the fall of Hitler and the Third Reich, Savitri Devi returned to Europe in an effort to aid the resistance against the Allied occupation. The first text she composed was *The Impeachment of Man*, her animal and environmental rights manifesto that served also as a defense for the Holocaust. She wrote:

> Immediately after the Second World War, one could not but hear, more or less cleverly presented tales of "crimes against humanity" alleged to have been committed under National Socialism. They failed to change my attitude towards National Socialism, in part because I was never a "decent person," and then also because I already knew too much of the atrocities of other races . . . , not to find the alleged German crimes hopelessly amateurish in comparison. And in addition to that, I had heard or seen too much of all forms of exploitation of animals by man— from the daily brutalities one witnesses in the streets of Southern Europe and the Orient, to the appalling deeds perpetrated in the secrecy of vivisection chambers . . . , not to feel more than indifferent to the fate of human beings, save in the rare cases these happen to be my own brothers in faith.[16]

Savitri Devi makes asking why attention to the animal in India is so repulsive seem like an unnecessary—or, at least, very obvious—question. She

14 Devi, *And Time Rolls On*, 35.
15 Devi, *The Lightning and the Sun*.
16 Devi, *The Impeachment of Man*, x.

represents the link among radical ecology, Nazism, and the RSS—the RSS representing the "requiting," in Robert Cowan's words, of the long Aryan romance with India.[17] Murders of Dalits and Muslims by twenty-first-century *gaurakshaks* is directly tied to that early adoption of Nazi forms of intimidation and social control by Hindu anti-imperial nationalists. We see in Savitri Devi's corpus, too, the truth that vegetarian purism and the perceived innocence of nonhuman animals are not coincidental to fascism but are in every sense *inherent* to it.[18] These are simply inextricable ideologies with coterminous origin points in modern India and fin de siècle Western Europe. Savitri Devi justifies her disregard for victims of the Holocaust on the grounds that they and those who sympathize with them are themselves guilty of violence against other living beings. The moral difference lies for her in the ostensible innocence of the natural world and the potential for evil in man, the former a violent and prevalent construct I address in chapters that follow. This inextricability of radical ecology and what Francesco Buscemi calls "sacred vegetarianism" with fascism, while indeed repulsive, is not logically surprising.[19] Fascism is antihumanist in the most profound sense, rejecting liberal secular ideologies as too impotent for the world-historical transformation necessary in the war of races. The animal is not just an empty symbol weaponized for fascism, as I have been tempted at times to argue, but a real utopian alternative for it—a return to innocence and truth in a world seemingly devoid of its Aryo-Brahmin supremacist order.[20]

17 Cowan, *The Indo-German Identification*.
18 The distinction between vegetarianism and vegetarian purism is important. The historian Francesco Buscemi has argued that existing vegetarian practices provided the canvas for a fascistic striving for "perfection and purity" and is what transmogrified vegetarianism into an ideal ideology to foment racism and genocide: Buscemi, "The Sin of Eating Meat," 145–46. For alternative histories of vegetarianism, including its "progressive" and queer forms, see Gandhi, *Affective Communities*; Stuart, *The Bloodless Revolution*.
19 For more on the historical relationship between fascism and vegetarianism/veganism, see Buscemi, "Edible Lies"; Buscemi, *From Body Fuel to Universal Poison*; Buscemi, "The Sin of Eating Meat"; Forchtner and Tominc, "Kalashnikov and Cooking-Spoon"; Goodrick-Clarke, *The Occult Roots of Nazism*; Nützenadel, "Dictating Food"; Sax and Fischer, *Animals in the Third Reich*.
20 Of course, the perspectives on animality held by racists do not exhaust what animals are, represent, and demand in nonfascist otherwise worlds. It is also the case that whatever nonhuman nature has represented historically to fascist dictatorships, those regimes have consistently revealed the falsity of their claims to "protect" animals—or even, in fact, to actually *be* vegetarian, from Italian fascism and German

The Genial: Crystal Rogers

While vegetarian purism, radical ecology, and the purported innocence of the "natural world" are ideologically inherent to fascism, fascism is not inherent to all traditions of care for animals. In India, three distinct but overlapping lineages of animal welfare have shaped the contemporary landscape: (1) the pagan Anglophobic dharmic Aryo-Hindutva one (this side, unfortunately and hypocritically, claims Aśoka, Buddha, and Mahavira under the banner of Hindustan); (2) the liberal, Anglophilic Judeo-Christian one; and (3) the theosophical tradition that shares much with both the anti-Christian mysticism of Franco-German-Hellenic Aryavarta and the liberal compassion-centered affective ecology of the British Empire.[21] While the first is represented by Savitri Devi, the second is represented by a contemporary of hers, a genial Englishwoman named Crystal Rogers who was described in an *Outlook* magazine obituary as "the original *kutta-billi* activist."[22] The beginning and end of the similarities between the two women are perhaps represented in the titles of their memoirs: Rogers's is *Mad Dogs and an Englishwoman*; Savitri Devi's is *Long Whiskers and the Two-Legged Goddess: The True Story of a Most "Objectionable Nazi" . . . and Half a Dozen Cats*—scare quotes and ellipses in the original.[23]

In *Mad Dogs and an Englishwoman*, Rogers details that sight that compelled her, while en route to further travels in 1958, to stay in India: the flayed horse,

Nazism to contemporary Hindutva. On Hitler and ham, see Adams, *The Sexual Politics of Meat*. See also Buscemi, "The Sin of Eating Meat," 147. Chapter 7 deals with the present-day antagonism between fascism and so-called cow protection in India.

21   One representative of how these traditions overlap is Maneka Gandhi. She voices the Aryo-Hindutva lineage though, in fact, she came to animal welfare through Crystal Rogers and, via the Nehruvian line, Rukmini Devi, who was a respected colleague of Maneka's mother-in-law, Indira Gandhi. Indira had even asked Rukmini to make Maneka chairperson of the AWBI, but this didn't—and hasn't ever—come to pass. Maneka Gandhi had not heard of Savitri Devi until I told her about the Nazi animal-rightist in June 2019 while describing to her this chapter I was writing.

22   *Kutta-billi* means dog-cat, and calling someone a kutta-billi activist, like "animal lover," is usually a mild insult. *Kutta-billi* tends to be reserved for women—aunties—of a certain age. This obituary of Rogers, nevertheless, is tinged with respect: Karlekar, "Animal Passions."

23   Rogers intended to call her memoir *Battle for the Weak*, but in the posthumous publication, about which more later, the title was changed to the amiable *Mad Dogs and an Englishwoman: The Memoirs of Crystal Rogers*. I draw biographical details about Rogers's life from that book, unless stated otherwise. See also Devi, *Long Whiskers and the Two-Legged Goddess*.

its eyes pecked out by crows, surrounded by indifferent onlookers.[24] It was she who called the Society for the Prevention of Cruelty to Animals (SPCA); she who had the horse shot. And it was therefore she who needed to remain on the subcontinent, to disseminate a Christian ethic of love in a society dominated by a practice of indifference—what Parama Roy calls, from the perspective of John Lockwood Kipling, the "vegetarian cruelty" of the Bania Indian.[25]

This was not Rogers's first time in India. As a child she had traveled to India often—her father was a retired colonel in the Indian Army—and lived in the country from age six to ten. In her forties, during the Second World War and while Savitri Devi Mukherji was beginning her wedded career as a Nazi spy, Rogers drove ambulances and worked as a librarian for the Royal Air Force in England. There she fell in love with a younger man, a Canadian flight sergeant named Jim Currie, though it appears that, like Savitri Devi and Asit Krishna Mukherji, if for very different reasons, they never sexually consummated their relationship. Jim was killed while on ops one night, his body never found, except as seen by Rogers and her friends—an affable, curly-haired ghost keeping time to music, looking at Rogers with love. After the incident with the horse Rogers was debating her place in India, her fortitude for staying, when Jim communicated to her that she was guided by the spirit of Saint Francis of Assisi and would dedicate her life to the care of animals, whatever its costs or hardship.

Rogers founded a shelter called The Animals' Friend (TAF) with an Indian magazine editor and a Dutch doctor in October 1959. She attached a wire basket to the back of a bicycle as an ambulance to drive animals to and from the SPCA, as TAF had no land of its own. On the first day of 1964, TAF moved onto a plot of land in Mehrauli, then a sparsely populated area in southern New Delhi.

24 Rogers, *Mad Dogs and an Englishwoman*, 43. The Indian friend to whom she narrates this story begs her to stop, saying that he didn't notice a thing. This leads her to a digression on native apathy. Rogers explicitly rejects essentialist cultural arguments, but she does suggest that the "magnificent" "India of the Raj" is now, in its independence, a lesser place: Rogers, *Mad Dogs and an Englishwoman*, 44–45.

25 *Banias* refers to merchants and moneymen and is a caste designation among Hindus and Jains. Roy suggests that *bania* (like *brahmin*) was a term used in England as a synonym for vegetarian before "vegetarian" was coined in 1847: Roy, "On Verminous Life," 90. There is a story in Kipling's *Beast and Man in India* similar to the one Rogers tells. A horse is "surrounded by crows, which had already picked out both of its eyes," he writes. "There is nothing unusual in this, for it is the fate of all animals that serve the Hindu to be left to die." Kipling, of course, shoots the horse: Kipling, *Beast and Man in India*, 2.

Local Muslim farmers were, according to Rogers, angered that a memsahib was occupying land on which a mosque had once stood and that was still home to Mughal tombs and put a curse on TAF. Jim's Canuck ghost could not compete with a deceased fakir, and TAF moved out of Mehrauli by spring.

Rogers began dedicating equal time and effort to helping dispossessed humans, from ferrying people to and from hospitals to aiding a sweeper, Likhan, in a three-year court case related to the wrongful death of his son. Rogers's capaciousness did not sit well with some of her board members, and in the following years, as TAF struggled with finances—even after Rogers sold her dwindling shares to keep it afloat—and the effects of their own growing notoriety in the form of a deluge of abandoned and injured animals, to which Rogers never once said no, relationships became irreparably strained. Rogers was voted out by her board in 1979. Now in her seventies, she packed her meager possessions and moved to Jaipur, where she founded Help in Suffering (HIS) "for helping suffering animals," to which Rogers was now careful to add, "and all living things." Help in Suffering is active to this day, with this same motto.[26]

For all of Rogers's compassion and competence, it appears she was not an excellent judge of character, and after being robbed and undermined by her associates again, including other white women welfarists, Rogers turned HIS over to an Australian named Christine Townend and headed south to Bangalore.[27] There, in 1991, at eighty-five, she cofounded Compassion Unlimited plus Action (CUPA)—another animal shelter and hospital that is still among India's most effective and widely known.

In the summer of 2014 I met Geeta Seshamani in her office at Friendicoes–Society for the Eradication of Cruelty to Animals (SECA), a small and beloved animal shelter and treatment center under the Defense Colony flyover in South Delhi. I have spent a lot of time here as I researched this project and in the years before and after that. This was where my queer friends and I brought animals: a puppy hit by a car while we were shopping in Lajpat Nagar, a sick dog we passed by at Savitri Flyover, a neighborhood cat in Greater Kailash with a distended stomach. This was where two lesbian elders with rhyming names funded ambulance services and volunteered. It was where a Sangini support group

---

26 Help in Suffering was run for years by Timmie Kumar.

27 See Townend and Little, *Christine's Ark*. As further evidence of Rogers's poor judgment of character, none other than Savitri Devi Mukherji lodged with Rogers in Jaipur following a debilitating stroke in 1981: Johnson, "Savitri Devi's Communist Nephews." Rogers, who drove ambulances and lost her great love in that war, does not mention the odious shelteree in her memoirs.

member's friend who had lost his wife and struggled with alcoholism worked off both his grief and his disease by feeding animals, driving emergency vehicles, and swabbing the floors and kennels with Dettol.

Friendicoes, Dr. Seshamani told me, was among the many Indian animal shelters that owed its start to Rogers. When she was fifteen, Seshamani encountered a homeless black cat and asked her mother's permission to adopt it. But her mother, like mine, was superstitious about cats and wouldn't allow it.[28] Theirs was, however, like many Indian Army officers' families, an "animal loving" household, with a penchant for both dogs and hunting.[29] A family friend suggested to Seshamani's mother that they take the cat to a place called The Animals' Friend in Mehrauli, where she and Seshamani encountered Rogers emerging out of (in what is probably a childhood-tinted recollection) a crumbling hut trailed by half a dozen dogs and, in the background, the uneven tombstones of buried pets.[30]

28 My mom's superstitions were such that she demanded I destroy a cat poster I had in my childhood bedroom, convinced it was responsible for a recent family misfortune. The repeated visits of an elderly long-haired gray stray my mom named Ashley (for her hue, naturally) in the early 1990s finally wore her down, and she began letting cats inside our house—not only Ashley but also the next-door neighbor's cat, Felix. My cat, Zami, was staying with her when I was in grad school and in India one summer, and while Zami was playing in the backyard a dog bounded across the lawn and snapped her neck. My mother saw from the kitchen window while she was washing dishes, ran out, carried Zami in her arms, and raced her in the car to the vet, even though Zami was clearly dead. My mom still remembers how Zami's eyes turned purple as she ran with her and how beautiful she looked, as if, she said, she had died according to her own nature.

29 Her father was an avid hunter and would take Geeta along with him on some of his jaunts. One day he unknowingly killed a pregnant deer. Geeta "wept and wept," and her father never touched his guns again. Geeta Seshamani, interview by the author, New Delhi, June 12, 2014.

30 The Animals' Friend did have what is considered India's first animal cemetery. The image of the graveyard often accompanies recollections of Rogers, including by Maneka Gandhi in her foreword to *Mad Dogs and an Englishwoman* and in my interviews with Seshamani and Satija. Pet cemeteries are now common, among the largest in Delhi being that at Jeev Ashram, an animal shelter on the outskirts of the city that was featured in the Bollywood adaption of Jane Austen's *Emma*, called *Aisha* (2010), directed by Rajashree Ojha. Aisha's *kutta-billi* activity was used to represent her triviality that was, of course, finally resolved by heterosexual love. I fault Ojha for this, not Austen.

Friendicoes-SECA began as a Kindness Club founded by Gautam Barat after he heard Rogers give a lecture at the College of Jesus and Mary in 1976. Gautam was joined at the Kindness Club by his sister and Anuradha Sawhney (then Aggarwal), a first-time activist who would go on to become the director of PETA-India after a detour as a leather importer and followed by a career as an editor of vegan celebrity cookbooks.[31] Gautam and Anuradha formally registered the club as Friendicoes-SECA in April 1979 and appealed to Indira Gandhi's office for funds—the Gandhis had a reputation for compassion toward animals, even after the violence they had committed against persons and the democracy during the Emergency. The appeal trickled down to Sanjay and Maneka Gandhi, the latter of whom had also recently been approached by Rogers for funds—an encounter Gandhi credits with changing her life.[32] They gave the two shops under the recently constructed Defense Colony Flyover to Gautam and Anuradha in late 1979 in honor of Maneka's birthday.[33] Geeta's family vet had told her about the Kindness Club the previous year, and once Friendicoes was operational in the spring of 1980 she gave up her search for a respectable job and started swabbing kennels and cooking enormous vats of dog and cat food in her kitchen.[34] There were very few—Geeta, perhaps exaggerating a little bit, said five—vets for domestic animals (or, in Friendicoes parlance, "community pets" to refer to street dogs and cats) in the city, so Friendicoes members had

31 I conducted a lengthy interview with Anuradha Sawhney in the summer of 2013 at her home in Pune. After her break with Friendicoes she did work as a leather importer. She believed then that leather is a "mere byproduct" of meat. It was when she heard otherwise that she began to research the leather industry and came across PETA. She badgered them for a job interview and eventually rose to chief functionary of the Indian office. Sawhney served in that role for nine years, during which time she led numerous campaigns and became a well-known figure on the cover of multiple magazines, lauded especially for her corporate achievements as a woman. After leaving PETA, Sawhney started a vegetarian tiffin business and published the two-volume cookbook *The Vegan Kitchen: Bollywood Style!*

32 Gandhi, "Foreword," ix–xii.

33 Friendicoes expanded with a third shop in 1990 and a fourth one in 1999 to its current size and configuration, still and forever under the overpass. Friendicoes also runs an animal sanctuary in Gopalpur Khera, Gurgaon, about an hour and a half's drive from Defense Colony.

34 Gautam Barat, both Geeta and he agreed, handled the "people side of things," as he had a genuinely irrepressible personality, and Geeta was better with what they both called "the heavy work." Gautam died in 2011 of cancer. For more on Barat, see Sekhar, "Continuing Grace."

to train, too, in advanced animal first aid and advocate for government veterinary training beyond animal husbandry and abattoir inspection.

Rogers had been forced out of Delhi in the years since Gautam heard her speak, and TAF, too, was gone. Friendicoes became the center of animal welfare in Delhi, constellating both animals and a burgeoning number of young welfarists shaped by Rogers.[35] In addition to Seshamani, Barat, Sawhney, and Gandhi crossing paths under the flyover, Camellia Satija, the activist and owner of the Rio Grande, was central to Friendicoes.[36] Two major philosophical differences began to show among these welfarists at Friendicoes during the 1980s: around meat and euthanasia.

Despite having grown up in a meat-eating Punjabi family, Sawhney was "strict veg" when she joined the group and was opposed to feeding meat to the dogs in their care. (Cats are understood to require taurine, an amino acid found exclusively in animal flesh, and thus were considered a necessary exception to vegetarian purity.) Anuradha and Camellia, in fact, had created their

35 The Indian SPCA, which was first founded in Calcutta in 1861 by Colesworthy Grant, had a shelter in the Tis Hazari neighborhood of Old Delhi at that time, but it had a poor reputation for its treatment of animals, mortality rate, and overcrowded kennels. Many Indian advocates and welfarists hold the SPCA in low esteem. Activists such as Nitya Ghotge, cofounder of Anthra, an organization that advocates on behalf of agrarian communities, believe the SPCA has done more to undermine Indian animal welfare than to aid it. The SPCA was premised on a specifically British, pet-centric understanding of animal cruelty. The AWBI borrowed this British model, focusing on dogs and cats instead of the interspecies dependencies between humans and livestock that are understood in a range of Indic traditions. Ghotge and others thus argue that the SPCA made an ethos already present appear foreign and trivial. Welfarists have described SPCAs as everything from a "death chamber" to "diabolical," and there has been a fair share of court cases against them over the years on grounds of neglect. Still, it is mandated by the PCA that every district in every state have an SPCA. Seshamani sued the government of India for a breach of this obligation: *Geeta Seshamani v. Union of India and Another*, Supreme Court of India, 2001.

36 Later, Arpan Sharma, the founder of the Federation of Indian Animal Protection Organizations (FIAPO), was introduced to animal welfare through Friendicoes and considers Seshamani his "guru." Counted in this lineage, as well, is Jayasimha Nuggehali, onetime director of Humane Society International-India, preceded by stints at PETA, as well as Maneka Gandhi's People for Animals (PFA). Jaya narrates two life-changing moments. He read Gandhi's "Heads and Tails" column in a newspaper in ninth standard and wrote her a letter, to which she responded by sending him autographed copies of her book and the contact information for a Bangalore branch of PFA, where he began his career. The second life-altering event was hearing Rogers speak at around the same time in his life.

own recipe for a "scientifically nutritious" vegetarian dog food, partly in the hope that such an option would entice more *savarna* Hindus to adopt dogs. But Seshamani found this uneconomical, as well as sentimental. Anuradha left, but Camellia stayed on. She only left later, in 1991, owing to opposition to the shelter's practice of compassionate euthanasia, which, even more than cooking and feeding meat, felt in conflict with her understanding of *ahimsa*, or noninjury. "Hindu philosophy," she said, "does not permit it." There was no animosity in her departure, she insisted. All three women believed in the Friendicoes motto of "service before self," and her leaving—ultimately to start the advocacy organization KARE in that same year—was just another form of service to animals. Cleaning kennels, cooking food, and rescuing animals from monsoon sewers and electrical circuit boards, anyway, does not leave much time for other kinds of labor, such as lobbying against vivisection, a central priority of KARE, building on the legacy of Rogers, a vocal antivivisectionist, and that of Rukmini Devi.

While Satija moved on to KARE and Sawhney moved on to varied vegan future, Seshamani stayed at Friendicoes with Gautam Barat and remained in touch with Rogers for the rest of Rogers's life, a connection unbroken from her first childhood encounter.[37] After leaving Jaipur—and after her exile from Delhi—Rogers wound up in Bangalore, living, as it turned out, in a small rented room with a menagerie of animals just behind Seshamani's father's estate. Seshamani met Rogers in the by-lanes of their neighborhood and learned from her that her room was haunted by a poltergeist. Rogers needed to move but had little money or connection, so she called upon an old friendship with an amateur welfarist, Suparna Ganguly, who would take care of Rogers through the last day of her life.

Like Satija, Sawhney, Barat, and Gandhi, Ganguly had heard Rogers speak in Delhi in the mid- to late 1970s. She was seventeen at the time and joined the board of TAF. The young Ganguly was unable to prevent the board from ousting Rogers and, disillusioned, she moved to Bangalore, where, by her own account, she lived a pretty quiet middle-class life, married with kids, until the reencounter with Rogers in 1990. Within a year, Ganguly and Rogers cofounded CUPA. Rogers was poor in health and resources, but Ganguly and the four other

---

37 In 1995, while still with Friendicoes, Seshamani cofounded Wildlife SOS, a conservation organization known in part for its efforts to end the practice of "dancing bears" by funding and "rehabilitating" members of the Muslim Kalandar community. For more on Wildlife SOS and the fate of those no-longer-dancing bears, see Venkat, "Iatrogenic Life."

women who started CUPA did what they could to support her. Rogers died in 1996. Ganguly was at the shelter and had asked General A. K. Chatterjee, chairman of the Animal Welfare Board of India (AWBI), to look in on her. He said that her last words, as he held her hand surrounded by cats and dogs, was, "Please don't let CUPA die!"[38] Rogers's memoir was unfinished when she passed away, but Suparna and other CUPA friends edited it posthumously. Suparna has Rogers's curling, typewritten manuscript in a glass-cased bookshelf in her home office. I remember only that it began and ended a little differently from the published version.[39] Suparna had Rogers's other material possessions in that display case, too: the first five issues of *Animal Citizen*, overseen by Rukmini Devi, and several mildewed books on the supernatural.[40]

---

38 Also in the "poignant last words" category is a contemporary of Rogers, a woman named Norah Nicholson, who is among the subjects featured in William Dalrymple's travelogue *City of Djinns* and was played by Zohra Sehgal in the 2007 stage adaptation. Nicholson claimed aristocratic British lineage, though the historical facts of her background are vague. Like Rogers, Nicholson chose to live in India after Independence and practiced a life of both material poverty and rich social connection. She was briefly a nanny to Rajiv and Sanjay Gandhi, or so she says—a claim that has taken on the social life of fact among the welfarists who speak of her. When Dalrymple met her in 1984, she was living in a makeshift structure composed of tin, plywood, and a tarp given to her by her benefactor, Indira Gandhi, who was assassinated that same year. Nicholson was another *pagal memsahib* (crazy Englishwoman) whose madness was represented in part by her affection for animals. In addition to a cobra who lived uninvited under her bed, Dalrymple says, she had four dogs, many cats, and a partridge or two. She was killed in 1987, bitten by the cobra while feeding it milk. Dalrymple's narrative differs from the one I heard from Seshamani. In the former, Nicholson's body was found a day later only because of the howling of her dogs; in Seshamani's version, someone was holding her hand as she died and heard her final words: "Don't you dare kill that snake!" According to Seshamani, Nicholson had willed her modest patch of land to Friendicoes—as well as her animals, of course—but the will was disputed, and the Delhi Jal Board expropriated her land.

39 In the preface to *Mad Dogs and an Englishwoman*, the editors explain that CUPA compiled the book from "a diversity of material—Ms. Rogers's personal diary, the draft manuscript *Battle for the Weak*, letters, poems, essays, inter alia" (xv).

40 This relationship between attention to nonhuman animals and attention to nonhuman spirits appears, in different forms, throughout this book. As Mayanthi Fernando argues in "Uncanny Ecologies," the multispecies turn—and even the ethnographic turn to god—in the Western academy, despite its other departures from traditional humanism, evinces an attachment to secularity and to that which we can touch and see. I suspect this reluctance to take ghosts and gods seriously as historical agents, and as objects of care, is related to certain formulations of "mattering," or a political

The Luminous: Rukmini Devi Arundale

We are not yet finished with eccentric Englishwomen and occultish white people, even though the narrative bends toward something new. The white woman here is Annie Besant (1847–1933), the theosophist, socialist, and Indian nationalist who was among the prime influences on the life and work of Rukmini Devi Arundale.

Because there is so much written about Besant, I'll limit my sources largely to Gauri Viswanathan's *Outside the Fold* (1998), a book on conversion that has resonance for this story about animals, too.[41] Viswanathan begins the chapter on Besant by considering why biographers insist she led a wildly inconsistent life, devoid of moral integrity—converting from atheism to socialism to occultism.[42] Viswanathan rejects claims of inconsistency because Viswanathan's theory of conversion is fundamentally premised on noncontradiction: of conversion being the activity of "overlaps and convergences" rather than radical breaks. I return to conversion—it is among my answers to the question that frames this chapter—but let me first discuss some significant overlaps and convergences, particularly between the odious Savitri Devi Mukherji and the luminous Rukmini Devi Arundale.

Like the former, Besant was an occultist who held to a cyclical theory of time in which war is a necessary stage toward the achievement of an ultimate unity.[43] Both Mukherji and Besant were Indophiles of the Franco-German tradition, and both, as it happens, served time in British prisons as enemies of the state (Savitri Devi as a Nazi; Besant for anticolonial activities). I'm not certain as to Besant's lifelong commitment to animals, but we do know that she cheekily told the famous vegetarian George Bernard Shaw, who publicly admonished her conversion to theosophy, that vegetarianism must have "enfeebled her mind."[44] But it is also clear that she was an impassioned antivivisectionist, an offshoot of both her distrust of science and her naturalist leanings toward

gradualism in which the turn to animals must still insist on other exclusions. Or, perhaps, it is simply to ward off the dreaded assignation of crazy cat person! Nevertheless, for many of those who populate this book, animalism entails a keen awareness across human, animal, and supernatural or nonmaterial domains, the last of which are not isomorphic with religion.

41 Viswanathan, *Outside the Fold*.

42 Among these biographers of Besant are William James, Arthur Nethercot, George Bernard Shaw, Geoffrey West, and Anne Taylor.

43 Besant presented her "final unity" as an "empire without subordination," exemplifying how her philosophy shaded in and out between anti-imperialism and imperialist race theory: Viswanathan, *Outside the Fold*, 205.

44 Shaw, *An Autobiography 1856–1898*, 142, cited in Viswanathan, *Outside the Fold*, 183.

monism—or the single substance of the universe—a theory she adopted while translating Ludwig Büchner's *Mind in Animals* in 1880, a book on the nonduality of anthropos and animal.[45] It is worth remembering in this vein of convergences and overlap with Savitri Devi that Besant was a committed antinatalist who, despite her skepticism toward science, advocated any means necessary for the curtailment of the human population (a point of convergence, too, of course, with the Emergency-era Gandhis).

This was the towering if diminutive figure—unhappily married and now more happily divorced—who, when Rukmini Devi accepted George Arundale's proposal of marriage in Madras, asked her, "Are you brave?" and when Rukmini said, "Yes. I am," replied with a kiss on the young woman's head, "You will do," and blessed her into adulthood.[46] Rukmini Devi is today an icon of the animal welfare movement in India. Her garlanded portrait was the image that greeted visitors to the original AWBI office in Chennai; the board's headquarters have since moved closer to the capital, in Haryana, as the AWBI was absorbed by, of all things, the Ministry of Fisheries, Animal Husbandry, and Dairying in 2019.[47] The AWBI has existed since 1962, instituted by order of the Prevention of Cruelty against Animals Act (PCA) of 1960 that was introduced by Rukmini Devi herself in 1954. She had been elected to Parliament two years earlier. Her speech to the Rajya Sabha in 1954 not only invoked the tradition of dharmic thought via Aśoka, Buddha, and Mahavira, but also looked to Europe for examples of how to fulfill an Indian destiny of compassion toward animals.[48] Jawaharlal Nehru, an animal lover in the bourgeois sense of that phrase, was taken with Arundale's speech. So moved was he that he asked her to withdraw the bill, claiming that the issue was too dear to let fail and that he should oversee the process. Arundale acquiesced to Nehru, but with unexpected consequences: she drafted the bill to curtail animal experimentation and slaughter for food. Nehru's version—the one that passed in 1960 and is still in effect—made animal experimentation, entertainment, and slaughter for food the three *exceptions* to cruelty law.[49]

45 Büchner and Besant, *Mind in Animals*, cited in Viswanathan *Outside the Fold*, 194.

46 Ramani, *Rukmini Devi Arundale Birth Centenary Volume*, 18.

47 I have not visited the Haryana office but assume that Rukmini Devi's portrait still occupies pride of place.

48 "Prevention of Cruelty to Animals," in Kalakshetra and Arundale, *Speeches and Writings of Rukmini Devi Arundale*, 2:33–44.

49 Chapter 4 of the PCA permits animal experimentation under welfarist conditions, and sec. 11(3) excludes "destruction of animals . . . for food for mankind."

Rukmini Devi, her convictions notwithstanding, was not an iconoclast. She had no desire, she once wrote, to "convert" anyone. She only asked people to open their eyes so she could provide a glimpse into her understanding of the world.[50] And she was no less pragmatic in some ways than Nehru. As the chairwoman of the AWBI when it was established in 1962, she proudly accepted gifts from the RSPCA in London to alleviate what she knew to be the inevitable suffering of animals: three modernized electrocution cabinets for stray dogs and twelve cash captive bolt pistols for buffalo slaughter.[51]

Rukmini Devi was born Rukmini Sastri in Madura, Tamil Nadu, in 1904 but was raised in Chingleput and then Adyar, which has been home to the Theosophical Society of India since its founding in 1882.[52] Her father, Neelakanta Sastri, the engineer son of a Sanskrit scholar, was opposed to caste, child marriage, and animal sacrifice, representing a historical pre–World War I moment when animal sacrifice was opposed on the same liberal, Brahmo grounds as the opposition to child marriage, the prohibition of widow remarriage, the practice of sati, and caste oppression. It would be interesting to trace how and when concern about the killing of animals, whether for religious or secular purposes, became delinked in India from liberalism and associated so thoroughly with fascistic principles. The rise of Aryo-pagan Nazism across Europe and India, and its version of "sacred vegetarianism," is certainly central to that moral-political rupture.

This racialist lineage bisected Rukmini Devi's liberal one through the complex figure of Annie Besant. Rukmini Devi's father was initiated into theosophy in 1906. Neelakanta Sastri had married off two of his daughters when they were twelve or younger. One of them returned home after years of abuse from her husband, and he refused to send her back to her conjugal home, despite the risk of social censure. Theosophy offered Neelakanta a new beginning. He, along with others, swore an oath to Besant to reject child marriage. Besant, in turn, supported the returned daughter's medical education in Banaras and, later, London.

Still a child herself—either thirteen or fourteen, the date varying in her own renderings—Rukmini Sastri met her future husband, Dr. George Arundale, at a party thrown at the Madras Theosophical Society by George's aunt and

50 Kalakshetra and Arundale, *Speeches and Writings of Rukmini Devi Arundale*, vol. 2.
51 *Animal Citizen*, July–September 1964.
52 Biographical details in this paragraph and the following are from "Rukmini on Herself" in Ramani, *Rukmini Devi Arundale Birth Centenary Volume*; Kalakshetra and Arundale, *Speeches and Writings of Rukmini Devi Arundale*, vol. 1.

adoptive guardian, the English theosophist Francesca Arundale.[53] The handsome George Arundale was Besant's "trusted lieutenant" who had moved to Madras to serve as editor of her anticolonial paper, *New India*. Besant, of course, blessed the wedding of Rukmini and George, but Madras high society did not. So they married in Bombay in 1920—Rukmini was sixteen—then traveled the world. On Dr. Arundale's arm, Rukmini Devi met the occultist author and theosophist Charles Webster Leadbeater and saw Anna Pavlova dance, the latter inspiring in her a lifelong reverence for the art.

Rukmini Devi became a devoted student of dance when she returned to India, taking up Bharatanatyam, a form then scorned by elite *savarna* society for its association with *devadasis*. A pivotal performance of hers in 1932 began to change local perceptions, converting even the likes of C. P. Ramaswami Iyer.[54] Together, the Arundales agitated for Indian independence, operated the Besant Theosophical School, and visited Shantiniketan—six years after Savitri, that one-woman pack of Nazis—where Rukmini danced for the poet and conjured designs for her own academy, Kalakshetra, that she founded in 1936. George Arundale's health began to deteriorate the next year. Wikipedia says that he died peacefully at home in 1945, but the truth, or at least the truth-force of local hagiography, is something different.

In July 2013, I went to Kalakshetra, Rukmini Devi's dance academy in Chennai. Rukmini Devi Arundale died in 1986, and Kalakshetra was now being run by Leela Samson, a student and devotee of Rukmini Devi's as well as her biographer.[55] Samson is perfectly upright and slender, with strong, muscular hands and feet. She welcomed me and brought me a cup of milky chai that, for some reason, I drank every drop of rather than politely refusing. Samson tucked her dancer's feet under her on the sofa and told me stories about Rukmini Devi, truth and myth force: how a bird once sat on her shoulder, and

---

53 Ramani, *Rukmini Devi Arundale Birth Centenary Volume*, 15.

54 Sir C. P. Ramaswami Iyer plays other minor roles in this story. He and Besant began as foes, as Iyer represented Jiddu Narayaniah against Besant in a custody trial and won. Iyer and Besant eventually came to a mutual respect. Years later, Iyer aided Arundale in the founding of the Indian Vegetarian Congress, and Arundale, in turn, was a founding member of the C. P. Foundation upon Iyer's death in 1966. The C. P. Foundation is directed by Nandita Krishna, granddaughter of Iyer and wife of Chinny Krishna, another legendary figure in Indian animal welfare and the founder of Chennai Blue Cross, among many, many other activities. Chinny's parents were also theosophists. For more on Chinny's work in Chennai, see Srinivasan, "Remaking More-than-Human Society."

55 Samson, *Rukmini Devi*.

woman and bird sat silently, looking into each other's eyes. There is a photograph of Arundale beperched with birds, reproduced in many places and among the first images to appear in a Google search of her name. (She never cooed at animals, Samson said. She met them in silence—person to person, object to object.) Samson told me how Arundale, at a dinner at Pandit Nehru's, confronted a maharaja—confronted them all—as they boasted about their great appreciation for animals while filling their bellies with meat. She talked about Arundale's capaciousness: she opened Kalakshetra's grounds not only to parrots and peacocks and mutts but to child widows who needed a home and livelihood.

Samson told me about a trip she and other students had taken with Arundale to Spain in 1968. The students, on a free day, thought it would be interesting to attend a corrida, not knowing that Arundale was there to lobby the Spanish government against bullfighting. A local journalist delighted in the sight of these beautiful girls in saris, and a photo of them rapt at the arena ran on the front page of the next morning's paper. That day was agony. In the evening they were finally called to their guru's room. "You could feel it in the air," Samson said. "She wasn't angry. It was more like we'd cut her to the bone, and it was trust you knew you would never earn back." As she said this, Samson started to cry. She elegantly pulled on her nose, trying, I think, to keep the tears from dropping. (Ah, yes, this is when and why I drank all of the chai.) Then there was the time they rode through Delhi, Arundale and Samson, while in the city for a performance, looking for soap and sandals made without flesh. Time ran out, and they were forced to give up. "No soap for us then," Arundale had said. "Water is fine." It seemed that these principles went beyond hygiene and footwear. George Arundale, influenced by his wife's opposition to animal experimentation, shared her refusal of allopathic medication and treatment. A diabetic with nerve damage and infected limbs, who refused to medicate or be seen by anyone but a single disciple in his final days, George Arundale did not, according to Samson, die a peaceful death.

The Theosophical Society largely abandoned Rukmini Devi after George Arundale died in 1945, thinking perhaps that she had strayed too far from them toward dance, crafts, and animals, all of which Besant had encouraged, but she, too, was now gone. During these years between 1945 and the establishment of the AWBI in the early 1960s—while the grieving Rogers was experimenting with spiritualism and planning the trip that would lead her to India, and while Savitri Devi was imprisoned for espionage and penning Nazi tracts—Arundale continued to build her life as an artist, politician, and animal advocate. In 1959, she founded the Indian Vegetarian Congress, of which she remained president until she stepped down in 1974. In 1964, in her capacity as chairperson of the

AWBI, she instituted a new and still extant government body, the Committee for the Purpose of Control and Supervision of Experiments on Animals (CPCSEA).[56] In 1977, Prime Minister Morarji Desai asked permission to nominate her for president of India; Arundale declined.

Among Arundale's many tasks as chair of the AWBI was overseeing *Animal Citizen*, a journal published by the AWBI beginning in 1963 under the editorship of a British expat named Peter Hoffman.[57] *Animal Citizen*, with many articles and columns written by Arundale, demonstrates her commitment to animal welfare, including to the issue of animal experimentation for which George Arundale, as myth would have it, gave his life thirty years earlier.[58] India was, until 1978, a major exporter of rhesus monkeys to Britain and the United States for research, the number reaching as high as 200,000 per annum in the 1940s and 1950s. According to a report in the *Bombay Sentinel*, the monkeys were usually caught in Uttar Pradesh, taken by train 260 miles from Lucknow to Delhi, and then flown from Delhi four thousand miles to London. Of those that survived the journey, some were flown three thousand miles farther, to the United States. The suffering of these animals gained international attention when a transport van at a London airport, transferring Indian monkeys from one plane to another, was left unventilated for more than two hours. When the van was opened, nearly four hundred of the 457 had died of suffocation.[59]

This brings to mind Timothy Pachirat's story of the wayward cow who escaped a slaughterhouse transport van in Omaha and was shot by police, leading to outrage even though the cow was going to die at the slaughterhouse, and probably a more painful death.[60] The moral of Pachirat's story is of the societal desire

---

56 Camellia Satija was a member of the CPCSEA when it temporarily disbanded in 1977. She then joined Friendicoes-SECA.

57 Hoffman was the husband of a Kalakshetra dancer and was an avid reader of international literature on animal welfare. He and Rukmini Arundale were close friends. Amala Akkineni, who appears in chapter 6, was a student at Kalakshetra between 1975 and 1985 and considered Peter Hoffman "like a father" to her. Akkineni says that Hoffman helped Arundale draft the version of the PCA that she introduced in Parliament, a copy of which Akkineni has in her personal archive.

58 In another publication, the *Indian Vegetarian Congress Quarterly*, Arundale reminds readers that vegetarianism includes the rejection of medicine manufactured through animal exploitation: "Vegetarianism is not [limited to] food. Vegetarianism is a way of life, a spiritual mission for which we are all working": Arundale, "Vegetarianism Is a Way of Life," 90.

59 *Animal Citizen*, July–September 1964.

60 Pachirat, *Every Twelve Seconds*, 1–3.

for not seeing, for once the eyes are open, ethical responsibility risks spreading like a fire. Rukmini Devi understood this drive to not see, this compartmentalization of culpability, as being at the heart of the failure of *ahimsa* as a guide for moral action. *Ahimsa* for Arundale functions less as a doctrine for compassion than as a moral-hygienic practice of keeping one's own hands clean by way of both delegating and concealing violence.[61] Perhaps we do not kill these animals ourselves, she wrote in 1954 in her address to Pandit Nehru, but we send them to foreign countries for "a fate even worse than death"—a phrase that appears often in *Animal Citizen* in relation to vivisection.[62] This justification and delegation of violence was especially consequential, Arundale argued, in light of the rise and ostensible defeat of Nazism, and she dared in Parliament to make what is often called the "dreaded comparison" but is more aptly a brutal resonance: "There were many Nazi doctors who thought that without human experiments there were certain remedies and techniques which could not be discovered. And so, the moral issue, *of using any means to achieve your ends*, is the most vital issue [to fight against] of all."[63]

The End of the World

We come full circle, then, with the evocation of the Third Reich, to how Savitri Devi, Rukmini Devi, and Crystal Rogers are linked in history, all through the figure of the animal and all in the midst of the rise of fascism and the afterlife of empire. But as I promised at the start of this chapter, the answer to the question, *Why is moral attention to the animal so repulsive?* cannot be settled entirely by its links to fascism or to the affective history of European liberalism. Reading Savitri Devi, Rukmini Devi, and Crystal Rogers together offers at least three other explanations for that repulsion, all of which tie back to the heteropatriarchal fundaments grounding fascism and liberalism: queer nonreproductivity, or fear for the end of the world; the hatred of women, or fear for the end of the world; and the fear of conversion, or fear for the end of the world.

All three women in this chapter are, shall we say, without child. Barren. Nil. Not only lacking in fecundity—a small mercy, to be sure, in Savitri Mukherji's case—but all appeared by their own and others' accounts to be at least *heterosexually* celibate, devoid not only of issue but of the physical love of men.

---

61 I say more on *ahimsa* in chapter 6.

62 "Prevention of Cruelty to Animals," in Kalakshetra and Arundale, *Speeches and Writings of Rukmini Devi Arundale*, 2:42.

63 "Prevention of Cruelty to Animals," 2:42–43, emphasis added.

Savitri's heterosexual celibacy was the product of her racism, but that did not deter her same-sex expressions. Not often mentioned by her right-wing fanboys, Mukherji had sexual relationships with women, including, most famously, Françoise Dior of the French house of fashion.[64] Rogers, for her part, was in love with a ghost for most of her life, and yes, while Demi Moore was able to have sex with Patrick Swayze through the medium of Whoopi Goldberg in a pottery studio, and Rogers did claim to develop "direct communication" with Jim, this is, by any measure, a highly not-straight, nonreproductive kind of love. Rukmini Devi was not queer, though it is obvious that persons of all and no genders and kind fell in love with her. Nor was she necessarily celibate, though an Arundale celibacy would certainly square with Besant's teachings, particularly the ones she was developing most forcefully in 1920, when the Arundales wed.[65] Whether the two were busy or not, the natalist view of their union on the family tree is a decisive, vacant, "Nil."[66]

Not only did Mukherji, Rogers, and Arundale not procreate—or, possibly, participate at all in the sexual-contract part of heteropatriarchy—but they also embodied in different ways the dangers of conversion. Conversion was implicit in the previous chapter, where I presented it in the positive, perhaps impermanent Deleuzian gloss of becoming. Yet the moments of becoming other that I have presented across both of these chapters are, in fact, lifelong, permanent, and demanding. They constitute, in other words, conversion, an activity that Gauri Viswanathan, to return to her once more, calls "one of the most unsettling political events in the life of a society."[67] Both Savitri Devi and Rukmini Devi, for all of their other differences, trace their moments of conversion to animal sacrifice; Rogers traces hers to a visit to India when she saw a beaten

---

64 Margaronis, "Savitri Devi." Françoise Dior was, not incidentally, a Nazi financier.

65 Besant's *Britain's Place in the Great Plan* (1921) developed, as Viswanathan explains, an explicitly nonreproductive ("calm and sterile" in Viswanathan's words) alternative to the biological family: Viswanathan, *Outside the Fold*, 195–96. Viswanathan suggests that Besant's nonreproductive brotherhood allowed her to smuggle back in her commitment to population control, which Madame Blavatsky had ordered Besant to recant as the price of admission into the Theosophical Society in 1890. For Blavatsky, population control was incompatible with reincarnation, for if the population dwindled, there would be fewer bodies for reincarnated souls to reside in. Blavatsky died in 1891.

66 Ramani, *Rukmini Devi Arundale Birth Centenary Volume*, 2.

67 Viswanathan, *Outside the Fold*, xi. See also Jaaware and Rao, *Practicing Caste*, 69. Jaaware argues that conversion is "repulsive" in caste-based, or what he calls "inheritance," societies.

horse with crows pecking out its eyes. All ostensibly, through no agency of their own but accidents of fate, became converts to a way of life in which soap and shoes are optional; in which human death entails necessary suffering; in which poverty of love, riches, or both are likely; in which, like Arundale and Rogers, one is, however determined, alienated from the values of their time and kind. As Viswanathan argues, conversion destabilizes society because it signifies the "departure of members from the fold."[68]

Stewart Cole demonstrates in "'Necessary Murder': Eating Meat against Fascism" how George Orwell and W. H. Auden—both also avid commentators on India and the Raj—formulated a hypermasculine carnophilic opposition to vegetarianism in the 1930s as a response to the rise of European fascism and its threats to the humanist subject. For each, differently, vegetarianism constituted a dangerous dictatorial puritanism and an effete affront to the commonality of humanity, a commonality that had to be insisted on in the face of fascism's "violent hierarchizing *within* the human species."[69] Carnivory was, in fascist Europe, and is still—perhaps in India more than any other place in the world—understood among the left as keeping intact the human fold, a gustatory bulwark against threats to the species posed by right-wing genocidal orders.

Yet the bulwark that is meat eating also takes the form of what Parama Roy, in another context, has called a "culinary masculinity," or "carnivoracity," that takes as its antithesis the sterile or effete.[70] Cole, for example, quotes from a poem by Auden called "Letter to Lord Byron:"

The Higher Mind's outgrowing the Barbarian,
It's hardly thought hygienic now to kiss;
The world is surely turning vegetarian;
And as it grows too sensitive for this,
It won't be long before we find there is
A Society of Everybody's Aunts
For the Prevention of Cruelty to Plants.[71]

---

68 Viswanathan, *Outside the Fold*, xi.

69 Cole, "Necessary Murder," 75. Orwell's "Reflections on Gandhi" took aim at the Mahatma's seemingly uncompromising vegetarianism, arguing that such saintly purity rendered him—on point—inhuman.

70 Roy, "Meat-Eating, Masculinity, and Renunciation in India," 66, 71. Roy borrows "carnivoracity" from Maggie Kilgour's *From Communion to Cannibalism*.

71 W. H. Auden, "Letter to Lord Byron," reproduced in Cole, "'Necessary Murder,'" 83.

In Auden's poem, Cole points out, the "proverbial spinster aunt['s] lack of a nuclear family of her own leads her to bestow maternal affections upon . . . lesser forms of life."[72] And we see, in this carnophallophilic poetics, how anti-vegetarianism is doubly fearful for the end of the world as we know it: rightly resisting the end of humanity, it trembles, too, at the end of Man.

72 Cole, "'Necessary Murder,'" 83–84. Kareem Khubchandani's collaborative initiative, Critical Aunty Studies, has much to say about the aunty's remove from the center of hetero-narrative. This remove is what makes her "urgent for the work of survival and care," Khubchandani says, "complicating the shape of kinship" as we claim to know it—complicating, we might say, the very concept of what we consider the fold: Khubchandani, "Welcome to Critical Aunty Studies."

CONTRADICTION. How Is the Otherwise Exhausted?

Many of us have a go-to story, our perfect and most telling ethnographic vignette. For many years now, mine has been this: in the summer of 2012, I was doing fieldwork in Bombay with Welfare for Stray Dogs (WSD). The organization's philosophy is to try to heal animals on the streets where they live rather than giving in to the sentimental impulse to rescue them into shelters, which are often miserable and lonely spaces. Welfare for Stray Dogs has many volunteers, mostly young and enthusiastic ones, who meet every Sunday at 9 a.m. in the center of town, splitting up into small groups to administer first aid to animals that are listed by location, description, and ailment. In addition to the Sunday volunteers there are salaried fieldworkers, such as Dipesh.

Dipesh covers the city six days a week, from South Bombay to the Matunga suburb, by foot, bus, and train. I watched him heal goats and donkeys, hens and crows, cats, cows, and dogs. Dipesh then was in his early thirties, with thinning hair, dark skin, and a strong, thick body. He wore the same pair of light-gray pants every day, with sun-bleached, peach-toned button-down shirts and thin black shoes with holes in them. He walks fast, despite his heavy first aid bags, and is often on his cell phone consulting with the volunteer help line operator back at the office. He doesn't stop to eat or drink but has chai in the morning and a meal at 10:30 when he goes back to the *chawl* he shares with his parents. Dipesh is unmarried but has two siblings, both of whom have families of their own. I asked him once why he hadn't married. "Aa badha maate," he said, sweeping his arm as if to include all the animals of the city. To have time for them, he continued in Gujarati, "main life cycle finish nathi karyu" (I haven't become husband and father).

Dipesh was whistling and chatting with me as we walked one day, and he suddenly turned and kneeled near a motorbike, from under which he pulled an old, horrid-looking dog with a tail like thick, tapered rope and huge patches of fur missing, all pink and scaly under there like an armadillo. Still whistling, Dipesh pulled a string from the pocket of his pants and casually tied the dog's snout and carried her into the partial shade of an apartment building. With his free hand, Dipesh grabbed a discarded newspaper, which he placed under the dog's butt. He lifted the animal's tail and applied medicine inside her anus with a dropper. Maggots emerged in the dozens, wriggling and wiggling, and Dipesh took his tweezers, with which he entered the dog's ass, and pulled out dozens more, placing them methodically on the newspaper, by which time they had all stopped moving. When he finished the job, Dipesh applied talcum powder and an anti-infection cream and unmuzzled her. As Dipesh wadded up the newspaper, looking for a place to dispose of it, the dog walked unsteadily into the street and took what looked like a very uncomfortable shit as cars and motorcycles dodged her. As a car nearly hit her, I screamed, and Dipesh turned to see. He shrugged and said, *she's old*.

What could something like this mean? What does it mean to kneel bareheaded in the heat of the midday sun, pulling maggots deep from the ass of an unknown animal, whistling a tune to soothe her trembling body—and then, when she walks headlong into her death, to shrug and say, *she's old*? This is what I have thought it means: an ethics that is immanent and not categorical, indifferent to the principle of conviction.[1] Dipesh did not heal the dog because she had life and therefore must live. Dipesh healed the dog because he saw her, and what else could he do?[2] It has also meant for me an ethics without future, an ethics shorn of promise, indifferent to the principle of continuity. Dipesh

---

1 On contradiction, dialectics, and abandoning the principle of conviction, see Price, "Before Politics."
2 As Sara Salih put it, "Our moral actions are ridiculous; but there's nothing else to do." Salih, personal communication.

worked but with little regard to the consequences, to how the dog would, in health, represent his labor.[3] In that immanence, and in that ethics without futurity, I have seen a radical solitude: not the solitude of man who stands alone, but a solitude that expresses a fullness of being in every present moment.

That is what I have made of that story. I tell it often. I think it has served me well.

But then one afternoon as I was reading through my field notes, I came across an uncomfortable detail, something I hadn't noticed before or, perhaps, had subconsciously repressed. Dipesh, like another notoriously self-effacing welfarist called the Birdman, did not like to have his picture taken. I took many pictures when we were together but never of Dipesh's face, with or without an animal in the frame—until, that is, the day of the dog with the maggots in her bum. "You should take a picture," he said. "All right," I said, as I readied my camera. "I won't get you in it." *Tik hai*, he said, with a wave of his hand, "I can be in it!" He even pointed out good shots and paused once to look into my camera.

Oh, no, I thought when I read this. My entire argument had been wrong. Dipesh was not indifferent to consequences. That act was not ordinary to him but as special and remarkable as it became to me. And that act *was* a representation of him, and the dog *did* represent his care and humanity. And he did want that image, that self, that other, to endure.

Well. I *could* just kind of forget about it again. As ethnographers, we omit things all the time—out of necessity, but also sometimes, let's admit it, for narrative convenience and coherence.[4] But, really, what would be the point? Already what people enjoyed most about this story was finding all the holes in it.[5] This isn't about ethics, some would say. It's about labor. Dipesh is an employee and was simply doing his job. Or, others would argue, he was clearly interested in futurity and continuity: he took you with him, didn't he? His ethics are not immanent, others would say, but culturally determined and even doctrinaire: the Bhagavad Gita tells us to act without regard to consequences. His ethics are not immanent, others would add, but discriminatory and categorical: he

3   I thank Aniruddhan Vasudevan for pressing me on this point. Does indifference to continuity shun instrumentalist or consequentialist ethical actions made necessary by structures of dispossession? No. The political burden of what I call for in this chapter lies squarely on the shoulders of the tyrants.
4   For essays that address ethnographic omission, see Das et al., *The Ground Between*.
5   As my friend Christian Novetzke pointed out when he read this: "Yes, including all the assholes!" Thanks for the analysis, Christian.

heals dogs with care but kills maggots without thought. And now, the issue of the photographs: yet another contradiction.

But in temporary service of continuity and conviction, I will lean on Dipesh after all, even if to make a different point from the one I originally anticipated: that contradiction is an unseemly fixation, both because it is ever present and because it is nonexistent. And by focusing on how things lie, we fail to see how the matter stands.[6] And how *does* the matter stand? It stands that life is full of contradiction (or, to put it differently, that life is not moral and cannot be grasped morally). And that when ethics is ethics at all, it is immanent, never consistent.[7] And the practice of finding contradiction—the enlightened false consciousness of cynicism—is how we ensure that things stay the same: the triumph of the norm, the triumph of the way things already are.[8]

When I first met Timmie Kumar, the director of what was once Crystal Rogers's Help in Suffering, we connected instantly and had a long and meandering talk. Her commitment to her work is evident, but so is its toll. "I have to stop now," she said. "I just have to. I didn't want to do nothing. But somehow, nothing became everything, and I started to drown." Her words affected me at the time and have continued to trail me. Why would a person like Timmie have to drown? I realized later that she is made to drown because of the logic of contradiction, the hermeneutic of skepticism, which steals the *something* that she needs for her ethics to persevere. The logic of contradiction, in service of a normative moralism, demands that any ethics in an oppositional or oblique relationship to the normal—to the way things are—account for its apparent inconsistencies or contradictions.[9] Under the logic of contradiction, or the tyranny of consistency, an act such as rescuing a pig raises the question of why Timmie does not rescue every pig—or, for that matter, every four-legged

---

6 Peter Sloterdijk, in the preface to *Critique of Cynical Reason*, cites Erich Kastner, a German poet and author of children's books who wrote, "I don't want to say how things lie / I want to show you how the matter stands": Sloterdijk, *Critique of Cynical Reason*, xxxii.

7 A consistent ethics, Judith Butler argues, is little more than "commitment to a commitment": Butler, "Response."

8 "Enlightened false consciousness" is from Sloterdijk, *Critique of Cynical Reason*, 5 and throughout.

9 Toni Morrison calls this white supremacy. "The function," Morrison said, "the very serious function of racism is distraction. *It keeps you from doing your work*. It keeps you explaining, over and over again, your reason for being. . . . None of this is necessary. *There will always be one more thing*": Morrison, "A Humanist View." The emphasis is from the original keynote address at Portland State University in 1975.

animal and avian being. Or an act such as healing a dog raises the question of why Dipesh does not rescue maggots and, for that matter, whether those shoes he wears are made of leather. These questions remind me of a story Julian Barnes tells in his novel *Love, Etc.* There's a girl named Sophie who announces to her parents that she's become a vegetarian. They ask her, with a healthy dose of self-satisfaction, "What are your shoes made of?" Sophie replies, "I'm not proposing to eat my shoes, am I?"[10]

The logic of contradiction sees in such inconsistencies ethically nullifying contradictions but fails to acknowledge two uncomfortable truths about itself: (1) as Sophie points out, the convenient absurdity of our equivalencies, reflective not of moral truth but only of a language ideology in which a pig, all animals, a maggot, and a shoe are even thinkable together; and (2) that the normative man, when acting normatively, is rarely called on to account for his contradictions. In fact, we can probably define the normative as that which is allowed to be and remain in self-contradiction without existential consequence.

Contradiction thinking has one primary, and deceptively ordinary, function: to *exhaust*—and I mean, literally, to *make people tired so that they give up*. It is a primary modality of what Peter Sloterdijk calls "cynical reason," the combatant consciousness of enlightened modernity (the combination of enlightenment with resignation and apathy) in which reason is put to the service of "maintaining us without extending us"—that is to say, of "hindering" what might be new.[11] So this is my argument about what contradiction as a politics *does*: it seeks to exhaust the ethically otherwise through a descent into obligation.[12] "If this thing, then why not that thing also? Yes, yes, you're right," until eventually all the world stakes a moral claim on you. Timmie drowns in infinite responsibility; Dipesh disappears into the quandary—however legitimate—between maggot and dog, responsiveness and footwear.

That is what contradiction thinking as a politics (a political antipolitics) does. But if it is logically sound, can we still fault it for its social effects? So although I am already tired, let me try to address some of the logico-moral flaws of contradiction.

In the Case of the Missing Something, in which Timmie didn't want to do nothing, but somehow nothing became everything and she started to drown,

10 Barnes, *Love, Etc.*
11 Sloterdijk, *Critique of Cynical Reason*, 379.
12 I borrow the phrase "ethical otherwise" from Povinelli. On exhaustion and the otherwise, see Povinelli, "The Will to Be Otherwise."

let's say that an example of "something" would be Dipesh relieving the pain of a dog with a maggot-ridden infection in her body. The *something* that somehow becomes *everything* in this case would take the form of either "relieve the pain of every living thing" or "the maggot also has life."[13] One specific word in each articulation—*every* and *maggot*—is representative of a key principle in contradiction thinking: *every* represents the principle of continuity and accumulation, while *maggot* represents the principle of representation/identity/analogy.

My attraction to the concept of immanent ethics—why it brought me pleasure to interpret Dipesh's act the way I initially did—emerged out of a dissatisfaction with the cynicism of contradiction thinking: that this action (helping the dog) contradicts that (not helping the maggot) and therefore *this* is nullified, brought back to the hegemonic That (not helping anything but yourself and your own). My attraction to immanence, then, was to the idea that *every moment might be its own ethical universe*—as Deleuze puts it, a "pure event—at its own time, on its own plane," or, as Judith Butler has said, "commitment . . . as the agreement to commit oneself anew, time and again, precisely when circumstances change."[14] That I might have, all my life, believed one thing and then, at some moment, for reasons untold but possibly tellable, I perform a moral action inconsistent with that belief, or inconsistent with all my previous actions, and have that neither (1) nullified by what came before, (2) *nullify* what came before, or (3) have any determinative consequence for what I may do or believe later. What is interesting in putting it this way is how bankrupt it sounds, how willy-nilly, how purposeless. But that is only because normative morality is so invisibly indebted to the principle of continuity and accumulation (the basic principle, I think, of *imminent* ethics, with an *i*, the belief that "out of this must come that").[15] At stake in the idea that every moment might be its own ethical universe is an indifference to the principle of continuity; to

13 "The maggot also has life" is from Davé, "Something, Everything, Nothing." This phrase was uttered by the manager of a *gaushala* in response to a visitor (not me) complaining that a calf was suffering from a maggot infection. I use this utterance as an example of a seemingly noncontradictory ethical stance, but one that results in an inability to act.

14 Butler, "Response," 238; Deleuze and Parnet, "Many Politics," 133.

15 In a line of verse about Lincoln, the poet Delmore Schwartz wrote that "he lived hand to mouth in moral things!": Schwartz, "Lincoln" (https://www.poetryfoundation.org/poems/51750/lincoln-56d22fb2f29a5). I love this turn of phrase for its nonaccumulative, fleeting, and immanent concept of moral action. I am reminded also of Paul Gilroy's "small acts," actions that do not totalize and, in fact, exist in oblique relationship to what is totalizable, ontologizable, and consumable: Gilroy, *Small Acts*. All this puts me in mind of Roland Barthes's quotation of Léon

say that ethical practice has no truck with accumulation; and that the measure of our ethical consciousness cannot possibly be a board game in which we go about collecting chips, committed to a designated path, hoping—if you dare depart from it—not to land on the wrong spot: *Sorry! You've committed a contradiction! Forfeit your capital and return to Go!*

I can understand wanting to ask, surely there must be *some* measure of ethics, some way to discern whether and how I live more or less ethically. Certainly. But that is not a measure of ethics; it is a measure of *me*. And the "I" that can be measured, like "dog" and "maggot" and the chips I collect, is frankly just an identity, a representation. What in contradiction thinking we think of as ethics is nothing more than the measure of the stability of a world-given concept, as arbitrary as the sign. Merely a commitment to a commitment.[16]

And this lies at the heart of the second principle of contradiction thinking: that of identity, of being identical. Another attraction for me to the idea of immanence emerged from a disillusionment with the politics of conviction, which manufactures duality where there is—in fact and in essence—no duality at all. The politics of conviction frames the world as this and that (a process, Gregory Bateson reminds us, designed to help avoid the complexities of reality, the lived paradoxes of abstraction, the paradoxes without which there would be no creative life) and treats those frames as reality instead of as frames: human and animal; life and nonlife; now and later.[17]

Let's come back to the dog and the maggot, to the assertion that killing a maggot contradicts saving a dog. Take away the concepts, maggot and dog. Imagine them as never existing. Wipe them away. Now? There is no contradiction. Take away the concept of the ethical actor, accumulating or depreciating over time. Imagine it never existing. Now? There is no contradiction. Take away the concept "animal," within which dog and maggot are thinkable together, are comparable equivalencies, and in which the human stands apart as moral actor and adjudicator. Take away that concept. Now? There is no contradiction.[18]

My point is simple: contradiction exists only internally to its terms; therefore, to believe in the principle of consistency is to assume an existence that is

---

Bloy, "There is nothing perfectly beautiful except what is invisible and above all unbuyable": Barthes, *The Neutral*, 13.

16 See Butler, "Response."

17 Bateson, "A Theory of Play and Fantasy."

18 On the ethical work of concept loss, see Diamond, "Losing Your Concepts." See also Povinelli, *Between Gaia and Ground*, 6: "Concepts knot and create habits in the field of immanence. . . . Thus, no concept explains the world."

purely representational, to conflate *ethics* with nothing more than a philosophy of representation, in which, as Deleuze argues, all of existence—including *what might be*—is already incarcerated within the logic of similitude and analogy.[19] In such a life, nothing unthinkable is possible; everything is only *imminent* to conceptuality.

Against such a dull and illusory existence, Brian Massumi adopts Spinoza's principle of noncontradiction.[20] Spinoza argues that there are two types of contradiction: a contradiction in terms and a contradiction in Being. A contradiction in terms means nothing. It is ethically meaningless because it concerns only meaning (the meaning, say, of *dog, maggot, human, shoe*). But a contradiction in Being? That, Spinoza says, is even more of a fallacy: a contradiction in being is morally impossible, because everything *is*. Massumi takes this to heart, rejecting the law of exclusive oppositions—the law without which there would be no contradiction, no forced rending of reflection and existence—and calls instead for a *supernormal politics of the included middle*, an ethics of lived abstraction: the freedom to live in what appears to us, and most certainly appears to others, as paradox—where, as Bateson told us, life actually is.

Massumi invites us to call contradiction thinking, or any desire to avoid lived abstraction, "politico-pathological" and to refer to those who deploy such thinking "normopaths."[21] I'm happy to do so. And in fact, I do. Often! But I also think it's worth placing some of the responsibility for contradiction thinking not on normativity first, but on its dialectical foundations and, specifically, on the slippage of dialectics as dialogics toward dialectics as ontology.

The critique of contradiction as represented by, say, Jean Hyppolite or Deleuze or Massumi, is almost invariably antidialectical: a refutation of dialectics and a critique of Hegel.[22] I, however, have no problem with dialectics (now *that* is truly antidialectical)—no problem with dialectics as what Sloterdijk calls a rhythmics of difference or with dialectics as a "doctrine for argumentation."[23] In dialectics as a doctrine for argumentation, contradiction exists only as a contradiction between *terms*, the essences of which are then shown to be, and to have always been, in nondualistic relation. The problem only emerges

---

19 Deleuze, *Difference and Repetition*.

20 Massumi, *What Animals Teach Us about Politics*.

21 Massumi, *What Animals Teach Us about Politics*, 69–70. He borrows *normopathy*, or "neurotic normativity" from Jean Oury, cited in Guattari, *Chaosmosis*, 72.

22 Deleuze, *Difference and Repetition*; Sauvagnargues, "Hegel and Deleuze;" Vitale, "Deleuzo-Hegelianism."

23 Sloterdijk, *Critique of Cynical Reason*, 369.

when, as Sloterdijk puts it, "a contradiction in concept is staged in reality . . . where dialectics sets foot in ontology."[24] The error arises when the thinker forgets that the disputatious dialogue is only a war of logic (between "dog" and "maggot," "dog" and "shoe") and not a war in lived reality (that dog, that day, that suffering, that man, those maggots).[25]

But there is another problem, too, that applies to dialectics as dialogics, as well as to its slippage into ontology: in both, the two parties in dispute are never actually equals. This was the realization of negative dialectics and of the near-fatal critique of Hegelianism. Dialectics is a cannibal. In the dispute between the first party (the already existing, the hegemonic) and the second party (the new), the third party that emerges from the dispute is, as Sloterdijk puts it, "the first again, but worse," now fatter and more righteous with the cannibalized soul of the second. In the ontological case of the dog and the maggot, the first (do nothing for anyone but yourself and your own) meets the second (do something for which I have no good reason), producing the third (fine, then, do everything), which is only the first again, but worse (do nothing for anyone but yourself and your own). Massumi describes this as the dialectical elimination of the supernormal; Sloterdijk, as the suffocation of the antithesis at its source; Povinelli, as the extinguishing of the will to be otherwise.[26]

How Else Is the Otherwise Exhausted? On Context

I sent an early version of the first half of this chapter to a friend, a South Asian South Asianist in a far-off discipline. She enjoyed it—in the "argumentative Indian" sort of way—but something troubled her.[27] This is India, she said. One can't talk about animal protection just however one wishes or through conceptual abstractions. "I mean, how about some context?" And then, with a laugh to soften the insult, "You're an anthropologist, for fuck's sake!"

24 Sloterdijk, *Critique of Cynical Reason*, 369.
25 Either way, "to reduce this otherness to contradiction is to reduce everything to violence and war": Serres, *The Parasite*, 21. Rainer Maria Rilke, likewise, writes that this tendency to place representation before the agent of representation reduces humans to a fate of closure: "That is what fate means: to be opposite/ to be opposite and nothing else, forever": Rilke and Hass, *The Selected Poetry of Rainer Maria Rilke*, cited in Santner, *On Creaturely Life*, 3.
26 Massumi, *What Animals Teach Us about Politics*, 38; Sloterdijk, *Critique of Cynical Reason*, 378; Povinelli, "The Will to Be Otherwise."
27 Sen, *The Argumentative Indian*.

As I, too, am an argumentative Indian, I appreciated her provocation. I later responded with the following text:

The dog Dipesh and I called Julie—because that is what the paanwala near Opera House called her—was probably, based on the condition of her teeth, born around 1999 or 2000. Phenotypically she is a pariah dog, with a slight curve in her tail, sharp ears, short, coarse fur, and a relatively long snout. Most of her white coat is missing due to mange, leaving exposed scaly, pinkish skin. Her anus, like that of most canines, is approximately one centimeter in length and divided into three zones: columnar, intermediate, and cutaneous. Within the columnar and intermediate zones are tubular sweat glands known as anal glands, or sacs. In most canines, the anal glands are abundant with semi-oily secretions that are strong and odiferous enough to actually gag maggots to death. (This is true, so please don't say you didn't learn anything from my paper!) Julie's glands were deficient and thus she was particularly susceptible to anal myiasis, a maggot infestation common in warm, wet weather like that we were having in Bombay in July 2012. Those maggots were producing an enzyme that was actually breaking down Julie's rectum, surely contributing to the uncomfortable defecation that nearly ended her life.

Of course this was not the context my friend was looking for, and I both did and continue to understand what it is she wanted from me—and why. Her request for context asked me to situate my reflections on Dipesh's act and the responses it generates less through a praxis of immanence and more firmly within the linked narratives of Hindu fascism and Western liberalism—contexts that I, too, understand as important (*vital*) enough to have shaped the early chapters of this book. But are there other contexts, too? The dog herself was a context. That day was a context. This world and what will become of us in it was a context. And so I'd like to think about how calls for context function similarly to demands for consistency: to normalize, to exhaust, and to restore otherwise gestures to existing, familiar, lines of force.

I was expecting my friend's demand, as it's one that's made by most of my other friends, colleagues, and everyday associates in India and the diaspora. For convenience, I'll call them the leftist secular humanists, though if longer names were not too unwieldy, I would add "elite but ashamed of it" and other such good-natured barbs. The leftist secular humanists are not antianimal per se (many love dogs and, as do we all, cat videos) but are against—or, more accurately, disdainful of—any *politics* by and for animals. Their position rests on three planks: opposition to high-caste Hindu cow protectionism (antifascist antivegetarianism);

the related belief that, in a place like India, caring about animals is antihuman; and the problem of anthropomorphism.

In their refusal of the fascistic violence of cow protectionism—a refusal that no nonpsychopath does not unequivocally share—some leftist secular humanists will go to great lengths. Many of them, upper caste or *savarna* themselves, will, in an act of pronounced solidarity with Dalits, eat beef. A Dalit activist, upon hearing this, said, "If they're really in solidarity, tell them to clean their own toilets." But more to the point, as a group of young Dalit activists in Hyderabad said to me, such performance is the very essence of Brahminism: capitalizing on a practice for which others are oppressed, maimed, and killed. "Consuming our struggle," Sudarshan and Kotesh called it. "Consuming as a performance of struggle."[28]

Undeterred, the leftist secular humanists believe that animal activists are essentially *out of place*. Even if they are able to disentangle the *gaurakshaks* from people like Dipesh, they base their argument on the notion of a "real India," or a radical fidelity to context. In India, vegetarianism is violence; in India, people have more important things to worry about. In other words, to have a politics around animals in India is—so context tells us—to commit a political sin. But not only is animal activism out of place, the political sin. It anthropomorphizes—an *intellectual* sin.[29] Animals do not suffer; humans do. Animals do not labor; men do. Animals cannot be exploited; humans are.[30] The interesting thing about their objection, though, is that it itself is out of context. Anthropomorphism as a concept is radically out of place in India.

For one thing, anthropomorphism was discovered through European racism, as enlightened cynics revealed the fallacies, not of how people represented animals but of how they represented gods. Anthropomorphic idols, mostly from the East and certainly from India, were sources of amusement for those who felt they had discovered the projective mechanism and, by extension, the deception of religion, not only abroad but also at home.[31] Second, while Europeans

---

28 Sudarshan and Kotesh, conversation with the author, Osmania University, Hyderabad, May 13, 2013.

29 Lorraine Daston and Gregg Mitman's *Thinking with Animals* unsettles this notion of anthropomorphism as an intellectual or "scientific sin."

30 See also Wilderson, "Gramsci's Black Marx." Wilderson argues that Marxism is premised on a disavowal of white supremacy, exemplified by its preoccupation with "exploitation" rather than "accumulation and death"; the latter state, Wilderson says, is the condition of Black and animal life.

31 Sloterdijk, *Critique of Cynical Reason*, 27–28.

used India as an egregious example of the anthropomorphic tendency, anthropomorphism itself has little meaning in Indic thought—or, to put it differently, it has never really bothered people much.

To anthropomorphize—let's say, to borrow language from the Orientalists, to *project* human qualities onto a nonhuman—requires a clear demarcation in the first place, ontological but also conceptual, between human and non. But the idea that such a demarcation exists is itself a European projection, for as scholars of India have so often shown, humans and animals can share morphology, as well as personhood. Jains say that humans and animals, along with all living creatures, share immortal souls and the ability to suffer.[32] Other traditions, exemplified by the Buddhist *Jatakas* and the Hindu *Panchatantras* and *Gita*, demonstrate the fluid existence of human, god, and animal. But leaving spiritual texts aside—which, anyway, only prove the Western cynics right—everyday life in contemporary India accepts and grapples ethically with the ever-shifting lines between humans and animals. Anthropologists of South Asia, including Radhika Govindrajan, Annu Jalais, Muhammad Kavesh, Nayanika Mathur, and Bhrigupati Singh, have shown how people think fluidly, if often ambivalently, of animals as kin, as moral beings, as companions, and as persons.[33]

This is all just to say that the leftist secular humanists, who base their disavowal of animal politics in part on a principled fidelity to context, espouse a critique of anthropomorphism that is quite *out* of context in India.

What a contradiction!

I keep running into this problem. I want to show the fallacies and impoverishment of contradiction thinking, yet I find myself doing so by calling out the contradictions of others. That itself, I realize, is a contradiction but—I hope to convince—a potentially *vital* one. The problem returns me to a question I left unaddressed earlier. To put it simply: Is there "good" contradiction but also "bad" contradiction? I say yes, and that the difference is a vital one.

As a former student of mine, Alex Dawson, pointed out to me, the world does not change without someone recognizing, and seeking to resolve, a contradiction.[34] In Dipesh's case, it went something like this: *I am alive. That dog is alive. I hate to suffer. That dog must hate to suffer.* Between what he knows (a shared desire to avoid suffering) and what is before him (one of them is visibly suffering), Dipesh sees

32 See Chapple, *Jainism and Ecology*; Laidlaw, "Ethical Traditions in Question"; Miller and Dickstein, "Jain Veganism"; Taylor, "Rethinking Non-violence."

33 See Govindrajan, *Animal Intimacies*; Jalais, *Forest of Tigers*; Kavesh, *Animal Enthusiasms*; Mathur, *Paper Tiger*; Singh, *Poverty and the Quest for Life*.

34 This is a basic tenet of Marxism.

a contradiction that he seeks to resolve by addressing the dog's wound by killing the maggots. This is Contradiction Set 1. But then comes another contradiction, which begins with the effort to ethically annul Dipesh's act by pointing out its internal contradictions but is *itself* a contradiction because the man pointing it out surely, like the rest of us, lives a morally contradictory life *but*, unlike most of us, rarely has to worry himself about it. His is Contradiction Set 2. In both, there is a *recognition of contradiction* that leads to the *committing of a contradiction*. What is the difference between the two sets?

The difference lies in a contrast Massumi draws between "vital" and "sterile" paradox.[35] Vital paradox, or contradiction, gives rise to the world; it is the generative source of dissensus. Sterile contradiction seeks to contain generativity, or, to return to Sloterdijk, to "maintain us without extending us."[36] The vital and sterile also correspond to the slippage between dialectics as dialogics and dialectics as ontology. The vital paradox—paradoxical as it may be in the context of a normative system of representation—cares not, for it exists in lived reality and addresses what is present in its dynamic, processual unfolding. Sterile paradox, by contrast, constitutes the lived experience of being *all cramped up* with concerns about structure, boundaries, and the proper relationship between concepts (India and animals; maggot and dog; human and animal). Most of all, I think, sterile contradiction deserves critical notice because it *puts us at war with the world*, which is altogether different from a world at war with you and with me.

Dipesh's contradiction, I feel quite comfortable arguing, is a vital one—or, at the very least, one far more vital than it is sterile. (We, too, must resist the binary mind machine.) He gives rise to the world by performing an act for which there are far more reasons not to perform. But just as important, we know that his contradiction is vital because it is *livable* for him. The vital contradiction—and this, too, is key—is far less livable for the person who points it out, whose ground is unsettled by the vitality of the apparent paradox. We see this in the case of Sophie, the not-yet-exhausted girl from the Julian Barnes novel, whose contradiction between diet and footwear is perfectly livable but is far less so for her parents, who seek to squash it. The fact that the vital contradiction is livable for Dipesh, the fact that he is not *all cramped up* with a concern for boundaries, also means that he is not at war with the world. (One might say that he is at war with maggots, but if, indeed, he is not guided by the principles

35 Massumi, *What Animals Teach Us about Politics*, 67. Massumi usually refers to "vital" paradox as "productive" paradox, but I prefer the former.
36 Sloterdijk, *Critique of Cynical Reason*, 379.

of conviction and continuity, who is to say he will not spare the maggots next time?) The man from Contradiction Set 2 *is* at war with the world. He is at war with lived paradox, with vital ambivalence and strange constellations; at war with what is new and queer.[37] However, I acknowledge that his is only a war of logic, one that does not necessarily set foot into ontology. So let's return to our secular humanists. They, I believe, are at war with the world, and in their case the slippage between concept and ontology is quite complete. They are at war with the animal, a concept made real in something to seek out and performatively consume. This is a manifestation of the passionate *investment* in difference rather than an indifference to it, a normative morality in which we forget that the frames are only frames.[38]

I argued earlier that contradiction thinking assumes an existence that is purely representational, in which ethics is nothing more than a philosophy of representation. But somewhere between an abstracted philosophy of representation and a lived ethics that is immanent is another modality of being that I have so far left aside: the modality of the political. So I'll begin by suggesting that contradiction thinking—the sterile paradox of warring positions— assumes an existence that is not just purely representational but only ever *political*. And I'll define the political as that which is always determined by context, by which I mean *overdetermined* by a given frame.

It feels, at first, odd and uneasy to speak of context with a critical valence. Being attuned to context is supposed to be a good thing, right? It makes for

---

37 "Vital ambivalence" is from Singh, *Unthinking Mastery*, 158. "Constellations" is from Benjamin and Steiner, *The Origin of German Tragic Drama*.

38 The performative consumption of animals is an *active* example of the political investment in difference—where it compels an action, however rote. There are "negative" examples, too, by which I mean where the objective of the political investment in difference is inactivity. (Both the active and negative forms are ultimately stagnant, and both, I believe, are at war with the world.) I'm thinking here with Sharmila Rege's "Dalit Women Talk Differently." Rege, an Ambedkarite feminist, argues that the framework of "difference" has enabled a *savarna* feminist movement in India to treat caste as the responsibility of Dalit women, even if the claimed motive is respect or nonappropriation. This investment in (respecting) difference, Rege writes, "hinders the dialectics," which is to say that it serves to prevent the ongoing revisioning and sharpening of both parties—we might say, maintaining both without extending them. Rege calls for a moving on from the politics of difference toward a politics of focusing on the "social relations which convert difference into oppression": Rege, "Dalit Women Talk Differently," 39–40. I thank Ridhima Sharma for reminding me of Rege's argument and how it connects with my own.

grounded thought, smooth communication, and efficacious strategy.[39] But as literary theorist Rita Felski argues in *The Limits of Critique*, the demand for context—like the critical-cynical triumph of finding contradiction—is far more often in service of what Eve Sedgwick called "paranoid reading."[40] In "seeking to explain everything," Felski says of contextualization, "it explains very little."[41] Bruno Latour puts the critique in a more curmudgeonly fashion: "'Context stinks!' It is a way of stopping the description when you are tired or too lazy to go on."[42]

I, a principled antiproductivist, have no problem with laziness. In fact, I think the problem of contextualization, contra Latour, is not laziness at all but precisely that it *makes everything work*, that it renders the ineffable, the queer, the odd, and the strange *useful* for the already given. In her essay "Out of Context" (1987), Marilyn Strathern argues that this making useful for the already known is precisely what characterizes the contemporary discipline of anthropology.[43] Strathern says that central to the Malinowskian ethnographic revolution of the 1920s—the break with armchair anthropology and the bibliophilic pastiche of James George Frazer—was the instruction to place alien phenomena within "their context" through immersive fieldwork in order to make those phenomena comparable with "ours," no longer as a hierarchical difference of evolutionary stage but as simply a relative one of differing contexts. What might seem amazing to the untrained eye at first—not to worry!—is not so amazing after all but perfectly sensible after having been professionally placed within the larger context of, say, Trobriand life.[44] Everything through this narrative—through context—can be mastered. This is what makes Kathleen Stewart's move, in *A Space on the Side of the Road*, so masterfully unmasterful: in offering a litany of the many contexts in which an ethnographic moment *could* be placed, she shows simultaneously the arbitrariness of rote ethnographic

---

39 I confess that I intend for these supposed virtues to sound a bit unctuous. I'm thinking with a former undergraduate student of mine, Jennifer Su, who wrote for my literary anthropology course that "social context, for both artist and anthropologist, serves as a site from which to generate market value."

40 Sedgwick, *Touching Feeling*.

41 Felski, *The Limits of Critique*, 183.

42 Latour, *Reassembling the Social*, 148. Latour borrows the sentiment that "context stinks!" from the architect Rem Koolhaas. It also serves as the title of Felski's chapter on the matter.

43 Strathern, "Out of Context." I thank Bharat Venkat for pointing me to this article.

44 Malinowski, *Argonauts of the Western Pacific*. See, by contrast, Frazer, *The Golden Bough*.

practices of contextualization and the manner by which authorized contexts work to smother the "texture and desire" of otherwise worlds.[45]

Stewart's otherwise writing cannily demonstrates its obverse: that when we contextualize an affect, a gesture, an event, it is to reassure ourselves that we knew it already, that whatever occurred was always inevitable. Let's think, for example, of the contexts I tend to provide to place a familiar frame around our dog and her healer and her maggots: the culturalist context in which Dipesh's actions and nonactions speak to Indic religiosity; the historicist context in which an urban devotion to animals suggests an adoption of Western values; the presentist context in which Dipesh's actions and nonactions speak to the rise of a Hindu fascism he, in fact, deplores. These contexts, while all legitimate, represent, arguably, the most "common knowledge" about the thing at hand rather than the juxtaposition of reparative reading, and they do so as if history or context is stable enough ground to *explain* events rather than being radically transformed *by* those events.[46] And like the contradiction thinking that takes the form of a paranoid critique of anthropomorphism, these rote practices of contextualization are also, ironically, contextually out of place in South Asia, products of an imperial pedagogy into the "real" operations of time and space.[47]

If contextualization so often serves this paranoid function of exhausting otherwise readings and queer juxtapositions, why do so many of us, myself included, persist in its reproduction?[48] Felski suggests that reading that takes the form of demands for context "has become an ethical and political duty: a sign

---

45 Stewart, *A Space on the Side of the Road*, 18. I thank Alex Blanchette for making this connection for me. Other anthropologists experimenting with context appear alongside Stewart in Pandian and McLean, *Crumpled Paper Boat*.

46 "Common knowledge" is from Latour, *Reassembling the Social*, 144. "Reparative reading" is from Sedgwick, *Touching Feeling*. In a conversation on the subject of context, William Mazzarella asked, "What if we thought of context as immanent or emergent, rather than as what is already there preceding and determining what we see?" This resonates with Kathleen Stewart's call to "inhabit a context of strict immanence," as well as with Paul Dourish's notion of "interactional" context, in which contexts are not stable containers but, rather, "relational properties occasioned through activity": Dourish, "What We Talk about When We Talk about Context," cited in Seaver, "The Nice Thing about Context Is That Everyone Has It," 1105; Stewart, *A Space on the Side of the Road*, 50.

47 Chakrabarty, *Provincializing Europe*; Felski, *The Limits of Critique*.

48 On authorizing contexts and the aversion to queer, surprising juxtapositions, see Khailikova et al., "Commitment, Citation, and Context."

that one is on the right side, fighting the good fight."[49] As unequivocal as I am on behalf of laziness, I am one for fighting good fights. I mean, I fight with people all the time, and I take pleasure and pride in an enemy almost as much as I do in a good friend. I suppose the question is: Is the overdetermination of an action, a gesture, a thought by context in the name of the political, a *good* fight?

It is not a coincidence that I feel almost as uneasy being critical of context as I do being critical of "the political." They work in tandem, or they do the same work: they enclose, they embag, they settle, they *surround*.[50] So much has rightly been made of Fred Moten and Stefano Harney's unsettling of the university in *The Undercommons*, but far less of their attendant rejection of the political in the first essay of the book, "Politics Surrounded."[51] Their argument is that politics, by surrounding "what it cannot defend but only endanger," is that against which *the surround* must defend itself.[52] Insofar as politics is "the subject and principle of decision," it is a "correctional" and "anti-social energy" that determines rather than generates.[53] "An abdication of political responsibility?" they ask—extremely rhetorically. "Ok. Whatever. We're just anti-politically romantic about actually existing social life."[54] I'm personally uncomfortable claiming an "antipolitics"—I think too much of my self-understanding is wrapped up in what I've understood to be political fights—but what I can borrow from Moten and Harney's antipolitics is something more like the *depolitical*: an ongoing refusal to be determined, decided for, enclosed, made useful, or made sensible through and for lines of force.[55]

---

49 Felski, *The Limits of Critique*, 161. The rest of Felski's sentence reads, "against the retrograde ranks of aesthetes and litterateurs mumbling into their sherry glasses." I know a lot of aesthetes, but only two actually drink sherry, so I omitted this part.

50 The word *embag* is from Povinelli, "After the Last Man," though I am using it against her meaning, which is aligned with immanence and the surround. With *settle*, I am thinking with the epistemological settlements in Mazzarella, *The Mana of Mass Society*.

51 Harney and Moten, *The Undercommons*.

52 Harney and Moten, *The Undercommons*, 18.

53 Harney and Moten, *The Undercommons*, 19–20.

54 Harney and Moten, *The Undercommons*, 20.

55 Further, just as I see being antidialectical as being dialectical, I see being antipolitical as being political—and neither in very efficacious ways. In my use, the *de*political signals not an "anti" stance but a being "indifferent to the rote demands of," which enables an ongoing reflection on what is called for in a moment and what is not. I'm thinking, too, with Julietta Singh's preference of *dehumanism* over its alternatives (post-, anti-, in-) and seeing the central practice of dehumanism in the act of reading—of reading reparatively, in our discomforts, and with faith in meaning that

Immanent gestures, too, have a context: What is here before me? But here is the difference, I think, between an existence that imagines itself as purely political and an existence that experiences itself as actually lived: the existence that imagines itself as purely political not only forgets that the frames are just frames but believes that the frames that exist are the only ones imaginable, the context that matters determined from the start. Not this butt, this dog, this day, these organisms, this world, but always first: this culture, this system, this war. The existence that experiences itself as lived creatively invents its frames, generates its own context. This invention is, of course, not out of nothing at all, and the action made possible within it is not pure event in the sense of transcendence or a rejection of this world. The immanent act has a history, as well as a context—just not the history or context of the authorized cut.

To talk about animal ethics in India tends to raise two sorts of questions. The first, in the realm of ethics, the problem of contradiction; the second, in the realm of politics, the matter of context. Both problematics share one main feature: the normopathic function of normalizing the anomalous and exhausting the otherwise—of explaining things away but *doing* very little. They imagine an existence that is only ever at war—a depressing existence but, perhaps more significant, an illusory one. But this is not to say that a rethinking of context, a refusal of its rote demands, is apolitical. Indeed, I want to end by asking, how do we nurture a politics that is not sterile, that is not *all cramped up* with concerns about structure, boundaries, and the proper relationship among concepts? Perhaps this is where ethics sets foot into conviction, where the immanent sets foot into futurity and continuity: committing to a nomadic creativity of inventing queer frames—anuses and hours and streets and universes—tracing the queer lines, making the oblique cuts.[56] Or, in honor of Julie, living an unconstipated life.

cannot be settled by inherited contexts or fields of interpretation: see Singh, *Unthinking Mastery*, 24.

56 "Queer cuts" is inspired by Sara Ahmed's "queer lines," which run obliquely and in killjoy counterproductivity to lines of force: Ahmed, *Queer Phenomenology*. "Oblique cuts," is borrowed from Clarice Lispector. In her novel *Agua Viva*, she writes, "How can I explain it to you? I'll try. It's that I'm perceiving a crooked reality. Seen through an oblique cut. Only now have I sensed the oblique in life. I used to only see through straight and parallel cuts. I didn't notice the sly crooked line. Now I sense that life is other": Lispector, *Agua Viva*, 61.

SOUND. Can the Subaltern Be Silent?

I decided to give this chapter the subtitle "Can the Subaltern Be Silent?" but I might have also chosen this: "How Might We Listen through Queer Tongues?"[1] What is the soundscape of relation?

Animals and Other Subalterns

The nomenclature of contemporary animal welfare organizations in India is multilingual and runs the affective gamut from pity to combativeness. *Daya* (sympathy or pity) is common, as are claims to sacrificial care work such as *seva* (service) and *karuna* (compassion). On the more warring side, *defense* tends to signal cosmopolitan, rights-based approaches to animal politics; *raksha* (protection) indexes moral and political proximity to Hindutva; and the deceptively

---

1 "Into the wind and waves, my child dances across the beach as she calls to me: *Amma! Amma! Amma!* / What I hear is bird: *Caw! Caw! Caw!* A simple reminder that she is animal, that her mother listens through queer tongues": Singh, *No Archive Will Restore You*, 101.

understated *for*, as in Maneka Gandhi's People for Animals, in actuality means "by any means necessary." Largely, but not entirely, gone from signboards and logos are explicit references to the muteness of animals, but the sentiment lingers. The premise that other animals are voiceless, and thereby innocent, is foundational to animal politics in India and elsewhere and may well be its most counterproductive praxis.

The celebration of World Animal Day in 1988 was observed in New Delhi on October 2, to coincide with Mahatma Gandhi's birthday. General A. K. Chatterjee, then president of the Animal Welfare Board of India (AWBI), quoted in his opening speech a letter Gandhi wrote to Jawaharlal Nehru: "Cow protection to me is infinitely more than mere protection of the cow. The cow is merely a type for all that lives. Cow protection means protection of the weak, the helpless, the dumb, and the deaf. Man becomes then not the lord and master of all creation but he is its servant."[2] While Gandhi tries vainly to equate the cow to "all that lives," we know cows are not just "any" animal in India. And his expression of animal protection, even if accidental, turns out to be precise: the premise that animals are "helpless, dumb, and deaf" gives the impression of human servitude to a greater good while invoking the imperious imperative to protection.[3] Shortly after the World Animal Day celebrations, the AWBI announced that it had "released an attractive poster with the caption, 'Protect the Dumb Animals from Cruelty.'"[4]

The purported muteness of animals is, as the poster has it, tied up with cruelty in both its conceptualization and its practice. The Krishi Gau Seva Sangh (Community for Service to the Cow) also goes by the name the Institution Speaking for Mutes and Innocents. The Gau Seva Sangh is a particularly litigious group, whose primary activity is to abduct cows from illegal transport vehicles on nighttime highways, brutalizing the usually Muslim transporters who are often working as middlemen to Hindu dons, and confiscating the cattle.[5] Lawsuits ensue, but the cows go only from confinement to confinement. I asked Samir Dubey, a *gaurakshak* who runs a department store in Bhopal, how he justified the deaths of Muslim transporters in the name of cows. Is he against killing in

---

2 Mahatma Gandhi to Jawaharlal Nehru, letter, 1925, in Gandhi, *The Collected Works of Mahatma Gandhi*, vol. 31, 199, reported in *Animal Citizen*, vol. 26, no. 1, 1988.

3 As Jacques Derrida writes, "'I protect you' means . . . I oblige you, you are my subject, I subject you": Derrida, *The Beast and the Sovereign*, 73.

4 *Animal Citizen*, vol. 26, no. 2, 1989.

5 On the violence wrought by Hindu vigilantes on Muslim families in relation to cattle transport, see Sur, "Time at Its Margins."

general, I asked him, or only against killing cattle? "The cows are mute and dumb," he responded a bit hotly in his office full of mannequins. "And therefore it is only a courtesy to use our voices to protect them." The purported muteness of animals establishes their innocence, which in turn establishes the cruelty of those who would harm them, which in turn establishes the civilizational "courtesy" of those who would protect them—by any means necessary. Alok Gupta and I have more to say about cows, innocence, and Hindu anthropatriarchy in chapter 7.

This attachment to the narrative of animal silence, the innocence it confers, and the violence that such innocence justifies is not limited to illiberal fundamentalism. It is also a feature of liberal animal rights discourse. Young activists in Bangalore, protesting against a traveling circus, held up placards that read, "Speak for the Speechless!" College student filmmakers against animal sexual abuse urge viewers to "keep this conversation going on behalf of the victims who cannot speak for themselves."[6] A prominent animal rights lawyer based in Bangalore said that when she goes to court on behalf of animals—unlike, say, in defense of a man—the stakes are higher because "the animals are always 100 percent innocent, no exceptions."[7]

One day I joined Jayasimha Nuggehalli, the Indian director of Humane Society International (HSI) India, at a hotel café in the Jangpura neighborhood of South Delhi. He was hearing a pitch from a young white woman representing a North American philanthropic organization I'll call Gully Dog Global. Gully Dog Global's plan was to sell gourmet dog food to North American patrons and use the proceeds to feed dogs living in Indian slums. Jayasimha and I said we thought it was unethical to feed dogs but not support the people with whom those dogs live. The philanthropist was not persuaded. Her contributors, she said, are "animal lovers" who feel that humans are responsible for their own lives. Dogs, who "are voiceless" and therefore innocent in relation to their circumstances, are the ones deserving of charity.

Animals are not voiceless; neither, as my discussion of animal political action will demonstrate, are they innocent. To claim that they are exemplifies what Gayatri Spivak meant in at least one of the iterations of her argument that the "subaltern cannot speak." Spivak's 1988 essay has as its central case study the life and suicide of Bhuvaneswari Bhaduri, a middle-class Bengali

---

6 From Pratik Rajankar, dir., *Bestiality—The Unheard Rape* (documentary video, posted May 8, 2018), https://www.youtube.com/watch?v=5TWefdOSjjw&noapp=1&client=mv -google&app=desktop. For more on this film, see chapter 7.
7 Brinda Nandakumar, interview by the author, Bangalore, July 2015.

woman who was a relation of Spivak.[8] Bhaduri was a freedom fighter who had received an assignment to assassinate an enemy. Unable, unwilling, or both, Spivak tells us she took her life by hanging. But versed as she was in the Indian genre that is the unmarried woman's suicide, Bhaduri knew her death would be interpreted as shame over an illicit pregnancy. And so—or so Spivak says—she purposefully waited to take her life until she had begun menstruating. Bhaduri spoke at least two truths that day: I can no longer live, and I am not pregnant. Yet years later, when Spivak attempted to speak to Bhaduri's nieces about her death, they reprimanded her for her unseemly interests and said that Bhaduri was just a girl who got caught up in illicit love. Spivak, caught up herself in the spiral of feminist disappointment and patriarchal resignation, then argued, "The subaltern cannot speak."

The essay attracted fame and notoriety in equal parts, inspiring numerous variations on the theme, as well as intense detraction.[9] If, by Spivak's own analysis, Bhaduri "intervened" in the patriarchal text that interprets unmarried women's suicide as sexual shame, then was not Bhaduri's act a speech act? And by attributing a coherent rationale for Bhaduri's suicide—her inability to kill for the resistance—does Spivak not speak for Bhaduri and therefore exemplify her own lament that the subaltern cannot speak (for themselves)? Spivak's 1999 revision concedes that, yes, her lament was "an inadvisable remark." But Spivak does not entirely acquiesce and turns the question back to her readers: What is at stake for you in insisting that the subaltern *does* speak?[10]

What Is It to Speak?

Fred Moten—through Saidiya Hartman's impossible writing of Frederick Douglass's sonic archive of his Aunt Hester's pain—argues that Marx was wrong in claiming commodities do not have voices. "Commodities," Moten says, "do speak and scream."[11] Objects, he says, can and do resist.[12] By commodities, Moten

---

8 Spivak, "Can the Subaltern Speak?" In the 1999 version of the essay, Spivak reveals that Bhaduri was her grandmother's sister. For histories and careful readings of the iterations of Spivak's well-known essay, see Morris, *Can the Subaltern Speak?*; Srinivasan, "Can the Subaltern Speak to My Students?"

9 The points of detraction below are articulated, for example, in Nivedita Majumdar's "Silencing the Subaltern."

10 Spivak, "Can the Subaltern Speak?" (1999).

11 Moten, *In the Break*, 214.

12 Moten, *In the Break*, 12.

means human persons—laborers treated as objects to be bought and sold—but he also therefore means commodities (objects bought and sold). Marx denied that the commodity can speak, because to speak is to have intrinsic value, and the commodity's value is precisely not intrinsic but found in exchange. This impossibility, Moten says, serves as "the final refutation of whatever the commodity will have said."[13] But Moten listens queerly, as do Douglass and Hartman, and beyond the realm of "the proper" hears "where shriek turns speech turns song"—the object's dysarticulate refutation of the proper itself.[14]

Moten often uses the verb *sounds* instead of *speaks*, not as a lesser form of "to speak" but a more expansive one that disrupts as much as it confirms. The anthropologist Lisa Stevenson turns to *soundings*, too, to consider the sonority of Inuit people transported, institutionalized, and let die. Stevenson calls these recordings *soundings* because they are less *information* than what Roland Barthes calls acts of speech as opposed to speech acts, "appeals, modulations, should I say, thinking of birds: songs?—through which a body seeks another body."[15] Soundings, Stevenson says, require a different kind of anthropological listening, less the rooting around that is proper to our proper than like listening to song: a creaturely, avian patiency; just body seeking body.[16] Janet Napolin calls this *resonance*: a sympathetic vibration; "the fact of the more than one."[17] Tobias Menely calls it *sensibility*: "receptivity to the affect sign."[18] The

---

13 Moten, *In the Break*, 10. This is similar to Jean-Francois Lyotard's formulation of a *differend*, in which a class is "divested of the means to argue," thereby exploited, and finally stripped of "the means to prove the damage:" Lyotard, *The Differend*, cited in Menely, *The Animal Claim*, 29.

14 Moten, *In the Break*, 22. "Dysarticulate" is from Berger, *The Disarticulate*.

15 Barthes, *The Grain of the Voice*, 4–5, cited in Stevenson, "Sounding Death," 74. In his monograph on the claims animals make—to humans and to one another—regarding injury and interest, Menely offers a soft distinction between speech acts and creaturely (panspecies) sensibility. While the speech act is associated with "intention and self-extension," sensibility concerns "receptivity, a susceptibility to the signs of others": Menely, *The Animal Claim*, 15. I'm not as invested in the difference between speech acts and, say, soundings, cries, or felicitous silences insofar as (1) receptivity is built into the speech act, particularly in its perlocutionary form; and, (2) as Menely himself insists, the creaturely claim of animal expression is an *address*, which is to say that it is "directed, sent forth," rather than lacking purpose or intent: Menely, *The Animal Claim*, 19. I thank Parama Roy for pointing me to Menely's book.

16 Stevenson, "Sounding Death," 73. For a political philosophy of sounding, see also Havis, "Now, How You Sound."

17 Napolin, *The Fact of Resonance*, 4.

18 Menely, *The Animal Claim*.

queer tongue hears this "hum of the world" and attends to what is not proper.[19] And this resonance is where "effects take place."

So drawing from Napolin and Barthes, Stevenson and Moten, what is it *to speak*? May we define it as to affect and have effects? I, for one, cannot think of a reason why not.[20]

J. M. Coetzee's *The Lives of Animals*, his Tanner Lecture thinly disguised as a novelistic portrait of a thinly disguised Coetzee in the form of Elizabeth Costello, also asks what it is to speak.[21] What is it to have effects? What is it to have one's speech disregarded as the ramblings of an old woman caught up in food faddism? After giving her lecture, Costello debates Professor O'Hearne, who represents the reason of the proper. He argues that animals are not persons because they cannot communicate symbolically: "The best performance the higher apes can put up is no better than that of a speech-impaired human being with severe mental [disability]. If so, are not animals . . . thought of as belonging to another legal and ethical realm entirely, rather than being placed in this depressing human subcategory?"[22] Costello refutes O'Hearne—including his ableist notions of what is and is not depressing—by telling a story about the young Albert Camus. When Camus was young and living in Algeria, his grandmother asked him to bring a hen in from the cage outside. He did and then watched as his grandmother cut its head off with a kitchen knife. "The death-cry of that hen," Costello says, "imprinted itself on the boy's memory so hauntingly that in 1958 he wrote an impassioned attack on the guillotine. As a result of that polemic, capital punishment was abolished in France. *Who is to say, then, that the hen did not speak?*"[23]

19 Kramer, *The Hum of the World.*
20 This is not to suggest that *other* people can't think of reasons why not. But because those reasons tend to stem from, rather than lead to, the sundering of human from animal, I'd like to remain indifferent to them. That said, I do not seek to argue that human and nonhuman (or object) speech is "the same," as sameness is but another manifestation of the prior investment in difference. We might say that two things do not have to be (are not) the same to be continuous, to be in common. Or, thinking with Claude Lévi-Strauss, who wrote that sympathetic identification precedes totemic differentiation, we might say that (indifferent) Difference precedes difference(s) and that I am interested in what occurs when we place ourselves before difference.
21 Coetzee, *The Lives of Animals.*
22 Coetzee, *The Lives of Animals,* 62.
23 Coetzee, *The Lives of Animals,* 63, emphasis added.

"Donkeys have ignored commands. Mules have dragged their hooves. Oxen have refused to work. Horses have broken equipment. Chickens have pecked people's hands. Cows have kicked farmers' teeth out. Pigs have escaped their pens. Dogs have pilfered extra food. Sheep have jumped over fences."[24] So goes Jason Hribal's only partial litany of the ways animals say no to labor and captivity.[25] As Hribal points out, those owners and imperialists and workmasters who are on the receiving end of what Jack Halberstam calls "animal anarchy" recognize these acts for precisely what they are: political resistance to a political system through political speech.[26] Historically, those who rely on the labor of animals have responded to these acts of animal anarchy in three distinct ways.[27] One is to treat animals better, with the understanding that a happy worker makes for better productivity. The second was to strengthen and expand carceral and punitive networks, including zoos and circuses, and public displays of punishing noncompliant animals with death and torture. This second strategy, one of disciplinary power, was attached to an ideological shift, which was to cast animals as dumb, incapable of speech, pleasure, or pain—that is, incapable of being the political actors they clearly were in necessitating these strategic inventions to suppress their voices in the first place.[28] *There is a material history to the representation of animals as voiceless: it is coincident with the intensification of capital, and arose in the West as a strategy of worker suppression.*

An important point for Hribal is that nonhuman animals did not refuse in obscurity or in vain—it was not only capitalists who heard them; other workers did, too. Their acts of resistance informed the labor movement, as well as abolitionism—noted, for instance, in a passage in *My Bondage and My Freedom*, by Frederick Douglass, who saw his struggle represented in an ox, "a wild young working animal" recruited into "life-long bondage."[29] The more-than-human

24 Hribal, "Animals, Agency, and Class," 103.

25 See also Hribal and St. Clair, *Fear of the Animal Planet*. For more true tales of animal resistance, see Burton and Mawani, *Animalia*; Halberstam, *Wild Things*; Meijer, *When Animals Speak*.

26 Halberstam, *Wild Things*, 162. Of course, not all animal speech is political speech—or, as one reader put it, "a *J'accuse*." Animal speech, too, is sometimes, if not often, indifferent.

27 Hribal, "Animals, Agency, and Class," 103–4.

28 As Menely puts it, "The very deflection of the animal sign is evidence of its irrepressible eloquence": Menely, *The Animal Claim*, 34.

29 Douglass, *My Bondage and My Freedom*, 207, cited in Hribal, "Animals, Agency, and Class," 107. I believe it is a mistake to analogize animal captivity to the enslavement of human persons. If I am reading this passage by Douglass correctly, he is offering

solidarities forged by acts of refusal across circumstance is what leads Eva Meijer to the concept of "interspecies civil disobedience," which views other animals not as objects for human political activity but as activists.[30] After all, Hribal notes, the third and final strategy that animal refusal has necessitated is nothing short of the "end to labor" itself.[31]

I once knew a cow who brought about an end to labor. She belonged at the time to Retired Brigadier-General S. S. Chauhan, whom I first met at his *gaushala* in Gurgaon, on the outskirts of New Delhi. I was taken with his gentle appearance, his white mustache, his corduroy pants and pageboy cap, and sneakers caked with grass and manure. He looked more like a boy than my image of a retired brigadier-general. Yet his boyishness belied an ardent passion: the man is *mad* about cows. His wife refers to his cows as his mistresses, with arch humor, but he thinks of them more as his collective mother. "We have an obligation to accept her gift," he said to me, an almost equally ardent refuser of milk, about why he milks his cows and sells their milk, though they are ostensibly there for shelter and care alone. When I raised playful objections to his treating his cows as unpaid laborers, he would shake his head in genuine sadness: "Why would you not drink your mother's milk? That is why she is here! What else is she going to do?"[32]

I arrived at his *gaushala* early one morning after having been away for a year. He led me around the grounds, quizzing me on his favorite breeds to see what I had retained from my last visit. I was doing well but then got a bit distracted by a Gir heifer who was mounting another heifer, with all the associated sounds of ecstasy. Chauhan steered me away by the shoulders: "Yes, that's the unnatural cow. She believes she's a bull, and even when she gets pregnant she miscarries."

Ah, but then he spotted his favorite cow, Kamadhenu, who would never refuse a duty. He held her face in his hands, kissed her, and stroked her ample dewlap, all while cooing, "Isn't she beautiful?" Her name means *wish cow*. Chauhan bestowed the name on her because, like the original Kamadhenu, she always had milk to give and could grant any other desire, too. He told me to whisper a wish in her ear. I did; he beamed.

a moment of recognition between human and animal in their state of what Joshua Bennett calls "living property," giving rise not to analogy but, again, to what Bennett calls "commonality and even comradeship" across species: Bennett, *Being Property Once Myself*. See also Ahuja, "The Analogy of Race and Species in Animal Studies."

30 Meijer, *When Animals Speak*.

31 Hribal, "Animals, Agency, and Class," 104.

32 See also Narayanan, "Cow Is a Mother."

Legend has it that the original Kamadhenu was cursed by Indra to live on Earth as an ordinary cow; to be relieved of this curse, she carried water from the Ganga in her ear to perform a rite (*abhishek*) on the Siva lingam. Siva, in a fit of pique, threatened to kill this ordinary, intrusive cow, and Kamadhenu asked only that he allow her to complete her *puja* of him first.[33] It was this abundantly self-giving nature of the *gau-mata* (mother cow), embodied most perfectly by Kamadhenu the actual and mythical, to which Chauhan returned to explain his consumption of milk, his breeding of purebred cows for Ayurveda, and his milking of cows for cash. And because of the company he kept as a member of the Animal Welfare Board, which included some people like me, he *was* asked to explain himself from time to time. But always his response was the same: "Why would you not drink your mother's milk? That is *why she is here!* What else is she *going to do?*"

But then a funny thing happened. One morning, between 4 and 5 a.m.—the time of day that Chauhan tends to receive communication from his cows through dreams—he dreamed of Kamadhenu. She came to him and said, "I have been mistreated. I was left out in the cold. A worker abused me." When he arrived at the *gaushala* that morning he looked for her immediately and asked the workers what had happened, whether any of this was true. One admitted that Kamadhenu had refused to give milk lately, and maybe he had been a bit rough with her udders.

And from that day on, retired Brigadier-General Chauhan gave up milk, and curd, and the sale of anything acquired from his cows.

( ) Refuses: When the Subaltern Is Silent

Kamadhenu was an articulate cow. She spoke because she knew she would be listened to by someone who could hear what she had to say: that her labor was just that—labor, not a gift—and her working days were through. But what about those women and other animals, commodities and other objects, who choose not to speak? How does the refusal of the imperative to voice help us conceptualize not an expanded humanism but a *de*human politics?[34]

Where a critical response does exist to the (il)liberal humanist, capitalist, anthropodenialist conception of the voiceless animal—the subaltern who cannot speak—it tends, understandably, to insist that animals *do* speak, thus

33 Ferro-Luzzi, *The Self-Milking Cow and the Bleeding Lingam.*
34 "Dehuman[ism]" is from Singh, *Unthinking Mastery.*

broadening political community to include their expressed perspectives, needs, and desires. I am not opposed to this response, which is why I tell the story of Kamadhenu and the Retired Brigadier-General Who Listens with a Queer Tongue. But I also know this response misses something vital, which is that sometimes—often—the subaltern does *not* speak, and that this is a politics, too. It is a politics of the right to opacity; an ethic of *non*relation.[35] And this not speaking to Man takes at least two forms: indifference to the politics of Man and commentary on the politics of Man.

I'm reminded here of another Coetzee novel—I apologize; it's an occupational hazard of thinking with animality: *Life and Times of Michael K.* Michael K is the largely silent protagonist, born harelipped to a mother who could not bear the look of him.[36] K and his mother lose their home during a civil war in apartheid South Africa, and once alone, after his mother has died, K begins to starve—not out of apathy but, rather, a recognition of the violence that inheres in eating. Emaciated and alone, he is misrecognized as an enemy and captured by authorities. The narration then shifts from third-person omniscient to the perspective of an unnamed military officer whose increasingly desperate attempts to make K "yield" to his entreaties—to speak, to eat—demonstrate the officer's attachment to his own humanitarianism, which is dependent on the grateful compliance of the other. Julietta Singh, in her dehumanist reading of the text, shows how this Foucauldian "incitement to discourse" is crucial to the constitution of humanitarian mastery, one that dehumanizes in order to speak for and to make speak.[37]

Many of the political actors who populate the anthropologist Banu Bargu's work cannot be compelled to speak in the conventional understanding of the term: they sew their lips shut to ensure it.[38] Migrants and refugees to Western European nations, many Kurdish and Iranian, have this "violently embodied silence" with which to protest and confront a carceral state.[39] Silence as political action for Bargu is an agency that is noninstrumental (like K's), asking

---

35   The "right to opacity" is from Glissant, *Poetics of Relation*, 190. "Ethic of non-relation" is from Giraud, *What Comes after Entanglement*, 2.

36   Coetzee, *Life and Times of Michael K.*

37   Singh, *Unthinking Mastery*, 111. Pooja Rangan's *Immediations* makes a similar argument: that humanitarian violence performs itself in and through the incitement of the subaltern to speak. See also Wagner, "Silence as Resistance before the Subject," 141, which concludes with the argument, "Not only is the subaltern unable to speak; in some situations [they] can't even remain silent."

38   Bargu, *Starve and Immolate.*

39   Bargu, "The Silent Exception," 5.

for nothing and yet expressive in its noncompliant materiality: silence is "the *announcement of a refusal to participate in the articulation of the good and the just . . .* the rejection of belonging to a common community of speech."[40] I see shades here in a tradition of feminist and Indigenous scholarship, from Doris Sommer to Trinh T. Minh-ha to Audra Simpson, which says that silences are a refusal to participate in anthropological malconceptualizations of the right and the good.[41] Indeed for Bargu, silence is what Foucault called *parrhesia:* an embodied practice of radical truth telling.[42]

What I want to propose is that the radical truth that silence—and, really, only silence—tells is the ongoing presence of *dominance* in what we think of variously as hegemony, entanglement, assemblage, intimacy, or even the social.

The Chengicherla Goat & the Mimic Man

One of the many traditions that the Italian autonomist Mario Tronti seeks to unsettle is assuming the importance of speech in political activity.[43] For example, Tronti offers two divergent models of worker revolt: one, a ten thousand-person march and contract negotiation in 1842, and the other, a day in 1871 in which prisoners who had participated in the June Days Uprising two decades earlier were ordered separated, shot, and killed. The temptation, Tronti says, is to interpret the first as an offensive action on the part of workers and the second as an act of repression on the part of capitalists; however, he says, perhaps it is quite the opposite.[44] The first, Tronti argues, is ultimately a positive development for capitalism because it improves it, adding the spectacle of consent. The second, though, is "a 'No'" that refuses to "manage" or "improve" society as it stands and therefore must be "repressed by pure violence."[45] While I'm not seeking to romanticize death as a political strategy, I do want to propose via Tronti two things: (1) that speaking and concerted action are not only unnecessary for radical politics but might also be antithetical to it; and (2) that living beings

---

40 Bargu, "The Silent Exception," 12–13, emphasis added.
41 Minh-ha, *Woman, Native, Other*; Simpson, "On Ethnographic Refusal"; Sommer, "Taking a Life." See also Malhotra and Rowe, *Silence, Feminism, Power.*
42 Bargu, "The Silent Exception," 17; Foucault and Gros, *"Discourse and Truth" and "Parrēsia."*
43 Tronti, "The Strategy of the Refusal."
44 Tronti, "The Strategy of the Refusal," 9.
45 Tronti, "The Strategy of the Refusal," 9.

under capitalism—whether donkeys, dogs, or men—must be dominated in order to work.

The modern abattoir is an obvious, but certainly not the only, site in which to see this.

My alarm went off at 3:45 a.m. It was May 2013, and I was living in the spare room, sparely but comfortably furnished, in the Hyderabad office of HSI India, at the invitation of Jayasimha Nuggehalli. Jayasimha is brilliant and driven—obsessed with the cause of reducing animal suffering. There are two stories about him that I love to tell. I had brought from Delhi two rather random gifts for his son: a stuffed dog and a wooden rattle. Jayasimha's desk was across the office from mine, and I looked up to see him playing with the toys himself, showing an employee how one might "humanely slaughter" a dog by "stunning it" in the head with the rattle and then using a letter opener to demonstrate how to slit its throat once it had been hung upside down. He caught me staring at him, my mouth open, and he blushed and put the toys away. The second story also involves his baby, whom he had brought to a restaurant and was crying inconsolably. We each bounced around with him, to no avail, until Jayasimha had an idea. "This is what I did when he was in the womb," he said, taking his child and reciting to him, from memory, entire passages from *Fast Food Nation* and statistics about factory farming. The baby, of course, in the embrace of their shared politics, fell peacefully asleep.

Jayasimha picked me up in his Subaru station wagon, which always smelled strongly of perfumed air freshener. We were driving to the Chengicherla Government Mechanized Slaughterhouse, in the Ranga Reddy District just outside Hyderabad in what was once Andhra Pradesh but is now Telangana state. As we passed through Begumpet, he spoke and I took notes. Chengicherla was designed and promoted by the Municipal Corporation of Greater Hyderabad, which sought to shut down hundreds of illegal butcher shops throughout the city, as well as the scattered legal *mandis* (live markets), and force butchers and consumers toward fully mechanized slaughter. Similar transformations had been wrought elsewhere in the country, including years earlier in Delhi, where *mandis* were forcibly closed down to relocate slaughter and sales to a behemoth market on the outskirts of the city in a village called Gazipur.[46] In both cases, the justification for the move was better hygiene, transport, and mechanization—animal welfare was even invoked—though, of course, the real

46 The privatization and relocation of *mandis* were among the issues that gave rise to the farmers' protests in India in late 2020 through to their victorious outcome in November 2021: see Sandhu, "Dispatches from the Farmer Protests."

reason was the smoother accumulation of capital. Wealthy entrepreneurs had begun investing in the machines that they touted as the wave of the future and used their political influence to ensure that future would be realized. Nothing proved smooth about Chengicherla, though. The mechanized abattoir was built, three stories and imposing, but within no more than a few months it lay vacant, windows shattered and derelict. Did the butchers refuse to come? Not exactly. They came but refused to use the abattoir. It was inefficient, they said, and the labyrinthine process meant that they were not certain that the carcasses they received were from the live animals they had brought. Instead, they began using the holding pens—one for goats and other small animals and one for cows and buffalo—as a collective slaughtering grounds.

The facility was running at a loss, but, Jayasimha said, it was politically productive even though it was costing butchers their livelihood. The fact that cows were more or less openly slaughtered at Chengicherla was important to show constituents that the MLA would stand up to *gaurakshaks*. "We will not be cowed," I said, finger in the air. Politely, Jayasimha laughed.

When we arrived, it was the sound that was stunning, like approaching a stadium while a game is in progress, the disembodied din of fifty thousand screaming persons. But where we stood there were only bunches of goats waiting around, rather placidly, and two-wheelers going past with live animals or bags of meat. A man threw a stick at a goat for no reason.

We walked to where the trucks were unloading. A man would grab a goat by the ear or a leg and let it hover momentarily before dropping it, where it either bounced first on the lip of the truck or fell straight down to the ground, several feet lower. Scattered around were downed goats, ones with unnaturally bent limbs, left in the sun to die or be dragged to the killing pens. Most had to be dragged anyway, even if they were not visibly injured. They were usually pulled by one back leg, the animal trying to gain balance on the front two to keep from being skinned along the stony path. Most cried out, and one in particular simply refused to go but had no choice in the end. He was dragged mightily, and finally another man came to help—or, rather, take over—who just pulled it up and along by the ear. The goat stopped for a moment while it tried to register this new sensation, then continued to groan and resist.

One of the things I found extraordinary about this scene is that the man who took over had been following the goat as it resisted, mocking its cries, "Bah," "wah," and so on, and acting as if he were being dragged (imagine an amateur actor pretending to be drunk) while chuckling to himself. It wasn't his meanness or lack of feeling that surprised me; quite the contrary. It was that the goat registered *that much* to him that he was compelled to imitate it: that its dysarticulate, noncompliant language drew "close enough to its object to make the sign ignite."[47] Belied here was his communicative contact with the goat, his *projective identification* with it.

Mimicry and mimesis are often valorized in studies of language as material, sensuous, nonsymbolic, nonspeaking forms of communicative contact between a self and an other. In *What Animals Teach Us about Politics*, Brian Massumi distinguishes between what Roger Caillois called mimicry and imitation.[48] The act of imagining oneself in another, *as* another, or another in oneself—which, of course, is all anthropomorphism really is—is a ludic, inventive gesture, a form of *sympathy* that cannot be reduced to liberal sentimentality. But some identifications, Massumi says, are mimetic ones, such as that of a child playing goat, while some are imitative ones, such as mocking a caged animal in a zoo. The goat—like Coetzee's K and the hunger strikers of Bargu's texts—did not give a name, did not negotiate, and refused to help improve, by word or spectacle, the conditions of its domination. The man, in imitating the goat in all its resistant corporeality, attempted to give it voice, to ventriloquize its demands, that incitement to speech in which the subaltern cannot only not be heard but is unable to remain silent, and yet still could not rid the scene of labor of its constitutive violence.[49]

But I want to offer an additional interpretation and say there is more to the sterile imitation than an expression of hierarchy. The man's identification still serves as a medium for conveying sameness of form. Notice, Massumi says, that animals never imitate humans. (They mimic but do not imitate.) Or, as Clarice Lispector put it, "The animal never substitutes one thing for another."[50] The interspecies mimetic gesture is a relational, "inventive 'thus,'" an excess of expectation rather than a mere reproduction of form. So why would an adult human imitate an animal? Because he seeks, however poorly, to be inventive and not rote. He seeks to stamp himself with an "animal motif."[51]

---

47 "Benjamin argued that language is the highest form of the mimetic faculty. This does not describe language as the system of signs we have come to understand it to be. Rather it describes a language that draws close enough to its object to make the sign ignite": Benjamin, *Reflections*, cited in Marks, *The Skin of the Film*, 162.

48 Caillois, "Mimicry and Legendary Psychasthenia"; Massumi, *What Animals Teach Us about Politics*.

49 The formulation of being *not-heard and yet also unable to remain silent* is indebted to Wagner, "Silence as Resistance before the Subject."

50 Lispector, *Agua Viva*, 42. This might be another way to articulate the critique of the race-species analogy.

51 Massumi, *What Animals Teach Us about Politics*, 82.

So here is what I want to suggest about the working man and the working goat who refused: (1) to refuse is inventive; (2) the fewer words used, the better; and (3) we stamp ourselves in hope and play with the inventive dysarticulate refusal. And that is what animals teach us about politics.

To Be Silent Alongside: Or, Listening to Goats with Queer Tongue

In Perumal Murugan's *The Story of a Goat*, translated into English from Tamil, the two human protagonists have no names to which we are privy.[52] They are an old woman and an old man. The old man happens upon a giant in the forest, and in the crook of the giant's arm is a jet-black kid the size of a kitten. The giant tells the old man that the kid comes from a line that yields litters of seven at a time. The giant leaves the old man with the kid and disappears. Being poor, the old man feels burdened yet possibly blessed if what the giant says is true. He returns home, and the old woman, despite her protestations, is enamored of the baby goat. She names her Poonachi after a long-lost cat. That night, the old man and the old woman talk as they haven't for years, pleasant chitchat about the old days. Poonachi has loosened their tongues.

Murugan, as is common across Indic literary traditions, is not cramped up about whether animals speak or think or feel.[53] He knows they do. It's just that usually only children and other queerdos want to hear them.[54] Nor is Murugan anxious about anthropomorphism, which, after all, is just a concept invented by European racism. Murugan writes, which is to imagine oneself into and express the form of something else—as much the old woman as the goat kid. Anthropomorphism implies that there is a human, separate from its (other) wordly mimetic relations, that can be crudely projected onto those severed

52 Murugan, *The Story of a Goat*. For another reading of Murugan's novel, see Thiyagarajan, "Inevitable Lives."

53 For just a small sample of talking, feeling animals in South Asian literature, see Bhattacharya, *Upanyas Samagra*; Chattopadhyay, *The Drought*; Hussain and Kidwai, *The Mirror of Wonders and Other Tales*; Lenin, *My Husband and Other Animals*; Mitra, *Mosquito and Other Stories*; Roy, *The Hundred Names of Darkness*; Roy, *The Wildlings*; Roy, *Animalia Indica*; Sajad, *Munnu*. For examples in recent-ish film, see Rishi Chandna, dir., *Tungrus: A Family, a Cramped Apartment, and a Problematic Pet Rooster* (video, posted January 29, 2019), accessed August 6, 2021, https://www.youtube.com/watch?v=4BzwEo5I-mw; Umesh Vinayak Kulkarni, dir., *Valu: The Wild Bull* (film, Netflix, 2008).

54 On talking animals and children in Indic literary traditions, see Olivelle, "Talking Animals."

things. But queer tongues come alive in imagined worlds. There is no such thing in such worlds—such worlds worth desiring and the only worlds worth reading—as anthropomorphism in the first place.

The old woman, like Poonachi, is special, and what makes her special is how she listens. When Poonachi cries, "though it sounded no louder than a blade of grass being ripped, the old woman heard it."[55] The bond between them grows as Poonachi does, and her soundings go from cries to narrative: "Every night Poonachi told the old woman everything that had happened that day in the pasture. Of what she recounted, the old woman would understand some things and not others. Nevertheless, she was always a keen listener."[56] She listens without having to understand.

The old woman's aural praxis reminds me of Kamala, a worker I knew at Animal Aid, a large animal shelter in Udaipur. Like most of the other employees, Kamala lived in a nearby village. One of her tasks at work was to sit under the tarp that shades the paralyzed dogs and massage them, which she does for nearly forty-five minutes each, every day, and while she does so she sings to them and pulls out their ticks. I was under the tarp with her one day and asked whether she wondered why she does work like this, with such love and sincerity, and others don't? She said she does it because she was raised well and that her parents loved animals and cultivated empathy in her. *Main insaan hoon*, she said. I am a human being, and it is human to care. But then, after thinking a moment, she added, *Insaan sab matlab se karte hai, lekin jaanver mein matlab nahi hai. Jaanver mein samajdar hoti hai, matlab nahi.* Humans do what they do with *matlab*—intention, meaning, purpose, interest, with and for reason/s. Animals are not *matlabi*, but lest I hear this as a demotion of animals, an argument for their lack of sense, she clarified that animals have something more vital than *matlab*: *samajdar*, understanding. The old woman in Murugan's tale, like many of us, may not have had this animal capacity. So she listened as she could: without having to understand.

I began this chapter with two questions: How do we choose to listen, and what do we choose to say? Here is what I would like to say about the soundscape of relation.[57]

---

55 Murugan, *The Story of a Goat*, 23.
56 Murugan, *The Story of a Goat*, 68.
57 Menely articulates the stakes, writing, "How we conceptualize communication— how we define what counts as a meaningful sign, claim, or mode of address—will determine the story we tell about the history of community": Menely, *The Animal Claim*, 13.

If we do not hear, it does not mean she has not spoken. I defined *to speak* in this chapter as "to affect and have effects." As is true of affect more generally, with which this definition finds affinity, the lived is in excess of what is articulated.[58] The flesh, after all, is faster than word.[59] Might we learn to listen with skin, if not word? Can we listen together with avian patience instead of the rooting around that is proper to our proper? "Can we listen together differently?"[60]

When we listen together differently (with skin, if not word), we know that the object (queers and other animals, commodities and other persons) speaks. With this knowledge of "the material form of the impossibility of silence," it now becomes possible to respect the chosen silences of the object (women and other animals, commodities and other persons) as the political will to not say.[61] Silence in this world is materially impossible. The whole world sounds, and there is no object-person-animal that does not speak. Silence, thus, is an effort of will, whether to (try to) silence another or to choose (that is, to attempt) to not sound. When an object attempts to not sound, out of indifference to being heard or known or as an act of resistance—when it exercises silence—that is, as Trinh T. Minh-ha writes, "a will not to say and a will to unsay."[62] Silence, Bargu writes, is not "simply the absence of sound" but often the "withholding of speech."[63] All those women and other animals, commodities and other persons who silently refuse and refuse with their silence know this way of sounding well. Silence, like the scream, is the object's dysarticulate refutation of the proper itself. The proper—in its offense against both mass and lonely movements of silent refusal, against the withholding of consent to its ways—ironically attempts to make the silent speak—even those, like animals and subaltern women, whose voicelessness is the proper's own invention.

When we listen together differently, we know that the object speaks. With this knowledge it now becomes possible to respect the chosen silences of the object as the political will to not say. This respect for mass and lonely movements of silent refusal of the proper is expressed through an ethos of being silent alongside, which is also to say, to listen alongside with queer tongues. Pranita, an animalist in Hyderabad, said to me as she crouched in

---

58 Williams, *Marxism and Literature*, 126.
59 Massumi, *Parables for the Virtual*.
60 Singh, *No Archive Will Restore You*, 61.
61 "Material form of the impossibility of silence" is from Kramer, *The Hum of the World*, 31.
62 Minh-ha, "Not You/Like You," 416.
63 Bargu, "The Silent Exception," 12. Bargu suggests, following Jacques Rancière, that this is the primary political modality of those whose speech is "reduced to sound by others": Rancière, *Disagreement*, 22, cited in Bargu, "The Silent Exception," fn. 47.

the dirt with a sick goat, that it is not for her or anyone to speak for animals; rather, it is for us "to be silent alongside." Alongside is the expression of relation. Alongside is the spatiality of the friend. Minh-ha writes, "I do not intend to speak about; just speak nearby," a sentiment that lent her documentary films the flavor of "anti-ethnography" to some.[64] If being nearby and alongside is the antithesis of ethnography, then so be it. Let's meet at the watering hole. Silence invites its own forms of ciphered solidarity.

Respect for mass and lonely movements of silent refusal of the proper is expressed through an anti-ethnographic ethos of being silent alongside, which is also to say, to listen alongside with queer tongues that fail and try to write the impossible. Sometimes we do speak (for) each other, object for object. To deny or reject that is to assume the sort of autological subject that does not exist in worlds worth desiring. In "Venus in Two Acts," Hartman writes about the calling to "construct a story from the locus of impossible speech."[65] Would writing about Venus, a girl killed by slave traders on the Atlantic, amount to an invention, a romance in the story of brutality? Hartman decides on "critical fabulation," which is to "listen for . . . the mutters, oaths, and cries of the commodity," but with "narrative restraint . . . and a refusal to fill gaps and provide closure."[66] Hartman's queer tongue writes an "impossible writing which attempts to say that which resists being said."[67] It resists being said not because it refuses to say, but because it is silenced. Sometimes we do speak each other, object for object—an act of critical fabulation necessary for any world worth desiring and in every world worth attending to.

64 "Speak nearby" is from Trinh T. Minh-ha, dir., *Reassemblage* (film, Women Make Movies, New York, 1982), https://www.wmm.com/catalog/film/reassemblage. The characterization of Minh-ha's films as "anti-ethnography" is discussed in Reed, "The Enduring Power of Trinh T. Minh-ha 's Anti-ethnography."

65 Hartman, "Venus in Two Acts," 3.

66 Hartman, "Venus in Two Acts," 12.

67 Hartman, "Venus in Two Acts," 12.

5

INTERLUDE. Take a Walk with Me

The absent man who walks exhausts no territory; he sets roots only in the sacred of the air and evanescence, in a pure refusal that changes nothing in the world. We are not following him in reality, because we always want to change something. But we know in the end that his traveling, which is not nomadism, is also not rambling. It traces repeated figures here on earth, whose pattern we would catch if we had the means to discover it.
—ÉDOUARD GLISSANT, *POETICS OF RELATION*

• • •

I met Abodh Aras, for the second time, on a Monday in May 2012. I had recently arrived in Bombay and was staying in a flat in Bandra. I took the local train south to Churchgate and walked across the maidan toward Flora Fountain to the Jehangir Art Gallery, where Abodh had suggested we have lunch. His workplace, the office of Welfare for Stray Dogs (WSD), was just behind the museum in Kala Ghoda on a *gali* known as Fabindia Lane.

Abodh is slim and handsome, with light black hair and gray-green eyes. Dressed in khakis, a white-and-tan checkered shirt, and inexpensive black dress shoes, he is friendly and attentive. Unlike most of the other "celebrity" animal activists I've met, he never interrupts. As we ate lunch, he asked me about my research that summer. I told him I was planning to work part-time at PETA's office in Juhu and that I would love to work the rest of the week with him at WSD. It was settled that I'd spend Wednesdays, Sundays, and Mondays with WSD for the length of the summer.

When Abodh was young, in 1995, he had come upon a sick, emaciated puppy near his home. He took the puppy to the SPCA, believing that to be the right course of action. The puppy contracted a disease and died within days.[1] Abodh completed his MBA, and while working as a customer service representative for the delivery company DHL, he began training with a veterinarian. In 1996, he approached WSD, then operated by Jain philanthropists, many of whom still sit on the Board of Trustees, and persuaded them to start an on-site first aid program that has since become a model for street animal welfare groups across the country and the world.

After lunch we walked to the WSD office, on the second floor of a building donated to the organization by the then MTV veejay Cyrus Broacha.[2] I met Lakshmi, a middle-aged woman who lived with her brother in an apartment near the sea and sold homemade artisanal chocolate. Lakshmi peoples the help line. When someone calls regarding an animal, she notes the species, description, location, ailment, and contact information for a nearby human. She then communicates the gist of this by phone to one of the WSD fieldworkers. Abodh works in the office most days with Lakshmi but does first aid himself on Sundays with a group of volunteers, often young Mumbaikars in their twenties. Under Abodh was a field manager named Dhanashree who oversaw the salaried fieldworkers—Dipesh, Arjun, and Milli. The organization owns two ambulances and a shelter near Dhobi Ghat, which was previously a municipal pound. It runs five programs: sterilization, on-site first aid, vaccination,

---

1 The mortality rate at shelters for young dogs is estimated at 60–70 percent. On shelter existence more generally, and a glimpse of what drove Abodh to create an alternative to it, see Guenther, *The Lives and Deaths of Shelter Animals*.

2 With its charismatic director and largely uncontroversial mandate of being nice to stray dogs, WSD has many influential supporters. The author, Jerry Pinto, runs free public awareness workshops for children. And several of our Sunday stops were to the Tata building in south Bombay, where security guards employed by the moguls watch over a pack of neighborhood canines. The Tatas also fund an education program that brings veterinarians from Cornell University to teach veterinary practices to WSD fieldworkers.

education, and adoption. Its mandate is the Island City, between Churchgate in the south and Mahim suburb to the north.

I first met Dipesh when he stopped in for that afternoon's field meeting. Abodh was looking forward to introducing us, as we both spoke Gujarati. He suggested we go on some walks together, and Dipesh, from the glance I saw him give Abodh, was not excited. Of course, I found this embarrassing—there is so much about fieldwork that embarrasses me—and yet I had a feeling it would be all right between us.

We arranged to meet at the start of his rounds on Wednesday morning. Dipesh was waiting for me at Study Centre, the public, always open reading hall across from the Oval Maidan, where he told me we would take a bus to Churchgate. I was a little disappointed. Dipesh was a mythical hero among the WSD staff: they talked of his stamina, how he had one cup of chai in the morning and then didn't eat the rest of the day so as not to lose time; how he had forty-two animals on his personal check-in list, in addition to the calls that came in each day from Lakshmi; how he walked nearly everywhere so as not to waste sweat idling under bus shelters. Yet we waited fifteen, twenty minutes for a bus, our conversation stilted. Finally it dawned on me that the bus was for my sake and I told him we could walk. *Chalenge*, he asked, shall we go? And we walked off, far more ease now between us.

Dipesh walks quickly despite the heavy and worn first aid pack he wears on his back and the duffel he straps across his torso. At the end of the summer I asked whether I could gift him a new backpack, and he said absolutely not. He knew where everything was in the one he was carrying, and he liked it that way. These are the backpack's contents: Wokadine or Betadine solution (for skin infections); 3 percent hydrogen peroxide (cleans wounds and removes dead flesh); Xylocaine ointment (gel form); chloroform (kills maggots, painful); Himax (smelly, rust-colored fly repellant); Nebasulf sprinkling powder (for skin infections); Scabnil Oleo (skin paste); Kailash Jeevan (Ayurvedic cream for treating anal fissures); Pendistrin SH (for teat infections); Neosporin (general); Ivermectin tablets (for intestinal parasites); Topicure spray (for maggot infections); eucalyptus oil and neem oil (general, soothing); Arnica (to treat osteoarthritis pain); Aconite (for shock after an accident or other trauma); Rescue Remedy (also for shock and stress); Glucose biscuits (for cajoling); and gauze, bandages, scissors, and forceps.

The first call that day was for a cat who lived behind a beauty parlor near Churchgate station. Half of her face was mauled in a fight, and the wound became infected by maggots. We caught a quick glimpse of her before she disappeared through the window of a house. Dipesh climbed the wall and peeked in, where a man with damp chest hair and wearing a towel said we should look in the garden, which is where the cat usually went after she raced through his house every day. He joined us, and the three of us searched, but we gave up when we realized she had escaped into the gutter system that ran the length of the nearby Brabourne Stadium, home of the Indian Premiere League cricket club, the Mumbai Indians. Dipesh and I knocked on the door of the beauty parlor to give the women who had called some Topicure to administer to the cat. The women offered us tea and water. I accepted the latter, while Dipesh looked ill at ease in the pinkish surrounds, doing nothing, and was ready to leave.

From Brabourne Stadium we walked north along Marine Drive, the sea-facing promenade with Art Deco architecture on one side and a seawall, populated by lovers and lounging dogs, on the other. Dipesh had been called by a family who lived under a tarp near Metro Cinema, with a parakeet and an ailing street dog. A security guard from the cinema joined the man, his wife, and a child to watch as Dipesh muzzled the dog with string he keeps in his right-side pants pocket. The dog had met with an accident, and its paw was bloody and filled with pus. Dipesh ascertained there were no breaks; treated his paw with hydrogen peroxide and Xylocaine gel; and cleaned mites out of its ear. The dog trundled off after Dipesh unmuzzled him, and his family thanked Dipesh with tilts of their heads and offers of refreshment, the latter of which he politely refused.

From there we walked northeast through the narrow lanes of the Zaveri Jewelry Bazaar to Mumba Devi Mandir, built in 1635 for the goddess Mumba, the namesake of Mumbai city. As we walked, I asked Dipesh about his life. Dipesh speaks Gujarati, Marathi, and Hindi and has comfort with some English vocabulary; we spoke to each other in Gujarati. Dipesh was unmarried and lived with his parents in a *chawl*, a form of collective tenement housing common to western Indian cities.[3] I asked him why he hadn't married. *Aa badha maate*, he said, sweeping his arm to indicate the animals of the city. *Aa badha maate, main life cycle finish nathi karyu*. So that I can care for these animals, he said, I haven't become a husband and father.[4] Dipesh finishes his WSD rounds at around 4 or 5 p.m., then takes care of animals in his own neighborhood until 9 or 10 at night. His mind is often busy, and he doesn't sleep until 2 a.m. or so. He was originally from

3 See Adarkar, *The Chawls of Mumbai*; Finkelstein, "Ghosts in the Gallery."
4 The Hindu concept of *dharma*, or duty, segments a man's life (a man's, specifically) into four stages, or *āśramās*: the student; the householder/father/husband; the retiree or forest-dweller; and the spiritual renunciate. It is less that Dipesh has not "finished" his life cycle, but that he skipped over the second stage of *grihasta*, or householder, and now occupies a transitional stage toward renunciation.

Bhavnagar, but he hadn't returned for more than ten years because he was busy with his animals. Dipesh hadn't always cared much for animals. He was drinking and playing cards one afternoon with friends, which was how he spent most of his days, he said, when a neighborhood man who then worked as a fieldworker for WSD scolded him (not the others; only him) for wasting his life. Dipesh and his friends laughed at the man and carried on with their game, but a week later Dipesh was training at WSD.

Dipesh asked the groundskeeper of the temple where the dog was to be found, only to be told he had disappeared. Dipesh was unperturbed; it seems this happens a lot. We continued northward to treat a dog at Khetwadi 4th Lane, where Dipesh bought me a bottle of Fanta. From there we walked back west toward the bay, Dipesh whistling. I didn't realize we were on the lookout for anyone when he suddenly stopped short, on a side lane near Opera House on Charni Road, and kneeled by a couple of two-wheelers parked side by side. With effort, he pulled an old, horrid-looking dog out from under the bike and, still whistling, tied her snout with the string. He pulled her into the partial shade of an apartment foyer and, with one hand on the dog, rummaged with the other through his knapsack for a pair of forceps. He grabbed some discarded newspaper from the ground which he placed at the end of the dog's butt. He lifted her tail and with a dropper placed a small dose of chloroform into her anus. Maggots emerged in the dozens, wriggling and wiggling, and Dipesh took his forceps, entered the dog's rectum and pulled out dozens more, placing them methodically on the newspapers by which time most of the others had stopped moving. Two people walked by. One looked briefly and then kept on his way. The other stood behind me and watched for most of the procedure. When he finished the job, Dipesh applied talcum powder and Himax to the area around the dog's butt and told me to undo the string around her snout while he disposed of the newspaper. The dog walked unsteadily into the street and promptly took what looked like a very uncomfortable shit as cars and scooters dodged her. When a car almost hit her, I screamed. Dipesh turned to see and waved his hand dismissively. She's old, he said, and walked me north toward Mumbai Central, where he had a dog to check on, and I'd catch a train back to Bandra.

THE FOLLOWING WEDNESDAY, I met Dipesh at 10:30 a.m. on Platform 1 of Grant Road Station. We started on the east side of the rail tracks, tending to a tailless dog with a bumpy skin infection (Wokadine followed by a sprinkling of Nebasulf). From there we walked east toward Dongri, a dense neighborhood near J. J. Hospital, one of the many landmarks on our walks named after the nineteenth-century Parsi philanthropist and opium lord Sir Jamsetjee Jejeebhoy.[5] Dongri looms large in the Mumbai cinematic imagination, in part for having served as headquarters of the gangster Dawood Ibrahim.[6] Dipesh pointed out the Damarwala building at the corner of Yaqoob and Pakmodia, a five-story structure with shops on the ground floor and rooms above in which Ibrahim lived before absconding to Dubai in the 1980s. We walked along Yaqoob and then down a narrow by-lane, where we were met by a well-built man with just a *lungi* around his waist—we seemed often to come upon people in half-dress. He told us the dog Dipesh had been treating was killed. She had an infected wound on her face and had been stoned to death for her deformity. I left Dipesh and the man to speak alone.

When Dipesh rejoined me, we walked eastward toward a cluster of auto garages near Sitaram Shenoy Garden. Dipesh said it was a false story (*katha*) that Muslims were intolerant of dogs: there are caring men like the man in the *lungi* and men like those who had killed the dog in every religion.[7] In his opinion, "posh" people were the worst where animals were concerned, and he carried a special annoyance for vegetarian Hindus who, on top of their cruelties, he said, could be hypocrites (*dhambi*).

I told Dipesh that when I was staying in Begumpet I had met a man called the Kuttawala Nawab—the Muslim Nobleman with Canine Companions. The Kuttawala Nawab's real name was Nawab Nazeer Yar Jung (1929–2019) and, like his late mother, the Begum, he was among the Paigah aristocrats of Hyderabad state.[8] When Jayasimha and I visited the Nawab, he lived in the penthouse of an aging building, with a large kennel on the upper-floor terrace. There were photos everywhere of the Nawab in glamorous days with glamorous people. The frames shared space with hundreds of ceramic dog figurines.

The story Jayasimha had told me about the Nawab was this: he was a famous breeder who once had upward of two hundred dogs roaming his palace. When the Begum died, mullahs refused to perform last rites because

5 For more on Sir Jejeebhoy in Bombay, see Prakash, *Mumbai Fables*, 37–39.

6 Among the films about Dawood Ibrahim are Anurag Kashyap, dir., *Black Friday* (Big Bang Pictures, Mirror Films, Mumbai, 2004); Ram Gopal Varma, dir., *Company* (Varma Corporation, Mumbai, 2002); and Milan Luthria, dir., *Once Upon a Time in Mumbai* (Balaji Motion Pictures, Mumbai, 2010). For more on Dawood Ibrahim in Dongri, see Zaidi and Chandra, *Dongri to Dubai*.

7 The place of dogs in Islam is contested, as the following conversation traces. For a discussion of specific hadiths concerning dogs, see Subaşi, *Dogs in Islam*.

8 The Nawab wrote a memoir about his life with animals: see Jung, *Strolling through the Jungles*.

they considered dogs unclean and proximity to them *haram*. Nawab Nazeer welcomed their abstention, saying he would perform the rites himself, as dogs are purer than mullahs anyway. The mullahs gave in, shamed by the Nawab's conviction, and the Begum was laid to rest appropriately. That, anyway, was the legend of the Kuttawala Nawab.

The Nawab himself, though, would have none of it. "Nobody would do that to my mother," he said angrily, after I related to him the story I had heard. "Everyone respected her too much. If they had a problem with the dogs, they would have kept it to themselves." He was sick, he said, of the stupidity around Islam and dogs, the same stupidity that had landed him with the ironic name Kuttawala Nawab, as well as the false story about his mother. There is nothing so unusual, he argued, about a Muslim loving dogs. The eighteenth surah of the Quran, Surah Al-Kahf (the Cave), extols a dog who protects its human companions by lying at the mouth of a cave. Muhammad Ali Jinnah, the founder of Pakistan, had a Doberman and West Highland Terrier, both of whom he openly adored. General Pervez Musharraf posed in an official portrait with his two Pekingese, and in his biography he memorialized his deceased dog, Whiskey.[9] The Nawab did, however, make two concessions to prejudice: "Only pedigreed people should have pedigreed dogs" and, "street dogs, frankly, should be shot." Dipesh, despite himself, laughed hard at this surprise ending.

When we arrived at our next destination, in Dongri, Dipesh asked an auto parts dealer where the dog was, to which the dealer replied, *Voh andar rehtha hai. Key use lijie.* So we went to the cycle shop man across the street, who used a key to undo a padlock on an aluminum door that opened into a garage full of stacked tires and three thin, chained goats standing in the dark. We called out for the dog, found him behind a stack of rubber, and pulled him into a shaft of light emanating from a hole in the tin roof, where Dipesh administered a treatment to the dog's infected paw. He checked on the goats and patted them—one in particular that nuzzled his hand.

From Dongri we walked south toward Masjid Bandar (Mosque Port) and the Mumba Devi Mandir. Dipesh had been called by a vendor at Manish Market, a bazaar of largely Gujarati and Marwari sellers of textiles, plastic home goods, toys, and clothes. The *thelawala*, or tote-bag seller, was a friendly fellow with a pockmarked face and mehndi-tinted hair who kept bowls of water under his tables. The dog he had called about was not around, though he searched for twenty minutes in the midday heat while Dipesh and I sat under his awning. The

---

9 See Doctor, "Political Pets."

dog was found, her snout tied with Dipesh's trusty string, and Dipesh cleaned maggots out of her ear—a horrifying sight. People gathered around to watch, which annoyed the bag vendor, and he shouted to the onlookers to beat it (*jao!*). Few obeyed. When Dipesh finished, the bag seller stayed, holding the dog's snout with one hand and the other resting on her ribs. You can let her go, Dipesh said. No, the merchant replied. When she's upset, it is very hard to calm her. One would never know this from looking at her then, peaceful despite having just been so strangely handled, penetrated by a stranger in a crowd of stares.

We were heading next in the direction of Victoria Terminus, the Gothic Revival–style railway station built in 1888 (now called Chhatrapati Shivaji Maharaj Terminus), but we took a detour through Crawford Market, a wholesale bazaar in the heart of the city, built in 1869 with Kurla Stone and redstone, punctuated with a clock tower and skylight. Dipesh led me to the infamous Pet Bazaar. Imagine the most depressing PetSmart adoption drive you've ever seen and turn up the sorrow a hundredfold. Not everyone can afford the Nawab's particularity, and lots of people want pets—mostly pugs and poms, mutts advertised as poodles, cats sold as Persian, none long for this world.[10]

We walked south to the Sir J. J. School of Art, another namesake of the philanthropist and opium trader Jamsetjee Jejeebhoy. Dipesh was here to apply Himax to the face of a blind dog named Lalu, whose eyes were often caked with pus from an infection that neither he nor Abodh could cure. The Himax at least would keep the bugs away. Lalu's eyes were bright blue with disease, his body all lumpy with age and tumors, but his tenure on campus meant he'd enjoyed a good life. He usually slept under a stone bench on the main lawn, relishing the favors of students from Mondays to Fridays. We petted Lalu and fed him Glucose biscuits. As we left, I pointed out to Dipesh the dean's bungalow, where I said Rudyard Kipling was born.[11] He ignored me.

We continued south toward Kala Ghoda, or Black Horse, today the home of an ignominious parking lot but once the site of an equestrian statue of King

---

10 For a media description of Pet Bazaar, see "Animal Crackers at Crawford Market." Crawford Market has been the subject of several public interest litigations filed by animal rights groups for its abuses of animals waiting to be sold and for alleged violations of exotic-animal trafficking law. Activists' agitation over the Crawford Market Pet Bazaar led in part to the passage of the Prevention of Cruelty to Animals (Pet Shop) Rules of 2016.

11 It was good that he ignored me, because I was wrong. Young Kipling was born nearby, but not in this bungalow. (Thank you, Parama Roy.) Rudyard's father, John Lockwood Kipling, the author of *Beast and Man in India*, was the first principal of the Sir J. J. School of Art, founded in 1857.

Edward VII and then, after protestors had him transported to a zoo in 1965, a statue of the seventeenth-century Marathi warrior Shivaji. Dipesh was met by Sumathiben, a diminutive woman who led him to a dog hiding underneath a taxi. Sumathiben called to a flower shop boy, who pried the dog out with a mix of sweet talk and leg yanking. Dipesh completed his treatment and, as we walked away, he told me that the previous year, Sumathiben was chasing after a dog who had been maimed in an accident. When she caught up to it, she threw her body over the animal in the middle of the road and lay there until Dipesh arrived. He found Sumathiben lying in the street in the monsoon rain in her widow's sari.[12]

Dipesh dropped me off at a South Indian spot near the WSD office while he ran upstairs to procure supplies. I scarfed down two idli with sambar and loads of chutney. Heavy now of stomach and spirit, I accompanied Dipesh northward to the *Times of India* office at the corner of Mahapalika and Manish roads. He, in his fasted state, was in a good mood and feeling philosophical. He talked to me about his life: "Everything I have is for my family. Everything I am is for others."

In an alley behind the building we were met by a waste collector (*kudawali*), an old woman slightly stooped, her head covered by the *pallu* of her sari. All it took from her was the sound of a single kiss and the dog emerged from under a car, with a little stretch, and loped over. The old woman stroked him. Dipesh's triage was quick: he searched the dog for ticks and maggots as he does every week, fed him some Glucose biscuits, and was on his way. As he gathered his things, Dipesh asked the old woman if she needed anything. Her husband, also a waste collector, had died of a stomach ailment, and Dipesh had contributed money for his treatment.

We returned south for an assignment at a roadside restaurant near the Oval Maidan. Dipesh had been there before and led us through the kitchen to the back, where the dog was tied on a short rope in direct sun. He was clearly suffering, cowering. I waited for Dipesh to say something to the owner—he had no qualms about lecturing people, especially people with money—but he was quiet. It turned out that Dipesh and the *malik* knew each other from nondog circles, and the *malik* teased Dipesh for walking around like a hobo instead of riding a motorcycle. Dipesh laughed uncomfortably; he's not a particularly chummy person, and I get the impression he doesn't love the company of men, especially back-slapping types. The *malik* reached into his well-stocked refrigerator and gave us a single bottle of water to share. Dipesh and I exchanged an annoyed look. Dipesh went to

---

12 I think of a line from Lawrence Cohen's *No Aging in India*: "The wanderer wanders because he has been abandoned, the *bakbak* dog lady barks because she has no one . . . Wandering and being lost point in several directions" (277).

the back, untied the dog and retied him under a patch of shade, and told the *malik* that the next time he was there he expected to see the dog sheltered.

Dipesh checked in with Lakshmi once again and was asked to go to Nariman Point, a once prominent business area now in a decline that could be sensed in the white-hot, vacant atmosphere. Even the dogs were gone. A year earlier, a neighborhood animal lover named Ravi had insisted on feeding hundreds of stray dogs on the footpaths of Marine Drive, despite Abodh's admonitions. Welfare for Stray Dogs is against feeding (besides, of course, the occasional Glucose cookie); they believe that animal populations should be allowed to recede naturally with urban waste levels, thus incentivizing modernized waste management and decreasing the overall number of street dogs. Welfare for Stray Dogs also views animal lovers such as Ravi as a public-relations nuisance, undermining hard-won sapien-canine relations by annoying rich residents. This is precisely what happened, and the Bombay Municipal Corporation, WSD's landlord, demanded that the dogs in Nariman Point be confiscated. Abodh felt he had to comply, and he oversaw the confiscation himself, hauling most of the Nariman Point dogs to the WSD shelter at Dobi Ghat.[13] But what the Municipal Corporation failed to understand is what happens when dogs are forcibly removed from their territory. A vacuum is created, and if there is trash, there will be dogs, so hungry new animals arrive from elsewhere, and internecine interspecies violence ensues.[14]

We were there that day because a Parsi shop owner had called in several complaints about a biting dog. Dipesh was skeptical; he believed that Parsis were particularly quick to complain about dogs. It was unlikely that the biting dog was just going to be hanging around on the seawall tetrapods in this heat, but we spent twenty minutes looking anyway. Dipesh found a group of *paanwalas* and hotel cleaning men hanging out in the shade and asked them about the biting dog. They laughed. They knew the dogs around there, they said, and agreed with Dipesh that it was likely a false report. But we wandered around for a while longer, along the seawall just for pleasure, and I asked Dipesh whether he knew about the Parsi Dog Riots of 1832.

13 The Animal Birth Control order of 2001 considers feeding a legal as well as a moral obligation, but only insofar as it does not pose a nuisance to the public.

14 For a range of perspectives on the relationship among feeding, waste, and sapien-canine violence, see Bhalla and Vanak, "Killing with Compassion"; Nag, "Feeding Abandoned Animals in the Pandemic"; Narayanan, "Street Dogs at the Intersection of Colonialism and Informality"; Parmar, "Canines, Campus, and Community"; Srinivasan, "Remaking More-than-Human Society."

I first learned about the riots from Abodh who, because he is light-skinned with green eyes, is often mistaken for Muslim or Parsi rather than Goan Saraswat Brahmin. He welcomes the errors, no less because they tend to come with surprise that someone who is not Hindu, Jain, or white does animal charity. His "No—in fact, I am not Parsi," or whatever else the mistake is, is always an opportunity for pedagogy about pluralistic interspecies solidarity, such as the tale of the Parsi Dog Riots of 1832.[15]

The colonial British, despite their dog-loving reputation, disliked Indian dogs, to which they gave the name "pariah."[16] In 1813, colonial officials passed an order to cull ownerless dogs between the hot months of April–May and September–October. In 1832, the dates were expanded into June, which overlapped with the Zoroastrian seasonal festival Maidyoshahem Gahanbar and the Muslim holy month of Muharram. On June 6, a Parsi holy day, dogs were being shot on British orders, and the local community of Parsis—colonial elites known then in part for their accommodation to empire—instigated a full-on rebellion.[17] Constables were beaten; the army's food supply was disrupted; and shops owned by Parsis, Hindus, Jain Vanias, and Muslim Ismailis (predominantly Gujarati-speaking all, Dipesh interjected) went on strike, each with their disparate relationship to dogs but a united rejection of colonial overreach into spheres of religious expression. By the next afternoon, thousands had gathered in the center of Bombay Town to protest the dog cull, and the colonizers had no choice but to relent. The Parsi Dog Riots predated the Sepoy Rebellion

15 All of the following historical details are drawn from Jesse Palsetia's "Mad Dogs and Parsis," which was also Abodh's source. Abodh is a true student of Canine History. The Parsi Dog Riots are also sometimes referred to as the Bombay Dog Riots.

16 The term *pariah* derives from the Tamil *Paraiyar*, a caste of ritual drummers (drum in Tamil is *parai*) who, due to their proximity to leather, were oppressed by dominant castes. People of the Paraiyar caste often worked as servants for British officers, who Anglicized the caste name as "pariah," expanding it to include street dogs and other social outcasts: see Agarwal, "Desi Dogs"; Zimmer, "Drumming Up the Origins of 'Pariah' States." Another common etymology traces to the Hindi word *pahi* (outsider), which has given way to the familiar term *pi dog*. Agarwal notes the irony of a native breed being cast by the British as an outsider and adds that, today, pariah dogs and street dogs are not the same kind of dog. Today's street dogs are mixed-breed, due largely to the rise of pet keeping and the abandonment and reluctance to sterilize such pets, while pariah dogs are considered a native breed with distinct characteristics, including a narrow waist, sharp snout, alert ears, and curly tail: see Bhavani, "These Aren't Stray Dogs, They're Native Indian Dogs"; Doctor, "Pomeranian Nation."

17 On the "crises" of identity faced by Parsis during, and in the wake of, the Raj, see Luhrmann, *The Good Parsi*.

by twenty-five years; the Raj had been issued a warning not to interfere with natives and their beasts.

Dipesh and I finally gave up on finding the biting dog. We caught a bus, and he dropped me off at Churchgate, where I boarded the local back to Bandra. I asked Dipesh the following week if anything had come of the biting incident. It turned out that yes, there had been a biting dog—or an assumed one—who was stoned by some teens, thrown into the bay, rescued by a passerby, and then died overnight at the SPCA.

WE MET AGAIN at Grant Road Station. Dipesh was on time, as always, but in unusual clothes: a bright yellow T-shirt and sandals. Our Grant Road dog was an old fellow, all black, with no name, but he had three security guards as caretakers, one of whom looked on anxiously as Dipesh checked up on the dog's tumor. We boarded a bus to Malabar Hill, where we rang the well-appointed flat of a well-appointed woman who was feeding ten kittens, all sired by a local tom. Calls about cats were a waste of time. We saw the tomcat and hoped to catch him and have him sterilized, but he was too nimble for us. Still, we gave chase across parking lots and a construction site. As we left, Dipesh grumbled that he needed a net.

Dipesh is one of the only men in the city who is qualified to dart dogs for sterilization, a central tenet of the Animal Birth Control (ABC) Program passed into law by the central government in 2001. Alok and I say more about ABC in chapter 7, but the rules were intended to replace culling—the practice inherited from British colonizers—with sterilization and rabies vaccination. Data from India and elsewhere showed that the ABC rules, if adhered to, would lower rabies deaths significantly and decrease the street dog population.[18] The latter has not come to pass, because the food supply for street dogs has not decreased, and sterilization efforts tend to be patchwork.[19] Welfare for Stray Dogs is very good at what it does, but most organizations have neither the resources nor the welfarian spirit required to turn the effort into something other than a mercenary project of capitalizing on animal extraction. (Nongovernmental organizations are rewarded monetarily per ovary and testis.)

18 See Srinivasan, "The Biopolitics of Animal Being and Welfare"; Srinivasan, "Remaking More-than-Human Society"; Srinivasan and Nagaraj, "Deconstructing the Human Gaze."
19 The AWBI minutes of March 22, 2011, reflect attention to the role that poor and casteist civic waste infrastructure plays in the inefficiency of sterilization efforts and the concomitant rise in dog-bite incidents.

During this summer of walks with Dipesh, dog sterilization erupted as an issue in Indian-occupied Kashmir. A three-year-old girl named Dua Meraj was attacked by a pack of dogs, leaving her face brutalized. Dog bites had been on the rise, by an estimated 80 percent in just one year. In one of many Kashmiri news articles about the attack, Meraj's bloodied visage was juxtaposed with a particularly moon-faced image of a smiling Maneka Gandhi, who, Mona Bhan and Purnima Bose note, represents to Kashmiri Muslims the violently misplaced priorities of the colonial state.[20]

In the wake of the attack on Meraj and the general rise in incidents of people being bitten and harassed by dogs, Kashmiris had begun to demand the instantiation of cull orders. Gandhi responded, jetting to Kashmir to gain assurances from officials that sterilization was still the norm, that culls would not be implemented, and that "dog welfare" was being maintained. One newspaper reported her visit this way: "While over 1,300 children have died at the sole pediatric hospital in the past year, the government is satisfied at 'zero mortality' of stray dogs undergoing sterilization at the pounds near the Zaberwan hills."[21] Bhan and Bose write powerfully about the weaponization of dogs against Kashmiris as part of India's counterinsurgency war. In addition to being recruited into the Indian Army as assault dogs, canines are discursively weaponized: online Hindutva zealots cast Kashmiris as evil for opposing sterilization in favor of culling, weaving fictions of mobs of dog killers on the loose.[22] This is a familiar historical narrative, one also illuminated by Bénédicte Boisseron in her book *Afro-Dog*: the pitting of canine life against (some) human life to consolidate supremacist, imperial power.[23]

Dipesh and I talked about cat nets and dog darts and the ethics of sterilization as we walked from Nepean Sea Road east to Dongri and a small lane in the shadow of the Dawood building. I helped Dipesh tend to a maggoted dog who had lost its tail in an accident or fight. A man walked by and asked

---

20 "The Trip," *Kashmir Times*, June 30, 2012. Bhan and Bose note that "more than one person expressed the desire to seek retributive justice against India by sending Kashmir's street dogs to Gandhi's New Delhi home": Bhan and Bose, "Canine Counterinsurgency in Indian-Occupied Kashmir," 351. Like Maneka Gandhi, Crystal Rogers once traveled to Kashmir, in the 1970s, seeking to prevent the killing of street dogs: Rogers, *Mad Dogs and an Englishwoman*, 156–58.

21 "The Trip," *Kashmir Times*, June 30, 2012.

22 The Indian military began recruiting pariah (or "desi") dogs, particularly the Mudhol hound, into its counterinsurgency ranks in 2017: Bhan and Bose, "Canine Counterinsurgency in Indian-Occupied Kashmir," 347–48.

23 Boisseron, *Afro-Dog*. See also Weaver, "Becoming in Kind."

whether everything was OK, a common occurrence, and Dipesh told him that the dog was fine. He packed up, and we walked fifteen minutes to Kamathipura, a neighborhood historically composed of migrant laborers (*kamathi*) and sex workers.[24] This is a bad part of town, Dipesh said as we got closer. I know, I replied, not because I agreed with him but because I knew he just meant it was the red-light district. One thing I had learned about Dipesh by now is that he is moralistic about how people treat animals but not about much else.

We walked into a market where vegetable sellers, fishmongers, and sex workers called out in Gujarati, Marathi, and Bengali. Dipesh had been called there by a sugarcane juicer to treat a white kitten who had an eye infection, but Dipesh was angered to see that the cat had gone blind. "Why didn't you call me earlier?" he barked as he rummaged through his backpack. He removed the pus from the kitten's eyes with a moistened cotton ball, treated her the best he could, and then placed her in a dirty crate, where she fumbled about. Someone brought another cat over since the healer was there—this one a large, healthy-looking black cat with scabs and a few bald patches. Dipesh thought the cat was fine but applied Scabnil to its wounds. A crowd had gathered by this point. Someone asked what he was doing, to which another answered, *Biladi ne mate seva kare chhe* (He is offering his service to the cats).

Two women and a boy got my attention and pointed urgently down the refuse canal, where a kitten was dying. A giant head on a body of ribs, she was lying amid the wet waste in the canal, still but for an occasional convulsing of her head. I tried to get Dipesh's attention, but he was busy giving instructions about the perfectly healthy cat with a bald spot. I raised my voice, compelling him to turn. He grabbed the kitten out of the canal by the scruff. It's dying of starvation and thirst, he said, angry. It's dying of weakness (*kamzoori*). Two sex workers were watching, talking to each other. One was toothless but handsome; the other, robust and voluptuous. They said the kitten was perishing from malnutrition. The wealthy who have moved into the developments keep pedigreed cats as pets but abandon their kittens in the market, lying to themselves that they will survive on refuse.[25] *Ketlu paap lagtu hashe*, the handsome one said several times to us all and to none of us in particular. How much sin must accrue?

We walked, not talking much at first but then lightening our spiritual load with conversation about Bombay real estate. (Dipesh knows a lot about the subject, which is all I am at liberty to say.) We headed south to Masjid Bandar

24 See Shah, *Street Corner Secrets*.
25 On redevelopment efforts in Kamathipura, see Kundu, "Nirmala."

and a building known as Ashok Chambers. The three security guards pointed Dipesh to a giant dog with an aural hematoma sleeping in a muddy stairway. Hematomas are usually addressed through surgery, which was not an option here, so Dipesh looked instead for the cause. It was a wound that the dog was repeatedly scratching, along with insects drawn to the sore. Dipesh treated the wound with Himax, the hematoma with Arnica, and on we walked in the direction of the Gothic spires of Victoria Terminus.

Dipesh had been called to Nagdevi Street, also called Chippi Chawl, a neighborhood of *masjids* and Hindu and Jain temples near Crawford Market. A family of Jains had recently found themselves caretakers for a litter of puppies outside their tenement building. The mother is not feeding her, they said in Marathi. The other pups were fat, all rolls and fur, but the one they were concerned about was indeed a sorry little runt. Dipesh held her up close to him and whispered something to her, a rare smile creasing his face, but as soon as he set her down, Dipesh began yelling at everyone, demanding to know why there were puppies in this area at all. Why were they not allowing the dogs to be sterilized? While he scolded the crowd, a dog with plump testicles trotted by, and Dipesh shook his head, exasperated. He returned his attention to the little runt, trying to sweet talk the mother into smelling it, but she just kept running away. Dipesh advised the family to keep trying what he had and to call again in a couple of days—punctuated, of course, with a demand to get their dogs sterilized. *Public*, he sighed. Dipesh was often complaining about *public*. Jains, he said, take good care of their animals but are among the least willing to intervene in the natural course of things.[26]

I told Dipesh I found it curious that we had just spent a half-hour on one puppy when there were thousands of animals languishing in cages across the street at the Crawford Market Pet Bazaar. Are those animals outside WSD's mission? They are not street dogs, he said, which made perfect sense. "They will probably become street dogs if they don't die there," he added, "and then I will treat them." In this rare case, the street, which normally represents the

---

26 Jain people do, of course, intervene in phenomena of suffering—for example, by limiting bodily movement to minimize harm to airborne beings or refraining from eating meat or even founding WSD in the first place. Dipesh's point, I think, is that in Jainism, practices of (human) self-restraint outweigh overt actions of manipulating or transforming the environment, and this position is rooted in knowledge of the inevitability and ubiquity of suffering. On Jainism and its resonances and dissonances with contemporary global ecology and animal welfare movements, see Laidlaw, "Ethical Traditions in Question."

cultural interstice for animal life, is actually a desirable destination, a locus for care.[27]

We walked toward the Sir J. J. School of Art at the behest of a married couple, domestic workers who live on the campus. We visited sightless Lalu on the way and gave him some Glucose biscuits. The couple lived in a shanty with a crucifix and an image of Jesus on the wall. They owned two Pomeranians, both acquired from Crawford Market and both in bad shape, with rheumy eyes and neurological tics, tied up all day but loved in their own manner. Dipesh yelled at the woman for not taking better care of her dogs and said that things would get worse when the rains started, jabbing a hand skyward. The woman and I exchanged a *boy, is he in a bad mood* look as we took our leave.

We walked for forty minutes toward the tip of the town, Electric House in Colaba. Dipesh had been called to the colonial-style bungalow of a lawyer who is a frequent caller to WSD. The lawyer was home for lunch and walked us to the footpath where the dog he was concerned about lives. He had been injured in a fight, with cuts on his face and a large wound at the base of his ear. He looked terribly sad. Dipesh treated the animal while the lawyer hovered nervously. After we said goodbye, Dipesh told me that the man isn't married and has no children because his life revolves around animals. *Please*, I thought. *That man is so gay.* I kept this to myself, not knowing how Dipesh felt about such matters and not having brought up how gay I am, either. I was rarely "out" to animalists except, of course, to all the queers among them. I was not sure what to make of my silence, though I suspect it was rooted in an understanding that most animalists harbor a haughty indifference toward every social issue that does not directly involve the abuse of animals.[28] I did not necessarily feel this way about Dipesh. I think I simply respected his monastic aloofness, his unhaughty indifference toward things that did not concern him.

In any case, whether or not the barrister was *so gay*, it was clear that he was lonely, and loneliness was what drove this world I knew most intimately of interspecies care—loneliness and emptiness and grief far more and more often than dogma. Men whose wives had died; women whose husbands had died; queer couples who had one or each been mistreated; queeny if closeted old single men; dykes whose praxis was forged as a rejection of the violent worlds of

---

27 On dogs and/as the interstice, see Cohen, *No Aging in India*.

28 I was out to Maneka Gandhi from the start, despite her being the only right-winger among my regular interlocutors. My revelation did not stop her from making clueless homophobic comments, but she did ask me with kindness about my relationships and offered to set me up once. Reader, I declined.

man and men; people alone; affect aliens from faraway galaxies. These people are not the ones who suck up all of the air, but they do, like Dipesh, walk the earth with attention, their errant paths carving grooves of grace.

Dipesh received a call from Lakshmi asking us to go back in the direction from which we had come—north toward Metro Cinema. He offered the bus, but I was glad to walk. We walked through Kala Ghoda, past Flora Fountain, past Churchgate station, and then down a broad, tree-lined lane of clothing stalls called Fashion Street, where I learned that Dipesh has a thing for clothes. I admit that I laughed, unbelieving. "I look like this when I'm working," he said, "but when I'm with my friends, I wear modern clothes and an earring in my ear."

We finally arrived at the crossroads near Metro Cinema. We walked through a sparkling pedestrian subway—clean because nobody uses these things; so clean that even the stair railings had been stripped for scrap metal. We emerged on the cinema's corner, and Dipesh tried to awaken a man who was sleeping on his side on the footpath under a makeshift awning that served as his shoe repair and shine shop. The *jootewala* was thin and wore shorts, a banyan, and a kerchief on his head. A puppy was tied up and cuddling against the soles of the man's feet, and two older dogs were tied up nearby on the sidewalk. "Why are you tying them?" Dipesh asked. "So they don't get killed," the shoeshine man replied. Fair enough. One of the older dogs had a paw injury. I inspected the paw for glass or other debris, applied hydrogen peroxide and then Xylocaine gel. Dipesh told the man to sterilize his dogs, and he refused, saying his dogs should be able to reproduce, to be parents (*Agar maa-baap honevale tho maa-baap hone chahiye*). Dipesh promised to send the BMC van. The man shrugged. *Public,* Dipesh muttered as we walked away.

The shoeshine man was our last stop for the day, and Dipesh offered to walk with me to Marine Lines Station. On our way, Dipesh was stopped by a boy in shorts and no shirt, holding a pink bottle of bubbles, saying that his mom needed help. The boy ran ahead, leading the way to his mother, who was sitting with a dog who had two ticks in its eye. Dipesh stood and held the dog between his knees. Not once had I seen Dipesh cringe, but cringe now he did, holding his contorted face as far as possible from the dog's while he squeezed the two ticks dead. There they were, hanging off the dog's eyelid. The mother thanked Dipesh while the boy blew bubbles. And we walked to Marine Lines Station.

6

TOUCH. Can Indifference Be the Basis for an Ethical
Engagement with the World?

When I scroll through my photographs, I see hands—more hands, to be sure,
than human faces: hands removing ticks from a dog's eye; hands delivering
a breach foal; hands witnessing a dying cow; hands holding a chicken's still
beating heart. Hands treating, hands killing: exposed and exposing. One could
interpret in these scenes something passionate in the labor of the hands, something interested or, at least, intimate. But the more I am exposed, the more
I believe that touch, when it is *creaturely*—by which I mean, with Eric Santner, when exposed to the apparent threshold between life and its other—it is
ethically *disinterested, indifferent, passive*.[1] When touch is creaturely, it neither
bridges difference nor resolves it but is passionately indifferent to its manifest
forms.

1 Santner, *On Creaturely Life*.

There is a story people often tell that is perhaps apocryphal but nevertheless apropos. The scene is a lonely stretch of road in northern India. A bull from a nearby farm is hit by a speeding lorry and is thrown onto another man's land. The sound of the bull's cries brings people from neighboring houses to see, most of whom are disturbed by the animal's injuries. He needs to be shot, which someone is ready to do, but the owner of the land on which the bull has fallen refuses, citing his adherence to *ahimsa*, or noninjury: this is *his* property and he will not be responsible for the bull's death. He tells the assembled crowd to move the bull ten feet to remove him from his land—and off of his hands, which he imagines as clean—and then they can shoot him, but this is an impossible task. The bull is bloody, broken, and afraid. He is also, well, a bull. The solution is to call someone with a vehicle to tow the animal off of this man's land and onto the road, where he can be shot. In the hours it takes to find such a car, with a willing driver, and amid the slow attrition of people who have other things to do, the bull eventually dies.

When people tell this story, it is not simply to lament the bull's death. They tell it to lay bare the practice of *ahimsa*, a central doctrine in Hindu, Jain, and Buddhist thought and one often invoked to laud the moral relationship between people and animals in India.[2] But in the story of the Bull Who Must Not be Touched, *ahimsa* is revealed to be *not* an injunction to act mercifully or compassionately, or to act at all. Rather, it is revealed as an abnegation of responsibility, a moral hygienic practice of washing-one's-hands-of.[3] Nonviolence, when invoked as *ahimsa*, is interested, impassioned touch, touch that takes the form of refusal. The interest, like that of the propertied man with the bull, is in staying intact; the refusal is refusal to expose oneself to being undone through the literal or figurative dirt on one's hands.

2 *Ahimsa* is theorized differently across and within these three traditions. In B. R. Ambedkar's reading of *ahimsa* in Buddhism, for example—a reading through which he critiques the hypocrisy of Hindu practice such as that of the propertied man—nonviolence is a collective precept rather than one of individual *dharma* or duty: Ambedkar, *The Buddha and His Dhamma*.

3 As Parvis Ghassem-Fachandi points out, the oppression of Muslims and Dalits in the name of vegetarianism reveals *ahimsa* to be not just an abnegation of responsibility but "a violent identification, re-appropriated as a psychological defense to one's own propensities for violence": Ghassem-Fachandi, "Ahimsa, Identification, and Sacrifice in the Gujarat Pogrom," 169.

Between creaturely touch and propertied nontouch, there is a third way, Abodh's way: of refusing little but also being rarely undone, though his hands are often dirty. I was with him on his rounds one Sunday morning, the day of the week that young volunteers in bright-yellow T-shirts join him for street-based first aid. I was in a group with Abodh and a college student named Surabhi. His first call was to the Oval Maidan. The *chaiwala* and his friends, upon seeing Abodh, stood and pointed him toward a dog lying on the sidewalk. Abodh put his hands on the dog—golden and furry—and knelt beside him as a crowd of people gathered around, all men and one boy in a soccer jersey. "How old is the dog?" Abodh asked the boy. One hundred and twenty-seven, he answered, eyebrows furrowed. Abodh laughed, and one of the men playfully smacked the boy on his head.

The dog seemed fine until Abodh turned him over and lifted his head slightly. There, on his neck, was a red, festering wound that I could smell from where I was standing. Abodh pointed out a fluorescent-green maggot wiggling around just under the pus and with a pair of tweezers picked it out and placed it in a cotton ball that Surabhi held out for him; she then closed it firmly on the fattened vermin, crushing it. Abodh placed medicine on the wound, his hands still naked, and finally, with his fingers, dabbed gobs of Himax over and just inside the wound. The crowd was rapt, and the *chaiwala* shouted at them, *Get to work! There's nothing to see here! Get to work!* Everyone ignored him. It was clear that the *chaiwala* liked the dog, too.

The animal now tended to, a different ritual began. Abodh stood up and looked at his hands. *Zara haath dhona hai.* Could I wash my hands? he asked no one in particular. The *chaiwala* gestured with his chin to another man, who rushed to a rusty spigot, filled a tumbler with water, and picked up a thin, crev-iced wafer of soap. Abodh held his hands out as the man poured water slowly over them, placing the soap between Abodh's hands, pausing as Abodh cleaned quickly under his fingernails, and then rinsing Abodh's hands of the dirt, the spent water spreading between them. The man stood up, taking the soap from Abodh's hands, and in this moment something transpired between them that I would call a glance or a nod but was less and more than either: a *minor gesture*.[4] This ritual occurred virtually every time Abodh treated an animal. That moment was always thick, the circuits of touch and intimacy medi-ated by the animal forging bonds of continuity between men of otherwise dis-

4 Manning, *The Minor Gesture.*

similar worlds. There are streets Abodh has trouble walking along because the hawkers and dwellers rush out to meet him, still insisting with smiles and back slaps on giving gifts for his healings of animals past. He refuses all of these gifts, but touch.

During the Monday morning field meetings at the Welfare for Stray Dogs office, I marveled at how *cleaned up* Abodh was—his baggy jeans, stained the day before with blood and Himax, replaced by pressed khakis; his yellow WSD T-shirt traded for a button-down shirt, his hands—once with grime and effluvia caked under his fingernails—now buffed like the hands of a salaryman. Among Indians who work on behalf of animals there is a general distinction made between "hands-on" and "hands-off" animalists. The former are the shelter workers, often but not exclusively women, who wear their hearts on their hands, live in the muck, get covered in fur, pick up feces, and offer their sanity to the gods of the present. The latter are the office types, the ones who attend conferences, plan campaigns, raise money, think of the future, preserve themselves and their sanity for what comes later. They are also known as the *laptopwala* or AC-*wala* (those who reside in air conditioning). The ones whose hands are on and not off are considered, if affectionately, crazy; the ones with hands off are considered, if much less affectionately, aloof but necessary. Abodh, whose hands are both dirty and clean, on even while off, is always thinking about the future. There is a method to his madness and a plan for his hands. I see it in the spectacle he creates wherever he goes.

There are three types of photographs I took most often when I walked with Abodh. One is of him healing others; the second is the ritual in which a stranger provides water so he can wash his hands; and the third is of the crowds that gather around him as he enacts his labors. They are most often men, sometimes boys, but not because women are uninterested. It was usually, but not always, women who took the initiative of informing Abodh in the first place of an animal in need; women who did things such as throw their bodies over injured animals in monsoon storms until Abodh or Dipesh could arrive.

The crowds that gather around Abodh on these Sunday mornings are rapt and, depending on the scene, sometimes three to four deep, straining to watch something as mundane as Abodh, perched in front of a storefront, placing drops in the infected eye socket of a blinded cat, his hand firmly on her scruff, tending to her with tenderness but an intra-ordinary matter-of-factness that says, "This is what to do." He does not say, "This is what *you* should do"; nor does he say, "This is what *one* should do." The touch is between him and the cat. He does not ask for volunteers; he does not admonish; and he does not instruct. He *touches*. And that is all.[5]

Scholars such as Erin Manning, Mayra Rivera, and Pablo Maurette have written about the simultaneity of touch—that singular characteristic of the haptic in which the sense that one exercises is sensed back onto the self.[6] To touch is to be touched, as Maurette puts it; touching something requires being touched *by* it, Rivera writes, too.[7] But both also point out something exceedingly ordinary, not singular at all, about touch: to touch, at its best, is also to see; to see, at its best, is also to touch. The interlacing is not just of touching and being touched but the coming into being of the synesthetic sensorium itself.[8] What Abodh understands is that to see—at its best, which is in that form of devotion that Simone Weil calls attention—is to wear your heart on your hands, to become yourself exposed.[9] His crowds are rapt; he invites that spectacle: to create what Maurette calls a "type of seeing that is like touching," or what Rivera calls a type of seeing that is "literally—a *palpation* with the look."[10] The touch is between him and the cat, but everyone has touched the cat.

Allow me to intervene in my own narrative with an exception, for I don't want my story to be overly clean. An exception in which Abodh is not creating a spectacle (or so I thought) and is not in any hurry to wash his hands. He was asked one Sunday to go to St. Thomas Cathedral, Mumbai's oldest church and the one for which Churchgate Station is named. A woman in a housedress who lives in a shanty nearby came to meet us, smiling when she saw Abodh. She led us to an alleyway where addicts hang out under an awning. We found the dog there, lying beneath construction refuse. The dog had maggots in his

---

5 Upon reading an early version of this chapter, Vijayanka Nair suggested that perhaps the crowds are not "rapt" but "passionately indifferent to, and hence paradoxically susceptible to, this intra-ordinary performance." I love and endorse this interpretation.

6 Manning, *The Politics of Touch*; Maurette, *The Forgotten Sense*; Rivera, *Poetics of the Flesh*.

7 Maurette, *The Forgotten Sense*, 6–7; Rivera, *Poetics of the Flesh*, 74.

8 "Interlacing" is from Rivera, *Poetics of the Flesh*, 75. For more on the synesthetic, see Buck-Morss, "Aesthetics and Anaesthetics"; Davé, "Afterword"; Farman, "Unlearning Pleasure."

9 Weil writes, "Attention, taken to its highest degree, is the same thing as prayer. It presupposes faith and love": Weil, *Gravity and Grace*, 170.

10 Maurette calls this type of seeing haptic, as opposed to optic: Maurette, *The Forgotten Sense*, 8. Rivera's "palpation" is from Merleau-Ponty. Merleau-Ponty, *The Visible and the Invisible*, cited in Rivera, *Poetics of the Flesh*, 75.

penis, and Abodh was holding it between the fingers of one hand and using the other hand to first clean the wound and then tweeze the maggots out. It was awful—even worse, I'm sure, for the dog than it was for me. When Abodh was finished, he teased the dog for having been a little humiliated, roughed him up a bit, and then we walked away, back toward the cathedral. Along our path we ran into a man who, in my recollection, was wearing a suit (which is unlikely) and whose daughter had once been into all this animal welfare stuff and thus knew Abodh. Abodh clapped the man on the back and shook his hand repeatedly with great bonhomie. I looked on with wide eyes, thinking only of this man's clothes, his hands—his unwitting exposure to compromised canine genitalia. Eventually they parted ways. Abodh knew of a little spigot nearby, and he washed his hands clean.

Now certainly, some of this reveals my own preoccupation with dirt and cleanliness, which I am sorry to admit to. Sick and dying animals can be messy business, and I was usually quite ritualistic about keeping the world of excrement, blood, and illness apart from the world of home, leisure, and writing: special clothes, of course, and a pair of Crocs (which are still my balcony shoes) that I thought of as my slaughterhouse slippers. I held tight to these distinctions until I didn't. And that moment came, oddly enough, at an abattoir. I returned to my room that afternoon and fell asleep in my rented bed in the clothes I had been wearing all day, including my bloody socks. It was the first time I became indifferent to the rituals of cleanliness—the time of an immersion so complete that there was no possible distinction between dirty and clean. Not because the world had suddenly become dirty, but because the abattoir was the whole world. (Mine is not a moral argument but an ontological one.) This was a place where dirt in Mary Douglas's conception, as matter out of place, *has* no place, because for matter to be out of place assumes that there is some other place for that matter to be—but there *was* no other place: the abattoir was the whole world.[11]

I'm reminded of a passage from Santner's *On Creaturely Life*, a scene from W. G. Sebald's *Austerlitz* in which the narrator recalls an exhibition in Antwerp about nocturnal animals: "The only animal that has remained lingering in my memory is the raccoon. I watched it for a long time as it sat beside a little stream with a serious expression on its face, washing the same piece of apple over and over again, as if it hoped that all this washing, which went far

11 Douglas, *Purity and Danger*. I am thinking here also of Vanessa Watts, who argues that dirt is not matter out of place but place-thought itself: Watts, "Indigenous Place-Thought and Agency amongst Humans and Non-humans."

beyond any reasonable thoroughness, would help it to escape the unreal world in which it had arrived, so to speak, through no fault of its own."[12] We wash to escape our worlds, until we realize there's nowhere else to go.

But in that *other* world, the world of Sunday morning walks with cheerful volunteers where people earnestly look for soap and water, Abodh and I had a conversation about a perception people often have—those who are perhaps trying to scrub their own hands clean—that people who tend to animals are by nature misanthropic and do nothing for people. He told me about a WSD fieldworker who, like so many others, puts a lie to that story. I should ask about it when I meet him, Abodh suggested.

That fieldworker, I would soon find out, was Dipesh. On one of our walks I mentioned having heard one of the fieldworkers had attempted to save a woman's life. He acknowledged that it was he. He was doing his rounds one day when he saw a woman lying on the side of the road. She had been thrown out of a taxi on the way to the hospital. She was dying of AIDS, and the wounds on her scalp were infected with maggots. Dipesh cleaned her wounds, picked her up in his arms, and took her to the hospital on foot. He paid for her treatment, twice a week for the three weeks before she died. The next time I saw him, Dipesh brought the intake document: "Gauri; 50 yr old female; weak; dehydrated."

How might we understand this touch? Unlike the propertied man with the bull, Dipesh will never keep his hands clean; he hasn't a property all his own, anyway. And unlike the propertied man with the bull, Dipesh is empty of refusals. He is, I think, what Julia Lupton has in mind when she describes passion as an *active* passivity: "perpetually becoming created, subject to transformations at the behest of the arbitrary commands of an Other."[13] What else is a stranger lying on the side of the road? The propertied man with the bull kept his hands clean, *washed his hands of*, by denying the stranger on his side of the road. Abodh put his bare hands in the body of an animal and asked, to no one in particular and with no particular urgency, *Could I wash my hands?* I never, not once, saw Dipesh perform that ritual. Surely he washed his hands. I just never saw. His is, I think, an indifference to the difference of others that is creaturely, where creature, Santner writes, is not a state of being "so much as the signifier of an ongoing exposure."[14]

12   Sebald, *Austerlitz*, quoted in Santner, *On Creaturely Life*, 144.
13   Lupton, "Creature Caliban," 1.
14   Santner, *On Creaturely Life*, 34.

But what does it mean to speak of indifference to difference in caste-stratified India, where untouchability persists as a practice and doctrine of violently differentiating social oppression? A doctrine that is linked in all manner of ways to the touch and untouchability of specific animals and of animality in general? In his posthumously published *Practicing Caste: On Touching and Not Touching*, Aniket Jaaware interestingly coins his own concept of indifference to difference—not as an indifference toward the politics of caste, of course, but, on the contrary, a critical commitment to the immanence of caste, and therefore its undoing, as it materializes in specific, observable operations of touch and refusing to touch.[15] Jaaware's deliberately clumsy neologism is *oublierring* (from the French *oublier*, "to forget," plus the English *err* plus the English *-ing*), which Anupama Rao, in her foreword to the text, defines as an act of "forgetting and thinking anew," an "attending to caste as if confronting it for the first time [and] approaching caste ignorantly . . . as an occasion to rethink the grounds of sociability."[16] But why would anyone want to be ignorant about caste? Well, for Jaaware it is because what we think we know about caste—its transhistorical tenacity, its subcontinental specificity—has abstracted the concreteness of its existence and, thus, the concreteness of its undoing: caste manifests and fails to manifest in specific acts of touching and refusing to touch, in—to quote Rao again—"the anarchic *facticity* of touch."[17] Shifting the focus from caste as a material concept to its specific operations also shifts caste ("anatomizes it," he says) from metaphysics or even, for that matter, anthropology to a problem of and for ethical practice—the quotidian, embodied acts of choosing one thing and therefore extinguishing another—that constitute being with others.[18]

Jaaware, like many scholars of the "haptic turn" in the West, emphasizes the primacy of touch within the sensorium. Unlike those Western scholars, though, who tend to emphasize the reparative, extimate, coconstitutive nature of touch, Jaaware, haunted and informed by caste, is always aware of touch's violent manifestations—notably, in the forms of refusal, disgust, and deletion.[19] But the singular promise of touch still lies for Jaaware in its sheer materiality,

15 Jaaware, *Practicing Caste*.
16 Jaaware, *Practicing Caste*, 2–3; Rao, "Foreword," vii–viii.
17 Rao, "Foreword," viii.
18 Jaaware, *Practicing Caste*, 11.
19 I thank Kajri Jain for this conversation about Western reparative readings of the haptic.

the simple fact that it is the largest sense of all, traversing the body, the skin. Touch is dispersed, *homeless*.[20] It is always potentially errant.

Unlike Maurette and Manning and Rivera, who speak of the simultaneity of touch (to touch is to be touched, and vice versa), Jaaware insists on a distinction between active and passive touch, *being* touched and touching.[21] Both touching and being touched provide an experience of otherness, but between the two it is *being* touched that is the more fundamental experience. Why is that? Simply because of the element of surprise. The toucher has a sense of what she is gearing up to do. But the touched? She is at another's mercy, a mercy that is vitalizing.[22] But in good dialectical fashion, there is a third element for Jaaware between touching and being touched, between action and passivity, and that is the "paradoxical passivity"—the power in contaminability—of the one who neither touches nor gets touched but *refuses* to touch.[23] This is the antithesis of passion, the interested touch that necessarily takes the form of a refusal: the touch that is not-one of the propertied man with the bull.

Jaaware borrows a story from within a story by Godse Bhatji to illustrate his point.[24] It is 1857, and a Brahmin and a Dalit soldier are at the river to drink. The Brahmin has a jug, and the Dalit soldier asks to drink from it. The Brahmin refuses, but in a peculiar manner. "I cannot *bring myself* to give it to you," he says. The Dalit soldier replies, "Your caste is all empty show. The bullets that you have put in your mouth are covered in cow fat and pig fat that I have handled." And alas, the Sepoy Mutiny begins. Jaaware emphasizes the "curiously passive form" of the Brahmin's refusal: "I cannot bring myself." The Brahmin self, like the propertied man with the bull, is a split self ("*I* cannot bring *myself*") where splitting is not the result of having *been* broken but of *the fear of* being broken, the refusal to risk breaking. And this is the difference between the split and the shattered, between, what I will come to later, the unlucky and lucky break. While the Brahmin's refusal is passive and gestures

---

20 Jaaware, *Practicing Caste*, 13. This notion of the homelessness of touch reminds me of Michel Foucault's conception of BDSM as a degenitalization, a total somatic dispersal of pleasure, which invites a profound undoing of sex and self—a liberation from sexuality or what Leo Bersani calls a "shattering": Foucault, *Ethics, Subjectivity and Truth*, 160–65. See also Bersani, *Is the Rectum a Grave?*; Halperin, *Saint Foucault*, 95–96.

21 Jaaware, *Practicing Caste*, 40.

22 Jaaware, *Practicing Caste*, 47. Jaaware's passive touch calls to mind Julia Lupton's rendering of passion as an "active passivity," a being subject to transformation at the behest of an Other: see Lupton, "Creature Caliban."

23 Jaaware, *Practicing Caste*, 98–99.

24 Bhatji, *Maza Pravas*, discussed in Jaaware, *Practicing Caste*, 49–53, emphases added.

only to metaphysics and failed abstractions that he himself cannot articulate, the Dalit soldier's response is rooted in hard reality: "I handled the fat myself." Jaaware's point is that to grapple with caste as a matter of and for ethics is to turn away from metaphysics and abstractions and toward the empirical and the ethnographic, toward what Rao calls, again, "the archaic and somewhat anarchic facticity of touch."[25]

I'll end this section on Jaaware with one final point, which is his central argument. Altruistic touch (picking up a stranger who has fallen on the side of the road; offering water from a jug) and sexual touch are the two most fundamental forms of touch, the generators of the social itself. Untouchability is the denial of altruistic and sexual touch. Insofar as touch always leaves a trace— think gooseflesh or the fingerprint—the refusal to touch and be touched is a refusal of the presence of the other, an act of social and moral deletion. Regulations on touch are thus regulations on relation—or, to put it another way, assertions of *unrelation*—that work through what he calls a "haptic dispersal": not only do I not touch the Other, but I do not touch the things that the Other might (have) touch(ed).[26]

Which brings me to the radical promise of a seemingly ordinary statement: "We're all hands-on people here. Everybody picks up poop."

Shattered, Not Split

Amala Akkineni is a South Indian actress who today is just as famous for being the cofounder and director of Hyderabad's Blue Cross animal shelter. Amala is one of the hands-on people, not a *laptopwali*. She is one of those who wears her heart on her hands. I arrived at Blue Cross ten minutes before our 11 a.m. meeting several years ago and looked through the open window to the office. There, among three or four mortals, was a woman of utter luminescence for which no Google search could have prepared me. It was easily the worst interview I have ever done. But in my defense, I don't think it was entirely my fault. There is a splitness to Amala—or perhaps *shatteredness* is the right word; certainly, it is not the split self of Brahminism. What I'm searching for is this: Amala is wary but not weary. *Exhausted.* Which, as Deleuze tells us, "is a whole lot more than tired."[27]

Hers is a way of being in the world that I recognize in other animal activists, too—a warmth with distinct limitations, a willingness to suffer fools or

25 Rao, "Foreword," viii.
26 Jaaware, *Practicing Caste*, 159, 163.
27 Deleuze, "The Exhausted," 3.

strangers or those not yet converted but with the hope that there will be some payoff, some sum-total transformation in the order of things. When that hope is extinguished, so goes the light they focused on you. But the exhausted keep moving, anyway—just away from those who refuse to be touched. They have what we might think of as an irrepressible resignation.[28]

Between eight and eighteen, Amala studied at Kalakshetra, the dance academy in Chennai founded by Rukmini Devi Arundale, who, of course, was such a staunch vegetarian that she was known to go without sandals and soap when plant-based products couldn't be found. (Was hers an effort, like that of the propertied man, to have morally clean hands? It was soap, not touch, that she refused.) Amala was also close to Rukmini Devi's friend Peter Hoffman, the husband of Amala's dance instructor and a paternal figure. Hoffman, the first editor of India's *Animal Citizen*, had stacks of vegetarian literature from England and the United States in his Kalakshetra bungalow, which Amala grew up reading. She became a vegetarian, not because she was convinced, but because, in the presence of Rukmini Devi Arundale, she said, what else would she be?

As we were talking about Rukmini Devi, a tall, slim girl wearing pink straight-legged sweatpants and a black T-shirt about animal compassion walked up to the open window. Amala commented to me on the cute shirt; I agreed that it was very cute, then one of the office staff told Amala that the girl, who had recently started volunteering at the shelter, had become a vegetarian. Amala turned the full might of her glow onto this defenseless child, saying, "Dear, let me tell you that when someone becomes a vegetarian, thousands of beings in the world rejoice." She spread her arms out like Jesus, and the girl, willed by the force of Amala's charisma, walked into the office and took Amala's hands. Amala repeated her incantation: "Thousands of beings, across the whole world, are rejoicing right now because of what you have done."[29] The girl mumbled "thank you" and seemed unsure of what to do. Amala released her and returned to our conversation.[30]

28 My thanks again to Vijayanka Nair for her irrepressible readings.

29 Amala's incantation echoes that of her teacher, Rukmini Devi. "Every time I think of the vegetarian movement, I hear in my inner ears the voice of animals saying, 'thank you,' and I feel we should earn thanks of the millions and millions of animals and creatures that are silently suffering": Rukmini Devi Arundale, *Indian Vegetarian Congress Quarterly*, June 1978, 90.

30 Many of the women who populate this book's narrative are, like Amala, charismatic iconic figures, from Rukmini Devi to Erika Abrams, including the more culturally repugnant figure of Maneka Gandhi. What seems to connect them all, as the ground for their devotional object energy, is the "irrepressible resignation" of the

I knew that Amala was a devoted student of Vipassana meditation, and I asked her about her practice—how it began and why. Maybe this was too personal, or maybe she had become tired, but something further receded. She said that shortly after starting Blue Cross in 1992, she started to experience "the dark night of the soul"—a reference, I assume, to the dark night of the soul in the epic poem the *Bhagavad Gita*. There, Lord Krishna, a chariot driver, counsels the young warrior, Arjun, who is in the midst of the dark night of his soul, that to act morally is to act free from passion and fear, to fulfill one's duty but without attachment to the consequences of those actions. Amala, then pregnant, was having trouble sleeping at night, the images of suffering she encountered at the shelter like "dark monsters" in her dreams. Her work, more often than not, felt meaningless, insignificant. In the midst of this dark night of her soul, Amala saw the face of Vipassana's leading teacher, Goenkaji, in a newspaper and embarked for the hills. Now, after years of the practice, she has begun to approach *something* like working without attachment to the consequences of her actions. The exhausted, as Deleuze says, are "not passive: [they] press on, but toward nothing."[31]

Amala began this work just like many of the others, all with their specific but recognizable tales of being shattered, converted, forever transformed. There is Crystal Rogers, of course, with the flayed, eyeless horse that she had to have shot. Her story resonates with that of the propertied man with the bull: the slowly extinguishing life, the passersby who do nothing, keeping their own hands clean. As it happens, Rogers tells a similar story in *Mad Dogs and an Englishwoman* to the one about the bull, which she concludes, imagining the logic of the landowner: "Kill the beast two inches away from my main gate, I don't care, but do not kill it on my grounds."[32] Such tales illustrate for English aliens to India, such as Rogers or John Lockwood Kipling, what Parama Roy calls the "vegetarian cruelty [of the] Baniya economy of preserving life":

exhausted. I'd suggest that their "carrying on, but towards nothing," as Deleuze puts it, is received by devotees as a maternal sign, a combination of sacrifice and self-annihilation that was also the basis of General Chauhan's filial devotion to the nonhuman female animal, Kamadhenu (until, that is, she was no longer resigned, no longer prepared to sacrifice). All of these female figures seem to differ, too, from Dipesh, whose heroism is solitary, less resigned than laborious, and who, in Parama Roy's words in a personal communication to me, "elicits admiration rather than devotion."

31 Deleuze, "The Exhausted," 4.
32 Rogers, *Mad Dogs and an Englishwoman*, 62–64.

those who refuse to consume but let die; those ostensibly clean of diet taking repressed pleasure in the spectacle of pain.[33]

And then there was Maneka Gandhi's conversion, sparked not by an eyeless horse but by a felicitous slur from a temperamental husband, resulting in a meaty broth scalding and scarring her skin. Maneka's scar would unfold into a history of scarring others, the scar showing that touch always leaves a trace, evidence of having been exposed. I wonder if Dipesh's intake papers from Gauri serve for him as a kind of scar: proof that he was touched, impressed on, discomposed.[34]

Amala's conversion occurred when she saw not a woman or a horse but a goat on the side of the road. Like the bull, it had been hit by a lorry. She and her husband lifted the animal into their car and took it to a government veterinary hospital. When the goat was partially healed, there was nowhere for it to go, so the goat went home with her, along with a few other invalids from the animal hospital. Before too long, a menagerie; and then a different kind of life. And that is why, as Jaaware tells us, regulations on touch are attempted regulations on randomness, dispersion, conversion—attempted regulations on queer, unseemly solidarities in favor of maintaining the fold.[35]

The cloud that had hovered over our conversation since I conjured the dark night of her soul suddenly lifted. "This is my happiest place," she said. "Getting my hands on the dogs. We're all hands-on people here. Everybody picks up poop." This has shades of a Gandhian principle, of course—this radical caste equality of the latrine; a form of cleaning one's hands (that of the self, the nation) that requires getting them dirty first; an active passivity that is counter, even when failed, to the paradoxical passivity of the one who "cannot bring himself" to touch that which has been touched by another whom he may not touch.[36] But what kind of touch is Amala's? Is it the touch of a Gandhian proj-

---

33 Roy, "On Verminous Life," 90.

34 Judith Butler says, "I am wounded, and I find the wound testifies to the fact that I am impressionable, given over to the Other in ways that I cannot fully predict or control": Butler, *Precarious Life*, 46. Julietta Singh connects this line from Butler to Elizabeth Costello's animal "wound, which I cover up under my clothes but touch on in every word I speak:" Coetzee, *The Lives of Animals*, 26, cited in Singh, *Unthinking Mastery*, 138.

35 Jaaware writes that conversions—the outcome of being touched, impressed upon— are especially "repulsive" in an inheritance society that is divided primarily by caste rather than by class or acquisition: Jaaware, *Practicing Caste*, 69.

36 The Gandhian haptic ethos of the latrine insisted that manual work, including that of sanitation, be shared across caste. In relation to casteist stratification—to which,

ect of national and spiritual betterment? Is there always a plan for her hands? All I know is this: when I left that afternoon, she was, sure enough, on her knees on a crap-splattered floor, her hands on the animals. As with Abodh, but whether she likes it or not, there is a spectacle wherever she goes. It is somehow impossible not to see her, and so all of us do: the workers, the visiting school kids, the stranger. The touch is between her and the dog. But everyone touches the dog.

Lucky Breaks

When I drafted this chapter in the spring of 2019, I was experiencing a strange repeated exposure. It seemed that everywhere I went I would find myself face to verse with Rainer Maria Rilke's "Archaic Torso of Apollo." The poem begins, "We cannot know his legendary head," and ends with the injunction, "for here there is no place / that does not see you. You must change your life."[37] This repeat encounter began when I reread Eric Santner's *On Creaturely Life*, then, on a whim, an article by Sara Salih, "Vegans on the Verge of a Nervous Breakdown."[38] And as I read these texts, I was stared at across the room by the blood-red spine of Peter Sloterdijk's *You Must Change Your Life*.[39] I wondered where this repeat exposure was taking me. Perhaps this chapter is its scar.

Like Rilke, Salih says she is "interested in pairs of absent eyes, in bodies we can't 'know' because we have limited access to them physically and ontologically."[40] How can that which we cannot see "round on us" and issue the order for us to change our lives?[41] And just as important, why does that injunction—or, rather, why do the absent eyes in unknowable bodies—resonate with some but

as Yamini Narayanan argues, animals are subject and of which they are constitutive (Narayanan, "Animating Caste")—it is interesting to consider why touching dog poop has a transgressive and defiling aspect while handling *gobar*, or cow dung, does not.

37 Rilke and Hass, *The Selected Poetry of Rainer Maria Rilke*.
38 Salih, "Vegans on the Verge of a Nervous Breakdown."
39 Sloterdijk, *You Must Change Your Life*.
40 Salih, "Vegans on the Verge of a Nervous Breakdown," 52.
41 Salih, "Vegans on the Verge of a Nervous Breakdown," 53. This rounding, which urges us to change our life, does not, of course, lead always to life. The disgraced narrator in J. M. Coetzee's *Disgrace* whispers to himself, "*Du must dein Leben ändern!*: you must change your life," as a vow to retaliatory violence (209). But earlier, upon witnessing a woman demonstrate grace to abandoned dogs, he thinks, "Do I have to change? Do I have to become like Bev Shaw?" (126).

not with others? This is not a question of epistemology but one of resonance, and that is what makes Rilke's poem—that final line—so startling. We do not change our lives because of what we know, or because of what we are told, or even because of what we see. People change their lives when *they* are seen, when they are themselves exposed, exfoliated, in a not precisely reciprocal exchange of gaze.[42]

J. M. Coetzee's Elizabeth Costello is one of these women exposed.[43] Flayed, even, descended into madness by what she cannot see but sees anyway, through what Salih calls "repeated efforts at imagination . . . to see what is not there to see."[44] Salih is interested in what she calls "the Elizabeth Costello moment," a breakdown "in self certainty and ease with one's universe, which can occur at any moment."[45] Why are some subject to the Costello moment and not others? Why, for instance, did Dipesh change his life one afternoon while sitting at a table playing cards, but the man next to him did not? How was it that Dipesh could see "aa badha"—all those unseen animals of the city—while I failed to? This might be the difference, as Toni Morrison put it, between being merely "touched but not moved" toward the "smashing."[46]

Salih turns to the psychoanalyst Jonathan Lear and his concept of the "lucky break."[47] Lucky breaks are indifferent to morality. They are moments in which virtue ends and there is a "rip in the world itself," rips that are caused by "too much of too much," opening life to new possibilities beyond the path of principle (beyond, that is, the compulsion to have clean hands, beyond the principle of sameness and Otherness).[48] Yet, still: why do some break, and

---

42 The Indic, primarily Hindu, concept of *darshan* is also Rilkean. In worship, the subject both sees and is seen by the deity in a kind of synesthetic mutual beholding of frontal gaze: see Eck, *Darsan*; Jain, *Gods in the Bazaar*.

43 Coetzee, *Elizabeth Costello*; Coetzee, *The Lives of Animals*.

44 Salih, "Vegans on the Verge of a Nervous Breakdown," 63.

45 Salih, "Vegans on the Verge of a Nervous Breakdown," 62.

46 Morrison writes that some readers (those touched but not moved) were led "into the comfort of pitying . . . rather than an interrogation of themselves for the smashing." As I interpret Morrison, it is in fact a kind of indifference to normative morality— the morality that finds comfort in, say, pity—that marks the difference between being merely touched and actually moved toward the break: Morrison, "Afterword to *The Bluest Eye*," 211.

47 Lear, *Open Minded*.

48 "Rip in the world" is from Lear, *Open Minded*, 119, cited in Salih, "Vegans on the Verge of a Nervous Breakdown," 63. "Too much of too much" is from Lear, *Happiness, Death, and the Remainder of Life*, 129, cited in Santner, *On Creaturely Life*, 136–37.

others do not? I suppose that's why they're called "lucky"—there is no rhyme or reason. Indeed, Salih leaves it here: that there is "some kind of predisposition to break and be broken."[49]

It is a good place to leave it, but to luck and predisposition I would add something else. There is a *disposition to be exposed*, to becoming indifferent, and that touch is the method and practice of that exposure. This disposition is the antithesis of the paradoxical passivity of the Brahmin with the jug or the moral-hygienic washing-one's-hands-of of the propertied man with the bull. This disposition is the antithesis of Brahminism, if we understand Brahminism not just as the practice of Brahmins—which, of course, it is—but also empirically as the refusal to be contaminated, as the interested nontouch of the propertied.

But why privilege touch as the practice most apt to conjure a lucky break? Probably for the same reasons that touch is the sense most privileged in preventing the lucky break from happening—all those prohibitions on touch that regulate shattering and attempt to prevent unseemly queer solidarities and repulsive conversions to new ways of life. It might be useful to return once more to the relationship between touch and sight, tactility and the spectacle.

In his essay "How to Open Your Eyes," Georges Didi-Huberman asks, "How to invest someone with knowledge who refuses to know? How to open your eyes?"[50] The image *qua* image is not the answer. Harun Farocki, in his film *Inextinguishable Fire* (1969), seeks to show the horrors of napalm in its use by American forces in Vietnam. But he is faced with what Didi-Huberman calls "an aporia for the thought of the image." Didi-Huberman writes: "If we show you pictures of napalm damage, you'll close your eyes. First you'll close your eyes to the pictures; then you'll close your eyes to the memory; then you'll close your eyes to the facts; then you'll close your eyes to the connections between them. If we show you a person with napalm burns, we'll hurt your feelings . . . and feel we used napalm on you, at your expense."[51] *Eyes close like umbrellas useless in a storm.*[52] In the face of closed eyes, the solution for Farocki, as well as for Didi-Huberman, is to reintroduce, to remember, the hands. Farocki, in the middle of his narration from Vietnamese testimony, reaches off-screen for a burning cigarette and presses it into his arm for three and a half seconds while a narrator compares the temperature of a burning cigarette to napalm. The

49 Salih, "Vegans on the Verge of a Nervous Breakdown," 64.
50 Didi-Huberman, "How to Open Your Eyes," 42.
51 Didi-Huberman, "How to Open Your Eyes," 41.
52 From Anne Atik, "Darcy," quoted in in Savas, "The Poet Upstairs."

image is not enough. To open your eyes, Didi-Huberman says, you must "put your hand in the fire."[53]

Yet hands, as we know, do not always lend themselves to attentiveness. We can be just as obtuse with them as we are with our eyes. India, again, can provide a sober, nonliberatory perspective on the workings of synesthetic hapticity. Vijayanka Nair, in her project on the Indian biometric identification program Aadhaar, focuses on the role of touch in the enrollment program: the mundane labor, for instance, of pressing people's fingers down onto scanners to capture and store their biometric data.[54] Despite the ocularcentric discourse of Aadhaar, she says, the program "descends into the population" and "gets its hands perhaps uncomfortably dirty." In India, "seeing is a kind of touching," and Aadhaar provides an example of what it is like "to touch like a state."[55] The caption to one of Nair's images reads, "Shreya is pressing the fingers of an elderly female enrollee on a finger-scanning machine while having a conversation with someone else."[56] Touching like a state: interested, impassioned touch, even when it takes the form of inattentiveness.

And so I end where I began, with images of hands. Why did Dipesh bring me Gauri's intake papers? Spread them out for me to see, the red stains like stray drops from a watercolor brush? Surely that is interested touch and not a sign of creaturely indifference? In a way. He did it in a world in which some, human and animal, are untouchable; where we wash our hands of and keep our hands clean, a sanitized world in which we build an island—or, perhaps, a pod—for ourselves and those we love, compelling touch from some out of fear of the touch and the nontouch of others. He did it so that I, too, in my relative isolation, might "palpate with the look." The simultaneity of touch was between him and Gauri. But as with Abodh and the one-eyed cat, perched before a crowd of onlookers, the intimate reveals only the extimate and we are—at our luckiest—returned toward the whole.

53 Didi-Huberman, "How to Open Your Eyes," 43.
54 Nair, "Becoming Data."
55 "Seeing is a kind of touching" is from Eck, *Darsan*.
56 Nair, "Becoming Data."

7

SEX. What Does Cow Protection Protect?

With Alok Gupta

A Cow Has Been Slaughtered

On May 8, 2020, seven Muslim homes in Faridpur Kadi village, in Uttar Pradesh, were pillaged by police as the daily Ramadan fast was being broken. Police assaulted the villagers, overturned food, and destroyed property. Several men were beaten and three were detained at the police station in nearby Bignor. The next morning, the village *sarpanch*, Iqbal, went to the police station to retrieve the detained men. No charges had been filed, but when pressed to state the reason for the raid, the police told Iqbal that they "came

Alok Gupta is an independent researcher based in Goa. He writes on queer and animalist politics in India and teaches animal rights at National Law School in Bangalore.

to the village on the basis of suspicion. They had been informed that a cow had been slaughtered."[1]

On July 25, 2018, a goat farmer named Aslup Khan, living in the Mewat region of Haryana, came upon three local men having sex with one of his goats while five others watched. They smashed the goat's head against a wall before absconding.[2] A group of villagers caught some of the men the following day and beat them up; Khan, for his part, filed charges. But the story of the pregnant goat "gang-raped by eight men," as one headline had it, took on a life of its own, propelled by the goat's pregnancy and the incident's occurrence in the only Muslim-majority region of Haryana state.[3] The hashtag #justiceforgoat trended, along with claims about the poverty, perversity, aimlessness, and backwardness of the men involved.

These two disparate narratives are united by a puzzle. In the first case, police justified their assault on the grounds that a cow had been slaughtered. In a country in which approximately thirty-nine million cattle are slaughtered each year for food and byproducts—about 170,000 per day—what could such an utterance mean?[4] What renders it sensible as a call to action? In the second case, both legal and vigilante procedures of redress were set in motion because a goat had been sexually abused. But that goat was the property of a farmer, and her pregnancy was likely the result of forced insemination in the first place, a practice that more than five hundred million farm animals undergo in India every year.[5] What rendered *this* act of sexualized violence outrageous?

Alok Gupta and I argue in this chapter that what separates permissible from perverse acts of interspecies sex in India—or husbandry from bestiality—is where it occurs geographically in proximity to an upper-caste, anthropatriarchal imaginary of a Hindu nation. We suggest that the state-sanctioned abattoir and its breeding facility are like the home: spaces of normalized exception in which violence is relatively permissible, and on precisely the same

1 Kashyap and Khan, "In Bignor, Muslim Villagers Allege U[ttar] P[radesh] Police Harassed Them."
2 Dhankar, "Haryana Police Arrest Two of the Eight Men Accused of Raping Pregnant Goat in Nuh."
3 Meyjes, "Pregnant Goat Dies 'after Being Gang-raped by Eight Men.'"
4 US Department of Agriculture, "India Animal Numbers, Cattle: Total Slaughter by Year," IndexMundi, n.d., https://www.indexmundi.com/agriculture/?country =in&commodity=cattle&graph=total-slaughter.
5 Government of India, "Twentieth Livestock Census," 2019. https://vikaspedia.in /agriculture/agri-directory/reports-and-policy-briefs/20th-livestock-census.

grounds.[6] In both the state-sanctioned abattoir and the home, permissible violence, which therefore must not be named violence, is imagined as reproductive, Hindu-national, symbolically central, natural or inevitable, and private.[7] For both, their constitutive alter-sphere of perverse violence, which justifies the existence of the permissible and therefore must always be made to appear as violence, is imagined as *un*productive, *anti*-national, at a spatial remove, unnatural or coercive, and requiring of surveillance.[8] It is not incidental that caste Hindu mobs commit lynchings of Dalits and Muslims in India over two perceived violations: the eating of (Hindu) cows and elopement with (Hindu) women. This coincidence that is not one is easy to explain: both are violations neither of cows nor of women, but of the sphere of permissible violence that is at the heart of Hindutva.

The Unheard Rape

In 2018, the director Pratik Rajankar, along with a group of Indian student activists, released an educational film about animal sexual abuse (ASA): *Bestiality— The Unheard Rape*. In its efficient twenty-two minutes, the film details six cases of ASA prosecuted by Mumbai-area NGOs.[9] The film begins abruptly, with two middle-aged women sitting on a bed facing the camera. One, petting a healthy white lap cat, repeats this several times: "She stopped walking. She just stopped walking." She is referring to a street dog named Ruby who once walked with a "swagger," but whose spine was broken after being raped. We see Ruby outdoors. The fur is shaved on her back end, and she has evident injuries on her legs. Ruby is attempting to walk but seems to have little control of what

---

6 A Delhi High Court judgment in 1984 declared that "the fundamental rights ensured to every Indian citizen by the constitution were not applicable to the family: these rights have to stop at the door of the home. Letting fundamental rights into the family would be like letting a bull into a china shop": quoted in Menon, *Seeing like a Feminist*, 6.

7 It might appear strange to call abattoirs symbolically central to India, but we include all of its facilities, including dairy and eggs, which are viewed as essential to national and familial growth.

8 On the communalist demarcation of legal and illegal slaughter in Ahmedabad in the name of *ahimsa*, see Ghassem-Fachandi, "Ahimsa, Identification, and Sacrifice in the Gujarat Pogrom."

9 Pratik Rajankar, dir., *Bestiality—The Unheard Rape* (documentary video, posted May 8, 2018), https://www.youtube.com/watch?v=5TWefdOSjjw&noapp=1&client=mv -google&app=desktop. All references to the film are to this source.

her hind legs are doing—they follow her at an odd angle and every now and then collapse.

The film cuts to a female voiceover, accompanied first by the title screen and then a montage of domestic animals. The narrator reads this script: "Animal sexual abuse, often referred to as bestiality, is the sexual molestation of an animal by a human. This kind of animal abuse includes a wide range of behaviors such as vaginal, anal, or oral penetration; fondling; oral-genital contact; penetration using an object; and killing or injuring an animal for sexual gratification." The images become darker in content over the course of her definition, to grainy and then infrared footage of a man, his buttocks exposed, penetrating a dog from two different positions.

The second section of the film focuses on Rinky Karmakar, a young activist from Save Our Strays. Karmakar wears a red kurta and sits in a park under the sun. Her manner is resolute. She explains that ASA occurs in "secluded places, slums, and areas where the population is really dense." As to why it occurs, she surmises: "Sexual frustration. Perverts to release their frustration." Animal lovers, she says, "have kept vigil, trying to trap these people." What disturbs Karmakar is that animal sexual abuse preys on trust and naivete. It is the friendly dogs who are usually victimized, she says: "They don't mind if humans touch them, and they don't know what is wrong and what is right."

The film's third section centers on an assault that occurred in Vartak Nagar, a neighborhood north of Mumbai, in Thane. A young woman activist, Aditi, sits on the edge of her bed flanked by two lounging dogs. She describes receiving a call one night that a society watchman had raped a neighborhood dog. We see closed-circuit television (CCTV) footage of the watchman taking the dog into a room and emerging nervously several minutes later. By the time Aditi arrived with a policeman, a mob had formed. She explains the mob's anger: "Today he is a raping a female dog. . . . [T]omorrow, what if it's a four-year old girl walking there, you know, or a boy?"

The fourth section focuses on Meet Asher, an officer of the Animal Welfare Board of India and an emergency responder for PETA. He speaks in hyperarticulate, staccato bursts while standing outdoors in front of a stone wall. Asher narrates two recent cases of human sexual assault of dogs, one of which, like the case in Vartak Nagar, turned on CCTV coverage of a rikshaw driver by day/watchman by night. Asher reminds us, though, that ASA is not limited to the cities. Large animals, particularly cows and buffalo, are common targets, particularly among those who work at *tabela*, or dairy farms. "The workers there," Asher says, "usually come from different parts of India not native to that particular place. Because of a lack of family, they use animals for sexual pleasure." As he speaks, we see grainy video of a man assaulting a buffalo in a pen. She kicks and resists, and the man backs away, appearing to buckle up his pants. But then he alters his direction and starts on her again.

The fifth and penultimate section of the film centers on Shakuntala Majumdar, a longtime animal activist in Mumbai. Like Asher, Majumdar argues that dairy workers specifically, and migrant workers in general, make up the bulk of ASA offenders, who are, anyway, "violent offenders, sex offenders, and the sexually abused."[10] These men, Majumdar says, are "away from their families for a very long time. . . . So, I guess they have to go to *somebody* to fulfill their desires, and the animals are the least expensive, economical, and affordable means of satiating their lust." Later, when discussing truck drivers who keep animals as sexual slaves, she says, "They are traveling, so obviously they cannot go to a prostitute or make out with anybody." Interestingly, Majumdar anticipates the connection of bestiality with animal husbandry. "See," Majumdar explains, "our animals are regularly artificially inseminated. They are *used to* being manhandled. And that is why they are accepting the act also. They think it is *done*, it is a *done* thing." Like Karmakar, Majumdar laments the exploitation of animals made trusting and docile by human intervention. Ironically, the human interventions that render animals trusting and docile, and thus vulnerable to sexual abuse in this schema, are, in the first place, sexual in nature: street dog sterilization and livestock insemination.

Bestiality—The Unheard Rape is premised on the distinction between permissible and perverse interspecies sex in India—that is, husbandry and paternalism from rape. Its field of permissible interspecies sex includes animal husbandry and population control of pets and strays, one of which reproduces in the name of economy and nation, and the other of which stanches reproduction in the name of the social. That sphere of permissible interspecies sex is bound up with a sphere of *permissible sex in general*, which is the home and the brothel, with the appropriate objects of wife and prostitute, both of whom are deemed in effect incapable of being raped by virtue of having "already consented" to belonging to the sphere of permissible violence. The field of *perverse* interspecies sex is defined by ASA discourse precisely by its distance from the sphere of the permissible. Animal sexual abuse occurs in secluded spaces and slums and is committed by those who come from "different parts of India." The narrators, in

---

10 Rosenberg points out that bestiality is often portrayed in cultural and scholarly discussion as "premodern desires emanating from communities marked by spatial remoteness and distance from capital": Rosenberg, "How Meat Changed Sex," 474. Our analysis in this chapter is indebted to Rosenberg's article.

contrast, stand in the sun or invite us, unselfconsciously, into a sphere of relaxed domesticity. Precisely because of the distance of ASA, symbolic and real, from the permissible, the sphere of the perverse demands surveillance—CCTV is a hero, as are those who lie in wait for offenders—which reinforces the autonomy and deserved privacy of the sphere of permissible violence. But this is how perverse interspecies sex is rent from its permissible forms according to one twenty-two-minute film. How does law conceive the separation?

The Unnatural, the Nonconsenting, and the Innocent

Section 377 of the Indian Penal Code of 1860, a remnant of British colonial governance, reads, "Whoever voluntarily has carnal intercourse against the order of nature with any man, woman, or animal, shall be punished with imprisonment for life." In India, as elsewhere in the British Commonwealth and beyond, sodomy laws perform this "double duty" of criminalizing both homosex and interspecies sex.[11] If, as Colleen Boggs argues, the advent of bestiality as a crime in Euro-America was a "founding moment for the criminalization of gays," the braiding of sodomy and bestiality works the other way, too: as sodomy laws have been reformed in the past quarter-century, an inadvertent consequence has been the legalization of bestiality.[12]

One of the barriers to repealing Section 377 in India is that it is the only existing law with which to prosecute the sexual assault of minors and sexual crimes between adults of the same sex, which in transphobic Indian rape law is thought to include the assault by men against hijras and transwomen.[13] Sections 375 and 376 of the Indian Penal Code criminalize rape, but they are gender-specific statutes that recognize only cismen as perpetrators and ciswomen as victims. They also do not recognize marital rape, or the rape of a woman by her husband, a subject to which we return.

With same-sex assault and sexual abuse of hijras, transwomen, and children in mind, queer activists were reluctant for decades to call for the striking of Section 377 in its entirety. They petitioned instead for a "reading down," which would decriminalize same-sex sex among consenting adults while retaining the rest as sex crimes. But in March 2000, the Law Commission of India issued a recommendation to make Section 375 gender-neutral, which would then

---

11 Rosenberg, "How Meat Changed Sex," 481.
12 Boggs, *Animalia Americana*, 106.
13 For a detailed analysis of Section 377 and its repeal efforts, see Davé, *Queer Activism in India*; Gupta and Narrain, *Law like Love*.

allow for a striking of Section 377 in its entirety. Aware that this would leave bestiality criminally unaccounted for, the commission said, "We may leave such persons to their just desserts."[14]

In more than 150 years of the existence of Section 377, only one case of bestiality entered the criminal records. That was *Khandu v. Emperor* (1935), in which Khandu was arrested but later found not guilty of inserting his penis into the nostril of a bull. The case reached the courts via the logic laid down in the 1925 case *Khanu v. Emperor* (a case of homosex, not bestial sex) which defined an unnatural act under Section 377 as "penetration of an orifice that does not lead to procreation."[15] We might note that nobody cared whether the bull minded or did not mind having a penis in his nose. This might sound either flippant or ridiculous or both, but it addresses a presumption at the heart of sodomy law, human and bestial: one cannot consent to an unnatural act, because it is by (un)nature irrational.[16] Both actors of an unnatural act—whether homosexual or bestial—are coconspirators rather than perpetrator and victim.[17]

Nevertheless, 70 percent of ASA cases are filed in India under what remains today of Section 377.[18] Numbers regarding ASA are difficult to come by. The National Crime Records Bureau does not keep statistics related to criminal acts against animals—animals are, in other words, not a class of victims. Yet organizations such as Voice of Stray Dogs (VoSD), the Federation of Indian Animal Protection Organizations (FIAPO), and All Creatures Great and Small (ACGS), and independent researchers such as Alok, have been collecting media reports, conducting interviews, and generating databases of ASA cases in India

14 Law Commission of India, "Review of Rape Laws," 35, emphasis added.

15 *Khanu v. Emperor* (AIR 1925 Sind 286) held that "the natural object of carnal intercourse is that there should be the possibility of conception of human beings, which in the case of coitus *per os* is impossible."

16 Bhaskaran, *Made in India*. See also Davé, *Queer Activism in India*, 230.

17 Rosenberg, "How Meat Changed Sex," 479.

18 In 2018, the celebrated *Navtej Johar* decision by the Supreme Court decriminalized sex between consenting adults in private. Bestiality and other nonconsensual sodimitic sex remain criminalized. A week before the *Navtej* judgment was announced, PETA petitioned the Ministry of Home Affairs seeking to retain the criminalization of bestiality on the grounds not of animal rights but the slippery slope from bestiality to pedophilia and other perversions: Valliyate, "Criminalizing Bestiality Safeguards Society." On efforts by American animal welfare groups to recriminalize bestiality in the face of overturned sodomy law, see Rosenberg, "How Meat Changed Sex."

since 2014.[19] They are predictably horrific. There are rapes of puppies, calves, dogs, monkeys, and goats. The crimes involve disembowelments, rods and screwdrivers, and human male sex organs. The cases, also predictably, generate much media attention, with their salacious stories about migrants and minorities, college boys and layabouts.[20] It is, of course, partly the brutal nature of some of these cases that attracts outrage and attention. But for most animal activists, what unites these cases, regardless of the means or intent of intercourse, is that ASA "is simply wrong because of the issue of consent. Animals can't give consent to what people do to them."[21]

This is the crux of contemporary transnational formulations of interspecies sexual assault: that bestiality, by definition, is sexual coercion or, as Gabriel Rosenberg puts it, that "nonabusive sex with animals is impossible."[22] As to why this is so, Piers Beirne, a criminologist of interspecies sexual assault, argues, "Animals are incapable of saying yes or no to humans in forms that humans can readily understand." He adds, "For consent to be present, both participants must be conscious, informed, and positive in their desires."[23] Indeed, *Bestiality—The Unheard Rape* ends with this voiceover: "Let's keep this conversation going on behalf of all the four-legged victims who cannot speak for themselves."

Are animals really incapable of being positive in their desires? A documentary about zoophilia titled *Zoo* centers on an erstwhile stallion named Strut who fucks a man with gusto, then so clearly enjoys being fellated by a mare that animal welfare workers castrate Strut, lest his sexuality again lead him

19 Voice of Stray Dogs is the first organization in India we know of to have compiled a report specifically on ASA; it was released in 2014 ("Sexual Abuse of Street Dogs in India"). More recently, FIAPO compiled a report in collaboration with ACGS that was published in 2021, "In Their Own Right."

20 Examples of headlines include: Express News Service, "Two Arrested for Raping Cows at Vizianagaram Farm" (*New Indian Express*); Ians, "Goa NGO Wants the Police to Probe Bestiality against a Dog" (*The Quint*); Kumar, "As Medical Students Stab and Burn a Monkey in Vellore, Activists Demand Stricter Animal Welfare Laws" (*Scroll*); "Man in Mumbai Let Off by Police After He Was Caught Having Sex with a Puppy" (*India TV News*); Singh, "Two Rape Dog, Drag Her to Death" (*The Pioneer*).

21 Seth, "Historic Trial for Dog Rapist."

22 That interspecies sexual assault is always sexual coercion is from Adams, "Animals and Women." The Rosenberg quotation is from "How Meat Changed Sex," 482.

23 Beirne, "Peter Singer's 'Heavy Petting,'" 50.

astray.[24] Strut's were, until his castration, positive and precise desires.[25] And although we didn't mention this at the time, *Bestiality—The Unheard Rape* opens with a voluble and positive rejection: the healthy white cat sitting on the speaker's lap is mewing with decisiveness, straining visibly to free herself from her cozy human jail. The speaker only tightens the adoring grip on her pet as she addresses us, a clear response to the cat's clear speech, and the animal intensifies her straining and mewing until she is finally released. Our point is not to cast aspersions on cat moms. It is simply to point out again that, of course, animals speak, and in ways humans register, if more rarely honor.

The casting of animals as innocent is never an innocent gesture. Deeming a class of beings innocent is what produces the sphere of permissible violence against them in the first place, whether human or animal.[26] We argue that innocence is construed in two main ways within Hindu anthropatriarchy. The first kind of innocence we call *innocent but consenting*. This is what constitutes the sphere of *permissible violence*, where *refusal on the part of the object is unthinkable*.[27] The second kind of innocence we call *innocent and nonconsenting*. This is what constitutes the sphere of *perverse violence*, where *refusal on the part of the object is inutterable* (table 7.1).

Many of those who work to combat ASA—innocently or not—produce this second kind of innocence: *innocent and nonconsenting*. Here, innocence is conflated with speechlessness (in which "no" is inutterable because it is physiologically not

24 Robinson Devor, dir., *Zoo* (documentary, THINKFilm, New York, 2008).
25 On the frenzy surrounding Strut in Washington State, see Brown and Rasmussen, "Bestiality and the Queering of the Human Animal."
26 For other critiques of innocence in relation to animal activism, see Govindrajan, "Beyond Cruelty and Innocence"; Ticktin, "A World without Innocence." Our only quibble with these works is that, in rightly critiquing the attribution of innocence to animals (and, by extension, the cruelty of "natives"), there appears to be little space to recognize violence against animals, examples of which are alluded to, for instance, as only "unhappy" occurrences. What we strive for here is a critique of innocence that enables a more rigorous analysis of how a plastic innocence underlies the systematic and coconstitutive exploitation of human and nonhuman persons, without that analysis furthering the abjection of animals. Our exemplars include Jackson, *Becoming Human*, and Kim, *Dangerous Crossings*.
27 Animal sacrifice provides an interesting counter. In this act of "permissible violence," an animal's refusal is not unthinkable; in fact, its permissibility is often premised on belief in the animal's consent: Singh and Davé, "On the Killing and Killability of Animals," for example, discusses *moor phodi*, in which a goat bangs his head on the altar as consent. Govindrajan, too, writes about *jharr*, in which a sacrificial goat shakes his body as a sign of consent: Govindrajan, *Animal Intimacies*, 33.

TABLE 7.1. Regimes of Hindu anthropatriarchal innocence

Regime	Moral Sphere	Refusal	Location	Examples
Innocent but consenting	Permissible violence (which therefore must not be named violence)	Unthinkable	Proper/natural sphere (home, abattoir, clinic)	Mother; wife; cow; pet
Innocent but nonconsenting	Perverse violence (which must therefore always be named violence and permissibly avenged)	Inutterable	Improper/ unnatural sphere (lair of thief or other nonmodern person)	Stolen wife, sister, daughter, mother; stolen cow; stolen pet; pregnant wildlife*

* In June 2020, a pregnant elephant in Kerala died after consuming a pineapple filled with explosives. Some animalists welcomed the national and global outrage, while others asked why the elephant's pregnancy was so important as a condition of empathy. Maneka Gandhi weighed in with communal rhetoric, suggesting that "intense criminal activity" was commonplace in this Muslim-majority district of Mallapuram (see "Kerala Elephant Death"). Her position was rejected by all thinking people in the animalist community. On the death of the elephant, see "India Outrage after Pregnant Elephant Dies Eating 'Firecracker Fruit.'" For critical reflection on how the elephant's death was received, including Gandhi's anti-Muslim rhetoric, see Nishant, "Who Killed the Elephant in Kerala?"

articulable or culturally unhearable or both). This, in turn, is conflated with a lack of physical and sexual agency, which renders the (non)subject docile even if nonconsenting. The innocent-but-nonconsenting (non)subject is *defined by her distance in space from the sphere of permissible violence,* which is to say, not by any inherent quality of her own. She has usually been forcibly wrested from her natural sphere (a perversity), which, in turn, justifies its own permissible violence: avenging the rape of cows, the killing of charismatic wildlife, or the elopement of women.[28]

In the sphere of permissible violence, animals and women are variously construed as *innocent but consenting,* where *refusal is unthinkable.* "Consent" is here

28 On Hindu anthropatriarchal fears of intercaste and intercommunal elopement, see Mody, "Kidnapping, Elopement, and Abduction."

assumed through the language of sacrifice and "patriotic motherhood," as well as a biological predisposition to be worked, killed, penetrated, or all three.[29] Refusal is unthinkable because of those predispositions, in which refusal to be worked, killed, or penetrated would constitute a breach of subjectivity and, thus, of the innocence bestowed by virtue of that feminine/animal subject position. This kind of innocence is defined *by proximity to the sphere of permissible violence*—that is, by being and remaining exactly where one is supposed to be.

For both figures of innocence, innocence is not bestowed to protect them. On the contrary, innocence carves out an opaque sphere of permissible violence precisely on the grounds that the innocent (non)subjects need protection and cannot speak for themselves.[30] Insofar as innocence is determined as an inability to consent (whether because refusal is unthinkable or inutterable), innocence marks an absence of reason and an absence of a desiring interiority—in other words, a deficit of personhood, the basis of killability and rapability itself.[31] Innocence prepares the body for violence by constructing it as less than human. And innocence prepares the body politic for violence by constructing *it* as the guardian and arbiter of that innocence.

The Agricultural (and Marital) Exception

India wrested its own independence from the guardianship of the British Empire in 1947, owing much to the nonviolent revolution led by Mahatma Gandhi.[32] The first prime minister of the new nation, Jawaharlal Nehru, was a friend and comrade of Gandhi and influenced by his philosophy of *ahimsa*, or noninjury. As Florence Burgat has noted, Gandhi's understanding of *ahimsa* generated for him a lifelong struggle of personal and national contradictions.[33] The interdiction against killing for Gandhi was nearly absolute,

---

29 "Patriotic motherhood" is from Hansen, *The Saffron Wave*, 98. The feminine/animal predisposition to be worked is from Adams, *The Sexual Politics of Meat*; Davé, "Kamadhenu's Last Stand"; Hochschild, *The Managed Heart*; Martin, *The Woman in the Body*.
30 See Ticktin, "A World without Innocence."
31 Innocence as an absence of reason is from Heidegger, *The Fundamental Concepts of Metaphysics*. Innocence as an absence of desiring interiority is from Rosenberg, "How Meat Changed Sex."
32 The subhead for this section is an homage to Rosenberg, "How Meat Changed Sex."
33 Burgat, "Non-violence towards Animals in the Thinking of Gandhi." For more on the conceptual cleavage of milk from beef in Indian animal welfare discourse historically, see Ahuja, "On Phooka."

except in cases of self-preservation or the preservation of one's wards.[34] But the problem of "harm" more generally—such as that required for farming—needed to be balanced against the nation's need for cheap and high-quality milk, even though he remained deeply conflicted about dairy in his own life and experimented with abstention.[35] His compromise was to promote dairy in the national interest as long as cows were sent to shelters (*gaushalas*) rather than to the "butcher's knife" to be slaughtered when dry. Gandhi's butcher figure (*kasai*) is explicitly Muslim, and however much he protested communal violence as a means to protect cows, the effects of his so-called compromise was one in which Hindus reap the fruit of bovine labor as long as the cow is ultimately protected from Muslim men.[36]

Nehru, too, had his compromise, though his was rather less tortured than Gandhi's. A self-avowed animal lover, like most of his dynastic descendants, Nehru considered it a point of pride to push through the Prevention of Cruelty against Animals Act (PCA). As I detailed in chapter 2, Nehru's revision to Rukmini Devi Arundale's draft made animal experimentation, animal entertainment, and slaughter for food the exceptions to the cruelty law.[37] The PCA thus essentially defines cruelty—and we're paraphrasing here—as that which is punishable if it does not contribute to the accumulation of capital. The PCA itself is pretty lousy in that regard, too: that which does manage to constitute cruelty, or "unnecessary suffering," even today brings in only a fifty rupee fine, or about seventy American pennies.[38]

34 Burgat, "Non-violence towards Animals in the Thinking of Gandhi," 225.

35 On Gandhi's experiments with what Larry David has more recently called "cream shaming," see Gandhi, *The Story of My Experiments with Truth*; Roy, *Alimentary Tracts*.

36 Gandhi also wrote in *Young India* that anyone who dispossesses a Muslim of a cow is an enemy of cows and therefore of Hinduism. Further, cow protection that resorts to violence "reduces Hinduism to Satanism." He points out, in any case, that cows end up at butchers only because they are sold to butchers by Hindus: Gandhi, *Views on Hindu Dharma*.

37 Chapter 4 of the PCA permits animal experimentation under certain limited welfarist conditions, and Section 11(3)E excludes "destruction of animals . . . for food for mankind" from the definition of cruelty.

38 David Bilchitz traces the root of the logic of "cruelty only as unnecessary suffering" to English Common Law, in which violence per se against an animal is not a straightforward crime but conditional against a test of "necessary suffering": Bilchitz, "When Is Animal Suffering 'Necessary'?"

As of this writing, the central government had proposed sixty-one amendments to the PCA of 1960. The proposed amendments increase monetary fines and prison

The Constitution of India demonstrates a similar ambivalence between wanting to claim a founding Hindu principle of noninjury along with the necessity of harm for economic progress. As Yamini Narayanan explains, Article 51A directs Indians to "cherish the ideals" that drove the Independence movement, citing as examples Hindu anti-cow slaughter agitations and the 1857 rebellion, which, long story very short, began as a revolt against invisible beef.[39] The Directive Principles in Article 48 of the constitution nevertheless prescribes that the state "organize agricultural and animal husbandry on modern and scientific lines and take steps for preserving and improving the breeds." Narayanan argues that these two articles are in contradiction.[40] But we might say instead that one necessitates the other. In exceptionalizing interspecies sex for the purpose of scientific breeding, the constitution requires a sphere of perverse bestial sex—the kind that fuels Hindu revolts, vigilantism, and communal violence.[41] What Rosenberg finds implicit in American law is more explicit here: legal structures dedicated to exceptionalizing meat animals reveal "the urge to disavow meat as the fruit of bestial coupling."[42]

Before we get to the part of the chapter where we justify calling artificial insemination (AI) "interspecies sex"—or, better yet, "bestial coupling"—we'll point out a parallel to the agricultural exception: that of marital rape.[43] As Krina Patel details, Sections 375 and 376—those pertaining to the rape of ciswomen—have undergone only three amendments since 1860, none of which managed to criminalize rape within the context of marriage.[44] The 1983 amendments recognized the rape of a woman by her husband *if they were separated and living apart.* Thirty years later, the fatal gang rape of twenty-two-year-old Jyoti Singh in Delhi, and the reckoning that followed, spurred another round of amendments.[45] The

sentences for animal abuse and create a new category of "gruesome cruelty" for bestial acts.

39 Narayanan, "Cow Protectionism and Bovine Frozen-Semen Farms in India," 26.

40 Narayanan, "Cow Protectionism and Bovine Frozen-Semen Farms in India," 28.

41 For more on the relationship between cow protectionism and animal husbandry in India see Adcock, "Preserving and Improving the Breeds."

42 Rosenberg, "How Meat Changed Sex," 475.

43 For more on marital rape in India, see Prasad, "Why It's Still Legal for Indian Men to Rape Their Wives." Narayanan also gestures to the connection between animal husbandry and the marital rape exception in "Cow Is a Mother, Mothers Can Do Anything for Their Children!," 6.

44 Patel, "The Gap in Marital Rape Law in India."

45 On the event and aftermath of the rape of Jyoti Singh, who was honored by the public as Nirbhaya (fearless) before her identity was released, see Shandilya, "Nirbhaya's Body."

late J. S. Verma, then chief justice of India, formed a committee to modernize Indian rape law. Among its recommendations was to repeal the marital rape exception, as it "suggests women are property."[46] But despite other changes, the marital rape exception held, reading: "Sexual intercourse or sexual acts by a man with his own wife, the wife not being under fifteen years of age, is not rape."[47] (In 2017, the age of marital rapability was raised to eighteen.) It is almost too glaring to point out: the home is the space of permissible violence, which must therefore not be named violence, and "consent" to sex is determined through the prior consent to be in one's proper sphere.[48] Patel notes that there are no marital exceptions for "lesser sexual crimes" committed by a man against his wife, such as voyeurism or intent to outrage modesty.[49] Rather than a contradiction in the law, this demonstrates only the coconstitutive nature of permissible and perverse sexual violence, where intolerance toward the latter displays the paternal humanity of a society that requires the former.

The ABCs of AI

In 2001, the government of India enacted a national policy requiring the sterilization of street dogs. ("Pet" dogs are a separate category, for which owners are held accountable for "responsible breeding and sterilization.")[50] The judgment was hailed as a victory by animal welfare activists in India, who had fought to institute sterilization as a humane alternative to starvation and municipal killing, the common lot of street dogs.

Animal sterilization is, however you slice it, "fully legal contact" with an animal's genitals.[51] And anyone who has been there knows there is nothing consensual about it. Animal welfare NGOs such as Welfare for Stray Dogs send

46 Patel, "The Gap in Marital Rape Law in India."
47 In her capacity as BJP Minister for Women and Child Development, Maneka Gandhi argued against repealing the marital rape exception in a speech to Parliament in 2016—another irony that is not one: see Sen, "Maneka Gandhi's Altered Stance on Marital Rape Angers Activists."
48 On the home as a space of permissible sexual violence against women, see also Menon, *Seeing like a Feminist*.
49 Patel, "The Gap in Marital Rape Law in India," 1526.
50 Animal Birth Control (Dogs) Rules, 2001, the Gazette of India Extraordinary Part II, Section 3, Subsection ii, page 2, published by Authority No. 929, New Delhi, December 24, 2001.
51 Rosenberg, "How Meat Changed Sex," 492. For additional critiques of ABC practices, see Srinivasan, "The Biopolitics of Animal Being and Welfare."

a van around a select area of the city; capture unsterilized animals either by tranquilizer dart (a high-skill job) or a catchpole; and drive them, squealing, in a freshly vomit- and shit-strewn vehicle to a shelter, where they await surgery. It is not only the animals who do not consent. I've watched a woman collapse next to the van, sobbing, pleading for assurance that her dog would be returned unharmed. I've seen men hide and shoo their dogs away when the NGO workers approached. There were a few beloved dogs, with especially plump testicles, to whom nobody could get near. I asked Abodh whether this might be a remnant of collective trauma from the forced sterilizations of the Emergency era.[52] "Don't overthink it," he said. "They just think animals have a right to have sex if they want to."

The Animal Welfare Board of India has published a lengthy guide to best animal birth control practices, and its authors, perhaps testicularly friendly, stress the need for a "female-centered approach."[53] They warn that one unsterilized bitch can birth up to twenty pups a year. And unneutered males are able to "protect territory" more effectively, guarding it from migrant dogs and the threat of rabies. Furthermore, the postoperative complications of castration are greater and—well, er, um—molestation is just "better tolerated" by females.[54] (Is there such a thing as canine anthropatriarchy?) In any case, once captured, male and female alike are subject to efficient but thorough sexual handling. Testicles are plopped into one jar of formaldehyde; ovaries into another. They are counted, and in exchange the clinic receives a modest bounty from the municipality for bringing the city nearer to a modern, stray-free future.[55]

While the reproduction of stray animals is stanched, requiring a tacit exception to the prohibition of sexual contact with animals, "unfree" animals—that is, livestock—are actively reproduced through artificial insemination.[56] Yamini Narayanan has laid the groundwork for understanding animal husbandry

---

52 On forced sterilizations see Prakash, *Emergency Chronicles*, 269–302.
53 Nagar and Animal Welfare Board of India, "Standard Operating Procedures for Sterilization of Stray Dogs under the Animal Birth Control Programme," 5–6.
54 Nagar and Animal Welfare Board of India, "Standard Operating Procedures for Sterilization of Stray Dogs under the Animal Birth Control Programme," 6.
55 There are a range of other legal sterilization and nonbreeding practices that involve extensive human contact with animal genitals, including Caslick surgery, in which copper wire is used to stitch the vulvas of racing mares and ponies to prevent "unwanted breeding."
56 For the distinction between "free-living" and "unfree" animals, where street dogs are among the "free-living," see Srinivasan, "Remaking More-than-Human Society."

as interspecies sex of the permissible kind.[57] Under what she calls Hindu anthropatriarchy—the ownership of female bodies as property, requiring sanctuary from a predator framed as male and Muslim—much is made, volubly and violently, about so-called cow protection.[58] As Narayanan points out, though, cow protection focuses obsessively on the end of bovine life, leaving not only life itself but its first industrial acts—semen extraction and artificial insemination—a normalized exception to so-called protection.[59] (Innocence, as we said earlier, is not meant to be protective; it is only a priming for violence.)

Artificial insemination has been a focus of Indian animal husbandry since the White Revolution, which began in the 1960s through initiatives by Verghese Kurien.[60] Kurien believed his revolution would not only bring high-quality milk to the masses, but would make India truly independent through autonomy from structurally uneven trade policies. Key to his plan was the crossbreeding of desi cows with productive foreign studs to produce high-yielding hybrids. His maximalist vision bore fruit. India has the largest number of bovines in the world.[61] It is the world's leading producer of milk and the second largest exporter of beef. At least 80 percent of these female bovines are artificially inseminated, and there are enough bulls to produce one hundred million of what the National Dairy Development Board calls "frozen semen straws"— each of which can impregnate between forty and one hundred cows.[62]

Narayanan has done extensive research at frozen semen farms in Maharashtra and Andhra Pradesh and describes the high-biosecurity regimes required to facilitate semen extraction.[63] Raw semen, unlike raw milk, cannot be treated, which means that bull studs must be kept in prime physical health. Bull studs

57 "Dairying involves acts that could be considered bestiality in non-'farming' spaces": Narayanan, "Cow Is a Mother, Mothers Can Do Anything for Their Children!," 6. See also "On Phooka," in which Ahuja refers to the "bestiality of the reproductive management of the cow in dairy production" (213).

58 Narayanan, "Cow Is a Mother, Mothers Can Do Anything for Their Children!"

59 Narayanan, "Cow Protectionism and Bovine Frozen-Semen Farms in India."

60 See Kurien and Salvi, I Too Had a Dream. For critiques of what Kurien and his revolution wrought, see Alvares, Another Revolution Fails; Baviskar and George, "Development and Controversy"; and Gaard, "Toward a Feminist Postcolonial Milk Studies."

61 Narayanan, "Cow Protectionism and Bovine Frozen-Semen Farms in India," 5.

62 National Dairy Development Board, "NDDB Organizes Workshop on Production and Processing of Bovine Frozen Semen under NDP I."

63 Narayanan, "Cow Protectionism and Bovine Frozen-Semen Farms in India." See also Gillespie, "Sexualized Violence and the Gendered Commodification of the Animal Body in Pacific Northwest US Dairy Production."

are confined starting when they are eighteen months old for an average of ten years when their semen quality drops and they are sold for slaughter. They are brought out of their pens twice a day to "provide service," which means mounting a dummy cow, who is actually a real bull with female pheromones slathered over its rear end, until erect and ready to ejaculate. A human worker anticipates the moment of ejaculation and greets the bull's penis with a temperature-controlled artificial vagina, which is then delivered to the lab and prepared for distribution.[64] Underperforming bulls, or injured ones that are unable to mount the "dummy," are subject instead to electroejaculation: electric shocks of up to twenty-four volts administered through the rectum.[65]

On the other side of the semen exchange, cows are kept in less healthful conditions in megadairies or *gaushalas*—cow shelters in name, though they usually serve as dairies, too (though we know of at least one recent exception, due to the labor strike of Kamadhenu, that articulate cow). *Gaushalas* without bulls purchase semen from the state's Department of Animal Husbandry and inseminate cows manually, a process that involves palpating the uterus through the rectum, manually removing dung from the rectum, handling vaginal lips, and inserting a gun into the vagina. When actual bulls are present, as Narayanan describes, they are usually given free-ish rein to choose a chained cow in estrous, a process that gives the impression of "keeping it natural."[66] All of these procedures, even when forced on ill or immobilized cows, are considered by *gaushala* managers a "virtuous service" that enables cows to achieve their destiny as mothers.[67] Asked whether a sick cow should be repeatedly impregnated, a manager told Narayanan, "Oh, she can handle it. Cow is a mother, and mothers can sacrifice anything for their children."[68] Of course, the flip side to this manufactured maternal consent is martial masculine

64 Murray, "In the Time of the Buffalo Clones."

65 Gillespie, "Sexualized Violence and the Gendered Commodification of the Animal Body in Pacific Northwest US Dairy Production"; Narayanan, "Cow Protectionism and Bovine Frozen-Semen Farms in India".

66 Narayanan, "Cow Is a Mother, Mothers Can Do Anything for Their Children!", 16 . Gillespie describes how bulls, particularly as the subject of jokes, are made a "scapegoat for the performance of the artificial insemination . . . and also used to naturalize" the procedure: Gillespie, "Sexualized Violence and the Gendered Commodification of the Animal Body in Pacific Northwest US Dairy Production," 1332.

67 Narayanan, "Cow Is a Mother, Mothers Can Do Anything for Their Children!"

68 Narayanan, "Cow Is a Mother, Mothers Can Do Anything for Their Children!," 16

imperative. "If anyone looks at my *gaumata* with bad intentions," says a *gaurak-shak* to Narayanan, "it will not take me long to kill him."[69]

Not all kinship metaphors, however, are in service of this virile Hindu militancy. Laura Murray, who earned a PhD in anthropology from New York University, conducts fieldwork in western India on bovine breeding and care. One of the chapters of her dissertation on buffalo breeding begins with a kinship metaphor that is intended as a joke among women.[70] Pinky, a junior scientist in a cloning lab, calls the buffalos she clones *beecha*, or child. When Laura asks what she means, Pinky laughs and dismisses it as a silly joke about being an overworked woman who will never have children of her own. But Murray sees something else in the *beecha* joke: recognition of the intimate "overlap of human and animal lives."[71]

Artificial insemination, Murray says, is viewed as the modern solution to "backward" rural breeding practices.[72] But as her ethnography illustrates, the techniques of this ostensibly modernized breeding are, despite its precision, raw and tactile—*sexual*. And perhaps only artificial because the cleavage insists on that designation. She describes how the farmer recognizes the animal in heat, rectally palpates the uterus, and manually inseminates their cow. "The animal must trust their keeper," Murray writes, "allow them to get close, and must know their touch and voice."[73] Though this is an uneven relationship between human and capital, there is in this "artificial" sex a "corporeal contiguity of a profoundly intimate kind."[74] The intimacy is such, Murray says, that "there is often something strange, something awkward in the event—perhaps even illicit—but always unspoken."[75]

This resonates with what Rosenberg argues regarding the cleavage that rents husbandry from bestiality. Drawing on Alex Blanchette's attentive descriptions of sow insemination, Rosenberg writes, "Humans go to elaborate and contradictory lengths to disavow these practices as sex, even as some workers explicitly recognize it as such."[76] There are many examples of this explicit recognition. Kathryn Gillespie writes about the rape jokes made by farmers

69 Narayanan, "Cow Is a Mother, Mothers Can Do Anything for Their Children!," 19.
70 Murray, "In the Time of the Buffalo Clones."
71 Murray, "In the Time of the Buffalo Clones," 143.
72 Murray, "In the Time of the Buffalo Clones," 159.
73 Murray, "In the Time of the Buffalo Clones," 160.
74 Murray, "In the Time of the Buffalo Clones," 160.
75 Murray, "In the Time of the Buffalo Clones," 160.
76 Rosenberg, "How Meat Changed Sex," 485, drawing on Blanchette, *Porkopolis*.

inseminating cattle; Temple Grandin's instructions for breeding sow is titled, "How to Make a Pig Fall in Love" (hint: you start by playing with a boar's anus just right).[77] But what Murray finds especially revealing of the truth of agricultural interspecies sex lies less in what is acknowledged than in what cannot be uttered.

She describes an embryo-transfer procedure conducted by a technician named Patil:

> To complete the transfer, Patil first reached one hand into the cow's rectum and methodically emptied it of dung. He did this quickly and without expression despite the indignity of the splat, splat, splat. Here, the collision of the enteric and the intellectual, the scientific and the beastly was managed through expression and gaze: If none of us laughed or otherwise acknowledged that my camera was covered in drool and Patil was up to his shoulder in shit, we remained in the temples of science, in the sterile realm of biotech, on a train rushing toward the future.[78]

In both the joke that makes Pinky laugh, and the nonjoke that Patil's friends must not laugh at, we find the same thing: a "vocalization of that which is excluded from social life . . . ; intimacies beyond the sayable."[79]

On Interspecies Erotics

Radhika Govindrajan concludes her *Animal Intimacies* with the chapter "The Bear Who Loved a Woman." It, like Murray's story, begins with a joke. A young woman named Mohini, known for her libidinous humor, says to Govindrajan, patting her cheek, "Watch out for the *bhalu* (bear). I'm sure he would love a city girl to do his work (*kaam*) with."[80] Govindrajan begins asking around among other women in Kumaon, who tell her, if at first reluctantly, of all the erotic configurations of woman and bear. Bears, she is told, are like men, only better: they are inexhaustible and have a particular fondness for licking the soles of women's feet. They are so virile that women might die from the sex,

---

77 Gillespie, "Sexualized Violence and the Gendered Commodification of the Animal Body in Pacific Northwest US Dairy Production," 1331; Johnson and Grandin, *Animals in Translation*.

78 Murray, "In the Time of the Buffalo Clones" (though this passage ended up on the cutting room floor).

79 Murray, "In the Time of the Buffalo Clones," 174.

80 Govindrajan, *Animal Intimacies*, 146.

but that is not enough to stop him: he will persist with her corpse. Bears can impregnate their women lovers. Their penises are rumored to be terribly large, though the hirsuteness of those members is a matter of some dispute. Govindrajan points out that these are not tellings about sexual assault, rape, or the perverse nature of bestiality (or, for that matter, interspecies necrophilia).[81] Insofar as they are a commentary on violence, it is not the kind that inheres in the erotically (semi)nonconsensual act of being taken by a bear and (semi) nonconsensually shagged by him. What these stories of interspecies sex—and the desire for it—speak to is, in part, the violence of (human) men's control over women's sexuality. The tellers posit themselves as "desiring subjects," thus "mounting a radical critique of rigid notions of sexual purity and control."[82]

Govindrajan's story about interspecies sex reminds me of a conversation I had with Savitri, then an employee of a women's NGO in Delhi. Savitri had returned from a feminist sex education workshop with rural women. They were asked to form small groups and list all of the sexual acts they could think of, but without specifying gender. In other words, each act had to be precise: which body part, where, and how. One group came back with 150, all recorded on a white board to general hilarity: toe in vagina, penis in ear, dog tongue on vulva. Someone erupted in laughter at the last one and mock finger-wagged, "No, only consensual acts!" Another replied, "Hum kilaathe hain, pilaathe hain. Esse hi thode kerthe hain!" We wine them, we dine them. It's not like we do it "just like that!" Others, still laughing, agreed: you get them in the mood; it's romantic; you can tell they like it by how they wag their tail.

What we come back to in both of these stories is what Govindrajan calls an imaginary of "another, radical, world in which norms separating the human from the animal are undone, and the shared tug of animal desire becomes a node of relatedness between human and animal."[83] That shared tug is premised on another thing shared, but one that must always be insisted on: a positive sexual desire, a wanting, an erotic capaciousness that has no business with innocence and its priming for violence. In recognizing that the bear wants, and the woman wants, and the dog wants too, we generate a queer outside to the permissible, where the perverse is only pleasure after all.

81 Govindrajan, *Animal Intimacies*, 152.
82 Govindrajan, *Animal Intimacies*, 170.
83 Govindrajan, *Animal Intimacies*, 171.

Exclusive Rights

In 2017, Sujatro Ghosh, a queer feminist artist based in Delhi, created a series of well-traveled photographs called, "The Cow Mask Project."[84] He photographed women in public and private locations in India, in everyday clothes doing everyday things such as visiting tourist attractions, buying food at the market, and even making out—but with their heads covered by rubber cow masks. The provocation was that cows are safer in India than women.

What does cow protection protect? We want to be clear. Cow protection does not protect cows, nor is meant to, nor does it seek to. Cow protection, like the protection of Hindu women, is but a sphere of permissible violence that necessitates a perverse other that can be permissibly avenged. *That* is its purpose. Or, to put it another way, cow protection protects the exclusive Hindu anthropatriarchal right to bestial sex.

84 Pandey, "Are Women Less Important than Cows in India?"

8

APPETITE. Does That Which Is Inevitable Cease to Matter?

Early on in my ethnographer-and-interlocutor relationship with Maneka Gandhi, she walked me around the garden of her bungalow in Lutyens' Delhi. It had just rained, and she was taking great delight in the mud squishing beneath her feet. Several of her dogs—how many there are, she has no idea—followed along. One was a blind and deaf Great Dane found abandoned in a gutter. Another came to her with its left eye hanging out of its head and its face swollen from an oral infection; everyone told her to put it to sleep, but she had its eye removed and its offending tooth extracted. Now the dog seemed as content as she. There were trees in this garden with lemon, curry *patta*, and avocado. There was one that grew sublime little cherries. "Pick that one," she said, pointing to a specific piece of fruit. "Eat it!" she demanded. "What does it taste like?" she wanted to know. I tried to describe its taste. "Interesting!" she replied. We continued this way—pick it! eat it! describe it!—until I was splattered with mud, and sticky with fruit. "Such a scent

I draw / Of carnage, prey innumerable! and taste / The savour of death from all things that live."[1]

That afternoon—like so many of the scenes I've traversed in this book while learning about the loving and eating of, and killing and caring for, animals—is suffused with carnality: a copresence of life and death (the trees, the fruit, the maggots, those near-death dogs with once-rotten teeth) that expresses itself in an intense nowness of being. Carnality is a bridge between the vitality that characterizes mere appetite and the bloodlust that characterizes the murderous. And I mean no offense here to carnivores. We find carnality just as true in a militant vegetarian's lust for hanging fruit, wet with recent rain.

The story I tell in this final chapter concerns this space—a space at once material and temporal—between lust and bloodlust, vitality and death. I seek to show (1) how a new form of carnality has been mattered forth in post-Independence India; and (2) that it is mattered forth within a specific temporality that is sometimes the No-Future and sometimes the Known-Future, but always has no otherwise to itself. I'll call this state of having no otherwise to itself, simply, "inevitability." And I will hunt down, with carnal vigor, other conceptions of time.

The Time of the Chicken

Sunil is a rich, kind, hospitable man. He and his brother own four roadside butcher shops in West Delhi that sell mostly mutton and chicken. I went to his shop on a Saturday morning in winter, along with a mutual friend, Nitin, who made our introduction. Sunil and three friends were sitting on rickety chairs with patchwork cushions. They welcomed Nitin warmly and all got up and offered me their seats. I accepted one as well as a Limca; Nitin had chai in a small plastic cup. Nitin and Sunil chatted about the weather and prices, the standard greeting among poultry men. Looking up at a sunny sky, they said in harmony that the price of chicken would be low tomorrow. Had there been clouds instead, the rates would be high, for chicken operates much like ripe, hanging fruit: rain intensifies the wanting. Few desire "hot" food like chicken or eggs when it is hot already (even the birds themselves eat less). And rain

---

1 In his *A Dictionary of the English Language* (1755), Samuel Johnson defines carnage as "slaughter," as well as "heaps of flesh." The latter definition is accompanied by these lines from John Milton's *Paradise Lost*. I thank Sandhya Shetty for this reading, drawing carnage to carnality.

makes for slow overnight traffic, which makes for fewer trucks arriving at the live markets, which—in the carnal appetite of rain—makes for seller-friendly rates for desirous buyers.

Sunil's shop was upraised, so one had to jump onto the platform or climb a few metal stairs. The chickens were kept on the ground in stacked, vented lockers so that customers could appraise them. Up near the butcher's block sat two boys, one of whom did most of the chopping. The walls were tiled in white, splattered and sticky. Everyone was smiling and happy.

There are four large pans in which different parts of the chicken are kept: legs, breasts, gizzards, carcasses. There is a scale. In a clump on the platform are the extra parts—the heads, beaks, feet, skin, and feathers. These are sold for fishmeal. A few customers came by for curry cuts, but none required a fresh slaughter. Nitin, having only recently made my acquaintance, felt this pacifism was a letdown for me and asked Sunil why his shop was suddenly the most boring spot in West Delhi? Sunil grinned and accepted Nitin's challenge, saying that his boys would butcher a few birds for me. I said this wasn't necessary, that I had seen animals slaughtered before and didn't want one killed for my sake. They laughed: they'll all be dead by night, they said, so you might as well see! Well, I *had* shown up wearing a camera.

On Sunil's signal, a tall man strode toward the stacks of cages. He had a broad, blank face and wore an oversize white shirt, gray pants with wide legs, and rubber slippers. He reached into a cage, rejected the first animal, and grabbed the one behind it. He handed it up to the butcher, who placed it, squawking and squealing, on the stump and chopped its head off in one fell swoop. The head lay there on the board, the beak moving, the eyes blinking. The broad-faced man dropped the body into the bleeding drum where it thrashed and kicked, the drum jerking across the ground. It was at least lucky to be the only one in there; when killing is heavy—say, first thing in the morning—the bird at the bottom kicks around underneath a growing pile, getting bled on and defecated on by other headless chickens before being unearthed an hour or so later. While this one continued to thrash (they do so for about four minutes) I filmed, watching the head chirping and the body flailing while the broad-faced man watched me with a smile on his face. I betrayed nothing, not that there was much to betray. About three minutes later, when he believed the bird had bled out long enough, he reached into the barrel, down to his shoulder, and pulled the bird out, still thrashing if more slowly. The head had just stopped chirping moments before, stopped at the end with a sudden alarmed opening of its eyes. The broad-faced man began to tear the bird, but Sunil stopped him *Aaram se!* he said, do it slowly, presumably so that I could better observe. *Aaram se nahi*, I said, *kar lo*. Just do it. But he took orders from Sunil, not from me, and so with exaggeratedly slow motion he puuuulled the wings off and puuuulled the skin off and tossed what was left, still pulsing, up to the butcher's block where the young man sat and reached into the hot body from the neck and pulled out its guts. *Dil dikhao*, Sunil said. Show her its heart. The butcher took the heart out, a slippery purply thing, and placed it photogenically on the blade edge of a knife, but it slithered this way and that. It beat for a while, not long this one, not as long another Sunil showed me, and I turned off my camera. Sunil apologized with a laugh: *kamzoor tha*. This one was weak.

In these few minutes there were many kinds of time. There was the slow time of easy hospitality (*aaram se*), but the slow time of hospitality was one and the same as the slow time of cruelty (pulling the skin off the still pulsing bird, all for me, who claimed not to want it but was there all the same). There was the No-Future of the chicken, who would certainly be dead by night, which was the Known-Future of the chicken, who would certainly be dead by night. This was a *jhatka* shop, involving a single severing chop to the head rather than the halal practice of the single slit of the throat (ostensibly immediate, pseudosecular time versus the elongated time of ritual).[2] The skin and feathers and heads were destined for a fishery that would then take its own remains—scales and heads and so on—and sell them in dried form to the poultry farm, where it would be fed to the hens who would lay eggs to make the Indian military and urban youth healthy and virile and fertile and strong. There are cycles here, re-generation, and they are one and the same with the full stops: the eyes opened for the very last time, the final beat of the *kamzoor* heart. There are many kinds of time, all bound up together. But there is no good time for the chicken.

The closest thing to a good time I saw for a chicken was in a meat market in Dimapur, Nagaland. Many of the other animals had it bad, as they would in any meat market, but the chickens were living a good, old-fashioned kind of life, not in battery cages but in natural deep litter, with all the food they could want. A well-dressed family of four came to purchase a chicken at about six in the morning. The shop owner picked the fattest bird up and held it with his left hand by the base of the wings. He lifted his right fist in the air and brought it crashing down onto the chicken's back with a deep, satisfying thud. He then tossed the bird into a Styrofoam box. And then: nothing. No movement, no dancing, no thrashing, no pulsing. That bird was *dead*. I asked him what he

2 *Jhatka*, from the Sanskrit for "at once," originated as a Sikh practice. *Jhatka* is also the preferred method of slaughter for Hindu and Buddhist consumers of meat in north India.

had done, and he said he had broken a rib that immediately pierced the heart. That's what we do here, he said, because the mostly Christian customers do not insist on halal.

But that was not always how it was done. An hour or so later, as the market got busier, I returned to the chicken shops. An adolescent boy was in charge now, and he was struggling to keep up with the demand. He, too, grabbed a bird with his left hand, mimicking the older man. He then raised his right fist and brought it down all about the bird, pummeling its back, its head. He didn't seem to know what he was doing. The bird was very much alive when he threw it into a pail of water made hot with an immersion coil and very much alive when he tossed its half-scalded body, likely full of broken bones, into the defeathering drum that, if you can imagine, is a large metal can with rotating and thrusting rubber spikes.

It is at times like this that one might imagine there is some benefit to the routinized, Fordist killing of the new mechanized slaughterhouses.

Modern Times

The day after my visit with Sunil, Nitin and I went on a road trip across the Barwala poultry belt in Haryana. He had planned our trip methodically, beginning in Delhi with roadside chicken and mutton stalls like Sunil's; traditional shops that had been run by Qureshi families for generations; Delhi Development Authority (DDA) "slum markets," which are the foil for the modernizers; "hypermarkets," or glitzy shops in malls featuring Styrofoam, plastic and high-tech temperature control; layer farms, both massive and medium; a mechanized, ultramodern slaughterhouse; a "further processor," which turns raw meat into value-added, export-quality edible form such as kebabs and sausage; and then finally back to one of India's largest live markets, Gazipur Mandi, on the outskirts of Delhi.[3]

I came to know Nitin through Jayasimha, our mutual friend at the India office of Humane Society International (HSI). Nitin had been working at Skylark, one of India's five largest poultry conglomerates, riding his motorcycle across the countryside to sell DOCs, or day-old chicks, to Barwala farmers, enticing them to become Skylark farmers for life. But there were two problems with this line of work. Nitin is Jain, and few Jains want to marry their daughter

---

3 For more on Qureshi butchers and on these built spaces of the northern Indian "meatscape," see Ahmad, *Delhi's Meatscapes*.

to someone who sells chickens for a living. (Not that Nitin wanted to get married, but that, like resistance to other inevitable things, does not always seem to matter.) Nitin also had debilitating nightmares about dying chickens. So he left Skylark and joined HSI, using his connections with the poultry industry to advocate a return to cage-free farming: the right opposite of what a massive integrator such as Skylark was promoting. His job with HSI didn't last, and Nitin returned to Skylark and began supplying the Indian Armed Forces with two and a half million eggs per day.[4] He is married now, with a lovely wife and child, but despite these riches, he is, he told me, "unhappy like anything." He doesn't want to sell chicken and eggs. He doesn't want to be a provider. He got into this line of work only because his sister is married to the director of Skylark. They are multimillionaires. But Nitin's sister is a strict vegetarian who "won't even touch an egg." How many times I heard this phrase from people in the poultry industry! Nitin's sister makes this make sense by reinvesting some of her fortune in the building of hospitals and temples and schools in their hilltop village in Himachal Pradesh.

I stayed at Nitin's home the night before our trip, and while I was eating breakfast he appeared neatly dressed in slacks, a blue dress shirt, and a corduroy jacket, smelling clean and cologned, and prayed in front of his Hanuman mandir that had flashing red lights and programmed music. His Blackberry was on the table, and it was pinging and buzzing, early on a Sunday morning, with rate updates on boneless chicken in Gujarat (jumbo, *mota*, medium, and tandoor) and urgent emails from Kentucky Fried Chicken. But he sat there quietly, bathed in the flashing red lights, surely not oblivious to the pressing time of capital.

We got in the car soon thereafter, saying goodbye to his wife and kid, and drove along the Grand Trunk Road.[5] We began with the multistory sheds of the Barwala layer farms. I should mention here that although I have used the word *chicken* many times, there is hardly any such thing in India as a chicken.[6] Those dual-purpose birds of yore are now either layers (females built

4 See Sujatha and Choudhary, "Army Jawans to Get Two Eggs."
5 Many of the big poultry farms originated in Punjab in the 1970s, but in the aftermath of the anti-Sikh massacres of 1984, the predominantly Hindu farmers moved to Haryana, formerly in eastern Punjab but since 1966 a Hindu-majority state. The Grand Trunk Road, which has existed since the time of the *Mahabharat*, runs from Kabul, Afghanistan, through Islamabad and Lahore in Pakistan and through Delhi east to Kolkata.
6 Although one of the protagonists of this story, Vinod Kapur, who was largely responsible for rise of Indian layers in the first place, also invented a real chicken called the

to lay eggs) or broilers (meat-producing monstrosities with chests so huge that their legs break from the weight). Barwala is layer country, with a population of one million layers producing one million to two million eggs per day in just a fifteen kilometer stretch of northern India. The air smells of feed and ammonia, at the same time nutty and suffocating. Long expanses of nothingness are punctuated by giant, windowless sheds, perched above-ground to allow for the passage of voluminous sewage. Most are two levels high, but some are three, each containing hundreds of thousands of hens.

Layer farming is considered "status farming," while raising broilers is more precarious. The layer farmers are well-off men, mostly Hindu and Sikh, with large plots of land, but they are still at the mercy of the integrators who decide how many DOCs to supply and determine the cost of feed and vaccines. Integration is exactly what it sounds like. A company such as Skylark, initially in the business of providing raw material in the form of chicks, integrates all other aspects of poultry farming into its activities, such as feed and vaccines for the raw materials, and equipment for the infrastructure on which they are raised. To keep profit margins high—say, in sunny times—it is not in their interest to help the farmers grow or maintain their supply of chicks. Given the integration of vaccine manufacturing, including vaccines and pharmaceuticals for humans, you can imagine the theories that circulate over evening pegs about chicken flu and other such economic avian disasters.[7] All told, it is a volatile business that breeds great unhappiness, man and bird alike.

Day-old chicks arrive at a farm not literally as day-old chicks, but somewhere between four days and twenty weeks old. They arrive in cardboard boxes. Though they are caged on arrival, they are often too small to be contained by the bars and end up pooling across the shed floor, yellow balls of energetic, hungry fur. When they are between three and five months they are debeaked with a guillotine, moved to another shed, and termed "growers," with nothing to do but, of course, grow. It is at about six months that the bird becomes a layer, the climax of her working life, and is expected to yield one egg every twenty-five hours. I don't need to describe these conditions: they live

---

Kuroiler: see Kapur, "Pioneering Micro-entrepreneurship through Poultry Breeding and Distribution in Rural India." For more on the history of chickens and chicken in India, see Staples, *Sacred Cows and Chicken Manchurian*, esp. chap. 5.

7 For these zoonotic dynamics in China, see Keck, *Avian Reservoirs*. In the context of the coronavirus pandemic in India, see Barua, "Virtual Virulence and Metabolic Life." The rumors of contagion Barua discusses were generated by online trolls for vast uptake rather than, in the cases to which I refer, privately by farmers themselves.

a life of perpetual darkness. And when their time should be over, just before they have laid their last egg, they are "force molted," which means they are starved until their feathers fall out and they regenerate internally, offering yet another cycle. This is usually done twice, and now she is finally worked dry. I am reminded of a line in the film *Fire*: "Sorry, madam, no eggs."[8] In *Fire* her barrenness condemns her to a lesbian existence. In Barwala, it condemns her to slaughter. There is an argument to be made that both outcomes are preferable to those that attained to her useful, fertile state.

We arrived in Panipat, Haryana, late that same morning. The ultramodern Skylark slaughterhouse, and others like it, is the product of a recent history that began with the ninth Five-Year Plan (1997–2002) and the drive to intensify the poultry industry, thanks in part to investment from American corporations that saw in poultry a "secular meat."[9] Likewise, in this modernization of poultry, which was at the same time a secularization of meat, ultramodern plants such as Skylark's pitted themselves directly against the long-standing *mandi* (live market) system, largely operated by Muslim brokers, which took a rough measure of the animals in market by dawn, and of the people arriving to buy them, and set a rate. This system began losing hold with the advent of mobile phones and the ability of farmers to communicate directly with buyers—often the multinational conglomerates themselves—untied to the rate set by the *mandis*.[10] The modernizers say they are not only more fair but more hygienic than the live markets and are what the Indian consumer will grow to want. And despite their openly anti-Islamic rhetoric, the "ultramodern" slaughter facilities make a show of being halal. But because a facility like the

---

8   Deepa Mehta, dir., *Fire* (Trial by Fire Films, Kaleidoscope Entertainment, Noida, India 1998).

9   There have been twelve Five-Year Plans, a Soviet legacy implemented in India by Nehru, beginning in 1951 and ending in 2017. To give a rough sense of some of their agricultural priorities: the Second Plan (1956–61) advocated for the efficient use of cow dung for sustainable agriculture; the Third Plan (1961–66) prioritized the import of foreign cows, helping to spark Kurien's White Revolution; the Ninth Plan (1967–2002) focused on intensification of the poultry industry; the Tenth Plan (2002–7) and Eleventh Plan (2007–12) sought to liberalize meat export (the Eleventh Plan also advocated a return to "backyard poultry" in response to the rural impoverishment wrought by the preceding plans); and the final plan, the Twelfth Plan (2012–17), again sought to accelerate and intensify poultry rearing and poultry consumption.

10   The farmers' protests of 2020 and 2021 were sparked by just these dynamics and the Modi administration's pivot toward an ostensibly freer market but that, in reality, resulted in a privatized agricultural system devoid of subsidies and other protections.

one in Panipat slaughters a thousand animals per hour, which is simply too fast for the recitation of anything, they say *kalma* only with the first bird of the day and the last, assuming comprehensive coverage for the ones who fall between. Someone from Halal India observes every day, in every such industrialized facility, the faithful execution of this compromise.

Remaining on the right side of this agreement is important to companies such as Skylark, not only to appeal to Muslim consumers in an otherwise meat-uneven country (about which more later), but to appeal to the most coveted consumer bloc in the country: HoReCa, or hotels, restaurants, and caterers. HoReCa includes everything from Domino's Pizza to the Michelin star restaurants in India's five-star hotels. HoReCa is where fancy and *firang* meet, creating unique—variously tasteless, tasty, and tasteful—amalgamations of taste.

Fast Times

Colonel Sanders came to India in June 1995. The first KFC franchise was launched in Bangalore amid the many shops and pubs of Brigade Road. Despite its promising landing location, KFC's Bangalore opening was contested by protestors and shut down on the grounds of using too much monosodium glutamate, and then, after reopening, operated for months under police protection. KFC planned a simultaneous launch in Delhi on June 1, 1995, but papers variously credited and blamed Maneka Gandhi for keeping that from happening. This was not, however, a concerted campaign by the BJP. In 1995, the BJP was shaping itself toward a promising electoral showing in the 1996 elections, ahead of its eventual 1998 victory. The right-wing Rashtriya Swayamsevak Sangh (RSS) had aligned with international animal rights groups to keep KFC out of India, but it was, as usual, far ahead of the BJP in terms of cultural fanaticism. In Parliament, it was Congress that was most vociferous about keeping fast meat out of India, while the BJP was establishing itself as a friend to multinational corporations. In a debate about KFC in the Lok Sabha, Member of Parliament Jaipal Reddy of the Congress Party shouted, "When tandoori chicken is far superior, why are imported tastes being rammed down the throat of the nation?"[11] Meanwhile, right-winger L. K. Advani capitalized on the economic foot-dragging of these socialist tandoori nationalists and suggested that, once in power, the BJP would scrap the Environment Ministry

11 "Waiting for Pizza Huts in Kalahandi."

altogether, as it was preventing multinationals such as Brands, Inc.—the parent of KFC—from implementing plans and making India rich. All of this, as astute journalists noted, was coterminous with an embarrassing alliance between the BJP and the scandal-plagued America conglomerate Enron, in which the party claimed in its defense that *"swadeshi* (self-rule) meant learning to deal with multinationals, not avoiding them."[12] (It should come as no surprise—except to those who somehow take the BJP's rhetoric about vegetarianism as sincere—that once in power, the BJP reintroduced subsidies to export-based abattoirs.)

Swadeshi and its discursive underbelly, compromised virility, were often invoked in the KFC debates. The conservative south Indian journalist K. Govindan Kutty wrote in an anti-Gandhi (Mahatma, not Maneka), pro-KFC editorial that, "by and large, people like to emulate a robust conqueror, not a famished sage."[13] He lamented the influence of vegetarianism on the RSS, dredging up historical evidence for Krishna's passion for deer meat.[14] Likewise, Indian youth were salivating for the taste of elsewhere. A twenty-year-old named Chandrashekhar, otherwise a vegetarian, was interviewed by the *Indian Express* outside of a KFC. "This is only the second time in my life that I have had chicken and I really relished it," he said. "It isn't every day that you get an international product in India, and I think the government is being very unfair."[15]

There is a saying in Hyderabadi Hindi: *Gar ki murgi, dal barabar.* It means that chicken cooked at home might as well be a bowl of lentils. The very point of chicken is that it represents the outdoors, an elsewhere: adventure, novelty, enjoyment of a different and possibly dangerous order.[16] It is not the meat itself that is pleasurable—for if cooked at home and alimented with neither excitement nor taboo, it is no better, alas, than legumes—but what it repre-

---

12 "BJP Ties Itself in Knots over Enron, KFC."

13 "Setting Menu for People."

14 "Setting Menu for People."

15 "Curiosity Keeps Customers Chewing on Chicken." Chandrashekhar exemplifies Parama Roy's argument about the "turn away from the aversions, scarcity, and ascetic habits of the colonial past and postcolonial present in favor of a metaphorics of abundance": Roy, *Alimentary Tracts,* 7. Chandrashekhar and his friends also embody what Parvis Ghassem-Fachandi has called *"enjoi,"* which is the pleasure in privileged vice such as that seen in upper-caste Hindus at Muslim meat stands late at night: Ghassem-Fachandi, "Ahimsa, Identification, and Sacrifice in the Gujarat Pogrom," 26.

16 On appetite and "longing for an elsewhere," see Roy, *Alimentary Tracts,* 4.

sents psychically: chicken is a mistress; chicken is enjoyment in the carnal consumption of the other. In a simpler way than Derrida could ever put it, *Gar ki murgi, dal barabar* argues that meat is not simply meat but *jouissance* itself—and we know the murderous envy that the enjoyment of others, enjoying the pleasure of the Other, incites in carnal mobs.[17]

Organizations dedicated to meat production in India have attempted to spread the enjoyment of meat across the land, regardless of caste or creed. And they find promise in poultry and egg, particularly, to avoid the violent national contests over beef: chickens provide a "secular meat" for a nonsecular land. Nitin and I met with Anil Sahni during our days in Barwala. Sahni is what is known as a "further processer," who produces sausage and kebabs, and other ready-to-heat-and-eat foods. To enter his facility, as at Skylark, we had to first walk through an antiseptic moat, then cover our shoes with disposable booties and the rest of us with lab coats and hairnets. I've been a vegan for more than twenty years, and Sahni's sausage facility smelled *delicious*. Everywhere were crates of coriander, carrots, chilis, and fat red tomatoes. Sahni and others in the business are marketing cleanliness and purity to a desired urban consumer: sausage is a health food; eggs are vegetarian because the chickens are.

Sitting in his spotless office in his spotless lab coat, Sahni told us that his objective is to see meat become an "ideal food" in India. I asked him what that meant. It means, he said, *chaahiye hi chaahiye*: you *have* to have it. He shook his hands, as if he were desperately anxious, to indicate an addict's yen. Meat has yet to become *chaahiye hi chaahiye* in India. He doesn't consider fish meat but uses the centrality of fish in West Bengal and Kerala as the *chaahiye hi chaahiye* he seeks to spread.[18] Another employee was listening and explained the problem this way: "There are two hundred days out of a year in which a Hindu or Sikh won't eat meat for one god or another." He continued:

No meat on Tuesday.
No meat on Thursday.
No meat on Navratri.

17 On Lacan, extimacy, and racism as hatred of the *jouissance* of the other, see Miller, "Extimity." On the Hindu right and Lacan, see also Sharma, "The Politics of Hindu-tva and Its Erotic Charge," which draws on the psychoanalytic analysis of Hindutva in Hansen, *The Saffron Wave*. The Derridean concept I'm alluding to is carnophal-logocentrism (the conceptual relation of carnivory and phallocratic power) in Derrida, "'Eating Well,' or the Calculation of the Subject."

18 Though on the rise of middle-class vegetarianism, particularly among women, in urban Bengal, see Donner, "New Vegetarianism."

No meat on Diwali.
No meat during Durga Puja.
No meat on Holi.

"Holy shit," I said. (Sahni had revealed himself to be someone who enjoys bad jokes.) He laughed. "It *is* shit. The domestic market is *holy shit*." There is hope, though. He said that one of the biggest days for meat consumption in India is the day that Navratri ends. "Three *times* the usual Saturday consumption. Check out the queue at a KFC on the day Navratri ends." Shaking his hands again, in that addict's way, he smiled: "*Chaahiye hi chaahiye.*"

CHAAHIYE HI CHAAHIYE

The ultramodern Skylark plant is one of the places in which this demand is met. The first truck of many arrived shortly after we did. A couple of workers in green jumpsuits began reaching into cages to pull out birds that had died during the journey, tossing them into a discard pile, one not yet fully dead but jerking around in the sun. There was a small boy there whom I had seen earlier on the road on a bicycle steered by his father. The boy jaunted, looking through the discard pile for a bird to play with. He found one—one of the ones that was not quite dead yet—took it to the unloading platform and began playing a game of catch with someone I could not see on the other side of the truck. Occasionally the boy would miss; the bird would fall; and the boy would stomp on it and scream at it and then, laughingly, throw it back again.[19]

The boy knew he was playing with something that had once been alive, and that was part of the pleasure and part of the defiance I saw in the eyes of the men who watched me watching him. Yet they couldn't have known that now I—caught bare and ashamed in this economy of totalizing gazes—had stopped thinking of these birds as being alive, as sharing anything with me other than participation in a relationship of power in which they were the losers and, my

---

19 In an earlier version of this story, I referred to the boy's actions as a kind of cruelty, even if in the context of panspecies pleasure in play: see Singh and Davé, "On the Killing and Killability of Animals." Shortly after, I read Milan Kundera's *The Book of Laughter and Forgetting,* in which he describes children rounding on a woman, Tamina, in a manner he likens to capturing and killing a calf: "If anyone is full of bitterness and hate, it is Tamina, not the children. Their desire to cause pain is positive, exuberant: it has every right to be called pleasure. Their only motive for causing pain to someone not of their world is to glorify that world and its law." But maybe this is an overly dark view of children, not to mention of women and calves: Kundera, *The Book of Laughter and Forgetting,* 185.

god, how. In this scene, their fate appeared even to me as having been always inevitable. They were weak little creatures squawking in cages and shitting all over each other and in no more than a few minutes, right after someone in a white lab coat gave a signal to a man in a green jumpsuit, the birds would be taken from the truck and thrown into milk crates and then carried inside and hung upside down by their feet and sent into a stunning machine from which they would come out like stiff little meaty stones with necks hanging off of them, necks whose vein would be cut by a woman with alarming regularity and with no regard for the blood splattering all over her as the birds morphed from stiff little meaty stones to flapping squawking art objects with bright red blood spurting from their necks and performing gymnastic feats in a failed attempt to free themselves from this endless ride.

Their ride began, in a sense, in 1967 when a man named Vinod Kapur founded Keggs Farms and made India the first developing country in the world to create its own parent stock of layer hen. The government of India began promoting egg production in the early 1960s (this was just before the advent of broilers), in the name of boosting the rural economy, but had to import parent stock from Canada and the United States, limiting both autonomy and productivity. I met Kapur in 2013 at Keggs Farms, which is on the Delhi-Gurgaon Highway, now a teeming, chaotic road with factories and hotels and malls but that had, as its very first shop back in 1968, a single tea stall to serve the workers on Kapur's farm. When he walked into his office where I sat waiting, he did so with the loose-limbed ease of someone rich, happy, and good-looking. He sat down in his leather chair and actually stroked his chin as he told me the story of buying germplasm from the United States and creating a line called the Keystone Golden that was all India's and perfectly produced for the Indian climate. He pointed at me with drama and said that where I sat (where he struck that deal with the Americans) "was the birthplace of modern India."

It was the birthplace of something new indeed. India has since become the third largest producer of eggs in the world.[20] India's behemoth poultry conglomerate, Venky's, started when its founder, B. V. Rao, competed with Kapur and bought its own pure line. The layer Rao produced had an advantage over Kapur's, which was that it was smaller and so more of them could be crammed into a single cage. We know how this story turns out: farms consolidated; battery cage systems proliferated; rural people became priced out of a product

20 See "Top Five Egg-Producing Countries."

geared increasingly to urban consumers; and Kapur took his fat birds and made a pretty fortune selling "cage-free eggs" at Nature's Basket, which is run by Godrej, itself a major integrator.[21] I give Kapur credit: his farm is a beautiful place, and the hens seem better off even than the ones who would get efficiently thumped in Nagaland. What happens when they're spent? I asked a staff person who was showing me around. They live a nice life here, he said. And then, more for himself, I think, than me: "Everything has to die."

Everything Has to Die

There are so many kinds of time in the time of the chicken, and all they tell us is that we're not really sure what it is to die, and *whether* things die, and we are not really sure what it is to live. A heart keeps beating outside a body with a decapitated, chirping head, its innards pulled out to please a guest who does not want it but is living off of it right now. Nitin does not want any of this, but the life course demands sacrifice, so he will pick up his pinging phone and deliver virility to the Armed Forces. The time of the nation is the time of replication, with the pure line that is the same all the way down, breeding cycles of chicken feet and fish heads, poverty and growth. *Everything has to die.* It is the very basis of our understanding of time, but is it even true? The birds on the truck in front of the Skylark plant: they were loathsome to me in that instant because they had lost the dignity of dying; from that point on, they could only be killed. Someone said to me once, during a conversation about the effects of agriculture's intensification, that "animals don't *die* in villages anymore." What she—Sagari Ramdas—meant is that in the tense of development, we don't have time for the abject to die.[22]

Rakesh Bhardwaj, the editor and founder of *Poultry Express*, agrees. He picked me up one afternoon from the Vishya Vidyalaya metro stop in Delhi. His car was outfitted like a race car, and he was listening to Jagjit Singh. He asked me about my research, and I told him I was interested in animal activism and, particularly then, action against the rise of factory farms. He laughed at me, even though he was otherwise a sweet man. "Poultry alone is a *64 crore rupee industry! 64 crore*! What do these people think they can do? And imagine: it's a 64 crore rupee industry even though people only eat meat three times per

---

21 Although nearly 70 percent of India's population is rural, 75–80 percent of eggs and poultry are consumed by Indians living in urban areas: see Datta, "The Chicken and Egg Question."

22 See Ramdas, "Reclaiming Endangered Livelihoods."

week—Tuesday no meat, Thursday no meat, this festival, this festival. Imagine how big it will be when we breach that."

Bhardwaj began his career as a journalist, covering politics in Haryana. He became interested in animal welfare issues and quit his job with the *Tribune*, starting his own newsletter called *The Truth about Animals*. His first call after quitting his day job was to Maneka Gandhi, who had a popular television show, *Heads and Tails*, and a newspaper column of the same name. They corresponded, but he became disenchanted with her as he learned more about the meat industry and how rapidly it was growing around them. Gandhi was ignoring all of this, focusing on dogs and cats and animal shelters: "Only doing eyewash," as Bhardwaj put it. So in 2004, he got into livestock journalism, out of awed curiosity for this world-conquering industry, and three years later founded *Poultry Express*.

I told Bhardwaj that I had just returned from Hyderabad, where I worked with cage-free farming activists who, like Nitin before he returned to Skylark, were going from farm to farm, trying to convince farmers that cage-free egg rearing would ultimately be more profitable, appealing to wealthy urban consumers and the restaurant business, and freeing them from the integrators. Bhardwaj shook his head: "What are these cage-free people trying to accomplish? If it's a cage-free chicken, it's going to get slaughtered. If it's a cage chicken, it's going to get slaughtered. And these people are doing nothing to slow demand for eggs. They are saying, 'Eat eggs, eat eggs, but only cage-free eggs.' But cage-free or not cage-free, all these chickens will die." I said it was important to try to alleviate suffering. He had once been an animal welfare activist, so surely he understood their point. He sighed. You've been to Delhi and Mumbai, he said:

> You've seen how people live one on top of the other. The population is only increasing, and every year we eat more meat. Before broilers came to India, we consumed zero kilograms of poultry. Now? We're fifth in the world. And you want to put chickens on the ground while we need to grow them up and while humans are living more and more one on top of the other? Maybe in US or Canada, where they have more land and have more future. But here, we live until seventy if we're lucky, so who cares? Here, we make money now, show off now, and don't worry about later because there is no later.

His father, though, lived until he was ninety. He was pure veg, Bhardwaj told me, "never even touched an egg."

An Old Man, Alone

The late Professor N. S. Ramaswamy was known, both affectionately and with some lighthearted fun, as Cartman Ramaswamy. CARTMAN was his creation—the Centre for Action, Research, and Technology for Man, Animal, and Nature—which, not incidentally, designed technologically forward bullock carts to be given away or sold at low prices to farmers so that bullocks could be made useful and, through that usefulness, allowed to live. One of the effects of India's White Revolution—which shares much with India's Pink Revolution, as meat modernization is known—is that cows, once a multipurpose animal as chickens were, became single-purpose machines through crossbreeding and through the economic emphasis on milk production. Male calves had little use in this economy and were starved or sent to slaughter, as even their dung became less felicitous with crossbreeding, as did their once prodigious humps for ploughing.[23] John Deere, a driver of the Green Revolution (so many food revolutions!) integrated tractors into Indian agriculture, which further pushed the bullock into the animal purgatory of uselessness. Ramaswamy's carts were a hopeful attempt to save them, to give them purpose, so they could live a dignified life in the fields and then die a dignified death.

Ramaswamy understands two things well: that everything has to die and that the slaughter of animals for food is a reality that no one, not even he, will ever curtail. Slaughter is a juggernaut, against which the pneumatic wheels of his compassionately designed bullock carts stood no chance. And yet, still. "Death without pain—that does not trouble me," he said to me on one of the many occasions we met. He had taken late in life to speaking into a tape recorder, which his wife would bring to him, with extra batteries, at the start of his meetings. "Death without pain does not trouble me. Needless suffering is what keeps me from resting at night." Like all of the animalists I know, Ramaswamy didn't rest much anyway. To experience the suffering of animals firsthand, he would walk alongside those destined for slaughter, sometimes two hundred kilometers at a time.

Professor Ramaswamy was appointed chairman of the Animal Welfare Board of India (AWBI) in 1989. It was a radical choice. His chairmanship was

23 One thing that both cow farmers and cow protectionists, normally at violent odds, agree on is the lesser ritual and everyday felicitousness of the hybrid cow: see Govindrajan, *Animal Intimacies*, chap. 3; Vasu, "Dung Is Gold Mine."

announced in an issue of the AWBI's magazine, *Animal Citizen*, under the heading, "New Directions":

> Prof. NS Ramaswamy has brought an additional dimension to the animal welfare movement. While he concedes that sentiment and kindness to animals should form the basis for animal welfare, real suffering of animals could be reduced only by upgrading the work animal system (ploughing, carting, and the meat system). Though he is a vegetarian, and has been championing the cause of vegetarianism, he had been the Chairman of two committees—Committee for the Development of the Meat Industry and also the Committee on Meat Research, both appointed by the Government of India. The objectives of these committees are to upgrade the meat sector, which will lead to reduced suffering to animals.[24]

This was not received well. Ramaswamy had a three-pronged plan to reduce suffering, and none of them made vegetarians, Jains, and Hindus in the organization (which is to say, virtually the entire organization) happy. One was to build rural abattoirs to prevent the long marches to slaughter that he had witnessed. For the unsentimental he had an economic argument, which is that animal wealth is rural wealth, and slaughtering animals in cities, to feed city people, steals from the poor and benefits the rich. Rural abattoirs would, by his calculations, increase rural wealth by 20 to 30 crores per annum.[25]

The second prong of Ramaswamy's plan was to introduce stunning to anesthetize animals, using a captive bolt system, or electric shock, a method that has become commonplace in Western countries.[26] He was given a stun gun by foreign friends and went from abattoir to abattoir, government office to government office, trying to convince anyone who would listen that it was compatible with halal; modern; efficient. This was linked to his third objective, which was to modernize slaughter in India, top to bottom.

---

24 *Animal Citizen*, vol. 26, no. 2, 1989.

25 Professor Ramaswamy's plan was laid out in the seventy-five-page "Report of the Expert Committee on the Development of the Meat Industry," which was submitted to the Ministry of Agriculture in 1987. Ramaswamy was chair of the twelve-person committee.

26 Ramaswamy was following in the pragmatic tradition of the first chairperson of the AWBI, Rukmini Devi Arundale, who, as I mentioned in chapter 2, accepted foreign gifts of captive bolt guns and other tools that she believed would reduce animal suffering.

Maneka Gandhi was appointed Union Minister of Environment and Forests when the Janata Dal briefly ascended in 1989, and among her first acts was to force Ramaswamy to resign. He did—he says Gandhi threatened his life ("A vicious lady, not a cultured lady")—and most members of the AWBI cheered his ouster. India's eighth Five-Year Plan (1992–97) was being drafted, and the last thing the AWBI wanted was someone from within advocating for the modernization of slaughter.[27] But slaughter is a juggernaut, and it happened anyway—just not how Ramaswamy would have wanted.

Ramaswamy was a beloved man, the CARTMAN office on the top floor of his Bangalore bungalow always full of people, others devoted to his pragmatic, compassionate, active ways. But he considered himself a failure: *I've had no success in my life at all; I'm old and sad and was never able to accomplish; I'm alone, and have no one to help me.* Professor N. S. Cartman Ramaswamy died, at age eighty-six, in September 2012. He once had a heart attack in a slaughterhouse. He did not have a *kamzoor* heart.

HOGA HI HOGA

In Varanasi in February 2013, I made the acquaintance of a man I'll call MKS. MKS is a high-caste vegetarian, mafia don, and pig transporter. When he worked for Indian Railways, he noticed the growing traffic in pigs transported from Agra to the northeast, where pork is consumed by a largely Christian population, but where the ideal agricultural conditions are lacking to grow pigs locally.[28] The middlemen, MKS told me, were mostly from backward caste communities and had less influence with the dominant-caste strongmen on both sides of the route. Payments were often missed, and the efficiency of the entire operation steadily sank. MKS overthrew the middlemen and, with his status, government railway connections, unspeakable charisma, and imposing physique, became a force in the lucrative transport business. (He took a bullet through the head from a gang of truck transporters, who were increasingly shut out of the trade.)

MKS is a man of contradiction, and while he was telling me about his brush with death we were on the road to visit a favorite place of his, the Buddhist pilgrimage site of Sarnath. We sat on a bench, yards away from the Dhamek Stupa, where the Buddha gave his first sermon after attaining enlightenment.

---

27 *Animal Citizen*, vol. 27, no. 3, 1990.
28 Pig rearing usually corresponds locally to the growth of sugarcane and thus is most common in states such as Uttar Pradesh (where MKS is based) and, to the south, in Maharashtra.

What is the point of animal activism? he asked me. To reduce or end the exploitation and suffering of animals, I suggested. Let me tell you what the activists do, he said, calling them, as he liked to do, the *laptopwala*. They come around, interfering with my business, trying to pass laws to ban our trade or to reduce the number of pigs in each train car or truck, telling us how much to feed them and what size the crates must be.[29] But do you know what the transporters do when the activists make our business impossible? Harass the train transporters, the transporters will use trucks. Ban the trucks, the transporters will break the limbs of animals and stack them into vans, even into cars. You've seen for yourself. The *laptopwala* live in a dream world, he said. In the real world, the demand to eat and kill and transport animals will always be there. *Ye sab hoga hi hoga*, he said. This will be. No matter what.

No Matter What

MKS liked to say that everything he had, he had built with his own hands. He had mattered forth a world—a world of pigs and bullets and sons and enlightenment, a world of pride and god and fortune. To build something, we must lose something, also. Making requires loss. He said this to me in the context of his relationship with his youngest son, who was very formal with him, almost afraid. This was the outcome of his absences, as MKS mattered forth his world.

There is so much building and so much loss in the modern time of the animal. Kapur's farms and Skylark's plants, Nitin's family and Sunil's business, economies and armies, hearts and beaks, wants and needs, time and its other. But is there an otherwise to the time of the chicken? *Yeh sab hoga hi hoga aur ye sab chaahiye hi chaahiye*. We are all pessimists now. Or is it optimism in fact? Either way, we are faced with the inevitable and the question is, does it matter? The answers are legion. What is the "it?" What is "matter" anyhow?

MKS said, *Everything I built, I built with my own hands. When that is the case, there is no shame in losing.* Professor Ramaswamy knew two things—no, one thing—well: that everything has to die. And yet he built his carts with pneumatic tires, a failure till the end.

29 MKS won a Supreme Court case against Maneka Gandhi in 2005. As environment minister in 2001, she had passed an order to halt all pig transport by rail. MKS argued that the government had offered no viable alternative, and won. But according to a more recent directive, the AWBI Transport of Animals (Amendment) Rules of 2009 (http://www.awbi.in/policy_acts_rules.html), MKS could transport no more than 104 pigs in each train car.

Jonathan Franzen—the cranky novelist who loves birds—makes a distinction between what he calls "eschatological time" and "Franciscan time."[30] The first is the time of the chicken: that which, like the climate catastrophe of which it is a part, cannot be grasped, cannot be halted. The second, too, is the time of the chicken: that thing before us, in an altered frame, that is not bound for anything, not in this situation now. He calls on us to "eschew eschatological time" for Franciscan—to respond, like Saint Francis, to what is before us—but there is no need for eschewal. Eyes wide open, like the chicken at its end, the pessimists confront what has always been true: Blackness as the other to whiteness, animal the other to Man. And find within that truth an ethics of "affectability," a "radical passivity" toward the future, a "properly decided, freely chosen passivity toward the social structure."[31] Does that which is inevitable cease to matter? Not in this, the time of the chicken.

30 Franzen, *The End of the End of the Earth*. This is different from Dipesh Chakrabarty's distinction in "Anthropocene Time" between Earth history and world history, or geological time and human historical time, in that neither are particularly Franciscan.

31 Sexton and Barber, "On Black Negativity, or the Affirmation of Nothing."

ACKNOWLEDGMENTS

INTRODUCTION

Thank you to the students in my winter 2021 graduate seminar, "Friendship," for conversations on opacity & relationality; Janine, whoever and wherever you are; my folks; the University of Chicago Patiencies & Passivities workshop, especially my discussant, Lisa Stevenson; and Bradley Dunseith, Celeste Pang, Julietta Singh, Muhammad Kavesh, Ned Dostaler, Noha Fikry, Parama Roy, Rachel Giese, Ridhima Sharma, Sophia Jaworski, Waqas Butt, and Wesley Brunson.

1. WITNESS

Thank you to the Abrams-Myers family, Amira Mittermaier, Anne Allison, Camellia Satija, Chandan Gowda, Christian Novetzke, George Mantzios, João Biehl, Joshua Barker, Kathryn Gillespie, Maneka Gandhi, María Elena García, Muhammad Kavesh, Ritu Birla, the University of British Columbia & University of Washington South Asia joint meeting, University of Washington Anthropology, and York University Anthropology.

2. BIOGRAPHY

Thank you to Alok Gupta, Chinny Krishna, Choudhary at the AWBI, the Codyraman family in Chennai (especially Frank Cody & Bhavani Raman), Columbia University's Institute for Religion, Culture and Public Life, Gayle Rubin, Geeta Seshamani, Leela Samson, Maura Finkelstein, Parama Roy, Ponni Arasu & family, Rajbir Singh Judge, Shakthi Nataraj, Suparna Ganguly, Vinod Kumar, William Mazzarella (for inspiring the title), and Yamini Narayanan.

3. CONTRADICTION

Thank you to Alex Dawson, Amira Mittermaier, Andrea Muehlebach, Aniruddhan Vasudevan, Atreyee Majumder, Bharat Venkat, Brian Price, Bruce Grant, Christian Novetzke, Columbia University Anthropology, Eduardo Kohn, Elizabeth Povinelli, João Biehl, Kajri Jain, Katie Kilroy-Marac, Nayanika Mathur, Ned Dostaler, the New School Anthropology, Oxford University Vegan Studies, Princeton University Anthropology, Reni Chang, Rice University Anthropology & Animal Studies, Samuel Peter Maull, Sara Salih, Sunila Kale, University of California, Berkeley, Anthropology, University of Michigan Anthropology, University of Texas, Austin, Anthropology, Veena Das, William Mazzarella, Yale University South Asia Studies, and Zoë Wool.

4. SOUND

Thank you to Jacob Bessen, Jayasimha Nuggehali, Julietta Singh, Kajri Jain, Kamala at Animal Aid, Muhammad Kavesh, Parama Roy, Rice University Anthropology, S. S. Chauhan, University of Zurich Anthropology, and Wesley Brunson.

5. WALK

Thank you to Abodh Aras, Dipesh, IRB (the person, not the review board), Lesley Esteves, and Muhammad Kavesh.

6. TOUCH

Thank you to Abodh Aras, Abou Farman, Akhil Gupta, Anand Pandian, Angela Garcia, Bharat Venkat, Christian Novetzke, Dipesh, Kajri Jain, Lisa Stevenson, Michael M.J. Fischer, Tyler Zoanni, University of California, Los Angeles, South Asia Center, University of Chicago Anthropology, Vijayanka Nair, and Zoë Wool.

7. SEX

Thank you to Abodh Aras, Alex Blanchette, Alok Gupta, Cassie Adcock, Elliott Tilleczek, Gabriel Rosenberg, Jaya Sharma, Jayasimha Nuggehali, Krithika Srinivasan, Laura Murray, Muhammad Kavesh, Radhika Govindrajan, Rajesh Kasturirangan, Savitri, and Yamini Narayanan.

8. APPETITE

Thank you to Anand Vivek Taneja, Bharat Venkat, Bhrigupati Singh, Columbia University's Institute for Religion, Culture and Public Life, Jayasimha Nuggehali, Julietta Singh, Mayanthi Fernando, Meghna Mehtta, Nandini Thiyagarajan, Nitin Goel, Parama Roy, Rachel Giese, Rajbir Singh Judge, Sandhya Shetty, Sumit Guha, Sunila Kale & Uzma Rizvi, and William Mazzarella.

I EXTEND AN overall thanks to Jaya Sharma, who has been my home in India for so many years. With this book I offer my gratitude and express my respect to the nonhuman persons who have worked with me, lived with me, and taught me. This research was made possible by a Social Sciences and Humanities Standard Research Grant, a fellowship awarded by the Jackman Humanities Institute, and my position at the University of Toronto. At Duke University Press, I am lucky to work with Gisela Fosado, brilliant, warm, and full of belief and vision in equal measure. My thanks, too, to the rest of the team at Duke University Press, particularly Alejandra Mejía, Courtney Richardson, and Ihsan Taylor. My thanks to Susan Deeks for the copyediting, and to Sharon Rodgers for the index. Thank you to Dhruvi Acharya for again permitting me to use her artwork on the cover of my book. To my extraordinary readers, Julietta Singh and Parama Roy—I cannot thank you enough for all your insights and inspiration, for the abundance and generosity of your thought. Finally, to Rachel Giese, who entered my life just as this book was beginning to leave mine: thank you for your care in reading me, your generosity in thinking with me, and most of all, for finding me.

This book is dedicated to the memory of my beloved friend, Wendy Coburn, who was never indifferent about anything, and so nor was I ever indifferent about her.

Adams, Carol J. *Animals and Women: Feminist Theoretical Explorations*. Durham, NC: Duke University Press, 1995.

Adams, Carol J. *The Sexual Politics of Meat: A Feminist-Vegetarian Critical Theory*. New York: Bloomsbury Academic, 2015.

Adarkar, Neera, ed. *The Chawls of Mumbai: Galleries of Life*. New Delhi: Imprint One, 2012.

Adcock, Cassie. "'Preserving and Improving the Breeds': Cow Protection's Animal-Husbandry Connection." *South Asia: Journal of South Asian Studies* 42, no. 6 (2019): 1141–55.

Adcock, Cassie, and Radhika Govindrajan. "Bovine Politics in South Asia: Rethinking Religion, Law and Ethics." *South Asia: Journal of South Asian Studies* 42, no. 6 (2019): 1095–1107.

Adonis. *Sufism and Surrealism*. Beirut: Saqi, 2013.

Agamben, Giorgio. *The Open: Man and Animal*. Translated by Kevin Attell. Stanford, CA: Stanford University Press, 2003.

Agarwal, Abhishek. "Desi Dogs: Everything about the Indian Pariah Dog Breed—DawgieBowl," n.d. Accessed April 15, 2021. https://dawgiebowl.com/blog/indian-pariah -dog-breed.

Ahmad, Zarin. *Delhi's Meatscapes: Muslim Butchers in a Transforming Mega City*. New York: Oxford University Press, 2018.

Ahmed, Sara. *The Cultural Politics of Emotion*. Edinburgh: Edinburgh University Press, 2014.

Ahmed, Sara. *Queer Phenomenology: Orientations, Objects, Others*. Durham, NC: Duke University Press, 2006.

Ahuja, Neel. "The Analogy of Race and Species in Animal Studies." *Prism: Theory and Modern Chinese Literature* 18, no. 1 (2021): 244–55.

Ahuja, Neel. "On Phooka." In *Meat! A Transnational Analysis,* edited by Sushmita Chatterjee and Banu Subramaniam, 213–40. Durham, NC: Duke University Press, 2021.

Alvares, Claude, *Another Revolution Fails: An Investigation into How and Why India's Operation Flood Project, Touted as the World's Largest Dairy Development Program, Funded by EEC, Went off the Rails*. Delhi: South Asia, 1985.

Ambedkar, Bhimrao R. *The Buddha and His Dhamma*. Chennai, India: MJP, 2019.

"Animal Crackers at Crawford Market." *Times of India*, March 28, 2003.

Arundale, Rukmini. "Vegetarianism Is a Way of Life." *Indian Vegetarian Congress Quarterly,* June 1978.

Bacchetta, Paola. "When the (Hindu) Nation Exiles Its Queers." *Social Text*, no. 61 (1999): 141–66.

Bargu, Banu. "The Silent Exception: Hunger Striking and Lip-Sewing." *Law, Culture and the Humanities* 1, no. 1 (2017): 1–28.

Bargu, Banu. *Starve and Immolate: The Politics of Human Weapons*. New York: Columbia University Press, 2016.

Barnes, Julian. *Love, Etc*. New York: Penguin, 2010.

Barthes, Roland. *The Grain of the Voice: Interviews 1962–1980*. Translated by Linda Coverdale. New York: Hill and Wang, 1986.

Barthes, Roland. *The Neutral: Lecture Course at the Collège de France*. Translated by Rosalind Krauss and Denis Hollier. New York: Columbia University Press, 2007.

Barua, Maan. "Virtual Virulence and Metabolic Life." *Society for Cultural Anthropology Online* (blog). April 17, 2020. https://culanth.org/fieldsights/virtual-virulence-and -metabolic-life.

Bateson, Gregory. "A Theory of Play and Fantasy." In *Steps to an Ecology of Mind: Collected Essays in Anthropology, Psychiatry, Evolution, and Epistemology*. Chicago: University of Chicago Press, 2000.

Baviskar, B. S., and Shanti George. "Development and Controversy: National Dairy Development Board." *Economic and Political Weekly* 23, no. 13 (1988): A35–43.

Beirne, Piers. "Peter Singer's 'Heavy Petting' and the Politics of Animal Sexual Assault." *Critical Criminology* 10:43–55, 2001.

Benjamin, Walter. *Reflections: Essays, Aphorisms, Autobiographical Writings*. Boston: Mariner, 2019.

Benjamin, Walter, and George Steiner. *The Origin of German Tragic Drama*. Translated by John Osborne. London: Verso, 2009.

Bennett, Joshua. *Being Property Once Myself: Blackness and the End of Man*. Cambridge, MA: Harvard University Press, 2020.

Berger, James. *The Disarticulate: Language, Disability, and the Narratives of Modernity*. New York: New York University Press, 2014.

Berlant, Lauren. "A Properly Political Concept of Love: Three Approaches in Ten Pages." *Cultural Anthropology* 26, no. 4 (2011): 683–91.

Bersani, Leo. *Is the Rectum a Grave? And Other Essays*. Chicago: University of Chicago Press, 2009.

Besant, Annie Wood. *Britain's Place in the Great Plan: Four Lectures Delivered in London, June and July 1921*. London: Theosophical Publishing House, 1921.

Bhalla, Shireen, and Abi T. Vanak. "Killing with Compassion: Why Feeding Dogs in Public Places Must Stop!" *Down to Earth*, July 2, 2020. https://www.downtoearth.org .in/blog/wildlife-biodiversity/killing-with-compassion-why-feeding-dogs-in-public -places-must-stop-72092.

Bhan, Mona, and Purnima Bose. "Canine Counterinsurgency in Indian-Occupied Kashmir." *Critique of Anthropology* 40, no. 3 (2020): 341–63.

"BJP Ties Itself in Knots over Enron, KFC." *Times of India*, November 13, 1995.

Bhaskaran, S. *Made in India: Decolonizations, Queer Sexualities, Trans/National Projects*. New York: Palgrave Macmillan, 2005.

Bhatji, Godse. *Maza Pravas*. Mumbai: Venus Prakashan, 1965.

Bhattacharya, Nabarun. *Upanyas Samagra*. Kolkata: Dey's, 2013.

Bhavani, Divya Kala. "'These Aren't Stray Dogs, They're Native Indian Dogs.'" *The Hindu*, March 21, 2019. https://www.thehindu.com/entertainment/movies/interview -filmmaker-jesse-alk-on-pariah-dog-documentary/article26599102.ece.

Bilchitz, David. "When Is Animal Suffering 'Necessary'?" *South African Public Law* 27 (2012): 3–27.

Blanchette, Alex. *Porkopolis: American Animality, Standardized Life, and the Factory Farm*. Durham, NC: Duke University Press, 2020.

Boggs, Colleen. *Animalia Americana: Animal Representations and Biopolitical Subjectivity*. New York: Columbia University Press, 2013.

Boisseron, Bénédicte. *Afro-Dog: Blackness and the Animal Question*. New York: Columbia University Press, 2018.

Brown, Michael, and Claire Rasmussen. "Bestiality and the Queering of the Human Animal." *Environment and Planning D: Society and Space* 28, no. 1 (2010): 158–77.

Büchner, Ludwig, and Annie Wood Besant. *Mind in Animals*. London: Freethought, 1880.

Buck-Morss, Susan. "Aesthetics and Anaesthetics." *Susan Buck-Morss* (blog). December 2015. http://susanbuckmorss.info/text/aesthetics-and-anaesthetics-part-ii.

Buck-Morss, Susan. *Dreamworld and Catastrophe: The Passing of Mass Utopia in East and West*. Cambridge, MA: MIT Press, 2002.

Bunch, Mary. "Posthuman Ethics and the Becoming Animal of Emmanuel Levinas." *Culture, Theory and Critique* 55, no. 1 (2014): 34–50.

Burgat, Florence. "Facing the Animal in Sartre and Levinas." *Yale French Studies*, no. 127 (2015): 172–89.

Burgat, Florence. "Non-violence towards Animals in the Thinking of Gandhi: The Problem of Animal Husbandry." *Journal of Agricultural and Environmental Ethics* 17, no. 3 (2004): 223–48.

Burton, Antoinette, and Renisa Mawani, eds. *Animalia: An Anti-imperial Bestiary for Our Times*. Durham, NC: Duke University Press, 2020.

Buscemi, Francesco. "Edible Lies: How Nazi Propaganda Represented Meat to Demonise the Jews." *Media, War, and Conflict* 9, no. 2 (2015): 180–97.

Buscemi, Francesco. *From Body Fuel to Universal Poison*. Cham, Switzerland: Springer International, 2018.

Buscemi, Francesco. "The Sin of Eating Meat: Fascism, Nazism and the Construction of Sacred Vegetarianism." In *Proteins, Pathologies and Politics: Dietary Innovation and Disease from the Nineteenth Century*, edited by David Gentilcore and Matthew Smith, 137–47. London: Bloomsbury Academic, 2018.

Butler, Judith. *Precarious Life: The Powers of Mourning and Violence*. New York: Verso, 2020.

Butler, Judith. "Response: Performative Reflections on Love and Commitment." *WSQ: Women's Studies Quarterly* 39, nos. 1–2 (2011): 236–39.

Caillois, Roger. "Mimicry and Legendary Psychasthenia." Translated by John Shepley. *October* 31 (1984): 17–32.

Calarco, Matthew. *Zoographies: The Question of the Animal from Heidegger to Derrida*. New York: Columbia University Press, 2008.

Candea, Matei. "'I Fell in Love with Carlos the Meerkat': Engagement and Detachment in Human-Animal Relations." *American Ethnologist* 37, no. 2 (2010): 241–58.

Chakrabarty, Dipesh. "Anthropocene Time." *History and Theory* 57, no. 1 (2018): 5–32.

Chakrabarty, Dipesh. *Provincializing Europe: Postcolonial Thought and Historical Difference.* Princeton, NJ: Princeton University Press, 2007.

Chapple, Christopher Key. *Jainism and Ecology: Nonviolence in the Web of Life.* Religions of the World and Ecology. Cambridge, MA: Harvard University Press, 2002.

Chatterjee, Sushmita. "Beefing Yoga: Meat, Corporeality, and Politics." In *Meat! A Transnational Analysis,* 96–120. Durham, NC: Duke University Press, 2021.

Chattopadhyay, Sarat Chandra. *The Drought and Other Stories.* New Delhi: Sahitya Akademi, 2014.

Chigateri, Shraddha. "'Glory to the Cow': Cultural Difference and Social Justice in the Food Hierarchy in India." *South Asia: Journal of South Asian Studies* 31, no. 1 (2008): 10–35.

Coetzee, J. M. *Disgrace.* London: Vintage, 2000.

Coetzee, J. M. *Elizabeth Costello.* New York: Viking, 2003.

Coetzee, J. M. *Life and Times of Michael K.* New York: Vintage, 2005.

Coetzee, J. M. *The Lives of Animals.* Edited by Amy Gutmann. Princeton, NJ: Princeton University Press, 2016.

Cohen, Lawrence. *No Aging in India: Alzheimer's, the Bad Family, and Other Modern Things.* Berkeley: University of California Press, 2000.

Cole, Stewart. "'Necessary Murder': Eating Meat against Fascism in Orwell and Auden." In *Literature and Meat since 1900,* edited by Seán McCorry and John Miller, 71–89. Cham, Switzerland: Springer International, 2019.

Cowan, Robert. *The Indo-German Identification: Reconciling South Asian Origins and European Destinies, 1765–1885.* Rochester, NY: Camden House, 2010.

"Curiosity Keeps Customers Chewing on Chicken." *Indian Express,* November 8, 1995.

Dalrymple, William. *City of Djinns: A Year in Delhi.* New York: Harper, 2011.

Das, Veena. *Life and Words: Violence and the Descent into the Ordinary.* Berkeley: University of California Press, 2006.

Das, Veena, Michael Jackson, Arthur Kleinman, and Bhrigupati Singh, eds. *The Ground Between: Anthropologists Engage Philosophy.* Durham, NC: Duke University Press, 2014.

Daston, Lorraine, and Gregg Mitman, eds. *Thinking with Animals: New Perspectives on Anthropomorphism.* New York: Columbia University Press, 2005.

Datta, Damayanti. "The Chicken and Egg Question." *Outlook Poshan* 2.0 (blog). July 16, 2019. https://poshan.outlookindia.com/story/poshan-news-the-chicken-and-egg-question/334312.

Davé, Naisargi N. "Afterword: For a Synaesthetics of Seeing." *Cambridge Journal of Anthropology* 39, no. 1 (2021): 143–49.

Davé, Naisargi N. "Indian and Lesbian and What Came Next: Affect, Commensuration, and Queer Emergences." *American Ethnologist* 38, no. 4 (2011): 650–65.

Davé, Naisargi N. "Kamadhenu's Last Stand: On Animal Refusal to Work." In *How Nature Works: Rethinking Labor on a Troubled Planet,* edited by Sarah Besky and Alex Blanchette, 211–24. Santa Fe: University of New Mexico Press, 2019.

Davé, Naisargi N. *Queer Activism in India: A Story in the Anthropology of Ethics.* Durham, NC: Duke University Press, 2012.

Davé, Naisargi N. "Something, Everything, Nothing; or, Cows, Dogs, and Maggots." *Social Text* 35, no. 1 (2017): 37–57.

De, Rohit. "Cows and Constitutionalism." *Modern Asian Studies* 53, no. 1 (2019): 240–77.

Deleuze, Gilles. *Difference and Repetition.* Translated by Paul Patton. New York: Columbia University Press, 1995.

Deleuze, Gilles. "The Exhausted." *SubStance* 24, no. 3 (1995): 3–28.

Deleuze, Gilles, and Félix Guattari. *A Thousand Plateaus: Capitalism and Schizophrenia* Minneapolis: University of Minnesota Press, 1987.

Deleuze, Gilles, and Claire Parnet. "Many Politics." In *Dialogues II*, 124–47. New York: Columbia University Press, 2002.

Derrida, Jacques. *The Animal That Therefore I Am.* Edited by Marie-Louis Mallet. Translated by David Wills. New York: Fordham University Press, 2008.

Derrida, Jacques. *The Beast and the Sovereign*, vol. 1. Chicago: University of Chicago Press, 2011.

Derrida, Jacques. "'Eating Well,' or the Calculation of the Subject." In *Who Comes after the Subject?* edited by Eduardo Cadava, Peter Connor, and Jean-Luc Nancy, 96–119. New York: Routledge, 1991.

Derrida, Jacques. *Of Hospitality.* Palo Alto, CA: Stanford University Press, 2000.

Descartes, René. *The Philosophical Writings of Descartes*, vols. 1–2. Edited by Whit Mason. Translated by John Cottingham, Robert Stoothoff, and Dugald Murdoch. Cambridge: Cambridge University Press, 1985.

Devi, Savitri. *And Time Rolls On: The Savitri Devi Interviews.* Edited by R. G. Fowler. San Francisco: Counter-Currents, 2012.

Devi, Savitri. *The Impeachment of Man.* Costa Mesa, CA: Noontide, 2008.

Devi, Savitri. *The Lightning and the Sun.* San Francisco: Counter-Currents, 2015.

Devi, Savitri. *Long-Whiskers and the Two-Legged Goddess, or The True Story of a "Most Objectionable Nazi" and . . . Half-a-Dozen Cats.* Reprint 3d. Raleigh, NC: Lulu.com, 2013.

Dhankar, Leena. "Haryana Police Arrest Two of the Eight Men Accused of Raping Pregnant Goat in Nuh." *Hindustan Times*, August 3, 2018. https://www.hindustantimes.com/india-news/haryana-police-arrest-two-of-the-8-men-accused-of-raping-pregnant-goat-in-nuh/story-WBpKwfKviqrldZuFm71UZN.html.

Diamond, Cora. "Losing Your Concepts." *Ethics* 98, no. 2 (1988): 255–77.

Didi-Huberman, Georges. "How to Open Your Eyes." In *Harun Farocki: Against What? Against Whom?*, edited by Antje Ehmann, Kodwo Eshun, and Nora M. Alter, 38–50. London: Koenig, 2009.

Doctor, Vikram. "Political Pets." *Times of India*, October 3, 2009. https://timesofindia.indiatimes.com/india/political-pets/articleshow/5083818.cms.

Doctor, Vikram. "Pomeranian Nation." *Economic Times* (blog). March 30, 2013. https://economictimes.indiatimes.com/blogs/onmyplate/pomeranian-nation.

Donner, Henrike. "New Vegetarianism: Food, Gender and Neo-liberal Regimes in Bengali Middle-Class Families." *South Asia: Journal of South Asian Studies* 31, no. 1 (2008): 143–69.

Douglas, Mary. *Purity and Danger.* New York: Routledge, 2002.

Douglass, Frederick. *My Bondage and My Freedom*. Edited by John David Smith. New York: Penguin Classics, 2003.

Dourish, Paul. "What We Talk about When We Talk about Context." *Personal and Ubiquitous Computing* 8, no. 1 (2004): 19–30.

Eck, Diana. *Darsan: Seeing the Divine Image in India*. New York: Columbia University Press, 1998.

Express News Service. "Two Arrested for Raping Cows at Vizianagaram Farm." *New Indian Express*, January 8, 2020. https://www.newindianexpress.com/states/andhra -pradesh/2020/jan/08/two-arrested-for-raping-cows-at-vnagaram-farm-2086702.html.

Farman, Abou. "Unlearning Pleasure." In *Shifter 24: Learning and Unlearning*, edited by Rit Premnath and Avi Alpert. Louisville, KY: Four Colour Print Group, 2019.

Federation of Indian Animal Protection Organizations and All Creatures Great and Small. "In Their Own Right: Calling for Parity in Law for Animal Victims of Crimes." Crimes against Animals Report. New Delhi, 2021.

Felski, Rita. *The Limits of Critique*. Chicago: University of Chicago Press, 2015.

Fernando, Mayanthi L. "Uncanny Ecologies: More-than-Natural, More-than-Human, More-than-Secular." *Comparative Studies of South Asia, Africa, and the Middle East* 42, no. 3 (December 2022): 568–83.

Ferro-Luzzi, Gabriella. *The Self-Milking Cow and the Bleeding Lingam: Motifs in Indian Temple Legends*. Wiesbaden: Otto Harassowitz, 1987.

Finkelstein, Maura. "Ghosts in the Gallery: The Vitality of Anachronism in a Mumbai Chawl." *Anthropological Quarterly* 91, no. 3 (2018): 937–68.

Forchtner, Bernhard, and Ana Tominc. "Kalashnikov and Cooking-Spoon: Neo-Nazism, Veganism and a Lifestyle Cooking Show on YouTube." *Food, Culture and Society* 20, no. 3 (2017): 415–41.

Foucault, Michel. *Ethics, Subjectivity and Truth: The Essential Works*, vol. 1. Edited by Paul Rabinow. Translated by R. Hurley. New York: Penguin, 1997.

Foucault, Michel, and Frédéric Gros. *"Discourse and Truth" and "Parrēsia."* Edited by Henri-Paul Fruchaud and Daniele Lorenzini. Translated by Nancy Luxon. Chicago: University of Chicago Press, 2019.

Franzen, Jonathan. *The End of the End of the Earth: Essays*. New York: Farrar, Straus and Giroux, 2018.

Frazer, Sir James George. *The Golden Bough: A Study of Magic and Religion*. Self-published, CreateSpace, 2018.

Gaard, Greta. "Toward a Feminist Postcolonial Milk Studies." *American Quarterly* 65, no. 3 (2013): 595–618.

Gandhi, Leela. *Affective Communities: Anticolonial Thought, Fin-de-Siècle Radicalism, and the Politics of Friendship*. Durham, NC: Duke University Press, 2006.

Gandhi, Maneka. "Foreword." In *Mad Dogs and an Englishwoman: The Memoirs of Crystal Rogers*, by Crystal Rogers, ix–xiii. New Delhi: Penguin, 2000.

Gandhi, Maneka. *Heads and Tails*. Goa: Other India Press, 2000.

Gandhi, Mohandas K. *The Collected Works of Mahatma Gandhi*. 98 vols. New Delhi: Publications Division, Ministry of Information and Broadcasting, Government of India, 1980.

Gandhi, Mohandas K. *The Story of My Experiments with Truth.* Translated by Mahadev Desai. Self-published, CreateSpace, 2016.

Gandhi, Mohandas K. *Views on Hindu Dharma.* Edited by Neerja Arun Gupta. New York: Routledge, 2017.

Ghassem-Fachandi, Parvis. "Ahimsa, Identification and Sacrifice in the Gujarat Pogrom." *Social Anthropology* 18, no. 2 (2010): 155–75.

Ghassem-Fachandi, Parvis. "The Hyperbolic Vegetarian: Notes on a Fragile Subject in Gujarat." In *Being There: The Fieldwork Encounter and the Making of Truth,* edited by John Borneman and Abdellah Hammoudi. Berkeley: University of California Press, 2009.

Ghosh, Sahana. "*Chor*, Police and Cattle: The Political Economies of Bovine Value in the India–Bangladesh Borderlands." *South Asia: Journal of South Asian Studies* 42, no. 6 (2019): 1108–24.

Ghosh, Shohini. *Fire: A Queer Film Classic.* New Delhi: Arsenal Pulp, 2010.

Gillespie, Kathryn. "Sexualized Violence and the Gendered Commodification of the Animal Body in Pacific Northwest US Dairy Production." *Gender, Place and Culture* 21, no. 10 (2014): 1321–37.

Gilroy, Paul. *Small Acts: Thoughts on the Politics of Black Cultures.* New York: Serpent's Tail, 1994.

Giraud, Eva Haifa. *What Comes after Entanglement?* Durham, NC: Duke University Press, 2019.

Glissant, Édouard. *Poetics of Relation.* Translated by Betsy Wing. Ann Arbor: University of Michigan Press, 1997.

Goodrick-Clarke, Nicholas. *Hitler's Priestess: Savitri Devi, the Hindu-Aryan Myth, and Neo-Nazism.* New York: New York University Press, 2000.

Goodrick-Clarke, Nicholas. *The Occult Roots of Nazism: Secret Aryan Cults and Their Influence on Nazi Ideology.* New York: New York University Press, 1993.

Gopinath, Gayatri. *Impossible Desires: Queer Diasporas and South Asian Public Cultures.* Durham, NC: Duke University Press, 2005.

Govindrajan, Radhika. *Animal Intimacies: Interspecies Relatedness in India's Central Himalayas.* Chicago: University of Chicago Press, 2018.

Govindrajan, Radhika. "Beyond Cruelty and Innocence: What the Death of an Elephant in Kerala Tells Us about Ourselves." *HuffPost India,* June 11, 2020. https://www.huffingtonpost.in/entry/pregnant-elephant-death-in-kerala_in _5ee1f662c5b67cba495cbbdc.

Guattari, Félix. *Chaosmosis: An Ethico-aesthetic Paradigm.* Translated by Julian Pefanis. Bloomington: Indiana University Press, 1995.

Guenther, Katja M. *The Lives and Deaths of Shelter Animals.* Stanford, CA: Stanford University Press, 2020.

Gupta, Alok, and Arvind Narrain, eds. *Law like Love: Queer Perspectives on Law.* New Delhi: Yoda, 2011.

Halberstam, Jack. *Wild Things: The Disorder of Desire.* Durham, NC: Duke University Press, 2020.

Halperin, David M. *Saint Foucault: Towards a Gay Hagiography.* Oxford: Oxford University Press, 1997.

Hansen, Thomas Blom. *The Saffron Wave: Democracy and Hindu Nationalism in Modern India*. Princeton, NJ: Princeton University Press, 1999.

Haraway, Donna. "A Cyborg Manifesto: Science, Technology, and Socialist-Feminism in the Late 20th Century." In *The International Handbook*, edited by Joel Weiss, Jason Nolan, Jeremy Hunsinger, and Peter Trifonas, 117–58. Dordrecht: Springer Netherlands, 2006.

Haraway, Donna. *When Species Meet*. Minneapolis: University of Minnesota Press, 2007.

Hardy, Kathryn C. "Provincialising the Cow: Buffalo-Human Relationships." *South Asia: Journal of South Asian Studies* 42, no. 6 (2019): 1156–72.

Harney, Stefano, and Fred Moten. *The Undercommons: Fugitive Planning and Black Study*. New York: Minor Compositions, 2013.

Hartman, Saidiya. 2008. "Venus in Two Acts." *Small Axe: A Caribbean Journal of Criticism* 12 (2): 1–14.

Havis, Devonya N. "'Now, How You Sound': Considering a Different Philosophical Praxis." *Hypatia* 29, no. 1 (2014): 237–52.

Heidegger, Martin. *The Fundamental Concepts of Metaphysics: World, Finitude, Solitude*. Bloomington: Indiana University Press, 2001.

Herzog, Annabel. "Dogs and Fire: The Ethics and Politics of Nature in Levinas." *Political Theory* 41, no. 3 (2013): 359–79.

Hochschild, Arlie. *The Managed Heart: Commercialization of Human Feeling*. Berkeley: University of California Press, 2012.

Hribal, Jason. "Animals, Agency, and Class: Writing the History of Animals from Below." *Human Ecology Review* 14, no. 1 (2007): 101–12.

Hribal, Jason, and Jeffery St. Clair. *Fear of the Animal Planet: The Hidden History of Animal Resistance*. Edinburgh: AK Press, 2011.

Hussain, Syed Rafiq, and Saleem Kidwai. *The Mirror of Wonders and Other Tales*. New Delhi: Yoda, 2020.

Ians. "Goa NGO Wants Police to Probe Bestiality against Dog." *The Quint*, July 31, 2018. https://www.thequint.com/hotwire-text/goa-ngo-wants-police-to-probe-bestiality -against-dog.

"India Outrage after Pregnant Elephant Dies Eating 'Firecracker Fruit.'" *BBC News*, June 4, 2020. https://www.bbc.com/news/world-asia-india-52918603.

Jaaware, Aniket, and Anupama Rao. *Practicing Caste: On Touching and Not Touching*. New York: Fordham University Press, 2018.

Jackson, John L., Jr. *Thin Description: Ethnography and the African Hebrew Israelites of Jerusalem*. Cambridge, MA: Harvard University Press, 2013.

Jackson, Zakiyyah Iman. *Becoming Human: Matter and Meaning in an Antiblack World*. New York: New York University Press, 2020.

Jain, Kajri. *Gods in the Bazaar: The Economies of Indian Calendar Art*. Durham, NC: Duke University Press, 2007.

Jalais, Annu. *Forest of Tigers: People, Politics and Environment in the Sundarbans*. London: Routledge India, 2011.

James, Robin. *The Sonic Episteme: Acoustic Resonance, Neoliberalism, and Biopolitics*. Durham, NC: Duke University Press, 2019.

Jha, Dhirendra K. "Guruji's Life: The RSS and M. S. Golwalkar's Undeniable Links to Nazism." *The Caravan*, 2021. Accessed September 6, 2021. https://caravanmagazine.in /history/rss-golwalkar-links-nazism.

Jobson, Ryan Cecil. "The Case for Letting Anthropology Burn: Sociocultural Anthropology in 2019." *American Anthropologist* 122, no. 2 (2020): 259–71.

Johnson, Catherine, and Temple Grandin. *Animals in Translation: Using the Mysteries of Autism to Decode Animal Behavior*. Orlando, FL: Mariner, 2006.

Johnson, Greg. "Savitri Devi's Communist Nephews," n.d. Accessed September 7, 2021. https://www.savitridevi.org/article-nephews.html.

Johnson, Samuel. *A Dictionary of the English Language: An Anthology*. Edited by David Crystal. London: Penguin Classics, [1755] 2007.

Jung, Nawab Nazeer Yar. *Strolling through the Jungles*. Delhi: Notion, 2016.

Kalakshetra and Rukmini Devi Arundale. *Speeches and Writings of Rukmini Devi Arundale*, vols. 1–2. Madras: Kalakshetra Foundation, 2016.

Kapur, Vinod. "Pioneering Micro-entrepreneurship through Poultry Breeding and Distribution in Rural India." *Innovations* (Winter 2008): 37–51.

Karlekar, Malavika. "Animal Passions." *Outlook India Online*, July 24, 2000. https:// magazine.outlookindia.com/story/animal-passions/209737.

Kashyap, Sunil, and Zubair Khan. "In Bijnor, Muslim Villagers Allege U[ttar] P[radesh] Police Harassed Them on Suspicion of Cow Slaughter." *The Caravan*, May 20, 2020. Accessed May 21, 2020. https://caravanmagazine.in/religion/bijnor-muslim-villagers -allege-up-police-harassed-them-on-suspicion-of-cow-slaughter.

Kavesh, Muhammad A. *Animal Enthusiasms: Life beyond Cage and Leash in Rural Pakistan*. New York: Routledge, 2020.

Keck, Frédéric. *Avian Reservoirs: Virus Hunters and Birdwatchers in Chinese Sentinel Posts*. Durham, NC: Duke University Press, 2020.

Kendall, Karalyn. "The Face of a Dog: Levinasian Ethics and Human/Dog Co-evolution." In *Queering the Non/Human*, edited by Myra J. Hird and Noreen Giffney, 185–204. New York: Routledge, 2008.

Kendall-Morwick, Karalyn. "Dogging the Subject: Samuel Beckett, Emmanuel Levinas, and Posthumanist Ethics." *Journal of Modern Literature* 36, no. 3 (2013): 100–19.

"Kerala Elephant Death: Maneka Gandhi Tears into Kerala Government over Elephant's Death, Says No Action Taken despite Frequent Incidents." *Times of India Online*, June 30, 2020. Accessed September 1, 2021. https://timesofindia .indiatimes.com/india/maneka-gandhi-tears-into-kerala-government-over -elephants-death-says-no-action-taken-despite-frequent-incidents/articleshow /76177703.cms.

Khalikova, Venera, Ned Dostaler, and Bharat Venkat. "Commitment, Citation, and Context: An Interview with Bharat Jayram Venkat." Society for Cultural Anthropology, 2017. Accessed October 20, 2021. https://culanth.org/fieldsights/commitment -citation-and-context-an-interview-with-bharat-jayram-venkat.

Khan, Naveeda. "Dogs and Humans and What Earth Can Be: Filaments of Muslim Ecological Thought." *HAU: Journal of Ethnographic Theory* 4, no. 3 (2014): 245–64.

Khubchandani, Kareem. "Welcome: Critical Aunty Studies," 2020. Accessed September 9, 2021. https://www.criticalauntystudies.com/01-welcome.

Kilgour, Maggie. *From Communion to Communism: An Anatomy of Metaphors of Incorporation.* Princeton, NJ: Princeton University Press, 1990.

Kim, Claire Jean. *Dangerous Crossings: Race, Species, and Nature in a Multicultural Age.* Cambridge: Cambridge University Press, 2015.

King, Tiffany Lethabo. *The Black Shoals: Offshore Formations of Black and Native Studies.* Durham, NC: Duke University Press, 2019.

Kipling, John Lockwood. *Beast and Man in India: A Popular Sketch of Indian Animals in Their Relations with the People.* London: Macmillan, 1891.

Kramer, Lawrence. *The Hum of the World: A Philosophy of Listening.* Berkeley: University of California Press, 2020.

Kumar, A. "As Medical Students Stab and Burn a Monkey in Vellore, Activists Demand Stricter Animal Welfare Laws." *Scroll*, November 24, 2016. http://scroll.in/article/822413/as-medi cal-students-stab-and-burn-a-monkey-in-vellore-activists-demand-stricter-animal-welfare-laws.

Kundera, Milan. *The Book of Laughter and Forgetting.* New York: Harper Perennial, 1980.

Kundera, Milan. *Immortality.* New York: Harper Perennial Modern Classics, 1999.

Kundu, Ratoola. "Nirmala: Kamathipura's Gatekeeper." In *Bombay Brokers*, edited by Lisa Bjorkman, 145–53. Durham, NC: Duke University Press, 2021.

Kurien, Verghese, and Gouri Salvi. *I Too Had a Dream.* New Delhi: Roli, 2012.

Laidlaw, James. "Ethical Traditions in Question: Diaspora Jainism and the Environmental and Animal Liberation Movements." In *Ethical Life in South Asia*, edited by Anand Pandian and Daud Ali, 61–82. Bloomington: Indiana University Press, 2010.

Latour, Bruno. *Reassembling the Social: An Introduction to Actor-Network-Theory.* Oxford: Oxford University Press, 2007.

Law Commission of India. "Review of Rape Laws: Report No. 172." New Delhi, 2000. https://www.legal-tools.org/doc/1c639d/pdf.

Lear, Jonathan. *Happiness, Death, and the Remainder of Life.* Cambridge, MA: Harvard University Press, 2000.

Lear, Jonathan. *Open Minded: Working Out the Logic of the Soul.* Cambridge, MA: Harvard University Press, 1999.

Lenin, Janaki. *My Husband and Other Animals.* Chennai, India: Westland, 2012.

Levinas, Emmanuel. "The Paradox of Morality: An Interview with Emmanuel Levinas." In *The Provocation of Levinas: Rethinking the Other*, translated by Andrew Benjamin and Tamra Wright, 168–80. London: Routledge, 1988.

Lispector, Clarice. *Agua Viva.* Translated by Stefan Tobler. New York: New Directions, 2012.

Lorde, Audre. "Eye to Eye." In *Sister Outsider: Essays and Speeches*, by Audre Lorde, 145–75. New York: Random House, 1984.

Lorde, Audre. *Our Dead behind Us: Poems by Audre Lorde.* New York: W. W. Norton, 1986.

Luhrmann, T. M. *The Good Parsi: The Fate of a Colonial Elite in a Postcolonial Society.* Cambridge, MA: Harvard University Press, 1996.

Lupton, Julia Reinhard. "Creature Caliban." *Shakespeare Quarterly* 51, no. 1 (2000): 1–23.

Lyotard, Jean-François. *The Differend: Phrases in Dispute*. Translated by Georges Van Den Abbeele. Minneapolis: University of Minnesota Press, 1989.

Mahmood, Saba. *The Politics of Piety: The Islamic Revival and the Feminist Subject*. Princeton, NJ: Princeton University Press, 2011.

Majumdar, Nivedita. "Silencing the Subaltern: Resistance and Gender in Postcolonial Theory." *Catalyst* 1, no. 1 (Spring 2017). https://catalyst-journal.com/2017/11/silencing -the-subaltern.

Malhotra, Sheena, and Aimee Carillo Rowe, eds. *Silence, Feminism, Power: Reflections at the Edges of Sound*. New York: Palgrave Macmillan, 2013.

Malinowski, Bronisław. *Argonauts of the Western Pacific: An Account of Native Enterprise and Adventure in the Archipelagoes of Melanesian New Guinea*. Oxford: Oxford University Press, 2016.

"Man in Mumbai Let Off by Police after He Was Caught Having Sex with a Puppy." *India TV News*, March 27, 2014. https://www.indiatvnews.com/crime/news/man-inmumbai - let-off-by-police-after-he-was-caught-having-sex-with-a-puppy-5720.html.

Mankekar, Purnima. *Screening Culture, Viewing Politics: An Ethnography of Television, Womanhood, and Nation in Postcolonial India*. Durham, NC: Duke University Press, 1999.

Manning, Erin. *The Minor Gesture*. Durham, NC: Duke University Press, 2016.

Manning, Erin. *The Politics of Touch: Sense, Movement, Sovereignty*. Minneapolis: University of Minnesota Press, 2006.

Margaronis, Maria. "Savitri Devi: The Mystical Fascist Being Resurrected by the Alt-Right." *BBC News*, October 28, 2017. https://www.bbc.com/news/magazine-41757047.

Marks, Laura. *The Skin of the Film: Intercultural Cinema, Embodiment, and the Senses*. Durham, NC: Duke University Press, 2000.

Martin, Emily. *The Woman in the Body: A Cultural Analysis of Reproduction*. Boston: Beacon, 2001.

Massumi, Brian. *Parables for the Virtual: Movement, Affect, Sensation*. Durham, NC: Duke University Press, 2002.

Massumi, Brian. *A User's Guide to Capitalism and Schizophrenia: Deviations from Deleuze and Guattari*. Cambridge, MA: MIT Press, 1992.

Massumi, Brian. *What Animals Teach Us about Politics*. Durham, NC: Duke University Press, 2014.

Mathur, Nayanika. *Paper Tiger: Law, Bureaucracy and the Developmental State in Himalayan India*. Cambridge: Cambridge University Press, 2016.

Maurette, Pablo. *The Forgotten Sense: Meditations on Touch*. Chicago: University of Chicago Press, 2018.

Mayo, Katherine. *Mother India*. Edited by Mrinalini Sinha. Ann Arbor: University of Michigan Press, 1927.

Mazzarella, William. *The Mana of Mass Society*. Chicago: University of Chicago Press, 2017.

McKenzie, Keisha. "Transcript: Toni Morrison at Portland State, 1975." *MacKenzian* (blog), July 7, 2014. https://mackenzian.com/blog/2014/07/07/transcript-morrison-1975.

Mehta, Vinod. *The Sanjay Story*. New Delhi: Harper Collins India, 2015.

Meijer, Eva. *When Animals Speak*. New York: New York University Press, 2019.

Menely, Tobias. *The Animal Claim: Sensibility and the Creaturely Voice*. Chicago: University of Chicago Press, 2015.

Menon, Madhavi. *Indifference to Difference: On Queer Universalism*. Minneapolis: University of Minnesota Press, 2015.

Menon, Nivedita. *Seeing like a Feminist*. New Delhi: Zubaan, 2012.

Merleau-Ponty, Maurice. *The Visible and the Invisible*. Translated by Alphonso Lingis. Evanston, IL: Northwestern University Press, 1969.

Meyjes, Toby. "Pregnant Goat Dies 'after Being Gang-Raped by Eight Men.'" *The Mirror*, July 29, 2018. https://www.mirror.co.uk/news/world-news/pregnant-goat-dies-after -being-12998644.

Miller, Christopher Jain, and Jonathan Dickstein. "Jain Veganism: Ancient Wisdom, New Opportunities." *Religions* 12, no. 7 (2021): 512–32.

Miller, Jacques-Alain. "Extimity." *The Symptom: Online Journal for Lacan* (blog), 2008. https://www.lacan.com/symptom/?p=36.

Minh-ha, Trinh T. "Not You/Like You: Postcolonial Women and the Interlocking Questions of Identity and Difference." In *Dangerous Liaisons: Gender, Nation, and Postcolonial Perspectives*, edited by Anne McClintock, Aamir Mufti, and Ella Shohat, 415–49. Minneapolis: University of Minnesota Press, 1997.

Minh-ha, Trinh T. *Woman, Native, Other: Writing Postcoloniality and Feminism*. Bloomington: Indiana University Press, 2009.

Mitra, Premendra. *Mosquito and Other Stories*. New Delhi: Penguin, 2004.

Mody, Parveez. "Kidnapping, Elopement, and Abduction: An Ethnography of Love-Marriage in Delhi." In *Love in South Asia: A Cultural History*, edited by Francesca Orsini, 331–44. New Delhi: Cambridge University Press, 2007.

Morris, Rosalind, ed. *Can the Subaltern Speak? Reflections on the History of an Idea*. New York: Columbia University Press, 2010.

Morrison, Toni. "Afterword to *The Bluest Eye*." In *The Bluest Eye*, by Toni Morrison, 207–16. New York: Penguin, 1994.

Moten, Fred. *In the Break: The Aesthetics of the Black Radical Tradition*. Minneapolis: University of Minnesota Press, 2003.

Murray, Laura. "In the Time of the Buffalo Clones: Population, Productivity, and Futurity on a Shrinking Planet." PhD diss., New York University, 2020.

Murugan, Perumal. *The Story of a Goat*. Translated by N. Kalyan Raman. New Delhi: Grove, 2019.

Nabokov, Vladimir. *Lolita*, 2d ed. New York: Vintage, 1989.

Nafisi, Azar. *Reading Lolita in Tehran: A Memoir in Books*. New York: Random House, 2003.

Nag, Aditya Kiran. "Feeding Abandoned Animals in the Pandemic." *Gastronomica* 20, no. 3 (2020): 66–67.

Nagar, Valmiki, and Animal Welfare Board of India. "Standard Operating Procedures for Sterilization of Stray Dogs under the Animal Birth Control Programme." Animal Welfare Board of India, Chennai, 2009.

Naipaul, V. S. *A House for Mr. Biswas*. New York: Vintage, 2003.

Nair, Vijayanka. "Becoming Data: Biometric IDs and the Individual in 'Digital India.'" *Journal of the Royal Anthropological Institute* 27, no.1 (2021): 26–42.

Napolin, Julie. *The Fact of Resonance: Modernist Acoustics and Narrative Form*. New York: Fordham University Press, 2020.

Narayanan, Yamini. "Animating Caste: Visceral Geographies of Pigs, Caste, and Violent Nationalisms in Chennai City." *Urban Geography* (March 2021): 1–21. https://doi.org/10.1080/02723638.2021.1890954.

Narayanan, Yamini. "'Cow Is a Mother, Mothers Can Do Anything for Their Children!' Gaushalas as Landscapes of Anthropatriarchy and Hindu Patriarchy." *Hypatia* 10, no. 10 (2019): 1–27.

Narayanan, Yamini. "Cow Protectionism and Bovine Frozen-Semen Farms in India: Analyzing Cruelty, Speciesism, and Climate Change." *Society and Animals* 26, no. 1 (2018): 1–21.

Narayanan, Yamini. "Cow Protection as 'Casteised Speciesism': Sacralisation, Commercialisation and Politicisation." *South Asia* 41, no. 2 (2018): 331–51.

Narayanan, Yamini. "Sperm to Slaughter: The Shocking Abuse of Bulls in Dairy Farming." *HuffPost India*, June 8, 2015. https://www.huffingtonpost.in/yamini-narayanan/sperm-to-slaughter-the-sh_b_7516454.html.

Narayanan, Yamini. "Street Dogs at the Intersection of Colonialism and Informality: 'Subaltern Animism' as a Posthuman Critique of Indian Cities." *Environment and Planning D: Society and Space* 35, no. 3 (2017): 475–94.

National Dairy Development Board (NDDB). "NDDB Organises Workshop on Production and Processing of Bovine Frozen Semen under NDP I." National Dairy Development Board, 2017. https://www.nddb.coop/node/1363.

Nishant, Vaidyanath. "Who Killed the Elephant in Kerala?" *The Wire* (blog), June 4, 2020. https://thewire.in/environment/who-killed-the-elephant-in-kerala.

Nützenadel, Alexander. "Dictating Food: Autarchy, Food Provision, and Consumer Politics in Fascist Italy, 1922–1943." In *Food and Conflict in Europe in the Age of the Two World Wars*, edited by Frank Trentmann and Flemming Just, 88–108. London: Palgrave Macmillan UK, 2006.

Olivelle, Patrick. "Talking Animals: Explorations in an Indian Literary Genre." *Religions of South Asia* 7 (2013): 14–26.

Orwell, George. "Reflections on Gandhi." Orwell Foundation, 1949. https://www.orwellfoundation.com/the-orwell-foundation/orwell/essays-and-other-works/reflections-on-gandhi.

Pachirat, Timothy. *Every Twelve Seconds: Industrialized Slaughter and the Politics of Sight.* New Haven, CT: Yale University Press, 2013.

Palsetia, Jesse S. "Mad Dogs and Parsis: The Bombay Dog Riots of 1832." *Journal of the Royal Asiatic Society* 11, no. 1 (2001): 13–30.

Pandey, Geeta. "Are Women Less Important than Cows in India?" *BBC News*, June 27, 2017. https://www.bbc.com/news/world-asia-india-40404102.

Pandey, Gyanendra. "Rallying round the Cow: Sectarian Strife in the Bhojpuri Region, 1888–1917." In *Subaltern Studies*, edited by Ranajit Guha, 60–129. Delhi: Oxford University Press, 1983.

Pandian, Anand, and Stuart J. McLean, eds. *Crumpled Paper Boat: Experiments in Ethnographic Writing.* Durham, NC: Duke University Press, 2017.

Parmar, Arushi Singh. "Canines, Campus, and Community: Case Study of Stray Dogs in Jawaharlal Nehru University." Master's thesis, Ambedkar University, New Delhi.

Parreñas, Juno Salazar. *Decolonizing Extinction: The Work of Care in Orangutan Rehabilitation*. Durham, NC: Duke University Press, 2018.

Patel, Krina. "The Gap in Marital Rape Law in India: Advocating for Criminalization and Social Change." *Fordham International Law Journal* 42, no. 5 (2019): 1518–46.

Patterson-West, JaBrea. "Julie Mehretu: On Black Abstraction, Futurity and Opacity as a Space of Liberation." *Flash Art* (blog), May 17, 2021. https://flash-art.com/article/julie -mehretu/.

Plant, Bob. "Welcoming Dogs: Levinas and 'the Animal' Question." *Philosophy and Social Criticism* 37, no. 1 (2011): 49–71.

Povinelli, Elizabeth A. "After the Last Man: Images and Ethics of Becoming Otherwise." *e-flux Journal* 35 (May 2012). https://www.e-flux.com/journal/35/68380/after-the-last -man-images-and-ethics-of-becoming-otherwise/.

Povinelli, Elizabeth A. *Between Gaia and Ground: Four Axioms of Existence and the Ancestral Catastrophe of Late Liberalism*. Durham, NC: Duke University Press, 2021.

Povinelli, Elizabeth A. *The Empire of Love: Toward a Theory of Intimacy, Genealogy, and Carnality*. Durham, NC: Duke University Press, 2006.

Povinelli, Elizabeth A. "The Will to Be Otherwise/The Effort of Endurance." *South Atlantic Quarterly* 11, no. 3 (2012): 453–75.

Prakash, Gyan. *Emergency Chronicles: Indira Gandhi and Democracy's Turning Point*. Princeton, NJ: Princeton University Press, 2019.

Prakash, Gyan. *Mumbai Fables*. Princeton, NJ: Princeton University Press, 2011.

Prasad, Pallavi. "Why It's Still Legal for Indian Men to Rape Their Wives." *The Swaddle* (blog), January 20, 2020. https://theswaddle.com/marital-rape-inda-decriminalized -crime/.

Preciado, Paul B. *Can the Monster Speak? Report to an Academy of Psychoanalysts*. Translated by Frank Wynne. South Pasadena, CA: Semiotext(e), 2021.

Price, Brian. "Before Politics: Contradiction in Aesthetic Experience." Unpublished ms., 2015. Shared with the author.

Ramani, Shakuntala. *Rukmini Devi Arundale Birth Centenary Volume*. Madras: Kalakshetra Foundation, 2004.

Ramaswamy, N. S. "Report of the Expert Committee on Development of the Meat Industry." Ministry of Agriculture and Cooperation, New Delhi, 1987.

Ramdas, Sagari. "Reclaiming Endangered Livelihoods: Untold Stories of Indigenous Women and Backyard Poultry." *World's Poultry Science Journal* 65, no. 2 (2009): 241–50.

Rancière, Jacques. *Disagreement: Politics and Philosophy*. Minneapolis: University of Minnesota Press, 2004.

Rangan, Pooja. *Immediations: The Humanitarian Impulse in Documentary*. Durham, NC: Duke University Press, 2017.

Rao, Anupama. "Foreword." In *Practicing Caste: On Touching and Not Touching*, by Aniket Jaaware, vii–x. New York: Fordham University Press, 2019.

Reed, Patrick J. "The Enduring Power of Trinh T. Minh-Ha's Anti-ethnography." *ArtReview Asia*, October 19, 2020.

Rege, Sharmila. "Dalit Women Talk Differently: A Critique of 'Difference' and Towards a Dalit Feminist Standpoint Position." *Economic and Political Weekly* 33, no. 44 (1998): WS39–46.

Riley, Denise. "The Right to Be Lonely." *Differences* 13, no. 1 (2002): 1–13.

Rilke, Rainer Maria, and Robert Hass. *The Selected Poetry of Rainer Maria Rilke.* New York: Vintage, 1989.

Rivera, Mayra. *Poetics of the Flesh.* Durham, NC: Duke University Press, 2015.

Rogers, Crystal. *Mad Dogs and an Englishwoman: The Memoirs of Crystal Rogers.* New Delhi: Penguin, 2000.

Rosenberg, Gabriel. "How Meat Changed Sex: The Law of Interspecies Intimacy after Industrial Reproduction." *GLQ* 23, no. 4 (2017): 473–507.

Roy, Nilanjana. *The Hundred Names of Darkness.* Toronto: Random House, 2016.

Roy, Nilanjana. *The Wildings.* Toronto: Random House, 2016.

Roy, Parama. *Alimentary Tracts: Appetites, Aversions, and the Postcolonial.* Durham, NC: Duke University Press, 2010.

Roy, Parama. "Meat-Eating, Masculinity, and Renunciation in India: A Gandhian Grammar of Diet." *Gender and History* 14, no. 1 (2002): 62–91.

Roy, Parama. "On Verminous Life." *Representations* 148, no. 1 (2019): 86–113.

Roy, Sumana, ed. *Animalia Indica.* London: Aleph, 2019.

Sajad, Malik. *Munnu: A Boy from Kashmir.* New Delhi: Fourth Estate, 2015.

Salih, Sara. "Vegans on the Verge of a Nervous Breakdown." In *The Rise of Critical Animal Studies: From the Margins to the Centre,* edited by Nik Taylor and Richard Twine, 52–68. New York: Routledge, 2015.

Samson, Leela. *Rukmini Devi: A Life.* New Delhi: Penguin Books India, 2010.

Sandhu, Amandeep. "Dispatches from the Farmer Protests." *The Caravan,* January 25, 2021. Accessed October 22, 2021. https://caravanmagazine.in/agriculture/dispatches -farmer-protests-delhi-border.

Santner, Eric L. *On Creaturely Life: Rilke, Benjamin, Sebald.* Chicago: University of Chicago Press.

Sauvagnargues, Anne. "Hegel and Deleuze: Difference or Contradiction?" In *Hegel and Deleuze: Together Again for the First Time,* edited by Karen Houle and Jim Vernon, 38–53. Evanston, IL: Northwestern University Press, 2013.

Savas, Aysegul. "The Poet Upstairs." *Paris Review* (blog), January 22, 2018. https://www .theparisreview.org/blog/2018/01/22/the-poet-upstairs.

Sawhney, Anuradha. *The Vegan Kitchen: Bollywood Style!,* vol. 1. Chennai, India: Westland, 2012.

Sax, Boria, and Klaus P. Fischer. *Animals in the Third Reich.* London: Yogh and Thorn, 2013.

Schwartz, Delmore. "Lincoln." In *Selected Poems: Summer Knowledge,* by Delmore Schwartz, 236–37. New York: New Directions, 1959.

Seaver, Nick. "The Nice Thing about Context Is That Everyone Has It." *Media, Culture and Society* 37, no. 7 (2015): 1101–9.

Sebald, W. G. *Austerlitz.* Translated by Anthea Bell. New York: Random House, 2001.

Sedgwick, Eve Kosofsky. *Touching Feeling: Affect, Pedagogy, Performativity.* Durham, NC: Duke University Press, 2003.

Sekhar, Rukmini. "Continuing Grace." *The Hindu,* November 4, 2011. https://www .thehindu.com/features/metroplus/continuing-grace/article2598259.ece.

Sen, Amartya. *The Argumentative Indian: Writings on Indian History, Culture and Identity.* New York: Farrar, Straus and Giroux, 2013.

Sen, Jahnavi. "Maneka Gandhi's Altered Stance on Marital Rape Angers Activists." *The Wire* (blog), March 12, 2016. https://thewire.in/politics/activists-angered-by-maneka -gandhis-altered-stance-on-marital-rape.

Serres, Michel. *The Parasite*. Translated by Lawrence R. Schehr. Minneapolis: University of Minnesota Press, 2013.

Seth, U. "Historic Trial for Dog Rapist." *Mid-Day*, September 1, 2009. https://www.mid -day. com/articles/historic-trial-for-dog-rapist/56082.

"Setting Menu for People." *Financial Express*, November 13, 1995.

Sexton, Jared, and Daniel Barber. "On Black Negativity, or the Affirmation of Nothing." *Society and Space Online*, September 18, 2017. https://www.societyandspace.org/articles /on-black-negativity-or-the-affirmation-of-nothing.

Shah, Svati P. *Street Corner Secrets: Sex, Work, and Migration in the City of Mumbai*. Durham, NC: Duke University Press, 2014.

Shandilya, Krupa. "Nirbhaya's Body: The Politics of Protest in the Aftermath of the 2012 Delhi Gang Rape." *Gender and History* 27, no. 2 (2015): 465–86.

Shange, Savannah. "Black Girl Ordinary: Flesh, Carcerality, and the Refusal of Ethnography." *Transforming Anthropology* 27, no. 1 (2019): 3–21.

Sharma, Jaya. "The Politics of Hindutva and Its Erotic Charge." *Kafila* (blog), June 24, 2019. https://kafila.online/2019/06/24/the-politics-of-hindutva-and-its-erotic -charge-jaya-sharma.

Shaw, George Bernard. *An Autobiography 1856–1898*. Edited by Stanley Weintraub. New York: Weybright and Talley, 1969.

Simmel, Georg. "The Stranger." In *The Sociology of Georg Simmel*, translated by Kurt Wolff, 402–8. New York: Free Press, 1950.

Simpson, Audra. "On Ethnographic Refusal: Indigeneity, 'Voice' and Colonial Citizenship." *Junctures: The Journal for Thematic Dialogue* 9, no. 1 (2007): 67–80.

Singh, Bhrigupati. *Poverty and the Quest for Life: Spiritual and Material Striving in Rural India*. Chicago: University of Chicago Press, 2015.

Singh, Bhrigupati, and Naisargi Davé. "On the Killing and Killability of Animals: Nonmoral Thoughts for the Anthropology of Ethics." *Comparative Studies of South Asia, Africa and the Middle East* 35, no. 2 (2015): 232–45.

Singh, Julietta. *No Archive Will Restore You*. Goleta, CA: Punctum. 2018.

Singh, Julietta. *Unthinking Mastery: Dehumanism and Decolonial Entanglements*. Durham, NC: Duke University Press, 2018.

Singh, Khushwant. *Truth, Love, and a Little Malice*. London: Penguin Books India, 2003.

Singh, S. P. "Two Rape Dog, Drag Her to Death." *The Pioneer*, December 16, 2018. https:// www. dailypioneer.com/2018/pioneer-exclusive/2-rape-dog–drag-her-to-death.html.

Skaria, Ajay. *Unconditional Equality: Gandhi's Religion of Resistance*. Minneapolis: University of Minnesota Press, 2016.

Sloterdijk, Peter. *Critique of Cynical Reason*. Minneapolis: University of Minnesota Press, 1988.

Sloterdijk, Peter. *You Must Change Your Life*. Cambridge: Polity, 2014.

Sommer, Doris. "Taking a Life: Hot Pursuit and Cold Rewards in a Mexican Testimonial Novel." *Signs* 20, no. 4 (1995): 913–40.

Specter, Michael. "The Extremist." *New Yorker*, April 14, 2003, 52–67.

Spivak, Gayatri. "Can the Subaltern Speak?" In *Can the Subaltern Speak? Reflections on the History of an Idea*, edited by Rosalind Morris, 21–78. New York: Columbia University Press, 1999.

Spivak, Gayatri. "Can the Subaltern Speak." In *Marxism and the Interpretation of Culture*, edited by Cary Nelson and Lawrence Grossberg, 271–313. New York: Macmillan, 1988.

Srinivasan, Krithika. "The Biopolitics of Animal Being and Welfare: Dog Control and Care in the UK and India." *Transactions of the Institute of British Geographers* 38, no. 1 (2013): 106–19.

Srinivasan, Krithika. "Remaking More-than-Human Society: Thought Experiments on Street Dogs as 'Nature.'" *Transactions of the Institute of British Geographers* 44, no. 2 (2019): 376–91.

Srinivasan, Krithika, and Vijay Nagaraj. "Deconstructing the Human Gaze: Stray Dogs, Indifferent Governance and Prejudiced Reactions." *Economic and Political Weekly* 42, no. 13 (2007): 1085–86.

Srinivasan, Ragini Tharoor. "'Can the Subaltern Speak' to My Students?" *Feminist Formations* 32, no. 1 (2020): 58–74.

Staples, James. *Sacred Cows and Chicken Manchurian: The Everyday Politics of Eating Meat in India*. Seattle: University of Washington Press, 2020.

Sterne, Jonathan. *The Audible Past: Cultural Origins of Sound Reproduction*. Durham, NC: Duke University Press, 2003.

Stevenson, Lisa. "Sounding Death, Saying Something." *Social Text* 35, no. 1 (2017): 59–78.

Stewart, Kathleen. *A Space on the Side of the Road: Cultural Poetics in an "Other" America*. Princeton, NJ: Princeton University Press, 1996.

Strathern, Marilyn. "Out of Context: The Persuasive Fictions of Anthropology." *Current Anthropology* 28, no. 3 (1987): 251–81.

Stuart, Tristram. *The Bloodless Revolution: A Cultural History of Vegetarianism from 1600 to Modern Times*. New York: W. W. Norton, 2008.

Subaşi, Věra. *Dogs in Islam: A Historical Survey of Islamic Sources*. Saarbrucken: VDM Verlag Dr. Müller, 2011.

Subramaniam, Banu. "The Ethical Impurative." In *Meat! A Transnational Analysis*, edited by Sushmita Chatterjee and Banu Subramaniam, 254–78. Durham, NC: Duke University Press, 2021.

Sujatha, S., and Shrimi Choudhary. "Army Jawans to Get Two Eggs, Poultries a Fat Biz." *Economic Times*, September 2, 2010. https://economictimes.indiatimes.com/news/economy/policy/army-jawans-to-get-2-eggs-poultries-a-fat-biz/articleshow/6477915.cms.

Sur, Malini. "Time at Its Margins: Cattle Smuggling across the India-Bangladesh Border." *Cultural Anthropology* 35, no. 4 (2020): 546–74.

Tarlo, Emma. *Unsettling Memories: Narratives of the Emergency in Delhi*. Berkeley: University of California Press, 2003.

Taylor, Sarah Pierce. "Rethinking Non-violence: The Spiritual and Emotional Lives of Animals in Jain Literature." Lecture presented at the University of Toronto, February 1, 2019.

Thapar, Romila. "Some Appropriations of the Theory of Aryan Race Relating to the Beginnings of Indian History." In *The Aryan Debate*, edited by Thomas R. Trautmann, 106–30. New Delhi: Oxford University Press, 2005.

Thapar, Romila. "The Theory of Aryan Race and India: History and Politics." *Social Scientist* 24, nos. 1–3 (1996): 3–29.

Thiyagarajan, Nandini. "Inevitable Lives: Connecting Animals, Caste, Gender, and the Environment in Perumal Murugan's *The Story of a Goat*." Special issue, *South Asian Review* 42, no. 4 (2021): 356–71.

Ticktin, Miriam. "Non-human Suffering: A Humanitarian Project." In *The Clinic and the Court: Law, Medicine, and Anthropology*, edited by Ian Harper, Tobias Kelly, and Akshay Khanna, 49–71. Cambridge: Cambridge University Press, 2015.

Ticktin, Miriam. "A World without Innocence." *American Ethnologist* 44, no. 4 (2017): 577–90.

Tonkiss, Fran. "The Ethics of Indifference: Community and Solitude in the City." *International Journal of Cultural Studies* 6, no. 3 (2003): 297–311.

"Top Five Egg-Producing Countries." *Business Standard* (blog), November 17, 2020. https://www.tbsnews.net/economy/agriculture/top-5-egg-producing-countries-2020 -159202.

Townend, Christine, and John Little. *Christine's Ark*. London: Momentum, 2012.

Trautmann, Thomas R., ed. *The Aryan Debate*. New Delhi: Oxford University Press, 2008.

Tronti, Mario. "The Strategy of the Refusal." *Italy: Autonomia Post-political Politics* 3, no. 3 (1966): 28–42.

Vasu, V. M. "Dung Is Gold Mine." Report, Viniyog Parivar Trust, Mumbai, 2012.

Valliyate, Manilal. "Criminalising Bestiality Safeguards Society." *Down to Earth*, August 20, 2018. https://www.downtoearth.org.in/blog/wildlife-biodiversity/ criminalising-bestiality-safeguards-society-61415.

Venkat, Bharat Jayram. "Iatrogenic Life: Veterinary Medicine, Cruelty, and the Politics of Culling in India." *Anthropology and Medicine* 29, no. 2 (2022): 123–40.

Viswanathan, Gauri. *Masks of Conquest: Literary Study and British Rule in India*. New York: Columbia University Press, 2014.

Viswanathan, Gauri. *Outside the Fold: Conversion, Modernity, and Belief*. Princeton, NJ: Princeton University Press, 1998.

Vitale, Christopher. "Deleuzo-Hegelianism, Part III: On Deleuze's Critique of Hegel and Hyppolite, Or, on 'the Concept.'" *Networkologies* (blog), August 10, 2011. https:// networkologies.wordpress.com/2011/08/10/deleuzo-hegelianism-part-iii-on-deleuzes -critique-of-hegel-and-hyppolite-or-on-the-concept/.

Voice of Stray Dogs. "Sexual Abuse of Street Dogs in India: An Analysis of the Phenomenon, the Law, First Hand Accounts, and Press Reporting." Report, Voice of Stray Dogs, Bengalaru, 2014. https://vosd.in/sexual-abuse-of-street-dogs-in-india-an-analysis -of-the-phenomenon-the-law-1st-hand-accounts-press-reporting.

Wagner, Roi. "Silence as Resistance before the Subject, or Could the Subaltern Remain Silent?" *Theory, Culture and Society* 29, no. 6 (2012): 99–124.

"Waiting for Pizza Huts in Kalahandi." *Financial Express*, June 4, 1995.

Watts, Vanessa. "Indigenous Place-Thought and Agency amongst Humans and Non-humans (First Woman and Sky Woman Go on a European World Tour!)." *Decolonization: Indigeneity, Education and Society* 2, no. 1 (2013): 20–34.

Weaver, Harlan. "'Becoming in Kind': Race, Class, Gender, and Nation in Cultures of Dog Rescue and Dogfighting." *American Quarterly* 65, no. 3 (2013): 689–709.

Weil, Simone. *Gravity and Grace*. Translated by Arthur Wills. Lincoln: Bison, 1997.

Wilderson, Frank. "Gramsci's Black Marx: Whither the Slave in Civil Society?" *Social Identities* 9, no. 2 (2003): 225–40.

Williams, Raymond. *Marxism and Literature*. Oxford: Oxford Paperbacks, 1995.

Yang, Anand. "Sacred Symbol and Sacred Space in Rural India: Community Mobilization in the 'Anti-Cow Killing' Riot of 1893." *Comparative Studies in Society and History* 22, no. 4 (1980): 576–96.

Yo-Ling, Daniel. "After Knowledge." *Daniel Yo-Ling* (blog), May 28, 2020. https://www.dylchen.com/post/after-knowledge.

Zaidi, S. Hussain, and Vikram Chandra. *Dongri to Dubai: Six Decades of Mumbai Mafia*. New Delhi: Lotus, 2012.

Zimmer, Ben. "Drumming Up the Origins of 'Pariah' States." *Wall Street Journal*, July 26, 2014.

ethics: animal ethics in India, 10, 72; ethnography as a tool for examining, 10–11; immanence and ethical responsibility, 22, 37–38, 50–51, 56–62; the ethics of choice that underlie touch, 108, 115, 117; the surrounding nonexploitation, 9; the surrounding opacity and indifference, 5–7, 82

fascists: the belief in intimidation and social control among Hindu, 36; *gauraksha* violence against Dalits and Muslims, 16; the rejection of humanist ideologies by, 36, 51; the vegetarian ideology of, 36–37, 53; the view among fascists that a natural world is utopian, 36; violence by against queers, 29; violence by portrayed as "animal protection," 16, 32, 34n12, 36–37n20, 47, 51. *See also* Nazism
Felski, Rita, 69–70, 71n49
fish, 104, 148, 149, 156, 159
fishmeal, 148, 149, 159
Franciscan time, 165

Gandhi, Indira, 17, 18, 37n21, 41, 44n38
Gandhi, Mahatma: the *ahimsa* of, 135; on cow protection, 74, 135–36; the vegetarianism of, 34n12, 53n69
Gandhi, Maneka Anand: the animal activism of, 13, 17–20, 73–74, 118–19n30, 120, 146; the Animal Birth Control (ABC) sterilization program, 19; conversion to animal activism, 18, 120; and Crystal Rogers, 14n1, 37n21, 41; early ties to the Congress Party, 17, 19; and Friendicoes-SECA 41; *Heads and Tails* 13, 42n36, 160; marriage to Sanjay Gandhi 17–18; opposition to a Kentucky Fried Chicken (KFC) franchise in India, 154; opposition to N. S. Ramaswamy, 163; People for Animals (PFA), 19, 42n36, 73–74; the rightist, anti-minority views of, 17n16, 37n21, 103, 106n28, 134, 138n47; ties to Rukmini Devi, 37n21; as Union Minister of Environment and Forests, 163; willingness to employ violence, 19–20
Gandhi, Sanjay, 17–18, 19n21, 41
Ganguly, Suparna, 43–44
Gaurakshaks, 15, 36, 65, 74–75, 141–42
gaushalas, 60n13, 80, 81, 136, 141
ghosts and gods. *See* supernatural beings
Ghotge, Nitya, 42n35
Glissant, Édouard, 3–6, 82n35, 91
Goa, 10, 15, 16n9
goats: as abused, 85, 126, 132; Amala's injured goat, 120; animal shelters, 27; as neglected, 97; Perumal Murugan's *The Story of a Goat*, 87–88; as sacrificial, 133n27; as sexually abused, 126; the slaughter of in holding pens, 85; the soundings and behaviors of, 85–87

Halal and jhatka slaughter methods, 149–50, 153–54, 162
Haraway, Donna, 2–3, 5

Harney, Stefano, 71
Haryana, 10, 46, 126, 150, 15n5, 153, 160
healers. *See* animalists
Hindus: the *ahimsa* doctrine, 43, 51, 109, 127n8, 135–36, 155n15; animal activist 23, 70; animal exploitation by 135–37, 140–42, 152, 156–57; the anthropatriarchy of many, 30, 75, 126, 133–34, 140, 145; the belief in the fluid existence of human, god, and animal, 66; the *Bhagavad Gita*, 57, 119; the concept of *darshan* among, 23, 122n42; the delineation of permissible and perverse violence by, 126–27, 137, 145; discrimination by against queers, 29n46; the employment of Muslim animal transporters by, 74; the female body regarded as property by, 47, 127n6, 140; the influence of *dharma* on, 94n4, 109n2; innocence as a duality for, 133–34; *jhatka* meat butchering, 149n2; leftist secular humanist, 64–65, 66; meat consumption by, 17, 149n2, 155–57; the Parsi Dog Riots (Bombay; 1832), 101; passivity toward animal deaths, 38n25, 43, 109; the reverence for Christianity among, 8; the sale of cows to butchers by, 136n36. *See also* caste
Hindutva: the Anglophobic stance of, 37; Aryo-Hindutva thought, 32–34, 37, 156n17; the cow protectionism of, 15n5, 16n10, 17n15, 31, 36–37n20, 73–74; the dominant-caste anti-minority politics of, 17, 34–36, 74n5, 103, 156n17; hate speech by adherents of, 17n16, 103; the Hindu Mission of Calcutta, 35; the influence of German ethnic nationalism on, 34, 46; espoused by Maneka Gandhi, 17n16, 37n21, 73–74; of Savitri Devi, 34; of the Rashtriya Swayamsevak Sangh (RSS) 34; the opposition of animalists to, 17; the pro-Nazi magazine *New Mercury*, 34; Swami Satyananda's support of Hitler, 35; the violence of as Indian nationalism, 34, 36, 127, 15n5. *See also* cow protection; politics; vegetarianism
Hitler, Adolf, 32–35, 36–37n20. *See also* Nazism
Hoffman, Peter, 50, 118
humanists: anthropocentric, 25–26, 28; the disdain of secular for animal politics, 64–66, 68; fascists versus, 36, 53; meat eating as a rejection of fascism for, 65, 68; the primacy of human welfare for, 65, 68
humanitarianism: humanitarian violence, 82n37, 83; the paternalistic, dominating aspects of, 82, 83, 138
humans: Bhuvaneswari Bhaduri's suicide as statement, 75–76; the bonding of otherwise disparate through animals, 104, 110–11; Costello moments and lucky breaks, 14, 121–22; the execution of June Days Uprising participants (France, 1871), 83; interactions between occasioned by animals, 106, 110–11; the interference of in bovine and porcine sexuality, 140–43; Lyotard on commodified, 77n13; Moten on commodified, 76–77; the rejection of domination by, 29–30, 79–80,

Acknowledgments

This book is the result of numerous conversations with many different people. First off, I would like to thank Edward Alpers and William Worger for sparking my interest in African studies during my years as a graduate student at UCLA. Other projects held my attention for far too long, but I am glad I could finally focus on a study I can only hope they find of interest. My deepest thanks also go to Carina Ray, Daniel Magaziner, Moses Ochonu, and Michelle Moyd for their interest in this topic and their willingness to include it as a part of the OSHA series. Ricky Huard at Ohio University Press performed sterling service in pushing this manuscript through the review process, and two anonymous readers provided valuable critical feedback that greatly improved my arguments. Tyler Balli and Jessica Zellers provided invaluable editorial services. Christopher Saunders, Jeremy Seekings, Jean Comaroff, and the late John Laband also shared their vast knowledge on South African issues with a peripatetic scholar looking for new things to say. Whatever faults or shortcomings that remain in what follows are, of course, mine, and mine alone. Finally, I dedicate this book to the memory of my father, Edward Vartavarian, a great storyteller in song and speech.

Introduction

*Theorizing Wealth Concentration in
South Africa and Beyond*

This book considers a fundamental question: How is it that, despite a long history of anticolonial struggle, South Africa has been so hospitable to wealth concentration? The loosening of British imperial control in the early twentieth century tightened white-minority privilege, while the advent of popular democracy in 1994 enriched a select number of well-connected African politicians and consigned the Black majority to griding poverty. Contradictions between democratization and persistent mass poverty are not particular to South Africa. Yet by focusing on its history, we can gain a wider understanding of why African societies remain so unequal.

I contend that the formation and evolution of privileged minorities paralleled the development of successful anticolonial movements. By *privileged minorities,* I mean small groups of people who dominate the politico-economic landscape of their respective societies due to the material assets and benefits they possess. Minority privilege is not necessarily synonymous with race, although race at times determined how privileges were secured and how wealth was accumulated. At several critical junctures, incumbent groups defended their privileges by extending economic benefits to other minorities. This study charts pathways to minority privilege taken by distinct sociocultural groupings and examines how such groupings interacted with each other over time. To understand these complexities, we must consider the full scope of South African history from the Dutch colonial period to the rise and decline of African National Congress (ANC) rule.

Debates on Economic Inequality in South Africa: Race, Class, and Synthesis

The origins of economic inequality in South Africa have generated extensive academic commentary. Mass poverty was not a natural phenomenon. It emerged from the deliberate dispossession of indigenous peoples by white settler communities and Black ruling elites. Most modern scholarship attributes impoverishment to either racial prejudice or class formation.[1]

I precede my gloss on these theorizations with an important caveat. The following classifications are ideal types. Authors' writings often evolve, and no single scholar can be neatly fitted into a single category. These labels merely provide shorthand approximations of their theoretical contributions.

Purportedly liberal scholars focusing on race claimed different sections of the white community treated Black people in different ways. This largely Anglophone school of thought developed in the nineteenth century and dominated South African historical studies until the late 1960s.[2] According to the liberal argument, Dutch-speaking colonists, progenitors of modern-day Afrikaners, viewed Black peoples they encountered as racially inferior beings deserving of unequal treatment. The importation of slaves from across the East Indies and wider Indian Ocean compounded this prejudice and consolidated an economic system premised on servile labor. Less affluent settlers attempting to establish leisurely lives along colonial frontiers captured peripatetic indigenes and converted them to bonded pastoral laborers. As virtual serfs subjected to a panoply of coercive sanctions, their condition was nearly indistinguishable from the slaves that worked the Western Cape's wine and wheat farms.

Liberal historians contend that the imperial transition to British rule at the turn of the nineteenth century alleviated racial injustice. British authorities removed restrictions on bonded labor and gradually emancipated slaves. The granting of a color-blind qualified franchise to the Cape colony in 1853, liberal historians argued, proved that British officials wanted to reduce racial divisions and include Black people in legislative processes.

Proto-Afrikaners, by contrast, rejected moves toward racial equality. They responded to emancipation by embarking on much-mythologized treks into the southern African interior, where they established republics that reconstituted racial subordination and unfree labor regimes. Liberal scholars saw racism as a product of the frontier. Fringe areas produced barbarous practices that negated social progress and perpetuated unsound economic systems. Areas remaining under British overrule formed mutually beneficial, if not necessarily equal, connections between settlers and indigenous societies. The coalescence of Afrikaner ethnonationalism undermined these connections and deepened divisions between races. Apartheid was, in a sense, the triumph of frontier racism over an interconnected multiracial nation. This resulted in economic maldevelopment and endemic social tensions.

Revisionist scholars inspired by Marxian theories of political economy challenged this liberal interpretation throughout the 1970s and 1980s.[3] Revisionism viewed Black poverty and white plenty as products of capitalism and class formation. British capitalists, rather than Afrikaner racists, imposed structural inequalities that advantaged big industrialists and commercial agriculturalists. The imperial state deprived Black people of autonomous means of subsistence and drove them into wage labor. Colonial conquests in the late nineteenth century demolished alternative centers of employment, expropriated land, and seized livestock. Hemmed into marginal territories, Africans had no choice but to work for white capitalists. Mines and farms premised profit margins on artificially repressed working costs. Pass laws, migrant labor systems, and carceral conditions at worksites kept wages down and repressed attempts at unionization. Hence, apartheid was not a product of atavistic racial regression but rather the culmination of coercive industrialization. Industrial conglomerates blamed racial excesses on Afrikaner nationalism while quietly taking full advantage of racist laws and labor regulations. When faced with industrial unrest, Anglophone capital called on coercive state power to suppress work stoppages and labor protests. Capital continued to benefit from the apartheid regime and would thus not mount a serious challenge to it.

Many revisionist scholars emphasized class over race for political reasons. Because they came from relatively privileged white backgrounds, African ethnonationalism made them uneasy. They wanted to play prominent parts in the freedom struggle and knew they would surely be marginalized if Black supremacist currents came to dominate the movement. In addition, the ANC's alliance with the South African Communist Party (SACP) allowed the former to mask its leaders' bourgeois ambitions behind the rhetoric of revolutionary stages. The SACP's theory of a two-stage revolution claimed that a bourgeois revolution, in which Black people would enter the economy's commanding heights, must precede a workers' revolution that would empower South Africa's laboring masses.[4] It is unclear if senior ANC leaders ever had any interest in this second stage. Yet the SACP propounded it to mobilize mass support for liberation from white-minority rule.

Attempts to synthesize racial and class theories on unequal wealth distribution took root in the 1980s. Merle Lipton, a prominent liberal social theorist, conceded that capital derived substantial benefits from racist labor legislation up to a point.[5] Anglophone corporate elites muted their criticism of racial oppression while it was economically profitable. Once it ceased to be so, big capital began to speak out. Pragmatism, rather than altruism, heightened this criticism. State repression could no longer secure private assets and had to be replaced with an alternative political arrangement that included African nationalist elites. Hence, class replaced race as the primary driver of inequality when a select number of Black people entered and reinforced the capitalist system.[6] Radicals continued to emphasize the inherently iniquitous nature of capitalism and the need for socialist transformation. Arguments against capitalism continued into the postapartheid period. As the ANC's turn to neoliberalism created a tiny group of African capitalists and a bigger Black middle class, left-wing theorists felt disillusioned.[7] Some claimed the ANC had sold out to global capital, while others stressed that African nationalist elites had always harbored bourgeois aspirations and merely used revolutionary tactics to seize power.

Conservative commentators took an opposite perspective, arguing that African nationalism was a fig leaf for creeping state socialism and would eventually lead to a Venezuela-style economic meltdown.[8] Ebrahim Harvey, in turn, has recently argued that race and class are inextricably intertwined. Capitalism was imposed on South Africa in a racialized manner, and if it continues to function, it will reproduce racial inequalities no matter which race its leaders belong to. In his view, only democratic socialism can break this vicious cycle.[9]

The Politics of Rent Seeking and Exclusive Advantage

Rather than formulate a new race/class synthesis that explains the initiation or perpetuation of indigenous dispossession, this study focuses on how minorities from various races and classes derived disproportionate material benefits from South Africa's evolving economic landscape. In a recent monograph, Steven Friedman attributes South Africa's current inequities to *rent seeking,* which he defines as "the search for profits which exceed those available in a competitive market."[10] In Friedman's view, repeated resorts to rent seeking by different elite groups created a structural path dependence that concentrated wealth within tiny minorities and inhibited inclusive economic development.[11]

However, Friedman's definition of rent seeking is in fact a description of monopoly profits, generally defined as excess earnings a corporation achieves by being the sole provider of a product or service. Rent seeking connotes the use of political connections to gain profits without creating wealth or adding value.[12] This form of rent seeking, which certainly contributed to South Africa's current inequalities, is a severe form of exclusive advantage used by select interest groups to skew economic opportunities in their favor. I define *exclusive advantage* as benefits, protections, and opportunities obtained by small sociopolitical groupings to facilitate material accumulation. Types of exclusive advantage include, but are not limited to, primitive accumulation, usually manifested as land and livestock seizures; racialized systems of slavery and indentured servitude; access to coercive organizations that expanded and secured assets; loose regulatory environments that allowed capital concentration by corporations; exclusive state expenditures; ethnopolitical economic empowerment schemes; and rent seeking. Such advantages are not necessarily limited to a single race, and certain variants can lead to economic growth. Yet when growth does occur, it generally accrues to select groups, mainly small oligarchies and exclusive middle classes. Favored groups deployed these advantages in various and shifting composite configurations, although certain elements tended to predominate over others during specific historical periods. Hence, exclusive advantages enabled the formation of privileged minorities over time.

Effective challenges by out-groups reformulated, rather than eliminated, minority privilege and attached new players to incumbent structures. These complexities created composite systems of accumulation and wealth concentration that privileged select minorities at the expense of large majorities. The following schema delineates cycles of exclusive advantage that created these minorities in South Africa.

Modes of Minority Empowerment from the Preindustrial to Postapartheid Eras

Prior to the mineral revolution, elites in southern Africa were multiracial and regional in character. Fluid systems of material accumulation, premised on mobile livestock, militated against macroregional centralization. Low barriers to economic resources made wealth accessible to a wide range of social groups. If quadrupedal animals could not be purchased, they could be plundered. Moreover, both colonial and indigenous elites lacked the administrative capabilities to assert their control beyond spatially circumscribed areas. White settlers encroaching on indigenous lands met protracted resistance from dispossessed populations. By the late eighteenth century, these conflicts caused widespread destruction of settler property and halted their territorial advance.

In addition, African kings never fully overcame political fissions that attenuated their state-building projects. Porous frontiers and multiple political jurisdictions provided zones of refuge for princes or lineages on the wrong side of succession disputes. More importantly, neither Black nor white polities succeeded in fully controlling free-floating service communities that provided manual or military labor to the highest bidder. Pastoralists and agriculturalists often doubled as war bands or native auxiliaries in colonial armies. Military service was a swift route to plunder. Indigenous allies accumulated land and cattle at the expense of African rebels. These material endowments gave a select number of loyalists privileged positions in emerging colonial orders, particularly in British territorial possessions. Preindustrial southern African society was too fluid for any one state to dominate.

Nonetheless, exclusive elites acquired significant wealth and status over regional areas. These elites ultimately derived material privilege from armed force because they could not impose sociopolitical systems that favored exclusive material accumulation without using coercion. Until the late nineteenth century, both white settlers and indigenous rulers accumulated resources by deploying various forms of military labor. Dutch settlers formed mounted commandos to kill rebels, seize land, and capture livestock. Indentured mixed-race laborers served on these commandos under compulsion, eventually making up around half of their personnel. Land-grabbing British settlers in the Eastern Cape faced massive resistance from Xhosa-speaking peoples and depended on direct assistance from imperial troops and indigenous allies. African kings organized violence by injecting military training regimens into male age-sets and establishing more direct control over the distribution of war booty.

These systems of military mobilization had their limits. Settler commando violence generated mass insurrections across the Northern Cape that halted further expansion. Settler militias also failed to overcome Xhosa resistance on the eastern frontier. Facing military defeat, the Cape Dutch turned to British power to bail them out. British power itself was never consistently applied. Despite the establishment of a lucrative wool trade in the 1830s, London viewed southern Africa as a financial drain and only backed settler interests with extreme reluctance. Metropolitan policymakers frequently halted or reversed colonial annexations that overextended British responsibilities. In addition, imperial reliance on African auxiliaries necessitated the transfer of certain spoils to loyalist communities, thus reducing quantities of looted land and livestock available for expropriation by white settlers. Finally, African kings faced constant internal challenges to their power from rival princes with autonomous access to cattle and armed retainers. European officials played on these divisions for strategic advantage, but they also rewarded and reinforced compliant African elites augmenting the military capacities of settler and imperial states.

Territorial unification, and by extension white domination, came through exogenous conquest. White settlers remained a minority heavily reliant on favorable public policies implemented and sustained by administrative coercion.[13] However, settlers could not have subordinated indigenous peoples without British military power. South Africa was constructed as an imperial conquest state by British proconsular officials seeking to homogenize administrative systems and labor regimes that obstructed an industrializing mineral economy. Deep-level mineral extraction required immense capital investment and naturally evolved toward oligarchic control. Mining magnates certainly had an interest in facilitating imperial expansion, as conquests lowered the cost of indigenous labor, but metropolitan plenipotentiaries ultimately determined when and how unification came about. London pursued annexation for geopolitical objectives and international prestige. Diamonds and gold were simply too important to leave in the hands of pro-German Boers. Imperial forces waged the Anglo-Boer War (1899–1902) to affirm British domination over an economically valuable area in danger of drifting into the orbit of a rival great power. The main beneficiaries of coerced unification were British mine owners and Afrikaner nationalists willing to cooperate with their new imperial overlords.

Afrikaners received state power in exchange for protecting the profits of an Anglophone economic elite. Protection came by way of repressing organized labor and thus sustaining low wages. Afrikaner workers were added to this nexus of minority privilege as white welfare programs espoused by ethno-populist politicians garnered sufficient electoral support. As cross-class white supremacist alliances coalesced, African nationalism embraced increasingly radical tactics centered on mass protests. Yet African political movements continued to be led by middle-class elites seeking to join, rather than overturn, a structurally unequal economic system.

Segregationist (1910–48) and apartheid (1948–94) regimes created productive modern economies. Twentieth-century South Africa saw an aggregate decline in economic inequality and developed impressive levels of infrastructural integration.[14] Nonetheless, a demographically contracting white minority acquired a disproportionate share of economic growth. Administrative restrictions and political oppression escalated whenever Black people gained greater material advantages from industrial and agrarian enterprises. Apartheid itself was instituted after a Black influx into urban manufacturing jobs during the Second World War.[15] Even after apartheid-era regulations began decreasing corporate profits, capital extended affirmative action programs only to select numbers of educated Africans. Liberal capitalists felt segmental incorporation would give "respectable" Black people a stake in the economic status quo. These initiatives proved unsuccessful. Mass protests escalated in intensity, and the international community began imposing sweeping economic sanctions in the mid-1980s.

Corporate profits could not be guaranteed without Black political empowerment.

Corporate conglomerates limited the economic impact of this empowerment by co-opting ANC elites into company boardrooms. Co-opted party leaders provided political protection from threats of nationalization in return for shareholdings and generous salaries. These arrangements attenuated tensions between racially bifurcated economic and political elites and delivered insufficient benefits to the unemployed and working poor. In addition, economic decline ensued when unqualified political cadres were deployed to parastatal agencies providing essential public services. Levels of graft escalated to overt economic predation under Jacob Zuma's administration (2009–18). Nonetheless, the ANC might have prolonged its political dominance had it not been for intraparty feuds between rival power networks jostling for privileged access to rents. South Africa under ANC rule was a fractious party state, in which a single political organization dominated the bureaucratic administration but failed to unify contesting party factions behind common interests.

Progressive structural reforms have been repeatedly attenuated by segmental incorporation. Selective compromises with ascending sociopolitical groups confined wealth circulation to privileged minorities. At critical junctures, incumbent minorities defended their privileges by privileging other minorities, thus perpetuating the cycle and preventing inclusive economic development.

Exclusive Elites and Contentious Rent Seekers: South Africa in Comparative Perspective

The rest of this introduction incorporates the concept of privileged minorities into the established literature on elite theory in Africa. I also draw more detailed comparisons between South Africa, Kenya, and Zimbabwe. In all three cases, ethnic or political insiders derived disproportionate material benefits from central states. In addition, postindependence party notables acquiring oligarchic wealth through exclusive economic advantages fell into chronic political feuds that fragmented their respective party states into rival factions.[16]

Social theorists often attribute African maldevelopment to neopatrimonialism. *Neopatrimonialism* is typically defined as a melding of traditional and legal-rational types of authority within governments. The concept's applicability to African case studies has generated sustained controversy among scholars, international donors, and public policy planners. In an African context, neopatrimonialism assumed decidedly negative connotations, as it resulted in the looting of public resources for private gain and prevented inclusive development.[17] South Africa was viewed as an exceptional case that evaded the worst aspects of predatory rule until the onset of state capture after 2009. Consequently, it too was categorized by neopatrimonialism's proponents as a decayed and criminalized state, if not a completely failed one.[18]

In the view of neopatrimonial theorists, African presidents prioritized the construction of loyal client groups over economic growth and disregarded the damage done to public assets. Legal-rational elements within neopatrimonial states either masked primordial ties between patrons and clients or permitted rent extraction from revenue-producing organizations. Certain leaders exercised more regulated forms of neopatrimonial rule at certain points, thus stabilizing political systems and achieving impressive economic growth, yet all too often, regulated patronage degenerated into overt predation.[19] Predatory plunder of state assets and commodities plunged Africa into a developmental morass from which it is still trying to fully extricate itself.

Revisionist scholarship has challenged neopatrimonialism's validity. Revisionists contend that the concept disregards variations between countries and within national governments. In addition, essentialized cultural explanations downplay global trade cycles and fluctuating commodity prices that prevent even well-intentioned elites from embarking on inclusive development programs.[20] More importantly, a few African countries have achieved impressive development despite, and at times because of, neopatrimonial rule. In Botswana, for example, sociopolitical ties between traditional rulers and mass electorates obligated patrons to deliver goods and services to their followers. Adroit negotiations with multinational mining companies also assured Gaborone a fairer share of mineral profits. Mauritius has moved beyond primary commodities and developed a successful textile manufacturing sector geared toward international markets. This created extensive employment opportunities in a value-added light industry. Rwanda's development is more controversial, given its pillaging of Congolese minerals, privileging of diasporic Tutsi, and heavy reliance on foreign donor assistance, yet it has delivered impressive growth through authoritarian governance.[21]

More generally, refusal to distribute wealth downward often frayed patron-client bonds and created openings for rival political leaders to market themselves as more generous patrons.[22] In addition, while some government ministries were mired in corruption, patches of administrative efficiency persisted and delivered essential services to subaltern social groups. Neopatrimonial theories constructed from African case studies also draw on problematic culturalist arguments, positing that primordial traditions encourage the worst features of personal rule. Such ethnic essentialism neglects the fact that neopatrimonial practices persist in advanced industrial democracies and presents African cultures as inherently antidevelopmental.

These criticisms are quite valid, yet they do not adequately explain why so much wealth remains concentrated in so few hands. At their core, patron-client relations are both transactional and highly unequal. Clients change patrons to obtain greater benefits from above. This shifts balances of power among rival elites without challenging hierarchical power dynamics. Ordinary Africans able to claw their way to the top of political hierarchies often join, rather than topple, incumbent elites.[23] Furthermore, patches of governmental efficiency are surrounded by rent-seeking seas. Taxation regimes must function effectively to pay public servants whose primary loyalties are to their patrons, political parties, or ethnic communities, rather than general publics. Government services, in turn, are selectively delivered or withdrawn depending on a constituency's political orientation or ethnic composition. Crucially, governments that construct dynamic economies generally privilege certain groups over others, directing most opportunities and entitlements to organized business interests and political supporters.

It is not, however, my intention to rehabilitate neopatrimonialism. The concept is altogether too broad and disregards particular historical trajectories throughout the continent. I instead narrow my focus to a group of cases in which minority empowerment was a product of ruling elites directing exclusive advantages to select ethnopolitical and entrepreneurial groups. As settler minority states, Kenya, Zimbabwe, and South Africa constructed relatively powerful administrative structures capable of penetrating and exploiting their respective societies. Profits and economic surpluses built on the backs of cheap Black labor benefited resident white minorities. These three states also fostered the formation of Black middle-class elites that used incumbent bureaucracies and economic systems for their own benefit. All three experienced protracted processes of decolonization with varying degrees of armed struggle. Nevertheless, Kenya, Zimbabwe, and South Africa all achieved majority rule through negotiated compromises that left exclusionary systems of wealth concentration in place.

Moreover, postcolonial elites did not distribute their newfound privileges coherently. Like the ANC, the Kenya African National Union (KANU) and Zimbabwe African National Union-Patriotic Front (ZANU-PF) were elite coalitions.[24] Rival factions maneuvered for political advantage and primacy of place for access to wealth. Over time, feuding political elites weakened the coherence of their respective party states. Rent seeking and oligarchy building took priority over party unity. In the end, KANU was torn apart by its ethnopolitical barons, ZANU-PF became little more than a forum for contending factional interests, and the ANC fragmented until it could no longer sustain its parliamentary majority. Kenyan and Zimbabwean similarities with the South African case are best illustrated by a discussion of their respective historical trajectories of minority empowerment.

From Rotating Authoritarianism to Oligarchic Democracy in Kenya

The British conquered and pacified Kenya's core areas from 1895 to 1914. Although colonial armies outgunned indigenous societies, they lacked sufficient personnel to impose their will. Hence, British officials tapped into independent war bands operating on an open military labor market. Free-floating warrior groups augmented and derived material benefits from an anemic colonial state in need of indigenous allies to make its presence felt beyond circumscribed strongpoints. Thus, the initial colonial intrusion redistributed material resources across a highly fluid political landscape. The decision to foster white settlement in 1902 spurred administrative consolidation. Vast settler estates produced tea, coffee, and sisal for global markets. Settler commodity farming precipitated extensive indigenous dispossession, particularly in Kikuyu-speaking areas and the Rift Valley. Politico-economic change altered coercive institutions and punitive practices. Colonial military commanders relied less on indigenous auxiliaries and more on uniformed soldiers and police.[25] A relatively powerful colonial state enabled settler accumulation and facilitated the formation of a racial oligarchy. Yet unlike South Africa, white settlers never managed to take full control of this state. They remained a tiny minority reliant on imperial power to guarantee their security.

Increasing land hunger, aggravated by state development projects, generated an agrarian insurgency in Kenya's Central Province in 1952. Kikuyu rebels, labeled *Mau Mau* by British officials, sought land and freedom from foreign rule. Imperial forces crushed the movement militarily, but their failure to reimpose political stability necessitated a negotiated settlement. Metropolitan plenipotentiaries co-opted moderate nationalist elites into these discussions, originally intending to turn Kenya into a loosely structured federal state that devolved power toward less radical, non-Kikuyu ethnic groups. However, London shifted its backing to Jomo Kenyatta's KANU as a likelier means to demobilize popular forces calling for land redistribution. Kenyatta's regime (1963–78) inherited a powerful bureaucratic apparatus able to apportion rewards and sanctions based on political loyalties.[26]

By 1964, Kenyatta's clique had established a centralized presidential regime and clinched alliances with tribal barons through strategic distributions of patronage. Kenyatta used land reform programs to endow his family with farms and forest reserves.[27] Politically connected Kikuyu also concentrated wealth through various redistribution schemes and became the core of postcolonial Kenya's state bourgeoisie. High commodity prices and administrative Africanization programs gave Kenyatta sources of patronage with which to placate non-Kikuyu party leaders while allocating key public positions to fellow Kikuyu. Only the Luo ethnic group under Oginga Odinga faced exclusion from state spoils. While Kenyatta's regime did not tolerate direct challenges to its authority, KANU's ruling coalition was held together by opportunities for elite enrichment and minority empowerment.

Intra-elite consensus gradually disintegrated during Daniel arap Moi's presidency (1978–2002). Moi lacked his predecessor's prestige and faced overt challenges to his authority. His 1982 declaration of a de jure one-party state did not forestall an attempted air force coup shortly thereafter. Moi cultivated loyalty by rotating rents away from the Kikuyu and toward his Kalenjin confederacy, with his fellow Tugen and closely allied Elgeyo subgroups receiving the richest rewards. Areas of the Rift Valley received greater infrastructural investments than the previously favored Central Province. However, Moi never fully succeeded in taming rival Kikuyu oligarchs.[28] Moi also prioritized political loyalty over professional competence, and this resulted in a deterioration of social services. Grand corruption and public sector scandals compelled donor organizations to tie further financial assistance to political reform.

Moi bowed to foreign pressure in 1991 by allowing multiparty elections the following year.[29] Former KANU Kikuyu elites founded rival parties, but personal animosities prevented them from forming a united opposition. A divided opposition, coupled with the formation of Kalenjin militias engaged in ethnic cleansing of anti-KANU constituencies, allowed Moi to retain power until 2002. KANU rule came to an end when Moi designated Uhuru Kenyatta, the late president's son, as his heir. This angered rival interests within the party and dissipated Moi's political support. When opposition elites managed to cobble together a unified coalition, single-party rule came to an end. KANU imploded, but its oligarchs remained and continued to dominate the political game.

President Mwai Kibaki's administration (2002–13) was initially dominated by a Kikuyu inner circle referred to as the Mount Kenya mafia. The profits of his purportedly technocratic macroeconomic policies flowed disproportionately toward regime insiders and fellow Kikuyu.[30] Kibaki himself had been a KANU stalwart and one of Moi's vice presidents. Kibaki's unwillingness to grant sufficient governmental powers to his coalition colleague Raila Odinga aggravated intra-elite tensions and triggered widespread communal violence after a hotly contested general election in 2007. All main contenders in this electoral contest bore responsibility for fomenting ethnic massacres and thus colluded with each other after the formation of an internationally brokered coalition government to avoid prosecution.

In 2013, Uhuru Kenyatta ascended to the presidency (2013–22) with William Ruto, a former Kalenjin militia leader and Moi protégé, as vice president. Both played leading roles in prior bouts of ethnic violence and agreed to protect each other from accountability. Ruto himself became president in 2022 and continued to direct exclusive advantages toward clients, hoping to pass on the costs, in the form of higher taxes, to the public. Legislated tax increases targeted the earnings of Kenya's multiethnic middle class and generated widespread social protests in 2024. Although state police violently suppressed demonstrations, middle-class anger coalesced into a broad-based reform movement. This threatened to undermine segmental divide-and-rule strategies used by ruling elites to fragment civil society. Consequently, Ruto scrapped tax hikes, engaged in a cabinet reshuffle, and co-opted Raila Odinga's opposition party without curbing elite privileges. His regime merely placed greater emphasis on debt financing as a source of patronage.[31]

African nationalism in Kenya was led by an elite coalition of ethnic leaders that never coalesced into a coherent group. Various KANU leaders played critical roles in the decolonization process and felt entitled to economic benefits and material rewards. Jomo Kenyatta distributed resources in ways that contained most intraparty conflicts. Moi's regime, by contrast, plundered the state to enrich itself but could not permanently sideline rival oligarchs that amassed wealth during the previous administration. These tensions fragmented KANU but did not dissolve the oligarchic interests within it. When violent clashes between rival elite interests nearly triggered a civil war in 2007–8, a new ruling coalition coalesced around more equal patronage flows and a need to protect its leaders from criminal prosecutions.[32] Much of Kenya's postcolonial political history has been driven by feuding elite factions seeking to accumulate and secure wealth. Most parties lack distinct political programs and operate as platforms to state spoils.

The Formation of Zimbabwe's Oligarchic Party State

White settler rule in Zimbabwe was wider and deeper than in Kenya. Initial settler incursions into what became Rhodesia were motivated by gold prospecting. When settlers found little gold, they turned to commercial agriculture worked by cheap African labor. In 1893, treaty disputes led the settlers to a short war with, and partial subjugation of, the Ndebele kingdom. As in South Africa, land expropriation and cattle confiscation deprived indigenous peoples of their means of subsistence. This pushed them onto white farms and drove down working costs. Property seizures, exploitative labor practices, and contemptuous treatment of traditional African leaders sparked a colony-wide rising from 1896 to 1897.[33] Without imperial reinforcements, the settlers might have been overwhelmed by rebel bands. After the rebellion, settler interests escalated the dispossession of Shona- and Ndebele-speaking peoples, driving them onto infertile and increasingly overcrowded native reserves. Settlers relied on migrants from these artificially impoverished reserves to cultivate commodities on their rural estates. Whites also developed a strong urban presence in major cities. The granting of responsible government in 1923 consolidated settler rule and confirmed African subordination.

Despite severe sociopolitical disadvantages, an educated African petite bourgeoisie did emerge and advocated for assimilation into the established order. When assimilation was rebuffed, African nationalism became more radical. Personal rivalries repeatedly divided nationalist parties.[34] ZANU itself was an organization that splintered off from Joshua Nkomo's Zimbabwe African People's Union (ZAPU) in 1963. The splinter parties themselves remained mired in factional conflicts. This further complicated the struggle against white-minority rule and set the stage for postcolonial strife.

As decolonization unfolded across the African continent, Rhodesia's white minority refused to relinquish its socioeconomic privileges. Ian Smith's government (1964–79) unilaterally declared independence from Britain in 1965 to preclude the possibility of Black majority rule. An international sanctions regime proved ineffective as South Africa extended material and military support to a fellow white-minority government. The Rhodesian state strengthened its coercive apparatus and pursued policies geared toward consolidating economic self-sufficiency. Smith's intransigence worked for roughly a decade, but by 1975, shifting geopolitical currents allowed ZANU and ZAPU's armed wings to escalate their respective armed struggles from bases in neighboring states. Attempts by frontline states to unite nationalist elites failed, and the two guerrilla armies remained separate fighting forces. British diplomatic pressure eventually resulted in a negotiated settlement at Lancaster House in 1979.[35] Although Robert

Mugabe's ZANU-PF wanted to continue the war until final victory, he settled on a diplomatic solution after Mozambique threatened to cut off military assistance.

After Rhodesia became Zimbabwe in 1980, widespread asset nationalization did not occur, and the cash crop sector remained under white control. Racial bifurcation between economic and political elites did not translate into immediate tensions. Mugabe placated white-minority interests to secure adequate infusions of foreign exchange and focus on constructing a one-party state. ZANU-PF cadres benefited from public sector employment, while the government unleashed its security forces on ZAPU supporters. State persecution eventually bludgeoned Nkomo's party into submission after an imposed unity accord in 1987.[36] ZANU-PF refused to share power with a coherent opposition party, but Mugabe did reward former ZAPU stalwarts with senior government positions after they agreed to capitulate.

Neoliberal structural adjustment programs in the 1990s gave ample opportunities for ZANU-PF leaders to benefit from privatization schemes. Burgeoning elite corruption bred discontent among impoverished war veterans. Large-scale protests in 1997 forced the regime to make massive financial payouts to aggrieved veterans, thus triggering a protracted economic crisis. Mugabe's decision to deploy troops to a collapsing Democratic Republic of Congo in 1998 reinforced the military's loyalty to his regime. Generals engaged in massive looting of natural resources and inflated contracts for military supplies. Foreign plunder endowed a praetorian oligarchy with great wealth and created a powerful interest group committed to the political status quo.

When Morgan Tsvangirai's Movement for Democratic Change posed a serious electoral challenge to the government in 2000, ZANU-PF chose to gain greater political support by seizing white farms. The ensuing economic meltdown and seizure of choice properties by party elites attenuated whatever positive impacts land redistribution had on Zimbabwean society. The middle class sharply contracted, with educated professionals largely relocating abroad. White Zimbabweans ceased to function as a cohesive privileged minority, although the regime continued to deal with individual white oligarchs able to circumvent sanctions and willing to contribute to party coffers. Senior security force officials grew richer and hence more determined to hinder efforts at political reform. Military officers allied with Emmerson Mnangagwa probably compelled Mugabe to remain in power after ZANU-PF clearly lost the 2008 harmonized elections.

ZANU-PF ministers retained control over security portfolios in the regionally brokered unity government (2009–13).[37] Furthermore, ZANU-PF elites encouraged the Movement for Democratic Change's fragmentation into rival parties and played various fragments off against each other, thus precluding the possibility of genuine cross-party power-sharing arrangements. However, ZANU-PF factionalism increased as Mugabe's health declined and party oligarchs fought over the succession.[38] Tensions escalated to the point where Mnangagwa's military-backed Lacoste faction launched a coup in November 2017 against an ascendant Generation 40 group nominally headed by Mugabe's wife, Grace Mugabe. Mugabe's subsequent resignation saw Mnangagwa assume the presidency and attempt to assert control over the praetorian elites who put him in power.[39] Mnangagwa rigged his way to reelection in 2023, yet elements within the security establishment appear to have autonomous access to rents and are pursuing separate agendas.

The ZANU-PF party state was powerful enough to eradicate or repulse external challenges to its supremacy but not coherent enough to contain rival interests within it. ZANU-PF elites that took part in the liberation struggle felt entitled to state rents and controlled client groups that assisted them in their pursuit of those rents. Mugabe balanced off rival factions as long as he could, but he was unable to secure a stable succession, and ultimately his own army overthrew him. Praetorian oligarchs had their own privileges to defend and could do without him.

Global Factors in African Inequality

Transnational currents have played an important role in determining domestic power configurations. However, elite African agency is not confined to national territories.[40] Numerous postcolonial governments received substantial aid by playing off superpower rivalries during the Cold War. The confines of global credit and commodity markets have loosened in recent decades with the reemergence of multipolar geopolitics. African leaders obtain security assistance from one great power while garnering economic investments from another.

While world economic systems cannot be discarded, wealth concentration is as much a product of elite political priorities. African elites acquire combinations of exclusive advantage to accumulate wealth and selectively extend or redistribute those advantages to defend wealth. Certain groups benefit from such redistributions, but large majorities remain excluded from economic advancement.

General scholarly consensus holds that the inability of African policymakers to follow Euro-American, or East Asian, developmental trajectories mired the continent in levels of economic stagnation that are proving extremely difficult to surmount. Earlier South African social theory focused on a unique history, mainly attributed to substantial white settlement and industrialization, that centered causal mechanisms for inequality on either race or class. Although more recent race/class syntheses add valuable nuance, these works usually overemphasize Black exclusion prior to the 1994 democratic transition. Deepening corruption under the ANC has made neopatrimonial theorizations more prominent in academic and public discourse. Yet neopatrimonialism assumes that African misrule is a product of primordial cultural characteristics, and its proponents tend to neglect the exploitative structures that European colonizers imposed.

This volume charts the development of privileged minorities through the allocation of exclusive socioeconomic and political advantages to select interest groups. Privileges were not always bestowed according to race and could be obtained by classes able to pressure established interests into making concessions. Moreover, exclusive advantages were not always squandered on conspicuous consumption and did at times contribute to impressive economic growth. Nevertheless, the benefits of growth were distributed exclusively. When incumbent elites felt threatened by progressive social movements, they selectively incorporated rival interests and protest elites into the politico-economic establishment. Newly incorporated power actors distributed patronage to select constituencies while deferring commitments to mass uplift. These exclusionary cycles are by no means unique to South Africa, and I have drawn some tentative comparisons here. Social theorists analyzing the persistence of mass poverty on the African continent can extend privileged minority formation to other cases.

1

White Gentries, Black Allies, and African Kings

Wealth Concentration in
Preindustrial South Africa

The subordination of indigenous societies in southern Africa was not a uniform or linear process. Although white settler communities subjugated indigenous peoples at certain points in certain places, they could rarely do so without African allies. Britain's imperial entry in the late eighteenth century increased the need for Black loyalists. British authorities frequently curbed settler landgrabs to cap burgeoning administrative costs and end ruinously expensive frontier wars. Prior to mineral discoveries, the imperial factor was inconsistent.[1] At times it slowed, but never entirely stopped, indigenous dispossession. Moreover, discontented subgroups within African polities, along with other free-floating service communities, allied with imperial authorities to accumulate and secure control over material resources. African monarchs also formed connections with European agents to export commodities, procure weapons, gain diplomatic advantage, and obtain prestige goods. These inputs bolstered their authority and weakened rivals.

From roughly 1800 to 1870, political power coalesced within a set of regional polities. States remained regional because wealth and labor remained mobile. For Khoikhoi pastoralists, white settlers, and African homesteaders, wealth was stored in livestock. If quadrupeds could not be purchased, they could be stolen. Commercial farmers transported produce to an expanding network of market towns. Mobile war bands and African kings commanding regimented military labor hired out violence to the highest bidder. Rich peasants, pastoralists, and warriors operated in a seller's market. If one buyer offered insufficient remuneration, or protection, producers and providers could turn to another. However, ample opportunities to market goods and services did not precipitate inclusive wealth distribution. Narrow groups in specific locales derived disproportionate benefits from interactions with colonial agents. Empire only privileged minorities.

Indigenous Dispossession and Settler Expansion in the Dutch Cape Colony

In 1652, the Dutch Vereenigde Oostindische Compagnie (VOC) established a foothold in southern Africa to consolidate trade networks across Asia. Its Cape Town waystation supplied company ships with provisions on journeys to and from eastern trading ports. Because the Cape of Good Hope lay astride strategic sea routes to those ports, whichever European power controlled it held an advantage over competitors sailing along it. Cape Town remained a vital transit point for commercial and military vessels into the twentieth century. It also rapidly became a central marketing zone for agropastoral products from the interior.

Indigenous pastoral peoples populating the Western Cape provided meat and other quadrupedal products in exchange for finished goods. Cape Khoikhoi groups functioned as small-scale peripatetic communities grazing cattle across seasonal pasturage zones and raiding weaker neighbors to make up for shortfalls in livestock.[2] Low population densities over vast territories enabled discontented elements in Khoikhoi communities to break off from chieftaincies and form their own bands. Raids, adverse ecological conditions, and fissiparous politics made it difficult to accumulate wealth. As a mobile resource requiring regular upkeep, cattle herds remained vulnerable to uncontrollable environmental factors and opportunistic predation.[3] Sustained deprivation compelled impoverished groups to enter the ranks of hunter-gatherer bands, now called San or Bushmen. Khoi communities may have originally emerged from San nomads that acquired cattle and consequently assumed more hierarchical sociopolitical structures. It was entirely possible for destitute Khoi/San to break back into pastoral status, provided they were able to recoup sufficient livestock. Lifeways, rather than genetic chains, determined ethnic labels.

For a time, Khoikhoi peoples provided livestock directly to the VOC without compulsion. Commercial interactions could and did operate to mutual benefit.[4] Yet when Dutch officials failed to secure provisions through trade, they turned to conquest. Extensive land-grabs commenced shortly after the VOC released several members from service to establish pastoral spreads in 1657.[5] White-owned farms required native land and labor. Since neither were transferred willingly, they had to be acquired coercively. Company soldiers and burgher militias possessed clear technological advantages over native warriors in the form of guns and horses. Mounted gunmen could ride up to, fire on, and ride away from Khoikhoi formations before they managed to muster adequate defenses.

Despite these advantages, the colonial state required indigenous military labor to augment its forces. At first, the Dutch supplemented their labor needs by aggravating preexisting rivalries between different Khoi chiefs. Fighting for the company gave indigenous allies opportunities to plunder their enemies and acquire a share of the spoils after hostilities. Such arrangements were sharply curtailed after a devastating smallpox epidemic in 1713. Khoikhoi communities lacked natural immunity to this contagion and consequently suffered widespread mortality. Indigenes decimated and weakened by disease proved easier to dispossess. Furthermore, the VOC gradually abdicated its responsibilities for conquest to white pastoral settlers. In 1715, a paramilitary commando system, populated by mounted civilians, was formally established and henceforth provided the primary means of frontier expansion.[6] Boer pastoralists used raids against recalcitrant indigenous groups to reclaim stolen livestock, seize native herds, and capture indigenous people. Captured indigenes provided semiservile labor on settler farms. Domesticated Khoi and mixed offspring, fathered by white men or slaves, fought alongside their masters on commando. By the mid-eighteenth century, indentured Black people made up roughly half of commando members.[7] Although this indicates frontier warfare cannot be reduced to a stark racial binarism, nonwhite participants did not derive any direct benefits from commando raids. These actions subjected them to retaliatory attacks by roving Khoisan bands. Farm servants defecting to these bands were mercilessly harried across arid terrain. Commando activities divided native peoples as much as they bifurcated settlers from indigenes. Moreover, Khoikhoi bondsmen soon began speaking their masters' language and practicing Christianity, further widening the gulf between acculturated servants and unconquered nomads.

Pastoral farmers considered nomadism a danger to livestock accumulation. Indigenous communities committed to a hunter-gatherer mode of subsistence added no value to the settler economy and were thus subjected to extermination.[8] These genocidal campaigns generated fierce opposition by San warriors. One Cape official estimated that between July 1786 and December 1788, indigenous raiders inflicted 92,191 rix-dollars in property damage throughout the colony, killed 99 horses, stole 6,299 cattle, and took 17,970 other animals.[9] Armed resistance was occasionally effective enough to temporarily turn back frontier expansion and inflict grievous damage to settler ranches and herds. Although recent research demonstrates that frontier farmers were far more affluent than previously thought,[10] this affluence was extremely fragile in conflict zones.

Landowners in the southwestern Cape faced far fewer dangers. Here, comparative stability and favorable climes resulted in the growth of wine and wheat farms worked by imported slaves. Slaves from the Indonesian archipelago and wider Indian Ocean could not easily find refuge in indigenous frontier communities if they managed to escape. Their diverse origins also made it difficult to construct overarching solidarities. Small-scale production prevented the emergence of disconnected subunits specializing in particular tasks. Slaves remained tightly controlled and violently disciplined.

Company agents in nearby Cape Town enforced racial hierarchies by subjecting disobedient or rebellious slaves to exemplary punishments. Continuing frontier conquests also grew the unfree labor pool. Dispossessed Khoikhoi streamed into Western Cape arable zones in search of work.[11] After entering agricultural service, they often became indistinguishable from legally enslaved chattel.

Slaveowners accrued substantial incomes thanks to subjugated workers and sympathetic company officials. However, slaveowners could secure status and respectability only by ostentatious expenditure. Dutch officials, planters, and ranchers strove to emulate metropolitan standards of consumption and comportment. Batavian fashions on Java set further standards on how colonial patricians should live. Pressures to meet such expectations were particularly intense on parvenus. More established elites could retain high status if they suffered a temporary decline in wealth. Newcomers, by contrast, had to look the part if they wished to enter exclusive social circles and power networks that opened doors to further advancement.[12] This led to many squandered fortunes and dissolved assets, although some managed to claw their way to the top.

Few frontier settlers got anywhere near this glittering world. Although their commandos rendered lands available for investment and their laborers supplied Cape Town with vital commodities, frontier settlers were always viewed as uncouth countryfolk unable to imbibe the social graces of their betters. Cape Town butchers bought up Boer meat supplies through intermediaries and sold them at markups across city markets. In addition, frontier farmers relied on urban centers for manufactured goods sold at higher prices than their animal products. Status divergence within the white settler community only worsened the condition of nonwhite peoples. Farm owners squeezed their slaves harder to maintain conspicuous consumption, while frontier pastoralists attempted to become masters of all they surveyed through force and violence.[13]

Settler coercion had its limits. By the late eighteenth century, protracted armed conflicts roiled the frontiers as the VOC went bankrupt. In the 1770s, Boers along the eastern frontier had come up against Xhosa-speaking agropastoral communities more firmly rooted in settler-coveted territories. As frontier ranchers migrated east, Xhosa princes and chiefs on the losing end of royal succession disputes trekked west with their client groups to found new polities. Boer attempts to expel the Xhosa from grazing grounds triggered the first of nine Cape frontier wars in 1779. Whatever forcible expulsions Boer commandos managed to achieve proved temporary as Xhosa easily flowed back into disputed areas and attacked settler farms in retaliation. Property destruction and white refugee flows undermined attempts at establishing profitable pastoral production. Attempts at further frontier accumulation could not proceed without greater imperial protection.

Imperial Contradictions and Settler Expansion Under British Rule

British rule in southern Africa had three faces. Metropolitan, missionary, and settler elites pursued contradictory objectives resulting in oscillations between colonial expansion and contraction.[14] While imperial incoherence was never deep enough to fundamentally endanger white settlement, metropolitan support was never consistent enough to ensure settler supremacy in frontier zones. Dutch-speaking and African peoples readily formed opportunistic alliances with the new colonial state's separate nodes to secure their own interests and property. British entry into the Cape may have strengthened state power, but it also added further sources of patronage for established Dutch elites and free-floating service groups. Understanding how British rule affected political economies of accumulation requires an elaboration of the separate concerns British officials, missionaries, and settlers represented.

Metropolitan policymakers in London primarily viewed the Cape in strategic terms. After losing its American colonies in the 1780s, the British Empire underwent a period of restructuring. By the 1790s, Britain's primary imperial concern was consolidating its hold on the Indian subcontinent and the strategic routes to South Asia. Conquest of the Cape in 1795, finalized after a brief interregnum in 1806, denied a resurgent France an established sea route to the east. London had little concern for southern Africa beyond the Cape Peninsula; however, the Cape's harbors could only be secure if interior areas achieved relative stability.[15] This drew the imperial state into settler politics and frontier wars. Initially, the British had not been keen on trekboer expansion. Settler intrusions into indigenous lands generated protracted conflicts that disrupted order and commerce.

After 1806, however, the character of British dominion became far more militaristic and far less sympathetic to African interests. This was linked to wider shifts in imperial governance and warfare. Britain administered its growing overseas possessions via a system of proconsular despotism. As embodiments of the British Crown, colonial governors assumed viceregal powers that allowed them to impose state directives on subject peoples and to mobilize military force to overcome resistance.[16] Proconsuls were usually senior army officers. They eschewed local political representation in elected assemblies, even for white settlers, and ran their territories as garrison states. The military contingents in these garrisons imported more destructive forms of warfare from continental Europe during the Napoleonic era. Rebellious elements on the receiving end of imperial ire were subjected to massacres and scorched-earth campaigns targeting livestock, crops, and other vital organic infrastructures. Such tactics were conducive to settler accumulation and indigenous dispossession, yet settler elites struggled to keep imperial troops in the field long enough to achieve complete conquest.

One reason for this was the missionary factor. Missionaries viewed Black peoples as benighted unfortunates fully capable of redemption via assimilation into British civilization. They only needed to be shown the way. Ministers founded frontier mission stations as points of contact and conversion wherein the gospel and Western cultural values could spread. The epistemic implications of religious indoctrination have generated much controversy among scholars.[17] It is nevertheless clear that missionary teachings took on a deliberately conservative hue. Natives had to don Western garb, dwell in European-style domiciles, work hard, embrace frugality, and fear God. These values and practices would turn heathens into obedient subjects who could be closely surveilled and easily taxed.[18]

Africans seldom saw it that way. Chiefs viewed mission stations as fixed points that provided access to valuable commodities. Moreover, missionaries advocated for chiefly interests and countered settler encroachments on grazing land and water sources. Tensions inevitably arose when chiefs and missionaries both claimed authority over African mission residents. Missionaries wanted converts, while chiefs wanted access to trade goods. When it came to Black people in colonial society, most church ministers strove for unequal integration rather than wholesale racial subordination. Missionary exertions produced diminishing returns over time as indigenes derived decreasing benefits from emulating Western lifeways. Agricultural improvements and cattle accumulation only made native lands more tempting targets for settler expropriation.[19]

Metropolitan officials facilitated British settlement in the Eastern Cape to promote frontier stability. British settlers would function as a buffer between the colony and disordered lands beyond. Settlement, in fact, produced the exact opposite effect. White settlers became a source of great instability as they began seizing indigenous lands.[20]

Post-Napoleonic politico-economic disorders gave the United Kingdom additional incentives to slough off surplus populations, but southern Africa never became a major destination for immigrants. Only about five thousand Britons arrived with the first wave in 1820. Downtrodden subalterns joined minor landed gentry fearing downward mobility at home and seeking greater aggrandizement abroad. Genteel individuals financed the passage of their poorer brethren, in the expectation that the latter would work for their sponsors on English-style country estates. Such hopes failed to materialize. Poor settlers refused to honor labor agreements and flocked to the colony's towns. Gentlemen also made poor agriculturalists. Economic viability came in the form of merino sheep farming. Although production never approached the levels seen in Australia, Cape wool contributed to the raw material inputs of Lancashire mills.

Landed proprietors on the eastern frontier began consolidating and enlarging their holdings. By the late 1830s, a few entrepreneurs, operating large spreads, dominated sheep farming. A select group of families stood atop white pastoral society. The Bowkers, Harts, Southeys, Gilberts, and others exported huge quantities of wool. In 1846, Richard Southey alone shipped fifty thousand pounds of fleece to Britain. James Howse pastured twenty-three thousand sheep on thirty thousand acres in Fort Beaufort district, while George Gilbert owned twenty-two thousand acres in the same area.[21] Gilbert lived in grand style; his estate at Sephton Manor lay astride three acres of land and was equipped with watchtowers to detect stock thefts.[22] Their domiciles were more akin to medieval fortresses than idyllic country houses. These men accumulated wealth on an incompletely conquered frontier and had to construct enclosed enclaves to defend their assets. Insecurity bred deep hostility toward unruly Black people. The prosettler *Grahamstown Journal* regularly hurled invective at Coloureds and Africans, presenting them as inferior races that only understood the language of force. Furthermore, wool farmers took a particularly uncompromising attitude toward indigenous sovereignty and chiefly autonomy. African polities beyond colonial control diverted labor flows away from settler-controlled pastoral production. By the early 1820s, when it became evident that there would never be enough white workers in the colony to exploit, settler farms had to draw in indigenous labor. Hence, settler elites strongly advocated for aggressive frontier expansion and land seizures.

Contrary to Dutch slave estates and Boer farmsteads, indigenous peoples were not integral components of British settler households. After being bludgeoned into submission, nonwhites were compelled to internalize their subordination. Administrative systems compelled natives to sell their labor to settlers at low cost and return to their reserves upon completing required tasks. Ultimately, Black people would only do so if they did not have alternative means of subsistence available.

This would not have been possible without imperial troops. British settlers formed militias that participated in frontier conflicts, yet they never managed to marshal the destructive power of Boer commandos. Metropolitan regiments and native auxiliaries, not settler paramilitaries, conquered Xhosa territories. As a result, colonial elites attempted to co-opt British governors into their expansionist projects. Sir Benjamin D'Urban's administration (r. 1834–38) was sympathetic to settler concerns and fought the Sixth Cape Frontier War (1834–35) in their interests.[23] The conquest and establishment of Queen Adelaide Province in 1835 presented new opportunities for pastoral expansion. However, London retroceded the territory in 1836 on the grounds that its seizure was unjust and uneconomical. Governor Sir Harry Smith (r. 1847–52) launched another frontier war with the intention of grabbing more Xhosa land. When the conflict degenerated into a protracted insurgency, he was replaced by Sir George Cathcart (r. 1852–54), who managed the transition to parliamentary representation with the caveat of a color-blind qualified franchise that gave propertied Africans the vote.[24]

Imperial power was both an enabler and inhibitor of settler expansion. Because of its global maritime supremacy, Britain could dispatch and reinforce field armies at will. Xhosa insurgents could and did attack settler farms but could not disrupt metropolitan supply ships. Whatever the merits or shortcomings of their field commanders, British units had access to greater resources than their enemies. Scorched-earth tactics targeting insurgent food supplies and dwellings meant starvation and exposure for those who continued to resist. Opponents engaged in irregular warfare were eventually exhausted, captured, or killed. Nonetheless, prior to mineral discoveries, the Cape colony was not important enough to subdue completely. London reined in proconsuls who went too far. At times, seized lands were returned or transferred from one group of Africans to another. The settler frontier advanced, and sheep barons continued to concentrate wealth as indigenous societies continued to resist territorial expropriation and proletarianization.

However, internal divisions impeded Xhosa resistance to the colonial onslaught. Dynastic tensions resulting in political fissions are well understood.[25] A surfeit of sons and wives inevitably triggered succession disputes and migratory flows led by disgruntled princes. More recent work has delineated developing socioeconomic cleavages within Xhosa polities.[26] By the early nineteenth century, certain households began subverting agricultural customs in pursuit of profit. Social mores upheld a gendered division of labor in which men tended cattle while women worked the fields. Homesteads that derived few benefits from such arrangements transferred male and animal labor to crop cultivation. Farms composed of migrants, possibly escaping disorders farther east, ranked very low on social hierarchies and could not hope to cull sufficient cattle through bride price distribution mechanisms that favored ruling elites. What cattle they had were used to plow fields and transport crops to market centers. The spread of colonial towns and trading posts further encouraged shifts to commercial cultivation. Households that accumulated wealth via proscribed labor practices faced spiritual condemnation. For prioritizing crops over cattle, they suffered social ostracism, witchcraft accusations, and physical violence.

Colonial territories to the west were hardly havens for indigenous capital accumulation, given settler hostility to Black agricultural competition. Nonetheless, African commercial farmers had greater opportunities under British rule and relocated accordingly. Around seventeen thousand migrants, labeled *Fingos* by colonial officials, entered the Cape colony in 1835. This exodus was no doubt prompted by the dislocations of the Sixth Frontier War, but many who migrated remained. Fingos, renamed the *Mfengu* by later scholars,[27] became British loyalists to serve their socioeconomic interests. Previous assessments, which view the Mfengu as a colonial construction driven by imperial divide-and-rule strategies, deprive Africans of agency.[28] Mfengus chose to live under British dominion because economic practices within those areas were more compatible with their own production systems. Many felt British identity transcended racial boundaries. Those able to cultivate for markets, convert to Christianity, and accumulate sufficient means could become Black Englishmen.[29] Most Africans allowed to vote under the Cape's 1853 constitution came from this affluent subgroup. Nevertheless, Mfengus remained a minority among Xhosa-speaking peoples, and the Black Englishmen among them were a tiny minority within that minority.[30]

Market enterprise was not the only route to Mfengu empowerment. Armed service in colonial armies proved equally important. Mfengu auxiliaries played a vital role in combat operations during the Seventh (1846–47), Eighth (1850–53), and Ninth (1877–78) Cape Frontier Wars.[31] Having been hounded out of Xhosa lands, they now returned with British regiments to seize land and cattle. Battlefield struggles between Xhosa and Mfengu were extremely fierce. British commanders encouraged but did not create these animosities. After conflicts concluded, Cape officials allocated certain plots taken from rebellious Xhosas to loyal Mfengus. Authorities felt native allies settled on conquered lands could provide the same buffer function between the Eastern Cape and Xhosa kingdoms originally attempted with the 1820 settlers. Yet Mfengu settlement had a similarly destabilizing effect as unpacified Xhosas attacked their assimilated counterparts and triggered further conflicts. When territorial dispossession and deepening socioeconomic deprivation produced the millenarian cattle-killing movement (1856–57), the Mfengu did not participate.[32] After an ensuing famine killed up to forty thousand people and drove destitute Xhosa refugees onto colonial farms, the Mfengu occupied abandoned lands. Since loyalist farmers retained their cattle, oxen soon furrowed new fields and transported grains to towns swollen with starving refugees. As most Xhosa speakers fell into penury, a small minority increased its prosperity.

Indigenous authority structures in Natal were more resilient because white settlers could not sustain imperial violence prior to the 1870s. In 1824, traders established a minor station at Port Natal, but its agents lacked the means to seize territory. They instead provided commercial and military services to Zulu monarchs who tolerated their presence to consolidate control over regional trade networks. Britain annexed Natal only in 1843 after Boer bands entering Port Natal posed a threat to frontier security and eastward sea routes. Intra-African wars had left large areas vacant. Clans and client groups fled factional conflicts in the Zulu kingdom and settled elsewhere. Minuscule administrative resources compelled Theophilus Shepstone, son of a Wesleyan missionary and secretary for native affairs from 1856 to 1877, to run the colony through indirect rule. After the Colonial Office vetoed his attempt to transfer the bulk of the Black population into a separate territory, Shepstone had to make do with demographic realities.[33] African chiefs who kept subjects in line could maintain control over their followers. When chiefs provided auxiliaries to punish recalcitrant colleagues, they received a cut of expropriated cattle. Although Shepstone has been portrayed as a figure that appropriated and manipulated indigenous traditions to wield despotic power over African societies,[34] the early colonial state lacked the capacity to impose centralized despotism. Rather, Shepstone molded administrative practices and procedures in ways that accommodated groups of local loyalist elites.[35] In doing so, he strengthened chiefly powers and made rulers less accountable to followers. Kholwas (African Christian converts), in turn, readily embraced commercial farming and sold their produce in colonial markets, much to the chagrin of white settlers. John Colenso, Anglican bishop of Natal from 1853 to 1883, became a staunch advocate for native rights and a vociferous critic of colonial abuses.[36] Furthermore, the neighboring Zulu kingdom posed a somewhat exaggerated threat to Natal's security. A tiny white population required loyal Africans if it hoped to remain viable.

The Western Cape Gentry and Voortrekkers in the Era of Slave Emancipation

London's main concern was to make its newly acquired southern African colony financially self-sufficient. Consequently, British administrators initially pursued economic policies that protected and encouraged gentry-dominated industries. In 1806, an enlarged colonial garrison prompted the administration to offer higher prices for wheat brought to Cape Town markets. A new grain committee headed by Dutch-speaking elites monitored wheat supplies and boosted production, although export levels remained modest, since London refused to reduce duties on Cape imports. Far greater profits came from wine making. In exchange for government support, producers agreed to improve their wines. In 1813, Governor John Cradock managed to reduce British duties on Cape wines by two-thirds. As a result, wine production grew by 151 percent from 1809 to 1823. In 1821, wine made up 63 percent of Cape exports. This wealth flowed to a select few able to expand acreage devoted to viniculture. In addition, owners of large estates bought more slaves and worked them harder in the fields. The wine boom was confined to a tiny enclave, with Cape Town and Stellenbosch districts producing about 93 percent of Cape wines in 1823. Winemakers remained a tight-knit community intimately connected through marriage alliances and social functions. Interelite economic alliances did coalesce as incoming British merchants bought wine directly from gentry farms, constructed storage facilities, and advocated for low duties in the metropole. Although British merchants and Cape producers did business together, for the most part, they remained culturally distinct.[37]

Slave emancipation brought the gentry few long-term benefits, although several palliatives cushioned the blows. Britain's ban on the slave trade, which came into effect in 1808, drove up slave prices and increased owners' net worth. Those in need of quick cash, however, sold off to richer colleagues. The wine boom resulted in urban slaves being sold to rural estates, transferring further wealth from town to country. Moreover, staggered emancipation kept ostensibly liberated slaves on estates as apprentices from 1834 to 1838. Despite these alleviations, severe labor shortages appeared soon after Britain banned the slave trade, cutting into agricultural productivity. Following full emancipation in 1838, a series of antivagrancy and squatting laws curtailed freedom's revolutionary socioeconomic potential. This prevented the emergence of an Mfengu-like Black peasantry in the Western Cape.[38] Yet what ultimately allowed former slave-owners to endure emancipation was the practice of partible inheritance and credit extensions across diffuse kin groups. Refusal to practice primogeniture inevitably meant estate fragmentation over time, but all heirs received some property and could thus cling to a genteel way of life. Below-market interest rates on loans to kinsmen staved off bankruptcy and gave landed gentlemen time to recoup losses and engage in more profitable pursuits.[39] The Cape gentry declined but did not fall.

Boer diffusion into the South African interior continued prior processes of frontier expansion. Contrary to mythologized nationalist narratives, trekking communities were not uniformly hostile to British rule. Their commandos augmented British military forces during frontier conflicts and seized Xhosa lands. Slave emancipation threatened social hierarchies, but interior migrations preempted Cape land speculators, compelling purchases from Boer owners and occupiers. In addition, local imperial officials encouraged extended white settlement because it provided a pretext for further territorial annexations. During the 1830s, roughly fifteen thousand settlers trekked out of the Eastern Cape in search of greener pastures.[40] Their encounters with African agropastoral peoples were hardly one-sided affairs. Boer migrants known as voortrekkers divided into separate parties, often working at cross-purposes to one another. They expanded by weaving their way into preexisting conflicts between African clans, chiefdoms, and princes. Voortrekkers frequently fought wars in coalition with native armies, and their coalition partners often gained as much from victories as their white counterparts. In 1839, the Boers allied with the Bakgatla to drive Mzilikazi from the highveld. In 1840, they backed Zulu prince Mpande in a successful bid to overthrow his brother, King Dingane.

In addition, the Transvaal and Orange Free State republics were established with British acquiescence. After a bitter struggle subduing Xhosa insurgents in the Eighth Frontier War, London had no desire to finance further conquests. The Sand River Convention of 1852 allowed Transvaal Boers to establish the South African Republic. The Orange River Convention of 1854 withdrew British sovereignty over that territory and handed it to Boer farmers. Pastoral farms across the South African interior continued to rely on bonded labor captured in commando raids. British commercial interests continued to dominate the Orange Free State's economy. The Transvaal remained a poorly governed agrarian backwater populated by powerful African polities, such as the Pedi kingdom, unwilling to accept white domination. South African Republic officials relied heavily on

Swazi military labor to raid the Pedi and deliver captives to be converted into indentured servants. Thus, white authorities contained Pedi power by bolstering Swazi strength. In addition, different Boer factions occupied far-flung locales and fought each other for access to state spoils.[41] The northeastern frontier remained a remote concern for imperial planners and capital investors until gold discoveries in the 1880s.

Black Kings and Regionalized Polities in Preindustrial South Africa

Political change in the South African interior resulted in the creation of regionalized polities with greater extractive capacities than the polities that immediately proceeded them. To be sure, early nineteenth-century state formation in southern Africa was not nearly as revolutionary as once thought. Complex civilizations with powerful kings and stone architecture existed centuries prior.[42] The Mapungubwe and Great Zimbabwe kingdoms were at least as impressive as any African state constructed after 1800. The set of polities formed at this time may represent a final phase in precolonial cycles of administrative dissolution and consolidation deeply rooted in macroregional history, although there is scant evidence of complex supralocal states in lower southeastern territories prior to the eighteenth century.[43] Developments from circa 1780 to 1850, referred to as the *Mfecane* (crushing) or *Difaqane* (scattering) by some scholars, have generated heated academic debates that remain unresolved. The controversy centers on which factor, or set of factors, triggered this process and drove it forward. Everything from psycho-historical speculations, ecological disruptions, conflicts over trade networks, population pressures, and European slave raiders has been considered.[44] What is beyond doubt is that state centralization, enabled by more lethal forms of warfare, concentrated substantial wealth within ruling families. Higher levels of military training within male age-sets produced warrior regiments. Kings attempted to directly control these regiments by removing or reducing the power of aristocratic intermediaries that traditionally mustered warriors on a monarch's behalf. This turned armies into extensions of monarchical households and enabled territorial expansion and cattle accumulation.

Due to intra-elite tensions, mountainous terrain, and multiple access points to trade products and prestige goods, transregional agglomerations did not fully cohere. No matter how powerful African kings became, unruly subordinates and royal kin caused severe ructions that precipitated civil wars or rebellions by exit. Detached segments did not necessarily wander across open country in destitute conditions. Rather, they operated as states on the march until they could locate and consolidate control over habitable territory. Some failed to do so and dissolved or degenerated into predatory brigandage. Others managed to reconstitute into powerful kingdoms replete with warrior regiments and tributary subordinates. Centralizing practices accrued in one area were grafted onto different locales. African peoples unable to centralize and amass sufficient coercive capacities either faced elimination or assimilation into more powerful polities. Incorporated peoples were often relegated to subordinate positions within political hierarchies and continued to face socioeconomic disadvantages long after their submission.[45] What follows is a selection of cases that exemplify pathways to regional consolidation.

Black politico-military elites pursued various options to increase their material wealth and human resources. Autonomous Cape Coloured peoples emulated white voortrekker lifeways and modes of warfare. Chieftains able to organize pastoral farmsteads and mounted gunners became paramount leaders of large communities, although some preferred predation to production. African elites across the southeast established militarized kingdoms. Although political legitimacy was concentrated within ruling dynasties, monarchs and princes engaged in violent feuds for supreme power. More cautious sovereigns combined coercion with diplomacy and attenuated colonial encroachments on their prerogatives. White settlers and British imperial authorities presented threats to and opportunities for further resource accumulation by indigenous rulers. Kings, princes, and chieftains attempted to incorporate and manipulate colonial forces to pursue their interests. Some proved more successful than others.

Cape Coloureds that managed to break free from labor bondage and migrate to the colony's frontiers often reverted to a nomadic existence, premised on raiding pastoral farmsteads. Certain groups pursued more complex forms of material accumulation. Life on Boer farms and commando service familiarized Coloureds with horses and firearms. Mixed-race males became particularly adept at riding and shooting. Fugitives used these skills to become mounted gunmen capable of imposing tributary systems on agropastoral peoples in fringe areas. Coloured war bands with sufficient firepower continued genocidal wars begun by white settlers against San hunter-gathers. In present-day Namibia, Jonker Afrikaner's retainers developed into a warrior elite extracting tribute from Herero communities.[46]

Other groups in Griquatown attempted to impose similar exactions on Sotho-Tswana groups with far less success. By contrast, the Griquas of Philippolis embraced Christianity and pastoral farming. This resulted in rapid stratification between farm owners and workers. Prosperous Griquas facilitated the establishment of mission stations. As in the Eastern Cape, missionaries provided valuable political contacts and presented Griqua enrichment as a sign of moral virtue. Agricultural prosperity had its downsides. Orange Free State settlers eyed Griqua farms with envy. Conflicts between the communities eventually compelled Philippolis Griquas to migrate southeast in 1861. The migrants consolidated a new settlement in Griqualand East, based at Kokstad, a few years later. Griqualand East reproduced the commercial pastoralism and socioeconomic hierarchies of Philippolis.[47] A representative council, or *raad,* placed limits on monarchic power, but Adam Kok III retained ultimate executive authority. Philippolis and Griqualand East were Boer republics in all but skin color. Yet white settlers could not overlook racial difference, and the two territories could not survive. The dissolution of Coloured polities resulted in mass socioeconomic dispossession. Within a generation, Griquas became indistinguishable from rural indigents eking out an existence on white-owned farms.

The Zulu kingdom provides an example of militarized accumulation. As its founder, Shaka kaSenzangakhona (r. 1816–28) represents best pathways to political centralization and wealth concentration by warrior kings. Born the son of a minor chief, Shaka gained prominence through military service with his Mthethwa overlords. The Mthethwa confederacy possessed large regiments under close royal control and sought out tributaries to secure access to labor and livestock. As an associate of King Dingiswayo, Shaka commanded field armies and raided cattle on his patron's behalf. In 1816, Dingiswayo supported Shaka's usurpation of the Zulu throne. This made a powerful Mthethwa tributary ruler of a subordinate chiefdom. After Dingiswayo was killed by Zwide, ruler of the Ndwandwe, Shaka incorporated most Mthethwa clients into the Zulu kingdom and launched military campaigns against neighboring states. As Shaka accumulated greater quantities of people and cattle, he fought more destructive wars against larger rivals and amassed ever more wealth. As one European witness later recounted, "The several bloody and exterminating wars of Shaka appear to have had no object in view other than to enrich himself with cattle of the conquered tribes; to obtain these was a sufficient incentive to engage in the most daring and arduous enterprise."[48] Shaka had authority to allocate all land acquired by conquest to clients, making him the primary source of state patronage. Nevertheless, chiefs responsible for territorial subdivisions often exercised that right in the king's name. Royal warriors also tended to royal herds, moving them across seasonal grazing zones and guarding them from rival armies.

The rapid incorporation of numerous peoples caused problems. After defeating the Ndwandwe, several prominent individuals refused to become vassals and withdrew northward with their clients. As a senior Ndwandwe military commander, Soshangane gathered a large following and founded the Gaza kingdom in southern Mozambique. Mzilikazi accepted Shaka's suzerainty for a time but soon decamped to establish his own polity. When his efforts to build a kingdom on the highveld failed, due to conflicts with voortrekkers and rival chiefdoms, he moved farther north and constructed a state in southwestern Zimbabwe.[49] These exits created alternative power centers to which other groups dissatisfied with Zulu rule could migrate. In addition, incorporated tributaries often came from prestigious bloodlines that gave them claims to material resources. Such claims clashed with the interests of a ruling house determined to concentrate livestock and grazing land in its hands. Shaka dealt with defiance through violent political purges. Chiefdoms and lineages deemed disloyal suffered mass executions and asset appropriations. When Shaka barely survived an assassination attempt, the Qwabe clan was deemed culpable, and thousands were wiped out.[50] Shaka faced greater dangers from family members. His father had sired many sons with different women, and royal mothers supported their sons' political ambitions. Some of Shaka's half brothers, led by Dingane, orchestrated his assassination after an unsuccessful military campaign against Soshangane in 1828.

Violent feuds racked Zululand for the next three decades as princes fought to displace incumbent monarchs. All contenders came from the same ruling family and sought to secure commercial and military assistance from European agents. Shaka died before Europeans appreciably impacted southeast African politics. King Dingane (r. 1828–40), by contrast, had to deal with unreliable Portuguese traders and intruding voortrekkers. Dingane's regicidal seizure of power compounded his political difficulties, and he never fully secured the army's loyalty. To gain military support, Dingane relaxed regimental discipline and did not act against contingents that relocated to Port Natal without his sanction. He also sought to accumulate prestige goods, guns, and horses from Europeans. By the 1830s, Portuguese officials at Delagoa Bay relied heavily on African military labor to capture slaves. Zulu regiments may have conducted slave raids in exchange for cloth, brass, and beads. Their material value was less important than the prestige they conferred on recipients. Yet Delagoa Bay's governor began withholding goods from Dingane and redirecting them toward Soshangane, who had access to more populous raiding zones. Consequently, Zulu forces launched an attack on Delagoa Bay that resulted in the governor's death.

The guns and horses Dingane expected from Piet Retief's voortrekker party would have bolstered his monarchic prestige and coercive capacities. When these items were not promptly delivered, Dingane's denigrated honor compelled him to order a massacre of Retief and his followers.[51] This act, in turn, precipitated a war with Andries Pretorius's voortrekker group. Dingane's attempts at consolidating power had not prevented his half brother Mpande from cultivating his own client base and seeking white settler support. The Boers backed Mpande's rebellion in exchange for land concessions. Mpande then seized power when Dingane was overthrown and killed in 1840.[52]

Mpande himself later was challenged by his son Cetshwayo. Even though Cetshwayo was Mpande's designated heir, born to the king's Great Wife, his father attempted to balance court factions by supporting Prince Mbuyazi, officially recognized as Mpande's son, though certain oral traditions claim he was fathered by Shaka.[53] Such an illustrious lineage may have aided Mbuyazi in forming a large following. Cetshwayo's position as crown prince and his close association with the Buthelezi clan gave him a wide-enough network to face down this threat. Mbuyazi's alliance with Boer leaders gave him access to firearms, but he could not match his rival's numbers. Cetshwayo's faction triumphed when the two princes clashed at the Battle of Ndondakusuka in 1856. Mbuyazi perished in the struggle and several of his half brothers were executed. Mpande stayed on as nominal sovereign while Cetshwayo wielded power from behind the throne. He assumed direct control over the kingdom after his father's death in 1872. Court plots and royal refugees continued to cause problems, but the Zulu state became more stable after 1856.

Overmighty sons, siblings, and subjects frequently challenged Zulu sovereigns for supreme power. These were mainly intra-elite conflicts that stayed within the family. Royal feuds did not fully dismember the kingdom, because all princes found usurpation more profitable than fragmentation. Migrations by powerful warlords such as Soshangane and Mzilikazi possibly spared Zululand further strife, since their departure reduced the number of elites that could internally challenge monarchic authority. Zulu elites mobilized human and material resources to seize or secure further resources. Through palace coups and predatory warfare, rulers accumulated assets they could strategically distribute to clients in exchange for loyalty. Acquired wealth circulated among a narrow elite and did not benefit the general population.

Other African kings accumulated power by offering refuge to local communities set adrift by disorder. King Moshoeshoe's mountainous territory in the Caledon River Valley provided greater security from incessant raids than open terrain. To dissuade enemies from launching attacks, Moshoeshoe claimed his highland base at Thaba Bosiu (Mountain at Night) grew taller after dark. He increased his following by allowing clients to come to him. Marriages, mounted warriors, guns, and missionary alliances expanded royal power, but diplomacy took centerstage in statecraft.[54] In the 1840s, Moshoeshoe leveraged support from his Paris Evangelical Missionary Society associates to block Wesleyan attempts to allocate lands to rival chiefdoms. Moshoeshoe also maintained close relations with British imperial officials to limit land-grabs by Boer settler groups. This policy was not always effective. In 1849, Moshoeshoe was compelled to cede a large tract of land, including more than one hundred villages and a few thousand subjects, to white farming interests. The Basotho king also lost authority over several migrant vassals. He was often compelled to restrain hardliners within his court who called for aggressive responses to colonial duplicity.

Tensions smoldered until Governor Cathcart's setback at the Battle of Berea in 1852. Imperial authorities took a more accommodating attitude toward Moshoeshoe after his refusal to exploit a temporary military advantage. Moshoeshoe used British support to good effect as Boer settlers in the Orange Free State incessantly encroached on Basotho lands. Despite the efforts of Moshoeshoe's warriors, Boer commandos inflicted crushing defeats from 1866 to 1867. To prevent complete dispossession, Moshoeshoe made his kingdom a British protectorate in 1868.[55] This rump state managed to avoid total submission to settler supremacy by maintaining the imperial tie.

* * *

By 1870, southern Africa was a patchwork of regional polities dominated by elites extracting wealth from subordinate populations. Race overlapped with class in areas where settlers established control over commercial agriculture and pastoral production. However, colonial intrusions prior to the mineral revolution did not uniformly solidify white domination. European agents could be utilized to enrich indigenous elites and allies. Powerful African kingdoms remained in place, and a thin stratum of affluent Black farmers was steadily accumulating capital. To be sure, colonialism only served a privileged few, but race was not yet the primary means to prosperity.

2

Wealth Concentration in an Age of Industrialization and Political Centralization

From the late nineteenth to early twentieth century, southern Africa experienced administrative centralization and accelerated indigenous dispossession. Diamond and gold discoveries triggered colonial consolidation. Aggressive imperial proconsuls dismantled autonomous African kingdoms and economic systems. Metropolitan authorities supported territorial amalgamation for geostrategic and commercial reasons. Britain's relative economic decline compelled more effective administrative control, lest now-valuable territories drift into the hands of rival imperial powers. As in the rest of Africa, modern transportation and military technologies facilitated conquest by foreigners. The superior coercive capacities of the British either overwhelmed or exhausted armed resistance.

The development of industrial mining further spurred administrative homogenization. Unlike livestock, minerals were obtained at fixed points and extracted from deep-level mines dug out and sustained with advanced machinery. Racialized property legislation, high capital requirements, and carceral labor conditions soon put precious minerals beyond the reach of African societies. Mining profits made white political and economic elites exponentially more powerful than their African counterparts. Small groups of assimilated Africans that participated in, or otherwise abetted, indigenous dispossession maintained a relatively privileged position. These privileged indigenes aspired to join, rather than overthrow, an iniquitous colonial order. Politico-cultural contradictions within the white community presented far greater risks to steady mining profits than traditional African societies. British officials instrumentalized intrawhite tensions as a pretext to consolidate imperial domination. This eventually triggered a protracted war between Britain and the Boer republics. Conflict was followed by compromise at Black expense. The result was a more perfect form of wealth concentration.

Diamond Discoveries, Industrial Mining, and Oligarchic Wealth

The discovery of diamonds in 1867 led to wealth accumulation that fundamentally restructured South Africa's political economy. The initial rush of prospectors panning along the Vaal River soon gave way to dry diggings in and around what became Kimberley.[1] As in the agricultural sector, mining ventures could not function without Black labor. Various factors drew Africans to the mines. In the 1860s, epizootic diseases, coupled with persistent drought, decimated indigenous cattle and crops. Young African males took up wage labor to assemble new herds, obtain guns, and purchase agricultural implements. Diamond digging also served elite interests. Chiefs dispatched work parties to Kimberley and took percentages of their subjects' earnings.[2]

The early mining industry was open to anyone with a set of tools and a team of laborers. Claim prices rose with increasing demand. Miners unable to afford full ownership bought shares in developing claims. Low barriers to entry resulted in a rapid proliferation of claims, overproduction, and declining diamond prices. As diamond prices dropped, the costs and dangers of mining rose. Mines became larger and deeper, requiring more labor. Rising labor demands meant higher wages for African workers. Deeper mines meant reef falls and flooding that shut down production for long periods. Only owners with sufficient capital could install or rent machines to clear fallen debris and pump out flooded shafts. Miners lacking the means to overcome these adversities sold claims to their more prosperous counterparts and either left the mines or became worksite overseers. Initially, downward mobility had little to do with race. Early on, several Black people managed to purchase claims and turn better profits than their white counterparts. As a result, downwardly mobile whites attempted to dispossess Black people of their claims through vigilante tactics. Beatings and home burnings became commonplace. Ostensibly anarchist movements for "diggers' democracy" were deeply racial, seeking greater privileges for white workers and more restrictions on Black competitors.[3]

Mining corporations had far greater means than white vigilantes had to repress Black labor. As small-scale diggers liquidated their holdings, entrepreneurs began buying up and amalgamating claims.[4] Amalgamation accelerated digger dispossession and capital concentration. By the early 1880s, a handful of firms dominated diamond mining. Joint-stock companies brought in industrial equipment to sink deeper shafts and process larger quantities of excavated earth. Deep-level mining required a regimented labor force ready to be mustered and deployed to rockfaces at regular intervals. Moreover, underground working conditions remained extremely hazardous. Rock bursts, mud rushes, and firedamp resulted in numerous deaths and countless injuries. Workers would fail to perform adequately without strict controls. Mine owners, in turn, would fail to profit if workers stole discovered stones. Diamonds stored great value in small packages, making them relatively easy to conceal and steal. White miners and company executives viewed all Black workers as inherent thieves eager to sell purloined stones outside corporate market channels. According to senior executives, thievish workers enabled illicit diamond buying (IDB). IDB cut into profits and had to be squelched at the source. As a result, mining sites, and by extension Kimberley's African areas, mutated into carceral spaces. Companies constructed closed compounds in which African workers had to reside for the duration of their contracts.[5] After their shifts, they were stripped and subjected to full body searches. On some mines, workers at the end of their contracts were required to remain in holding rooms until they had fully evacuated their bowels to preclude the possibility of smuggling out swallowed diamonds.[6] Africans in Kimberley had to present a pass on demand to police officers to indicate they either had a job or a reason for being about town. Failure to present proper documentation resulted in arrest and incarceration.

Although companies derived huge profits from criminalizing Black labor, the system did not work perfectly. Desertions, go-slows, and physical resistance undermined companies' panoptic pretensions. Africans with work experience in the mines informed migrant bands approaching Kimberley which companies paid the best wages. Certain employers found bureaucratic regulations irksome and hired undocumented Africans. Nonetheless, extra-economic coercion severely undermined labor's bargaining power and kept wages artificially low. For a time, Black workers still had enough discretionary income to invest in the rural sector when they returned home. But as rural areas became increasingly impoverished, dependents had to devote larger portions of mining wages to basic subsistence.

Unskilled white workers did not derive appreciable gains from Black subordination. White overseers avoided the denigrating treatment meted out to Africans but were also subjected to surveillance and controls. When white workers went on strike in 1884 over body search regulations, police and special constables opened fire on a marching crowd, resulting in six deaths and six injuries.[7] Capital further fragmented labor by pandering to racial solidarity. Whites had to unite if they wanted to keep Black people in their place. Closed compounds also made it harder to launch concerted strike actions and prevented union organizers from recruiting members. At the same time, corporations cultivated a separate class of skilled white workers operating or maintaining machinery along the edges of mining sites. Higher wages and better working conditions made skilled labor reluctant to embrace radicalism.

Mine owners obtained further supplies of cheap labor from the Kimberley convict station and other Cape colony prisons. Convicts proved more compliant and provided replacements for recalcitrant workers. Convict laborers, who could not strike, were subjected to harsher discipline and thorough body searches.

Companies kept them separate from other workers and confined their activities to surface labor such as loading carts, digging trenches, carrying rocks, and sorting gravel. Cape authorities provided convict workers free of charge; mining companies were responsible only for their upkeep. This decreased maintenance costs for Cape convicts and saved the colony around £20,000 a year by the 1890s.[8] This system gave enormous benefits to government and business at free labor's expense. As the number of convict workers went up, the number of wage laborers went down.

The indirect costs of coercive labor regimes compounded losses for small white businesses. Compound barracks and convict labor reduced customers for whites in the hospitality sector. Wholesalers concluded lucrative contracts with mining companies to supply company stores, but this locked out retailers and small shopkeepers. The mines choked off commercial activities that did not serve their interests.

With capital's ascent over labor, diamond profits depended on control of demand. Yet only a single source of supply could effectively manipulate demand. As long as than one company operated in Kimberley, corporations undermined competitors by flooding the market with stones and offering African migrants higher wages. Lower prices and higher working costs curtailed profits. An effective monopoly promised to solve both problems and pay steady dividends. Amalgamation could only be achieved by buying out competitors, and only a few mining magnates had the means to do so. Magnates who concentrated investments in blue earth excavation accumulated the most capital. Deep-level blue ground held far richer deposits than yellow diamondiferous soils near the surface. However, blue ground deposits had to be dug out with heavy machinery or blasted loose with dynamite. Large-scale operators plowed profits back into purchasing industrial equipment to obtain higher profits. Higher profits meant more money to purchase more claims and to buy out rival companies.

Although many magnates attempted amalgamation, Cecil Rhodes and Barney Barnato proved the most successful.[9] Both men accumulated vast fortunes developing deep-level mines. The struggle between Rhodes's De Beers Mining Company and Barnato's Kimberley Central Diamond Mining Company for mastery over the diamond fields has been heavily romanticized. Rhodes is often depicted as a visionary using his fortune to spread enlightened Anglo-Saxon rule across Africa. Barnato, by contrast, is portrayed as a rapacious Jewish capitalist and social climber eager to accrue riches at every turn. Rhodes's eventual triumph over Barnato signaled the triumph of progress over greed. To be sure, Barnato was more of a speculator than diamond digger, and there is strong evidence he took part in IDB transactions.[10] Despite their differences, both Rhodes and Barnato accumulated wealth by repressing Black labor. Their clash was, in fact, more akin to a modern-day corporate merger from which Barnato profited handsomely.

De Beers and Kimberley Central strove to gain ascendancy over the other by acquiring Jules Porgès's strategically placed French Company. Using connections with European financiers, Rhodes bought the French Company with a massive loan from the Rothschild Bank. He then sold the French Company to Barnato in return for a large stake in Kimberley Central. Shortly afterward, Rhodes inflated Kimberley Central shares to the point where many of Barnato's supporters started selling off. This allowed Rhodes to become the majority shareholder. He was nevertheless compelled to buy Barnato's compliance through massive payoffs. In early 1888, Barnato sold 11,333 Kimberley Central shares, worth £10 each, to De Beers for £66 each. A few months later, Rhodes bought out Barnato's Kimberley Central assets with a check for £5,338,650. Shortly thereafter, Rhodes and company incorporated De Beers Consolidated Mines. Barnato was appointed one of its life governors. After 36 percent of profits were allocated to dividend payments, life governors were entitled to divide up what remained.[11] Senior executives and managers received lesser perks, but wealth clearly flowed upward. Amalgamation concentrated the diamond oligarchy into a single corporation without unifying its members. Individual diamond magnates on the De Beers board still had means and motives to pursue contradictory objectives.

From a market perspective, however, De Beers Consolidated operated as a monopoly. It created artificial scarcity by selling predetermined quotas of stones to the London-based Diamond Syndicate, where Barnato was also a major shareholder. The syndicate sold the stones to retail traders who marketed them to consumers. Each stage along this marketing chain involved significant markups.

At the production end, De Beers's profits came from low wages and minimal investments in workers' welfare. Those who survived industrial accidents frequently lost fingers or limbs and suffered from chronic respiratory illnesses. Many lived as invalids after retiring to their rural homes. When stones glutted the market, De Beers cut production and retrenched its workforce. Production cuts tipped Kimberley into deep depressions as high unemployment stifled consumer spending. In 1899, the Kimberley mines employed two thousand Europeans and eleven thousand Africans compared to five thousand Europeans and twenty-five thousand Africans twenty-five years earlier. Average wages had also dropped 25 percent since the mid-1880s.[12] The town waxed and waned according to corporate boom-bust cycles and boardroom priorities. Monopoly brought tremendous wealth but concentrated it within a corporate oligarchy that had little concern for inclusive economic development.

Shifting Geopolitical Winds and a Resurgent Imperial Factor

Diamond discoveries in the South African interior coincided with seismic geopolitical shifts in the global balance of power. German unification on the European continent and rapid economic growth in the United States posed fundamental challenges to British commercial dominance. From roughly 1830 to 1870, Britain exercised global dominion through free trade. Naval supremacy gave Britain the means to knock down barriers to its products and to protect strategic shipping lanes connecting it to overseas markets and resources. City of London financiers bankrolled infrastructure projects in colonies and client states to facilitate trade flows and raw material extraction. As rivals rose, informal empire could not provide sufficient safeguards to forestall foreign penetration in areas of interest. More direct forms of imperial supervision had to be put in place to secure markets and commodities.

Mineral discoveries vastly increased South Africa's importance to metropolitan policymakers.[13] A coalescing mining sector located in the interior required efficient transport routes and abundant labor. Confederation, through conquest and annexation, promised to ease commodity flows and increase labor pools. An end to independent polities meant an end to internal customs duties and separate economic systems that tied up workers in alternative pursuits. Although the diamond fields employed far fewer workers than the Rand's gold mines, support services and railway construction exponentially increased required labor inputs. Mineworkers had to be fed, clothed, and sold consumer products. Railways transported these items faster than pack animals. After large-scale gold discoveries, Rhodes led a parliamentary coalition in the Cape that raised public debt to build railways to mining sites. Freight charges and customs revenues were then plowed back into extending rail lines toward mines. Only farms located en route to mining areas benefited from these burgeoning grids.[14] As lines and rolling stock expanded, larger numbers of commodity producers delivered their products to transportation hubs. These activities were predicated on an abundant supply of cheap African labor.

A major proponent of confederation was Sir Henry Bartle Frere. As high commissioner for southern Africa from 1877 to 1880, he pushed territorial amalgamation through belligerent pronouncements and deliberate provocations. Armed conflicts provided pretexts for aggrandizing British possessions. The first major move toward confederation came with the annexation of the Transvaal in 1877.[15] Boer commandos had fared badly against Pedi warriors under King Sekhukhune. The republic's ramshackle administrative structures could not mobilize sufficient resources to successfully prosecute the campaign, and British occupation spared Boer farmers further property losses.

Thereafter, the Ninth Cape Frontier War (1877–78) toppled what remained of Xhosa rule in the Transkei. Property disputes between Gcaleka Xhosas and Mfengus heightened tensions between these antagonistic groups. In August 1877, a brawl at an Mfengu wedding triggered war. Cape forces crossed into the Transkei to protect their Mfengu allies. Frere declared that Gcaleka territory would be occupied by white settlers and their warriors disarmed. These directives fomented wider resistance as other Xhosa groups rose in solidarity with Gcaleka rebels. Imperial reinforcements ground down insurgent bands in 1878, and the Gcaleka were subjugated.

Frere's wars for imperial unification then suffered a setback when British forces in 1879's Anglo-Zulu War faced unexpectedly fierce resistance from Cetshwayo's regiments. The Zulus inflicted a crushing defeat on British regulars at Isandlwana. This humiliation prompted the British to retaliate with a second, larger invasion in which they beat back Zulu attacks and sacked the royal capital at Ulundi in July 1879. However, when the British subsequently divided Zululand into chiefdoms, the area fell into disorder as feuding warlords maneuvered for political advantage, and London's appetite for South African amalgamation soon soured.

British troops and their Swazi allies defeated Pedi armies and captured Sekhukhune shortly after taking Ulundi. But this benefited the Boers as much as it did the British. Without powerful Zulu and Pedi rivals around them, Boer leaders had no need for imperial overrule. The Transvaal Rebellion (1880–81), also known as the First Anglo-Boer War, resulted in another shocking British defeat at Majuba Hill (1881). William Ewart

Gladstone's Liberal government (1880–85) was highly averse to further imperial adventurism. The Pretoria Convention of 1881 stipulated London's recognition of the Transvaal Republic under loose British suzerainty.

Efforts to disarm the Basotho triggered further reversals. The Basotho rump state had been under Cape administration since 1871. When the Cape government, with Frere's encouragement, moved to collect Sotho firearms, their chiefs refused to comply. In the ensuing Gun War (1880–81), the Basotho effectively defeated Cape forces, and Basutoland became a Crown colony in 1884, thus preventing its incorporation into a settler-governed state. Metropolitan policymakers had temporarily halted the confederation project.

African Loyalism and Indigenous Accumulation

Without indigenous allies, Britain's limited military gains would have been far more costly. Loyalism was predicated on material rewards and inter-African divisions. Over two thousand Mfengu auxiliaries took part in the Ninth Cape Frontier War. Conquest facilitated further wealth concentration by loyalist groups. After battlefield engagements, Mfengu troops plundered livestock, crops, and plows. Thousands of cattle could be stolen in a single day. Other looted items were sold for cash. This gave auxiliaries the means to augment herds and purchase more agricultural implements. Mfengu settled on abandoned Transkei lands and used confiscated cattle to farm acquired properties. Their methods of capital accumulation were not that different from those of white settlers. Some Mfengu secured their holdings by obtaining individual titles, while others merely squatted on abandoned territories and began commercial farming. Although nearly thirty thousand Africans had moved into the Transkei and adjacent areas within three decades, only a few had prospered.[16] Mfengu elites saw themselves as part and parcel of the colonial project, bringing progress to benighted lands with the gun and the plow. They viewed unpacified Xhosa communities as inherently unstable and irredeemably uncivilized.

Comparable intra-ethnic cleavages facilitated the British conquest of Zululand in 1879. Chiefdoms out of favor with the ruling Zulu house frequently found refuge in colonial Natal. Many could not return unless factional alignments shifted in their favor. Most Natal Africans viewed the Zulu kingdom as a looming threat to their lives and property. It thus came as no surprise that around nine thousand Natal native levies took part in the 1879 invasion. Thousands more provided essential haulage and carrier services.[17] Economic rewards proved elusive for most loyalists after the war, but a tiny kholwa elite remained committed to colonial administrative service and the benefits to be accrued therefrom.

In addition, Sir Garnet Wolseley's field force against Sekhukhune's Pedi included eight thousand Swazi warriors. Destruction of the Pedi kingdom removed a rival power from the eastern Transvaal and made it easier for Swazi regiments to raid Pedi communities.[18] Swazi monarchs generally accommodated imperial authorities and later provided labor for the mines. Britain recognized Swazi independence in 1881. After a brief period as a Transvaal protectorate, the kingdom reverted to indirect British rule in the early 1900s.

In certain respects, loyalism turned out to be a thankless task. Colonial authorities extended disarmament to Mfengu communities after the Ninth Cape Frontier War. Some were promptly rearmed to fight further campaigns, but coercive paths to material accumulation gradually closed off. Moreover, Natal underwent extensive land expropriation after the Anglo-Zulu War. Black loyalty was no longer vital to colonial security, and settler accumulation could proceed apace. Nonetheless, affluent African fathers began investing in their children's education. A new generation spent less time farming and more time learning. Learning gradually moved from mission stations to African-run schools. These schools generated wider elite networks as educators formed connections with pupils from affluent families. John Dube's Ohlange Institute instructed numerous future nationalist leaders, including the Msimang family and Albert Luthuli. Westernized elites strove to induct Africans into modernity under their careful tutelage.[19]

Early African nationalism did not escape the factional rivalries and personal animosities that typify elite-led anticolonial movements. Nevertheless, Black elites gradually homogenized their style and substance. This thin educated stratum came from all parts and peoples of southern Africa. English became their primary medium of communication and publication, and they soon dominated the lower rungs of colonial administration. A modern African petite bourgeoisie was in the making.[20]

Gold Mining, Randlords, and Elite Divergence in the Transvaal

The discovery of vast gold deposits along the Witwatersrand in 1886 magnified the socioeconomic effects of the mineral revolution. Yet it also led to a divergence between political and economic elites. Unlike in Kimberley, a foreign and increasingly hostile government held administrative jurisdiction over the Transvaal. Furthermore, most of the gold-bearing ore was deep underground, with diffuse deposits stretched across vast swathes of hard rock. Africans were almost immediately locked out of opportunities for independent prospecting. Surface digging was rapidly replaced by deep-level mining. Only Kimberley's corporate magnates had the capital to transport, install, and maintain the machinery required to excavate and process underground deposits. In addition, diamond barons had developed carceral methods of labor control ideally suited for complex mining operations. Hence, the gold sector was dominated by an incumbent mineral oligarchy. De Beers executives further augmented their vast fortunes, but businessmen with previous diamond mining experience also became prominent players. There was simply too much gold for any one company to monopolize. Consequently, the Rand's mineral elite operated within an oligopolistic framework. Gold-mining magnates, widely referred to as *Randlords,* were largely Anglophone and Anglophilic.[21] Many came from Britain and the wider Anglosphere; others migrated from Germany. A disproportionate number were assimilated Jews.[22] They all lobbied for procorporate policies conducive to profit making and wealth concentration, yet they were not a united group. Different oligarchic factions maneuvered for advantage over rival groups and amassed wealth in different ways.

Their main venue for asset trading became the Johannesburg Stock Exchange (JSE). First opened in 1887, this institution drew capital investors into the Transvaal and connected Johannesburg to global financial markets. Stock exchanges had already been established at Kimberley (1880), Pietermaritzburg (1881), and Barberton (1885), but none achieved the JSE's heft in southern Africa's financial markets.

The JSE had to overcome several economic contradictions. It needed to encourage capital investment while preventing reckless speculation. Barnato aggravated speculatory tendencies when he entered the gold market. His Johannesburg Estate Company, established in 1889, owned the JSE's central trade building and adjoining properties in the city center. Barnato supplemented rental income by raising JSE membership fees while simultaneously encouraging an influx of traders. He inducted members without thoroughly vetting their financial credentials and professional records. Dubious characters entered the trading hall in droves. Barnato may have been attempting to form a loyal client base, but his immediate interest was expanding the pool of fee-paying members. In 1890, unsound trading, combined with a slump in gold production, sparked a short-term depression.[23] Ensuing bankruptcies resulted in a contraction of officially listed JSE companies. Corporations with sufficient capital reserves managed to weather the crisis, and fewer companies reaped greater profits.

Rhodes himself diversified into gold mining when he founded the Gold Fields of South Africa Limited in 1887, and he devoted more time and resources to political projects that consolidated and expanded white-minority rule. Upon becoming Cape prime minister in 1890, Rhodes formed a parliamentary alliance with Jan Hendrik Hofmeyr's Afrikaner Bond political party. This political bloc passed regressive legislation that disenfranchised Africans and compelled them to seek work in the mines or on farms.[24] The 1892 Franchise and Ballot Act raised property requirements for voting from £25 to £75. This was followed by 1894's Glen Grey Act, which limited the amount of land Black people were legally entitled to hold and placed limits on agricultural productivity in nonwhite areas. By the 1890s, the mining sector had become so large that it required massive inputs of African labor to excavate, haul, and treat underground ore. Moreover, Afrikaner farmers wanted to remove African produce from the market and become the main providers of foodstuffs for a burgeoning urban population. The African agrarian elite contracted as these laws took effect. As farming became increasingly untenable, affluent Black people made larger investments in their children's education, and middle-class professions became alternative pathways to social prominence.

Transvaal Boers and Britons both benefited from deepening Black poverty. Yet they failed to forge an effective interelite alliance. As in the Cape, Boer farms depended on extra-economic coercion to maintain semiservile labor systems and favorable sharecropping arrangements with Black cultivators. Randlords, in turn, relied on artificially induced migrant labor systems to obtain cheap African labor. In addition, pass laws could not function without government cooperation. Given the poor quality of Rand ores, mineral profits depended on a low-wage workforce. Wages were kept low through imperial conquests and administrative compulsion. Separate segments of a white minority found common ground in exploiting southern Africa's Black majority. President Paul Kruger himself was not uniformly hostile to the mining sector. He even struck lucrative deals with individual magnates, such as the ubiquitous Barnato, J. B. Robinson, and Sammy Marks.[25] Corporate capital was not necessarily a bad thing. Pretoria itself engaged in a failed attempt to launch its own stock exchange and made no moves to impose government regulations on the JSE. Nonetheless, Kruger's administration felt

Anglophone *uitlanders* (outlanders) as a group posed an existential threat to Boer supremacy in the South African Republic. Uitlanders had the economic power to challenge, and potentially overturn, an established sociocultural order. Kruger therefore limited their avenues for political representation and placed onerous taxes on the mineral economy. Mining oligarchs unable to cultivate compliant political collaborators opted for regime change.

Aided by a selected group of Randlords and a British administrator named Leander Starr Jameson, Rhodes tried to overthrow Kruger's government in a corporate coup.[26] The Jameson Raid of 1895–96 ended in complete disaster. Uitlanders proved unable to rally sufficient support within Johannesburg, and Transvaal forces routed Jameson's troopers. Rhodes resigned as prime minister shortly thereafter, and several of his coconspirators spent time in prison. Cape Afrikaners put ethnic solidary before legislative expediency and sided with their Transvaal brethren against British colonial interests. Kruger began purchasing large quantities of modern weaponry from Germany and France as further armed conflict became all but inevitable.

Imperial Conquest, Scorched Earth, and an Anglo-Afrikaner Elite Bargain

Gold discoveries made southern Africa a major geopolitical concern for British policymakers. The Transvaal's mineral revolution shifted southern Africa's center of gravity away from British-controlled coastal cities and toward an unstable interior. After the Jameson Raid, Kruger's government moved to cement alliances with other great powers. By this point, Germany had carved out a colonial holding in South West Africa, present-day Namibia. This placed a hostile power on the Cape's doorstep and perilously close to pro-German Boer republics. If Germany replaced Britain as imperial suzerain in the Transvaal, its gold reserves would further strengthen a dangerous rival. Joseph Chamberlain, secretary of state for the colonies, had been sympathetic to Jameson's endeavor. When furtive means proved inadequate, direct pressure was applied. If Kruger's government could not be toppled, it would have to be annexed.[27]

When Sir Alfred Milner was appointed high commissioner for southern Africa in 1897, confederation was his top priority. After an extensive assessment, Milner concluded that lasting peace and progress was predicated on full political rights for Transvaal Britons. The continued oppression of British subjects by an "inferior" people would only sap national prestige and embolden rival powers to make further inroads into a vital sphere of influence. In 1898, Milner stated his determination to secure British rights during a speech in Graaff-Reinet, an Afrikaner Bond stronghold. He also urged Cape Boers to promote the benefits of British administration to intransigent Transvaalers. Milner's aggressive pronouncements only drove different Boer communities closer together. The uitlander issue divided South Africa's white population into two distinct ethnolinguistic camps. At the Bloemfontein Conference in 1899, Milner presented Kruger with an unacceptable ultimatum. In addition to immediate enfranchisement of uitlanders, Milner demanded the use of English in the Transvaal parliament and approval of all its legislation by London. War broke out in October 1899, when a military coalition between the Transvaal and Orange Free State launched attacks on the Cape colony and Natal.

The Anglo-Boer War (1899–1902) was enormously destructive.[28] Britain had not expected such fierce resistance from backcountry farmers and was compelled to mobilize massive resources and labor reserves to bring the conflict to a close. British forces encountered difficulties for two main reasons. First, Boer commandos had modern weapons. Magazine rifles and field guns fired from entrenched positions inflicted heavy casualties. It took several months before larger concentrations of British firepower could be deployed to break through Boer defensive lines. Second, the war shifted from a conventional struggle (1899–1900) to an unconventional counterinsurgency (1900–1902). British armies spent the war's opening months organizing the relief of besieged troops at Mafeking, Ladysmith, and Kimberley. After Lord Frederick Roberts relieved these sieges, he launched a full-scale offensive that captured the Boer capitals of Bloemfontein and Pretoria. When Pretoria fell, Roberts declared victory and directed his forces to mop up residual resistance. Such optimism proved premature. By the time Lord Herbert Kitchener succeeded Roberts in November 1900, it was apparent the Boers had merely changed tactics. A vicious guerrilla insurgency ensued, and the British lost control of territories beyond the reach of their military columns. As in all unconventional conflicts, Boer commandos maintained themselves in the field by drawing sustenance from the civilian population. To win the war, Britain had to sever civilian/insurgent links. Roberts initiated a policy of retaliatory home demolitions in the vicinity of guerrilla attacks. Under Kitchener, British forces systematically destroyed Boer property. By war's end, British units had destroyed around thirty thousand farms and slaughtered around seven million livestock.[29] Occupation authorities often commandeered huge herds of sheep and cattle to feed mineworks on the Rand. Boer units remaining in the field were gradually hemmed in by an expanding network of garrisoned blockhouses and ground down by Kitchener's incessant sweeps.

Rural inhabitants were driven into unsanitary and ill-provisioned concentration camps. When the resulting mass mortality of Boer women and children created a scandal, destitute families were simply left to wander the veld. As in past imperial wars, armed African levies augmented imperial forces.[30] The use of African troops fomented fears of racial violence against Boer civilians and played a part in compelling certain commandos to capitulate. However, British field commanders also subjected Africans to a brutal forced labor regime. African farm servants were removed along with Boer families during veld clearances. A majority ended up in separate camps. The British built at least sixty-five African internment sites during the war. Some Black people were slated to serve captive white families. Most African camps were situated along railway lines that led to Johannesburg. From these points, Black labor gangs were dispatched to work in mines, grow food for garrisons, maintain British blockhouses, and toil on white-owned farms. Cultivation was forbidden around camps to prevent commandos from using crops to screen their movements. British commanders withheld food and medical aid until Africans provided labor. Those refusing to work often died. According to rough estimates, around twenty thousand interned Africans perished during the war.[31] As sites that corralled African labor and rendered it available, these camps manifested the embryonic beginnings of later townships from which private and parastatal corporations extracted surplus value.

Scorched-earth tactics, Boer civilian internment, and levies of armed Africans compelled hardline Boer commanders to come in from the cold. The 1902 Treaty of Vereeniging was a generous one. The Boer republics came under Crown sovereignty but were promised eventual self-government. A section of the Boer elite, led by Jan Smuts and Louis Botha, collaborated with the British almost immediately, while more recalcitrant factions remained committed to noncooperation and Afrikaner nationalism.

As head of the Transvaal and Orange River Colony from 1901 to 1905, Milner pursued policies of socioeconomic reconstruction, administrative integration, and social engineering.[32] His performance was decidedly mixed. Randlords grudgingly accepted a 10 percent tax on gold-mining profits to fund recovery efforts. Railway infrastructure was restored, and the removal of internal customs barriers facilitated the flow of minerals to South African ports. When a labor shortage on the Rand reduced mining output, mine owners proved reluctant to hire white workers, as their wage demands were too high to make operations profitable. Milner accommodated executives by importing Chinese workers in 1904. This aggravated class tensions and deepened industrial unrest but kept working costs down. Milner's attempts to redress white demographic imbalances by encouraging British settlement in the former republics failed. His emphasis on anglicizing the South African countryside did not appeal to metropolitan Britons. Urban/rural socioeconomic divides between Anglophones and Afrikaners persisted. Yet this did not prevent the formation of a functional alliance between economic and political elites. Many Randlords accommodated Afrikaner nationalism as the surest means to keeping African workers in line. Certain capitalists supported Louis Botha's Het Volk Party, which won the 1907 Transvaal election. By that time, most businessmen had left politics and concentrated on lobbying for procorporate public policies.[33]

Cooperation between Anglophone mining elites and Afrikaner nationalist elites was premised on deepening Black economic subordination and political exclusion. Many Africans had rallied behind Britain's war because they hoped Cape voting rights would be extended to the former Boer republics. This did not occur. In 1908, a national convention was formed to discuss the constitution of a South African union. The following year the British Parliament accepted basic constitutional provisions through the South Africa Act. A 1909 Black deputation to Britain protesting nonwhite franchise restrictions was ignored.[34] London was prepared to hand over power to Afrikaner nationalists so long as Britain's mineral interests were secured. The Union of South Africa, established in 1910, was based on the principle of parliamentary supremacy. The judiciary had no power to contest the ultimate legality of legislation. This enabled segregationist laws that further impoverished Black communities and kept industrial wages down.

* * *

From 1870 to 1910, accelerating territorial dispossession, coupled with the conquest and dismemberment of African kingdoms, eroded indigenous means of subsistence. Journeys to the mines became necessary for basic survival. A thin stratum of westernized African elites benefited from this process either by taking part in colonial landgrabs or assisting in the administrative tasks that made capital accumulation possible. The oppression of a Black majority enabled South Africa's exclusionary economic growth. High profits derived from artificially low wages. Industrial production benefited an ostensibly divided white minority. Yet beneath these surface divisions was growing cooperation. An Anglophone mining oligarchy relied on an Afrikaner political class to pass and enforce legislation that repressed labor. Afrikaans-speaking politicians derived huge economic benefits from mining profits and utilized segregation laws to push cheap labor onto Afrikaner commercial farms. A dual elite divided the tasks of racial capitalism between them to concentrate wealth within a privileged minority.

3

White Amalgamation, Corporate Integration, and Struggles for African Elite Inclusion

Anticolonial nationalism dominated South African politics for most of the twentieth century. White Afrikaners sought to redress economic inequalities between themselves and their Anglophone counterparts by further exploiting African labor. This exploitation was premised on Black exclusion from political power. For their part, Westernized African elites sought inclusion within a capitalist system.

The staggered incorporation of more radical Afrikaner nationalist factions into the political establishment resulted in an expanding white welfare state. Whites succeeded in spreading prosperity among themselves because of a relatively small and shrinking demography. Making up roughly 21 percent of the population in 1920, they had shrunk to 10 percent by 1990.[1] When South Africa faced economic headwinds in the 1970s, declining numbers made proportionally fewer whites easier to care for. At the same time, corporate elites found racial protections increasingly unprofitable and included growing numbers of Africans in skilled and administrative positions. The elites pursued this selective co-optation to protect corporate profits; doing so did not undermine white-minority privileges.

Black political elites wanted to take part in these privileges and embraced increasingly radical methods of mass resistance to attain economic inclusion. The Cold War both facilitated and complicated the struggle for national liberation. Black nationalists obtained vital aid from the Soviet bloc, but white-minority governments received material and diplomatic support from Western states by presenting Black nationalism as a front for communist infiltration. As social disorder mounted, economic elites distanced themselves from apartheid and sought political partners better able to dissipate discontent and secure corporate assets. The rapid political ascent of the African National Congress (ANC) from the mid-1980s onward made it a prime candidate for corporate favor. Big business expanded its support for ANC leaders after the unbanning of liberation organizations in 1990. Black elites lacked wealth and wanted to reap material rewards after decades of struggle. The period 1910–94 thus saw new minorities gain economic privileges by obtaining exclusive advantages.

The Struggle for White Working-Class Inclusion and Black Exclusion

Jan Smuts and Louis Botha dominated national politics in the early period of the Union of South Africa. Both had been prominent commando leaders during the Anglo-Boer War, and they became leading proponents of British imperial interests shortly after that conflict concluded in 1902. After a stint as Transvaal premier, Botha became Union prime minister in 1910. Smuts assumed several cabinet positions, thereby turning the executive into a de facto dyarchy. The Botha/Smuts regime consolidated its position in 1911 by merging Het Volk with three other moderate nationalist parties to form the South African Party (SAP). Botha remained in power until his death in 1919, whereupon Smuts assumed the premiership.[2] Their government pursued policies that supported British imperial objectives and protected mining company interests. When it came to Afrikaner nationalists, the SAP favored Cape-based commercial farmers and private corporations. The Afrikaner-run life insurance company Sanlam, established in 1918, followed British corporate practices. Poor Afrikaners in the Transvaal and Orange Free State suffered neglect and seethed in resentment.[3] The Afrikaner Broederbond (Brotherhood) formed in 1918 as a secret society committed to uniting Afrikaans speakers and seizing political power. But divisions remained deep.

The SAP administration did not tolerate popular protests. When faced with demands it considered unreasonable, the state unleashed massive violence on social movements, irrespective of their racial composition. When tensions within the Afrikaner political elite resulted in open rebellion, the government response was uncompromising. In 1914, Botha and Smuts had secured South Africa's entry into the First World War despite fierce opposition from rival Afrikaner politicians. Shortly thereafter, army troops and police crushed a pro-German revolt led by former Boer generals unwilling to fight for Britain.[4] The killing, capture, and internment of former comrades-in-arms deepened intra-Afrikaner political divisions. Smuts and Botha's entry into the war and response to the rebellion tightened their commitment to the imperial tie. Hardline Afrikaner nationalists responded by playing up their perceived betrayal to gain political advantage.

Labor unrest on the Rand compounded political problems. These industrial actions did not transcend racial tensions and forge multiracial working-class solidarities. Rather, strikes manifested white working-class fears of downward mobility. Racial tensions in the mines had run high ever since Milner introduced indentured Chinese labor. Although Chinese mineworkers had departed by 1910, white fears of being replaced by cheaper alternatives persisted. Mine owners preferred African migrant labor to white employees. Migrants from Mozambique and Basutoland without support networks in local communities were far easier to control than white citizens with voting rights. When white workers became too demanding, mining companies turned to their more compliant African counterparts.

Industrial disputes were primarily based on wage rates. Because gold industry profits depended on low wages, mining companies expanding operations either had to hire and upskill more Black workers or drive white wages down to Black levels. White labor unions viewed both prospects as unacceptable. Afrikaans and English-speaking whites attempted to transcend cultural divisions in their struggle for racial privileges in the workplace. Formed in 1910, the South African Labour Party pursued wealth redistribution along racial lines. White workers hoped to secure higher wages by monopolizing skilled labor tasks from which Africans would be excluded through color-bar legislation. The Labour Party, and organizations like it, wanted to create a white labor aristocracy at Black labor's expense.

The struggle for white worker supremacy was bitter and bloody. In June 1913, British troops violently crushed a white mining strike. When several thousand Black mineworkers refused to work a few months later, government security forces drove them into the shafts at bayonet point. This was followed by a general strike in early 1914 by white workers protesting wage cuts and the hiring of cheaper Black replacements. The government mobilized sixty thousand troops to break the strike and resume business operations.[5]

Disease and war exacerbated economic problems in the Transvaal. An 1897 rinderpest epidemic, coupled with British scorched-earth tactics from 1900 to 1902, devastated herds and drove many poor white farmers permanently off the land. Afrikaners flooded into urban centers in search of scarce mining and manufacturing jobs. Johannesburg's white population swelled from forty thousand just before the Anglo-Boer War to almost two hundred and fifty thousand in 1914. Efforts to secure steady employment often proved futile, as cheaper African workers could always be found, and most white migrants fell into an urban underclass. Indigent whites frequently joined ethnonationalist parties advocating legal protections against Black competition in the labor market. Poor urbanites combined with affluent commercial farmers to make Afrikaner nationalism a potent political force.

Conditions on the Rand deteriorated further with a protracted post–First World War slump in gold prices. As the price decline accelerated throughout 1920 and 1921, mining companies restructured their workforces. Their attempts to maintain profit margins by cutting working costs sparked the Rand rebellion. Executives decreased wage bills by removing color bars, employing Black people in skilled positions, and hiring African supervisors. These moves set off a wave of strikes in January 1922. Unrest began at collieries and soon spread to the gold mines. After efforts to negotiate a settlement failed in late January, strikers formed armed commandos and seized control of various urban areas. This was not a proletarian revolution. Racially motivated killings of Black bystanders by white lynch mobs occurred in insurgent-controlled zones.[6] The revolt's main slogan was "Workers of the world, unite and fight for a white South Africa!" The government mobilized the Union Defence Force and launched full-scale assaults on rebel fortifications. Troops, artillery, and airplanes overwhelmed the resistance. The revolt and its repression caused over two hundred deaths. An incensed white electorate threw out the SAP in 1924's general election. J. B. M. Hertzog's National Party (NP), in coalition with Labour Party members of parliament, formed a Pact government committed to protecting white workers and strengthening exclusionary race laws.

White working-class empowerment completed the racialization of minority privilege. NP-dominated governments instituted a series of socioeconomic measures that gradually ended white poverty and raised white workers into the middle class. This was done in three ways.[7] First, Hertzog's cabinet solidified job color bars into a rigid caste system that excluded Black people from high-paying employment. Whites were entitled to wages that enabled "civilized" living standards. Thus, the Industrial Conciliation Act of 1924, the Wage Act of 1925, and the Mines and Works Amendment Act of 1926 made white workers into permanent employees guaranteed a panoply of rights and protections. Black workers, by contrast, were viewed as temporary migrants and denied these advantages. White workers received the right to unionize, minimum wages, trade apprenticeships, and job reservations for skilled positions. The second component of white worker empowerment was an extensive public works program that provided rapid relief to the unemployed. Building projects provided essential aid during the Great Depression. By 1933, an estimated fifty thousand whites were at work constructing irrigation systems, dams, roads, and railways. Government spending on infrastructure increased from 2.6 percent of the budget in 1930 to 15.8 percent in 1933. By 1939, an estimated ninety-eight thousand whites were on public sector payrolls, with over half that number engaged in construction work.[8] Finally, NP-led administrations invested heavily in social expenditure. White families received subsidized public housing, state-funded schools, and old-age pensions.

Such entitlements and opportunities resulted in a better-educated white population able to take on a growing number of managerial and bureaucratic tasks in a burgeoning parastatal sector. In addition to alleviating white unemployment, Afrikaner political elites wanted to prove that their people could run complex organizations efficiently. Since Anglophones dominated private sector corporations, the government founded massive parastatals. In 1923, the Electricity Supply Commission (later known as Eskom) was established to provide power to South Africa's growing urban population.[9] This was followed in 1928 by the Iron and Steel Industrial Corporation, founded to produce steel products for various industries.[10] These companies proved extremely successful in fulfilling their mandates. Mining companies came to rely on the parastatal provision of power and transport services, thus consolidating the centrality of the public sector in the South African economy. However, these services mainly benefited a white minority. African townships and rural communities remained in the dark and without modern amenities.

Private capital also thrived under segregationist polices. As the Rand transformed into a sprawling urban agglomeration, manufacturing industries servicing mining companies and urban consumers employed an increasing share of African labor. Moreover, the segregation era saw the development of huge mining conglomerates. The formation and expansion of Ernest Oppenheimer's Anglo American corporation exemplified this mode of wealth concentration.[11] As an anglified German Jew, Oppenheimer first came to Kimberley in 1902 to represent the Dunkelsbuhler diamond merchant firm. While looking after his company's interests, he became involved in municipal politics and served a stint as Kimberley's mayor. When a wave of anti-German hysteria cut his tenure short in 1915, Oppenheimer turned his full attention to business pursuits. In 1917, Oppenheimer partnered with J. P. Morgan and other American financers to establish the Anglo American corporation. Anglo took over several gold-mining companies on the Rand and expanded its interest in diamonds. In 1920, Oppenheimer bought confiscated German diamond mines in South West Africa from the Union government. Two years later, Anglo agreed to purchase diamonds produced in Angola and Congo. Further mine acquisitions in South West Africa eviscerated the De Beers monopoly. In 1929, De Beers was forced to appoint Oppenheimer as its chairman. Thereafter, Oppenheimer consolidated all his diamond businesses under De Beers's aegis and formed a new marketing body that took power away from sellers and gave it to producers. Over the next several decades, Anglo multiplied its income streams by diversifying into other commodities, construction, and manufactured goods.

Afrikaner uplift and Anglophone conglomerates relied on steady supplies of cheap African labor. African labor remained cheap because indigenous dispossession deepened. Armed resistance led by traditional leaders and millenarian prophets could not stand up to the state's coercive power.[12] Westernized African elites, in turn, refused to be involved with subaltern social movements driven by superstitious beliefs. The main concern of middle-class Africans was inclusion within a colonial system. Their educational achievements and civilized lifestyles entitled them to the same career opportunities and benefits as their white counterparts. The South African Native National Congress formed in 1912 to defend the privileges of an exclusive minority. After rebranding to the African National Congress, or ANC, in 1923, it attempted to facilitate mass mobilization by establishing a network of local branches, but these efforts remained cautious and conservative.

Consequently, the ANC could not halt increasing African impoverishment and sociopolitical exclusion. The 1913 Natives Land Act restricted Black landownership to around 7 percent of South Africa's territorial landmass. The act also severely restricted tenure agreements that allowed Black people to dwell on white-owned farms. These disadvantages encouraged migrant labor flows to the mines and drove agricultural wages further down. In 1936, Cape Africans lost their qualified franchise rights. As a form of compensation, the 1936 Native Trust and Land Act increased native reserves to slightly over 13 percent of South African territory. This incremental expansion proved woefully inadequate for a demographic group that constituted over 70 percent of the population. Some African cultivators tenaciously held on as sharecroppers and homeland farmers.[13]

Collaborating chiefs and headmen in the native areas managed to secure privileged access to fertile plots and livestock. Yet overpopulated African reserves suffered from soil erosion and declining agricultural productivity. Other native areas were located on barren lands unable to sustain their inhabitants without wage remittances from African mineworkers.

White Economic Amalgamation and Corporate Integration Under Apartheid

The apartheid state was a product of politics and war. Afrikaner voters sought to defend their newly acquired privileges and feared wartime socioeconomic shifts would erode those privileges. At the same time, splits within Afrikaner nationalism created more extremist political parties seeking to solidify racial divisions. After Hertzog's National Party consolidated a fusion government with Smuts's United Party in 1934, Dr. D. F. Malan's faction broke off to form the Purified Afrikaner National Party. Malan's support base was composed of farmers, Dutch Reformed churchgoers, and several pro-Nazi ideologues virulently opposed to South Africa's participation in the Second World War on the Allied side. Yet the reasons for resisting a pro-British policy went beyond ideological beliefs. Britain heavily relied on South African commodities and manufacturing capacities to prosecute its military campaigns. In 1939, Smuts again secured South Africa's entry in the face of fierce political opposition. As industrial production took off, huge numbers of Africans came to cities to work in mines and factories. Pass laws and segregated residence requirements were relaxed to facilitate production. Many whites feared being swamped by this Black influx. Malan promised to bring this influx under control if elected to office.[14] This platform gained him wider electoral support, although his political base remained in white farming communities. When Malan's NP won the 1948 general election, it implemented apartheid, deploying the national state to achieve a complete separation of racial groups and solidify white-minority privilege.

The early apartheid state's primary concern was to solidify spatial and biological divisions between racial groups. Authorities viewed Black townships as open-air prisons to be sealed off from white areas and closely surveilled. Residents without proper documentation were subjected to removal. Criminalized African communities proved easier to exploit and repress. National laws forbidding marriage and extramarital sexual relations between whites and nonwhites could not reverse several centuries of ethnocultural mixing. Yet they hardened social boundaries. As a closed racial caste, whites had to maintain their purity.

During Hendrik Verwoerd's premiership (1958–66), the NP embarked on a project of grand apartheid in which rural homelands would gradually be transformed into fully independent states. This policy's main objective was to strip Africans of whatever citizenship rights they retained in the South African Republic. Migrants seeking jobs in whites-only areas were regarded as guest workers without civil or economic rights. They were paid artificially low wages and had no legal right to strike. Influx control ultimately failed because apartheid bureaucrats attempted to achieve contradictory aims. Africans had to stay long enough to be exploited but not long enough to embed themselves in white areas. As the urban economy became more complex, Black labor had to remain near mines and factories for longer periods. They inevitably put down roots and in doing so enabled other Africans to follow suit. Nonetheless, apartheid's structural flaws did not prevent medium-term profit accumulation. As Black labor was squeezed, white prosperity burgeoned. By the 1960s, Afrikaners had achieved levels of affluence comparable to their English-speaking counterparts.

NP politicians did not restrict their ambitions to constructing an Afrikaner middle class. They also cultivated a small group of Afrikaner businessmen that could stand alongside Anglophone capital at the economy's commanding heights. This policy was not universally popular among Afrikaans-speaking whites. Popular attitudes painted corporate capitalism as a foreign implant, imposed by Jews and Britons eager to exploit a hardy frontier race. However, many upwardly mobile Afrikaners strove to emulate English upper-class standards and consumption habits. They desired to join, rather than replace, an incumbent economic elite.

Anton Rupert benefited from, but was not entirely a product of, these procapital policies.[15] In 1940, Rupert joined the Reddingsdaadbond (Rescue Action League), an organization attempting to improve the plight of poor Afrikaners. He headed a business section tasked with arranging loans for small companies. This widened his network of political and financial contacts. Rupert then purchased a small tobacco firm in partnership with Nico Diederichs, who went on to become minister of finance, and A. J. Stals, later a minister in Malan's cabinet.[16] The extent to which these political connections aided Rupert's corporate career is debatable. He did display genuine entrepreneurial talent, albeit in a permissive environment that favored his ethnic group. In 1948, Rupert's team founded the Rembrandt Tobacco

Corporation. It began producing cigarettes about a week after Malan became prime minister in 1948. Aggressive marketing campaigns entreated Afrikaners to buy cigarettes manufactured by their own kinsmen.

After a rocky start, Rembrandt began turning handsome profits, with net earnings of £105,000 in 1950. When Rothmans, a London-based cigarette company, came up for sale, Rupert offered to buy a controlling interest for £750,000. Rupert only had about £50,000 available and completed the purchase in 1954 with a £700,000 loan from Sanlam and Volkskas, an Afrikaner-owned bank.[17] The Rothmans transaction enabled Rembrandt to enter the European market, and Rembrandt obtained a formal listing on the Johannesburg Stock Exchange in 1956.[18] Rupert was a member of the Broederbond but was never considered an apartheid ideologue. He entered these networks because they opened doors to influential friends and generous credit lines. However, his primary concern was to secure his assets. As NP policies went increasingly against sound business practices, Rupert repeatedly proposed coexistence with African nationalists and attempted to facilitate the incorporation of educated urban Black people into the South African middle class. Rembrandt gave Rupert the resources to strike out on his own.

Rhetorical condemnation and threats of nationalization made English-speaking business elites more accommodating to Afrikaner interests. Yet the NP needed Anglophone capital to earn foreign exchange and keep the economy humming. Anglo American continued to reap massive profits from the migrant labor system and pass law regime. Upon Ernest Oppenheimer's death in 1957, his son Harry inherited the firm and further diversified its portfolio. Harry championed liberal values while serving as an MP for Kimberley and was never comfortable with the ethnonationalism espoused by Afrikaners or Africans. He did not, however, advocate universal suffrage, and he called for a qualified African franchise based on educational achievement. In addition, Oppenheimer readily called in coercive police power when faced with labor unrest on his mines. His primary concern was protecting company profits, not expanding political rights.

Aided by a tight-knit group of Oxford-educated personal assistants, Oppenheimer made Anglo a central player in the global commodities market.[19] By the 1980s, Anglo owned or controlled around 70 percent of companies listed on the Johannesburg Stock Exchange. At home, the Oppenheimer family's lavish lifestyle was a subject of intense interest among English-speaking whites. Abroad, Oppenheimer represented the "acceptable" face of white capital in an inherently racist state. With concerns in nearly every sector of the South African economy and close contacts with multinational corporations, Anglo became a virtual state within a state.

Gold mines in the Orange Free State provided another major profit stream. In 1936, a mining consortium consisting of Anglo, Union Corporation, Central Mining, and Consolidated Gold Fields purchased options for 145,000 hectares of land around Bothaville. When the African and European Investment Company drilled for coal further south in Odendaalsrus, it discovered rich gold deposits. This drew in Anglo, which gradually consolidated a block of landholdings throughout the 1940s. Anglo's first Free State gold mine began producing in 1951, with other mines coming onstream thereafter. The Free State mines generated huge profits, still premised on cheap Black labor. When Harry Oppenheimer proposed to allocate a portion of rising profits to constructing married quarters for Black mineworkers, he initially received some government encouragement. But as the NP's apartheid project took hold, Verwoerd's Ministry of Native Affairs would not permit Anglo to house more than 3 percent of its workers with their wives. Whatever interest Oppenheimer had in improving living conditions of African workers proved fleeting. Anglo never met the 3 percent ceiling.[20]

Oppenheimer's main economic achievement was the integration of Afrikaner capital into the gold-mining sector. Federale Mynbou began mining operations in the 1950s with support from Sanlam. In 1957, the fledging company won an Eskom contract to supply coal for the new Komati power station. Within several years, Federale Mynbou acquired other large collieries, branched out into asbestos mining, and began eyeing the diamond sector. Sensing the danger, Oppenheimer preempted a possible takeover by diverting Federale Mynbou into gold. From 1963 to 1965, Anglo allowed Federale Mynbou to acquire a controlling interest in General Mining, a gold-producing Anglo subsidiary, in exchange for abandoning its designs on De Beers's diamond monopoly.[21] Afrikaner capital's penetration into the English-dominated gold sector through corporate bargaining forestalled political efforts at nationalization and deflected attempts to undermine De Beers's stranglehold on global diamond supplies.

Anglophone/Afrikaner corporate integration was indicative of wider economic convergence within the white community. Afrikaners and English speakers continued attending different schools and adhering to distinct sociocultural traditions, but they were becoming more alike. Both derived substantial material benefits from a racial order that exploited a Black majority to privilege a white minority.

Shifting Strategies of African Resistance

Failure to obtain political concessions compelled African nationalists to shift strategies in their struggle against white supremacy. The formation of the ANC Youth League in 1944 radicalized protest politics without altering the fundamental aims of the wider party.[22] As Youth League organizers, Nelson Mandela, Oliver Tambo, Walter Sisulu, and Anton Lembede advocated for Black inclusion within an industrial capitalist economy. Calls for nationalization in the 1955 Freedom Charter did not necessarily mean a turn to socialism. Rather, public ownership of key assets provided a pathway for Black political elites to seize the economy's commanding heights. Mass action replaced reasoned persuasion, but the liberation struggle would be led by a small Black middle class, not workers or peasants. However, ANC leaders mobilized support in African townships through local *tsotsis* (thugs). Tsotsi bosses drew on criminal networks to foment disorder, partly because they stood to profit from such disorder. Unrest in townships made it easier to steal property and run illicit rackets. Joe Modise, who later served as Mandela's defense minister, began his career as an Alexandra township gangster engaged in car theft and smuggling rings. He continued these activities to supplement his income after he joined the ANC.[23]

The ANC's alliance with the South African Communist Party (SACP), tilt toward the Soviet Union, and revolutionary symbolism were products of political expediency.[24] The apartheid state declared itself an anticommunist bastion sitting astride strategic sea routes and gained extensive support from the west. The NP branded antiapartheid activism as a front for international communism that must be crushed. When the ANC failed to convince Western governments that it was an organization primarily concerned with national liberation, it looked east.

Mass action and Soviet bloc assistance had no appreciable effect on the freedom struggle until the 1970s. Apartheid security forces, spearheaded by the South African Police, violently crushed disobedience campaigns. A year after the 1960 Sharpeville massacre, ANC cadres launched an ineffective armed struggle against the state. Umkhonto we Sizwe (MK), the ANC's armed wing, sabotaged vital infrastructure but was incapable of taking on state security forces.[25] By 1964, senior ANC leaders were either in prison or exile.

Cadres in exile relied on donor contributions from sympathetic states and nongovernmental organizations to keep their cause afloat. Not all aid was properly accounted for, as certain ANC officials embezzled funds to live comfortable lives abroad. This generated fierce criticism in the party from far-left elements, led by Chris Hani.[26] Hani's group branded corrupt cadres as mere opportunists waiting for apartheid to collapse, whereupon they would claim the credit and reap the rewards. Hani's censure nearly led to his execution.

The armed struggle never posed an existential threat to the apartheid state. Nevertheless, the turn to violence profoundly impacted the ANC's organizational culture. Underground activities, infiltrated spies, and covert operations bred suspicions against outsiders. The party had to hold together under enormous pressure.[27] Internal dissent was not tolerated and, at times, was severely punished. Operating structures became opaque and unaccountable. Sub-rosa party cells engaged in infiltration forged connections with criminal networks that smuggled cadres and weapons across borders. ANC leaders able to reward and protect clients garnered strong loyalties.

Party spooks became senior leaders. After a ten-year prison sentence on Robben Island, Jacob Zuma continued to recruit MK members. He fled abroad in 1975 to avoid arrest and entered the ANC's National Executive Committee in 1977. Zuma conducted infiltration operations into South Africa from Mozambique until pressured to relocate to Zambia in 1987, where he directed the ANC intelligence department. Zuma cultivated a following in the intelligence community that would support his later political ambitions.[28] His actions were emblematic of a wider political culture. Loyalty to persons or subgroups, coupled with conspiratorial operating procedures, militated against transparency and legality. Armed struggle encouraged illicit accumulation.[29]

Although a few ANC cadres continued to operate within South Africa, internal dissent in the 1970s was mainly directed by the Black Consciousness movement. Black Consciousness propounded an overt form of African nationalism, distinct from the ANC's multiracial coalition approach. Africans did not need white sympathy or support and could achieve liberation on their own. Led by Steve Biko, Black Consciousness took root among Africans in schools and universities. Mass activism by educated youth generated organized protests that created a new generation of nationalists. Cyril Ramaphosa, the current president of the ANC, was one of many university students drawn into the resistance by Black Consciousness ideology. The state responded to this new challenge with further repression and ill-considered administrative measures to inculcate docility into African children. NP attempts to embed Bantu education and Afrikaans-language instruction into African school curricula lit the spark that set off a conflagration.

Apartheid's Decline and the Rise of an African Protest Elite

By the late 1960s, elements of apartheid were no longer economically viable. Both Afrikaner and Anglophone corporations required more stable workforces if they hoped to successfully expand operations. Deporting undocumented Africans was bad for business. Moreover, as South African conglomerates diversified into manufacturing, the demand for semiskilled and skilled labor increased. There were never enough whites to fulfill these tasks, and only Black people with long-term residency in industrial areas could acquire the skills necessary to fill the gap. Hence, corporate executives began to ignore bothersome bureaucratic restrictions on Black workers in white areas. Furthermore, job reservations for white laborers inflated wages and had to be done away with. NP officials, however, remained intransigent. Verwoerd's assassination in 1966 changed little. John Vorster's government (1966–78) pressed forward with grand apartheid and separate development for Africans in their own tribal homelands. After a series of wildcat strikes erupted in 1973, Anglo committed to upskilling more African workers and advocated for the legalization of Black trade unions.[30] Such palliatives benefited only a small number of Africans. In addition, when the 1973–74 oil shock slowed economic growth, state protections shielded whites from the worst of it, while Black impoverishment deepened.

The political implications of the 1976 Soweto uprising for African nationalism are well known.[31] Excessive force by police resulted in hundreds of deaths and further radicalized the antiapartheid movement. Newly installed Marxist governments in Angola and Mozambique provided sanctuaries for South Africa's Black liberation armies and student activists fleeing abroad. Vorster's cabinet attempted to balance brute force with divide and rule. The Transkei was granted complete "independence" in October 1976, followed by Bophuthatswana in 1977.[32] Most homeland presidents, ministers, and chiefs lacked popular legitimacy and could not provide an alternative focus for African nationalism. Homeland elites ran predatory regimes wherein private interests looted public resources and failed to deliver basic social services. Loyal client groups received patronage and other material perks, but affluent individuals did not invest in productive industries. Homeland governments remained dependent on centrally disbursed monetary allocations from Pretoria, and residents continued to rely on remittances from migrant laborers.

After Soweto, corporate conglomerates took their own measures to pacify the Black population. In December 1976, a group of company executives, led by Oppenheimer and Rupert, established the Urban Foundation.[33] This organization created clerical and administrative job opportunities for educated Black people, and its programs provided livelihoods to many disadvantaged Africans. Ramaphosa was among the first to benefit from its largess. Yet the Urban Foundation's architects were not motivated by altruism. They hoped to neutralize Black radicalism by co-opting its leadership. Comfortable jobs with prospects for advancement would instill respect for social order and corporate property. Moreover, a larger population of urban Black people with steady salaries would mean more customers for consumer products. Segmental co-optation had mixed results. Few Black people became obedient clients to white capital. Most Africans utilized newly acquired resources and social networks as a base from which to make further demands and build their own careers. Ramaphosa took full advantage of corporate largess. His association with the Anglophone mining sector allowed him to form the National Union of Mineworkers (NUM) in 1982.[34] NUM grew rapidly and won bargaining recognition from the Chamber of Mines. It soon became clear that Ramaphosa was not the compliant union boss corporate oligarchs had hoped for. Under Ramaphosa's stewardship, NUM conducted aggressive negotiations for improved wages and working conditions.

In late 1985, NUM became a core component of the militant Congress of South African Trade Unions (COSATU). Ramaphosa was a driving force in aligning NUM and the larger COSATU confederation with the ANC.[35] He followed this up with a massive mineworkers' strike in 1987 centered on stopping Anglo operations. The strike was unsuccessful because mine owners retaliated with mass dismissals and brought in the police. Several deaths and numerous injuries compelled a chastened Ramaphosa to call off further work stoppages. He had, however, cemented his position as a major player in the trade union movement. Black nationalists and white capitalists would have to accommodate him.

NP leaders attempted to maintain white-minority privilege through a combination of violence and reform. P. W. Botha's administration (1978–89) embarked on a "total strategy" to meet a total onslaught from Soviet-backed African liberation movements. Global currents initially flowed in Botha's favor. A resurgence in Cold War hostilities in the late 1970s tightened anticommunist military alliances. US and British policymakers saw South Africa as a central bulwark against the spread of communism in southern Africa. In addition, Botha's government subscribed to Western neoliberal economic policies and supported Cape Afrikaner corporations that advocated deeper linkages with the global economy.

Pretoria took full advantage of a favorable geopolitical context. The NP coupled police death squads and cross-border raids on ANC bases with support for traditionalist African elites. The NP formed an alliance with Mangosuthu Buthelezi's Inkatha movement. Founded in 1975, Inkatha began as an ANC-front organization but later spun off to pursue an exclusively Zulu nationalist agenda.[36] NP patronage emboldened Buthelezi's ambitions to become the Zulu nation's preeminent strongman.[37] By the mid-1980s, Inkatha cadres had received weapons and military training from state security operatives. Party militias in present-day KwaZulu-Natal and the Rand conducted a series of massacres against pro-ANC groups. ANC/MK-backed groups retaliated in kind.[38] The state also hired out violence work to township street gangs to sow further dissension within Black communities.

Botha paired bullets with ballots. The institution of a tricameral legislature in 1984 gave Coloured and Indian voters electoral representation in separate houses.

However, African exclusion from this arrangement ensured white political dominance. Most Coloureds and Indians boycotted the tricameral elections, and African nationalists escalated the freedom struggle.

In 1983, a plethora of civil society groups came together to form the United Democratic Front (UDF).[39] This multiracial coalition launched mass protests against white-minority rule and faced mounting state repression. Initially, the UDF had little to do with the ANC. Its members espoused an inclusive nonracial society to be achieved through mass action rather than armed struggle. The ANC's ability to associate with, and eventually incorporate, the UDF increased its logistical capacity to undermine apartheid. When President Botha declared a partial state of emergency on July 20, 1985, Oliver Tambo responded with a radio address calling on all antiapartheid activists to intensify resistance. As disorder mounted, economic elites reevaluated their commitment to NP rule. They did not do so because they believed in complete racial equality, but because apartheid could no longer guarantee sufficient profits and protect corporate assets.

Anglo led the way. Contrary to Botha's wishes, a team of Anglo executives headed by chairman Gavin Relly met senior ANC leaders in Zambia to discuss South Africa's future.[40] Relly's main goal was to dissuade the ANC from pursuing nationalization policies stipulated in the Freedom Charter. Although Tambo stated that the ANC could not "leave the large corporations operating as they do," he remarked that nationalization would not affect small businessowners or personal property.[41] This mixed-economy approach was an attempt to detach the white middle class from corporate elites, but most middle-class whites worked within the private and parastatal sectors. Thus, economic restructuring was bound to alter their conditions of employment.

Opposing pronouncements aside, the Anglo-ANC meeting began a process that resulted in cooperation between incumbent economic interests and a rising protest elite. Differences between the two groups were not mainly ideological. ANC elites wanted African empowerment within a broadly capitalist framework. Its leaders did not pursue nationalization to implement socialism nor to redistribute wealth from whites to Black people. Rather, party leaders and midlevel functionaries sought to join a white corporate sector operating a commodity-based extractive economy. Radical elements calling for structural reforms often found themselves marginalized in policy debates or sidelined in leadership roles. Socialism was a fig leaf for partial Black economic inclusion.

Political Compromise, ANC Divisions, and Incumbent Economic Interests

The negotiated settlement that ended apartheid has generated extensive commentary.[42] By all accounts, the NP government could have clung to power by escalating repression yet chose not to. President F. W. de Klerk's (r. 1989–94) decision to unban African liberation organizations and release Nelson Mandela from prison in February 1990 was driven by pragmatism. Liberation armies could not overwhelm apartheid's fearsome security apparatus, but the liberation movement was generating increasing socioeconomic disorder. The NP had no political legitimacy beyond the white community and could not impose a settlement favorable to that constituency through force. It had to negotiate a compromise solution with African political elites.

The ANC widened its political leverage soon after its unbanning. It established a formal tripartite alliance with the SACP and COSATU in 1990 and compelled the UDF to disband the following year. These mergers and dissolutions drove protest elites to new heights of political power. This did not, however, reduce factional tensions between the ANC's external and internal wings, which jockeyed for advantage and position. Ramaphosa and Zuma best represented the rising fortunes of domestic and exilic elites, respectively. As a driving force within COSATU, Ramaphosa became ANC secretary-general after 1991's national elective conference and led the transition talks to majority rule.[43] Zuma returned from exile in 1990, whereupon he left the SACP and was elected ANC chairman in southern Natal. Zuma utilized his Zulu roots to draw political support away from the Inkatha Freedom Party (IFP) and toward the ANC.[44] Zuma lost the 1991 elections for the secretary-generalship to Ramaphosa but won the contest for deputy secretary-general. The exilic faction gained further advantages when Thabo Mbeki was elected ANC national chairperson in 1993.

Political power brought the ANC material rewards. Corporate oligarchs dispensed these material rewards to defend their wealth. This strategy proved successful for two reasons. First, exilic and domestic ANC elites lacked material resources. Most, in fact, had little to no money.[45] Company executives saw nationalist penury as an opportunity to ingratiate themselves with incoming rulers. Corporations provided housing, office space, monetary donations, and connections to global financial institutions. As the ANC geared up for national elections in 1994, it needed all the campaign funds and friendly foreign creditors it could get. Because the collapse of the Soviet bloc from 1989 to 1991 deprived the ANC of its main benefactors, it required alternative sources of support. Second, economic inclusion within a capitalist economy had always been a primary objective for ANC leaders. Polemical tracts claiming white monopoly capital captured ANC leaders during the democratic transition are not convincing.[46] As an elite-led anticolonial movement, the ANC wanted to create a politically loyal Black middle class and a small group of Black capitalists allied to white corporations.

ANC officials unwilling or unable to form close connections with white conglomerates entered partnerships with maverick businessmen who brokered relationships between their political associates and capitalist interests. Zuma used Schabir Shaik to manage his parlous finances. Shaik himself worked in the ANC underground and had channeled donor funds from London to South Africa. He also served as financial adviser to ANC treasurer general Thomas Nkobi.[47] Shaik went on to serve as Zuma's business partner and arranged various gatekeeping schemes in which he collected bribes in exchange for access to his boss.

The 1994 democratic elections saw the ANC win over 62 percent of the vote. Even though it entered a Government of National Unity with the NP and IFP, the ANC was the dominant player and received the lion's share of corporate favor. Mandela had already embraced promarket policies at the 1992 World Economic Forum, but the ANC could still use its parliamentary majority to nationalize corporate assets if continued patronage did not keep it content. White capital needed politically connected Black partners to protect its profits.

***

Twentieth-century South African history can be viewed as a tale of two nationalisms.[48] Afrikaner and African nationalist elites pursued anticolonial agendas against incumbent corporate interests to obtain privileged access to material resources. Afrikaner nationalism ultimately succeeded because of a relatively small, slowly shrinking demography. NP political leaders could afford to extend socioeconomic privileges to the Afrikaner working class because Afrikaner workers amounted to a small percentage of the total labor force. Moreover, state support facilitated the formation of a small group of Afrikaner capitalists that equaled Anglophone oligarchs in terms of opulence and assets. Incumbent English capital allowed Afrikaners to enter the mineral sector and its associated industries to stave off threats of nationalization. Despite sociocultural differences, Afrikaans and English-speaking whites amalgamated into an economically privileged minority with vested interests in structural inequality. Some whites dissented from the apartheid system, but parliamentary opposition never posed an appreciable threat to state-sanctioned racial discrimination. White-minority rule was challenged, and eventually overthrown, by African nationalism. Yet moderate elites led Black nationalist movements. These elites aspired to join, rather than overturn, a commodity-based capitalist system that exported minerals to global markets. Black nationalists adopted more radical methods of protest when attempts at persuasion failed. Alliances with communist states provided military training, weapons, and logistical support without altering fundamental aims. The ANC sought inclusion, not revolution. Cold War NP polemics presented the freedom struggle as a communist front to justify Black exclusion from political power. Apartheid ended when white corporations and politicians accepted African nationalism for what it was, not what they wanted it to be.

4

A Privileged, and Fractious, Political Minority

The ANC in Power

South Africa's transition to majority rule shifted the primary locus of exclusive advantage from a racial to a political minority. While the first fifteen years of African National Congress (ANC) rule brought impressive social improvements, economic decline set in when predatory rent seeking became the primary concern of political leaders. Productive investments in basic education, trade apprenticeships, and infrastructure were not sustained, which concentrated wealth into the hands of fractious elites and, to a lesser extent, a politically connected middle class. Moderate ANC leaders were keen to join established private corporations. Party bosses espousing more radical ideologies plundered public resources for personal gain. Rival factions sought to defend material privileges, and inclusive economic development became incidental.

Many ANC macroeconomic policies were doubtless well-intentioned. However, too many cadres viewed party membership as a pathway to wealth. Few political checks existed to restrain their rapacity. The

ANC secured its dominance after the National Party (NP) left the unity government in 1996 and support for the Inkatha Freedom Party (IFP) drained away. The coalescence of the Democratic Alliance (DA) in 2000 created an official opposition, yet it never made appreciable gains among African voters and could not threaten the ANC's parliamentary majority.[1] This exposed the South African state to rent-seeking interests that manipulated policies to secure access to wealth.

Predatory plunder might have been avoided if intraparty feuds had not derailed developmental initiatives. Technocratic elements ascended to senior policymaking positions soon after the democratic transition. President Mandela focused his diminishing energies on racial reconciliation, select social causes, and international affairs, leaving economic issues to his deputy president, Thabo Mbeki. Mbeki's team of experts implemented procapital policies that favored multinational investors. Substantial public expenditures continued, particularly in public housing and electrification. However, Mbeki also provided ample opportunities for ANC elites to extract rents and accrue personal assets. Such material endowments enabled recipients to consolidate rival political networks that clashed for advantage within the ruling party. This exacerbated elite fragmentation. No single faction could assert total dominance over all others. Disgruntled ANC leaders either orchestrated palace coups to topple ruling factions or broke with the party to form their own organizations. Intra-elite feuding eventually eroded single-party dominance and compelled the formation of a multiparty government in which a rump ANC maintained disproportionate advantages.

Accommodating Capital and Politicizing Empowerment

The ANC succeeded in extending civil and political rights to a disenfranchised population. South Africa's 1996 constitution guaranteed basic freedoms and protections for society. Yet it stipulated none for economic development; constitutions seldom do. In parliamentary democracies, economic policies are formulated and implemented by ruling political parties. From 1994 to 2024, the ANC had an absolute parliamentary majority, enabling it to formulate and legislate economic policies of its choosing. Given the ANC's lack of administrative experience, the opening years of ANC rule witnessed impressive economic achievements. The Reconstruction and Development Programme (RDP), pursued from 1994 to 1996, provided government housing, piped water, and power lines to deprived Black townships. To be sure, RDP initiatives focused on quantity rather than quality, and rudimentary infrastructure later decayed due to lack of maintenance, but formerly deprived communities now found themselves connected to public infrastructures that improved lives.[2] Such successes must be balanced against ill-considered missteps. Soon after coming to power, ANC policymakers cut tariffs and lifted exchange controls. Cheap textile and footwear imports wiped out local industries while domestic corporations channeled profits onto first world stock exchanges. ANC polices gradually came to privilege politically connected officials and exclude Black workers. Salaries and perks mattered more than growth and jobs.

Governance failures were compounded by a lack of party discipline that aggravated factionalism and magnified economic dysfunction. Mbeki directly contributed to the political tensions that triggered protracted decline. In 1996, he consolidated his position as Mandela's heir apparent and scrapped the RDP for the Growth, Employment, and Redistribution (GEAR) strategy. Since effectively leaving the South African Communist Party in 1990, Mbeki had marginalized left-wing elements within the ruling party. He had reduced trade union influence by supporting Youth League leaders and managerial technocrats.[3] GEAR called for economic policies that would facilitate growth by encouraging foreign direct investment.[4] Procorporate public policies did not prevent capital flight. Conglomerates seeking less regulation and more secure capital markets transferred their primary listings overseas. In 1999, Anglo American moved its main headquarters from Johannesburg to London. Moreover, Mbeki's administration badly mishandled South Africa's dire HIV epidemic. The president's personal AIDS denialism aside, one reason the government resisted funding antiretroviral therapy (ART) for so long was because it was so expensive. Misguided public health measures focused on treating the illnesses of infected children rather than preventing mother-to-child transmission through ART distribution.[5] The administration's aloof top-down governing style detached it from the daily concerns of ordinary citizens. Expanding infrastructural spending in the early 2000s triggered modest job growth, but most of the working poor and unemployed relied heavily on social grants to meet basic needs.

Mbeki's team devoted considerable energy to empowering ANC cadres through parastatal employment and by cultivating a "patriotic bourgeoisie." Much like radical Afrikaner nationalists in the 1920s, Mbeki wanted to prove that Black people could run complex organizations. Cadres with few administrative qualifications assumed public sector posts and ministerial positions. They received high salaries, free cars, and government housing. These perks lifted them into a growing Black middle class. Cadre deployment made South Africa into a de facto party state in which officials from a single political organization dominated bureaucratic administration. In all fairness, ANC functionaries faced a far more daunting task than their NP counterparts seventy years earlier. NP ministers and bureaucrats served a small Afrikaner minority and neglected nonwhite needs, while the ANC had to uplift a large Black majority mired in poverty after decades of government neglect. Even so, cadres often lacked technical competence, and service delivery to deprived communities gradually deteriorated. Despite these failures, cadres were not held accountable for their shortcomings. The leadership masked errors and irregularities committed by fellow comrades. This only encouraged corruption and generated numerous scandals.

The largest corruption scandal of the 1990s was a controversial arms deal with Western defense contractors.[6] Arms embargoes and economic sanctions in the late apartheid period limited opportunities to sell advanced weapons systems to the South African military. Soon after South Africa rejoined the global community, arms manufacturers began lobbying senior ANC officials for defense contracts. Corporations bribed cabinet ministers with illicit payments, financial retainers, and personal gifts. Defense minister Joe Modise; South African National Defence Force chief Siphiwe Nyanda; minister of public enterprises Stella Sigcau; and deputy president Jacob Zuma all derived financial benefit from pushing the arms deal through.

In late 1999, the government signed massive procurement contracts costing thirty billion rand for corvettes, submarines, fighter aircraft, and helicopters. By all accounts, South Africa paid exorbitant prices for arms it did not need. The country faced no threats of external invasion, and its military did not require offensive weaponry. Calls to investigate financial irregularities resulted in a formal inquiry. A joint investigation led by the auditor general encountered ANC obstruction, and its conclusions exculpated senior ministers. Mbeki refused to involve the Special Investigating Unit and protected his colleagues from prosecution.[7] Mbeki was eventually compelled to remove Zuma from the deputy presidency in 2005 after Schabir Shaik's conviction for funneling illegal payments to Zuma in exchange for backing the arms deal.[8] Zuma's temporary political setback was a rare event in the Mbeki administration. Many other ANC officials were never held accountable for corruption.

The ANC circulated washed-out members back into different posts on multiple occasions. Efficiency and professionalism mattered far less than placing the party's people in top positions. Government and public sector wages were paid by taxing productive industries in the private sector. This cut into company profits and left entrepreneurs with less to invest in business expansion and industrial innovation. Again, like previous NP leaders, Mbeki facilitated the formation of a Black bourgeoisie because he felt Africans should assume their rightful place in the corporate world. He was also driven by personal motives. Business careers removed political rivals from government and consolidated his faction's control over party structures. However, unlike Afrikaner capitalists, most Black business elites extracted rents without adding value to their companies. Mbeki's empowerment policies were geared toward display and entitlement, not development.

Rent Seeking and the Rise of African Oligarchs

The transition to democracy sharpened distinctions between South Africa's political and economic elites. These distinctions had the potential to disrupt corporate profits. ANC leaders lacked material assets but possessed the political power to appropriate assets from capital through legislative action. Thus, business elites took measures to minimize that risk. They pursued policies defined as Black economic empowerment (BEE), or the provision of privileged access to company shares for influential Black politicians. The international business climate facilitated the unbundling of conglomerates. Once economic sanctions were lifted, corporations sloughed off subsidiaries deemed redundant in an era of free trade. In addition, corporate oligarchs sought to extend apartheid-era policies, aimed at Anglophone and Afrikaner capital amalgamation, to Africans. Anglo chairman Julian Ogilvie Thompson later claimed he "tried to do for the blacks what Harry did for the Afrikaners."[9]

White conglomerates empowered individuals rather than social groups. Corporations generally transferred assets to domestic leaders of the freedom struggle. Companies were more familiar with *inzile* (domestic anti-apartheid activist) types and felt they could more readily demobilize working-class protests. At no point did Black politicians become subordinate clients to white executives. Business elites did not have direct access to political power and could only influence government policies by dispensing favors to ANC policymakers. ANC officials in corporate boardrooms sustained links between the private sector and party structures in exchange for company shares. Preferential access to shares allowed a select group of ANC leaders to amass huge wealth. Part of this wealth was invested in party building. New ANC provincial branches had to be constructed, and the party needed campaign funds for future elections. As good earners, BEE businesspeople secured and maintained senior-level party positions, which raised demand for their services in corporate circles. The more in demand they were, the more they could ask for their aid. If one white conglomerate no longer served their interests, they could always find another.

Black empowerment ventures began before the fall of apartheid. In 1993, Sanlam set up New Africa Investments Limited (NAIL) to co-opt liberation leaders and dissuade them from implementing nationalization clauses in the Freedom Charter. Sanlam targeted individuals headed for parliamentary careers and senior positions in policymaking bodies. It made a percentage of shares from its subsidiary Metropolitan Life, a Cape life insurance company, available for sale to NAIL directors. Sanlam then borrowed money on behalf of NAIL leaders to enable them to buy those shares. A leading beneficiary of this transaction was NAIL chair Dr. Nthato Motlana. Motlana had been an ANC Youth League member, a leader in the Defiance Campaign, and Mandela's personal physician. In 1977, he became a member of the Soweto Committee of Ten that managed township affairs after the uprising. Under his direction, NAIL acquired interests in media houses, radio, and television.[10]

Anglo followed Sanlam's example in 1995 by unbundling Johannesburg Consolidated Investments (JCI) into three separate companies and selling shares in two of them, JCI and Johnnic, to Black companies. These moves launched Ramaphosa's business career. Ramaphosa resigned as ANC secretary-general in 1996 after losing out in the presidential succession dispute to Mbeki. However, Ramaphosa retained his position on the ANC's National Executive Committee and wove his way into the corporate world to obtain party funds and amass a personal fortune. He started out as deputy executive chairman at NAIL. When the NAIL affiliate National Empowerment Corporation bought a controlling interest in Johnnic, Ramaphosa was appointed Johnnic chairman, giving him a stake in hotels, casinos, and entertainment. A stream of executive and nonexecutive directorships in other companies followed.[11] These positions came with shareholdings, dividend payments, generous salaries, and other benefits. In 2001, Ramaphosa founded the Shanduka Group, a holding company with interests in mining, television, telecommunications, food and beverages, property, and financial services. Shanduka later made investments in Mozambique, Mauritius, Ghana, and Nigeria.[12] Ramaphosa's various ventures allowed him to acquire a net worth of some $450 million as of 2015.[13] He bought private estates, branched out into cattle farming, and built a game farm at Phala Phala in Limpopo.

Ramaphosa's fortune paled in comparison to that of his brother-in-law Patrice Motsepe. Although Motsepe did not begin his business career with the same high-powered political connections, his familial alliance with Ramaphosa generated opportunities for continued material accumulation, even though personal relations between the two men are, according to some, far from amiable. After a rough start, Motsepe founded Future Mining in 1994.[14] His company gleaned dust left over from blasting operations in gold mine shafts. Such low-level work meant less competition. Motsepe secured a steady stream of contracts and reserved company savings for future investments. He incorporated African Rainbow Minerals (ARM) with venture capital from Future Mining in 1997. Motsepe still needed large bank loans to purchase production shafts and had difficulty securing credit until pitching a proposal to Bobby Godsell, Anglo's chief gold and uranium mining executive. Godsell later commented that he "wanted to help black South Africans get into business. . . . I was seeking to create capitalists out of people who had no capital."[15] Anglo extended a 500,000 rand loan to ARM in exchange for a percentage of profits. Godsell's company AngloGold also sold off numerous marginal shafts to ARM, thus expanding its involvement in deep-level mining.[16]

Motsepe widened his political and economic network when his sister Tshepo married Ramaphosa in 1996. Much like Anton Rupert, Motsepe benefited from personal/political alliances without becoming overly dependent on them. ARM received a Johannesburg Stock Exchange listing in 2002 and merged with Harmony Gold Mining and Anglovaal corporations the following year. These acquisitions made ARM the premier Black mining conglomerate. In 2008, Motsepe became a billionaire. As of October 2025, he had a net worth of $3.5 billion.[17] Motsepe is one of the few BEE beneficiaries to engage in competitive entrepreneurship, yet it is unlikely he would have risen so far so fast without political connections. Both he and Ramaphosa have made extensive donations to the ANC, although Motsepe hedged his bets by making financial contributions to other political parties as well.[18] Motsepe joined a global capitalist elite and achieved celebrity status through philanthropic and environmental causes. His investments and involvements with soccer teams led to his election as president of the Confederation of African Football in 2021. Organizing matches and tournaments, coupled with selling broadcasting rights, provided Motsepe with further money-making opportunities. His wife, Precious, began her career in the public health sector but shifted over to high-end fashion as ARM took off.[19] Precious Moloi-Motsepe's promotion of African luxury designers propelled their products onto first world catwalks, yet expensive consumer items remained beyond the reach of ordinary South Africans. The Motsepe family's philanthropy opened doors for many individuals, but charity could not overcome structural inequalities that produced mass poverty.

Other BEE beneficiaries have followed political paths to wealth. Like Ramaphosa, Tokyo Sexwale began his career in the Black Consciousness movement. Sexwale then joined Umkhonto we Sizwe and went to the Soviet Union in 1975 to receive military training.[20] He was arrested for conspiracy to topple the government in 1976 and imprisoned on Robben Island. Upon his release in 1990, Sexwale returned to Johannesburg and was elected a member of the ANC Executive Committee for Pretoria-Witwatersrand-Vereeniging. After the 1994 elections, he became premier of Gauteng Province and formed personal connections with Johannesburg's Anglophone mining oligarchy. He was a frequent guest at social functions and became very close to the Oppenheimers. In 1998, Sexwale fell out with Mbeki and left politics to take advantage of empowerment opportunities. That same year, Sexwale created the Mvelaphanda Group, a holding company. Anglo sold a bundle of mining assets to assist Mvelaphanda, and in 2000 Sexwale's company acquired 22.5 percent of a mining company, Northam Platinum, from Anglo and Remgro, the successor to Rembrandt. Although platinum, gold, and diamonds remained core interests, Mvelaphanda diversified into car dealerships, business services, and banking.[21] In 2009, Sexwale declared a net worth of nearly $200 million. He utilized his private wealth to seek public office. Sexwale attempted to replace Mbeki in 2007 and served as Zuma's minister of human settlements from 2009 to 2013. Sexwale sold off his shares in the ABSA Group, a banking and financial services conglomerate, to finance his campaign for the ANC deputy presidency at the 2012 leadership elections.[22] After losing to Ramaphosa, Sexwale concentrated on his business ventures, embarking on murky mining deals on the African continent, and continued to campaign for the ruling party.

Saki Macozoma also used his struggle credentials to accumulate wealth and extract rents from white conglomerates. He was arrested at the age of nineteen for leading student protests and spent five years on Robben Island under Mandela's political tutelage. After his release, Macozoma was involved with United Democratic Front and ANC structures. He became an MP in 1994 and was elected to the ANC's National Working Committee the following year. In 1996, he became managing director at Transnet, a parastatal responsible for running ports, railways, and South African Airways. These political and bureaucratic connections made Macozoma a prime candidate for BEE ventures, and he was appointed to the board of Standard Bank in 1998 where he later became deputy chairman.[23]

In 2001, Macozoma purchased a 10 percent share in Safika Holdings, another BEE company. Several months later NAIL appointed Macozoma as CEO. When

Macozoma doubled his Safika stake in 2003, he and two other directors held 60 percent of company shares.[24] From 2003 to 2005, Macozoma orchestrated a reciprocal shareholding scheme with Standard Bank in a deal worth an estimated 4.3 billion rand. This transaction solidified Standard Bank's empowerment credentials while allowing Macozoma to maintain his 20 percent stake in Safika. His appointment to several other corporate chairmanships and involvement in manganese mining multiped his income streams. Although Macozoma has a reported net worth of around only $31 million, multiple corporate salaries constantly replenished his financial reserves.[25]

Conglomerates secured their wealth by co-opting ANC political elites into corporate boardrooms. Neither white executives not Black politicians were primarily concerned with creating entrepreneurial African capitalists. Rather, incumbent economic interests wanted to defend their assets, while senior ANC officials sought rents and sinecures. This project proved successful. Preeminent white oligarchs passed on their fortunes to their heirs without difficulties. Nicky Oppenheimer inherited huge wealth from his father Harry, as did Johann Rupert from his father Anton.[26] Beyond the great dynasts, white executives sustained control over corporate operations and prioritized private profits over public welfare. BEE was an elite pact that forestalled nationalization and enriched a few well-connected individuals.

Deepening Predation and Elite Fragmentation Under Zuma

Zuma's removal from the deputy presidency only aggravated growing tensions within the ANC. Mbeki's decision to retain Zuma despite mounting evidence of corrupt practices related to the arms deal was probably motivated by political considerations. Whatever affective ties Mbeki may have had to his fellow comrade, Zuma's shady side deals made him vulnerable and hence an unthreatening deputy president.[27] However, Mbeki miscalculated. Mounting pressures compelled him to replace Zuma in 2005, and this added another element to intraparty discontent. The South African Communist Party and the Congress of South African Trade Unions had voiced their dissatisfaction with neoliberal macroeconomic policies on numerous occasions. Deindustrialization dissipated their support base, and Mbeki's pan-Africanist platitudes shifted focus away from domestic working-class struggles. While Mbeki openly ignored communist and trade union concerns, Zuma at least appeared to care. In addition, BEE oligarchs building autonomous power bases within the private sector drew Mbeki's ire. In 2001, three members of the ANC—Ramaphosa, Sexwale, and Mathews Phosa—were investigated for organizing a plot to oust the president. The trio allegedly insinuated that Mbeki had a hand in Chris Hani's 1993 assassination.[28] Nothing came of the investigation, and it was clear that senior ANC figures posing a threat to the ruling faction would be subjected to politically motivated harassment. Disillusioned party oligarchs added weight to opposing factions.

Other pro-Zuma elements viewed their boss as a pathway to patronage and affluence. Zuma's network felt the political system had been dominated by neoliberal technocrats, committed to embedding themselves in globalized capital networks, for far too long. Disgruntled ANC elements associated elitist tendencies in the party with Mbeki's presidency. Mbeki's educated and articulate coterie imbibed the haughty, and at times ill-conceived, intellectualism of their leader. They premised their claim to power on specialized knowledge and technocratic expertise. These technocrats had also indulged in asset accumulation. As a result, Zuma's group felt it was only just that they have their turn at the feeding trough. Hence, their agenda was more reactionary than revolutionary.[29]

Zuma himself had secured new financial backers as Shaik's star began to fade. Ajay, Atul, and Rajesh Gupta were three brothers who migrated to South Africa from India in 1993 and made a fortune in IT distribution. The Gupta brothers used their wealth to purchase favors from prominent politicians. Never comfortable with incumbent corporate elites, Zuma chose instead to conduct business transactions with multinationals through intermediaries or sold political services to maverick entrepreneurs outside white monopoly capital. Freewheeling businesspeople outside established corporate channels were Zuma's primary path to enrichment. He saw to their political requests while they delivered money, sinecures, and material goods.[30] Both Zuma and BEE oligarchs used politics to accumulate wealth and engage in conspicuous consumption. Consumption signified status and the ability to command resources, thus attracting larger followings and further consolidating political networks. However, BEE oligarchs pursued those objectives from within incumbent corporate structures and consequently secured more stable wealth. Zuma accumulated money and material assets by blatantly selling political favors to businesses that threatened established economic interests. These contradictions eventually undermined the ANC's political dominance.

A Zuma-led coalition ousted Mbeki from the ANC presidency at the 2007 Polokwane Conference and had him recalled as state president the following year. Mbeki loyalists formed a breakaway party called Congress of the People in late 2008. The party received over 7 percent of votes in the 2009 elections and won thirty parliamentary seats but gradually petered out thereafter. Zuma clinched the state presidency in 2009 and had some early successes. His administration rolled out ART medication, and the economy received a short-term boost from hosting the 2010 FIFA World Cup. It soon became apparent, however, that Zuma's primary concern was enriching himself, his family, and his clients by repurposing state institutions to serve Gupta family interests. Law enforcement agencies and regulatory bodies were either politicized, criminalized, or hollowed out.[31]

The president's extensive political network received rents and bribes from his financial backers. The Zuma-Gupta nexus stood at the apex of a predatory system that reached down into provinces and localities. Zuma did not so much create this network as allow political bosses at various subnational levels to plunder public resources and consolidate their own client groups. Zuma culled substantial political support from an interprovincial bloc called the *premier league*. The Free State, North West, and Mpumalanga Provinces, led by Ace Magashule, Supra Mahumapelo, and David Mabuza, respectively, delivered votes in exchange for political protection from Pretoria.[32] All three provinces fell prey to grand corruption as fraudulent tenders, looting of public funds, land grabbing, and patronage appointments to parastatals collapsed service delivery.

Magashule manipulated Free State tenders to reward his cronies and Gupta family clients. This expanded his political network downward into provincial localities and upward into national government. As an example, the Free State Department of Human Settlements awarded a 255-million-rand contract to Blackhead Consulting in 2014 to remove asbestos from homes. Thereupon, a Magashule aide requested that a Blackhead subsidiary make payments to various third parties, one of whom was a Gupta client in need of money for a child's school fees.[33] Tender funds drained away and little asbestos was removed.

Mahumapelo siphoned off North West provincial funds with little regard for the effect it had on public services. Hospitals collapsed and refuse remained uncollected. One Mahikeng resident said of Mahumapelo, "He apparently calls himself *setsokotsane* (hurricane). Maybe that is the setsokotsane that had stolen all our money since he came into office." An associate of Mahumapelo made a deal with a Gupta-linked company in which a 30-million-rand prepayment was disbursed to provide a single mobile clinic, with a further 100 million rand set aside for the company to draw on.[34]

Mabuza ran Mpumalanga like a private fiefdom, holding court in his Barberton farm where he stashed suitcases full of cash, dispensed favors to supplicants, and passed money upward. In one instance, Mabuza made a financial contribution toward Zuma's wedding. In addition, Mabuza used land reform programs as a pretext to grab turf from nature reserve developers.[35] The construction of Mbombela Stadium for the 2010 World Cup generated dubious tenders involving politically connected contractors. Several whistleblowers attempting to expose these and other illicit transactions were assassinated.

Political violence also permeated several South African municipalities. Mayoral and local party positions brought access to various benefits, including lucrative tenders. Contenders for public office occasionally resorted to assassinating competitors, while incumbent officials hired professional assassins to gun down whistleblowers. Such killings became particularly prevalent in Mpumalanga and KwaZulu-Natal.[36]

Zuma's faction achieved dominance without hegemony. Powerful ANC figures pursued interests at variance with Gupta-controlled channels. Ramaphosa continued his close association with white mining companies. In 2012, he facilitated the violent repression of striking workers at a platinum mine in Marikana owned by Lonmin, a British producer of metals. Although Ramaphosa initially took a cautious approach to the strike, he came under pressure from Lonmin's chief commercial officer Albert Jamieson to brand protesting workers as criminals. Once Ramaphosa shifted to a hardline position, he lobbied government ministers, including the minister of police and the minister of mineral resources, to take firm action.[37] Paramilitary police units dispatched to the scene opened fire on protestors, killing scores and wounding many more. Taking a page from Mbeki's book, Zuma backed Ramaphosa's election to the ANC deputy presidency in December 2012. Marikana damaged Ramaphosa's reputation, thus making him less of a threat to Zuma's position.[38] Zuma followed this up by arranging Ramaphosa's appointment as deputy state president in 2014. Zuma did this to offload difficult administrative and diplomatic tasks onto his deputy while consolidating his faction's capture of the South African state.

Zuma proved unable to hold the ANC Youth League together. Its firebrand leader, Julius Malema, supported Zuma's initial rise to power but fell out with him shortly thereafter, purportedly because the president refused to implement a radical left-wing agenda. Malema's constant heckling and brazen insubordination eventually led to his expulsion from the ANC in 2012. He and close associate Floyd Shivambu responded by founding the Economic Freedom Fighters (EFF) the following year. The EFF espoused radical economic policies centered around nationalization and land expropriation without compensation. EFF members assumed the trappings and rhetoric of Venezuelan-style socialism, making significant political capital out of polemical pronouncements condemning state corruption. The EFF won over 6 percent of votes in the 2014 general elections and nearly 11 percent in 2019. With forty-four seats, it became the third-largest parliamentary party. Malema's polemical tirades against ANC sellouts may have been motivated by political opportunism and personal grudges, but his radical populism resonated with disenchanted youths. EFF leaders were not above using their growing political muscle to loot public resources. In 2018, it emerged that Shivambu had siphoned money from VBS Mutual Bank through a front account owned by his brother.[39] Malema himself garnered significant popularity among the poor because of his ability to steal from an oppressive state and build a lavish lifestyle. Relatively privileged Black university students also imbibed the EFF's radical rhetoric as their frustrations against the ANC establishment mounted.

The main source of societal anger was a decline in public services. Service delivery sharply deteriorated as the Zuma-Gupta network tightened its grip. Predation in the parastatal sector took place under the banner of cadre deployment. Those deployed to run state-owned enterprises soon became indistinguishable from the criminal mafias that looted plants and pilfered raw materials. Cadre-mafia amalgamation indicated an intertwining of public servants with organized crime. Government-sanctioned grand larceny led to chronic rolling blackouts, contaminated water supplies, and dysfunctional transportation systems. Consequently, the ANC lost political support, particularly in large metropolitan areas. Its share of the national vote declined from 65.9 percent in the 2009 general election to 62 percent in 2014 to 57.5 percent in 2019.[40] What kept the party afloat was the rural vote in the former homelands. These impoverished areas relied heavily on government social grants to meet basic needs, and rural voters feared such assistance would end if the ANC lost power.

Economic decline accelerated when global markets and domestic conglomerates soured on Zuma's administration. In 2016, public protector Thuli Madonsela released a damning report, *State of Capture,* claiming that the Gupta family had undue influence over government policies. This influence did indeed reach into the highest levels of government but had its limits. For example, when Zuma appointed a Gupta crony as finance minister in 2015, multinational investors compelled the president to reverse himself and reappoint Pravin Gordhan. Gordhan was eventually dismissed in March 2017, and credit agencies downgraded South Africa to junk status shortly thereafter. Zuma's faction attempted to polish its image by hiring British public relations firm Bell Pottinger. Bell Pottinger spin doctors focused public attention on the menace of white monopoly capital and the need for radical economic transformation. Johann Rupert baldly stated that Zuma's policy of radical economic transformation was "a code word for theft."[41] Senior party leaders reluctantly concluded that either the ANC would have to learn to live without Zuma or South Africa would learn to live without the ANC.

Zuma attempted to have his ex-wife Nkosazana Dlamini-Zuma elected as ANC president at the 2017 party conference, but she lost to Ramaphosa. Zuma resigned as state president in early 2018 and was replaced by Ramaphosa. Yet Ramaphosa's victory was not a triumph for the forces of renewal and reform. It was rather an instance of one oligarchic network gaining ascendancy over another.

Not wanting to yield further market shares to the Gupta network, incumbent corporate oligarchs backed ANC leaders more amenable to their interests. As a BEE oligarch, Ramaphosa was embedded in established economic interests and would be inclined to protect those interests. Ramaphosa had often used radical redistributionist rhetoric to keep private conglomerates off-balance. However, because he continued to extract lucrative rents from capital, he never mounted a sustained attack against it. As president, Ramaphosa passed progressive legislation geared toward downward distributions of wealth but never sustained the momentum necessary for successful implementation. Ordinary South Africans, in the main, failed to benefit from such laws. Furthermore, many state-capture looters were never brought to book. Opportunistic elements within Zuma's network rapidly shifted their loyalties to Ramaphosa and evaded accountability. Ramaphosa, hesitant to further aggravate internal party tensions, soft-pedaled prosecutions. Mabuza became vice president, while

Nkosazana Dlamini-Zuma held cabinet positions. Magashule was elected ANC secretary-general at the 2017 conference, and a warrant for his arrest was not issued until 2020.[42] Mabuza was replaced as deputy state president in 2023 by Paul Mashatile, head of a notorious tender syndicate from Johannesburg's Alexandra township, popularly referred to as the *Alex Mafia*. Such an accommodationist stance toward dubious characters prioritized party unity over justice.

Declarations of national renewal rang hollow as government reform initiatives failed to address systemic corruption. The Zondo Commission, an inquiry into state capture from 2018 to 2022, interviewed hundreds of witnesses and collected extensive evidence of administrative malfeasance.[43] Its final report called for criminal prosecutions that generated convoluted legal wrangles which have yet to be fully resolved. Ramaphosa's administration removed certain corrupt officials and went some way toward reforming the prosecution services, but too many people implicated in financial improprieties remained in government. The much vaunted "Ramaphoria" gripping South Africa after Zuma's removal was fading before COVID-19 came.

The pandemic generated fresh procurement scandals related to protective equipment for medical professionals. These problems were compounded by political instability. When Zuma was briefly jailed for contempt of court in 2021, his family and other loyal supporters fanned violent unrest in KwaZulu-Natal and Gauteng. The riots resulted in over three hundred deaths and extensive property damage.[44] Government reluctance to respond with lethal force probably forestalled further civil disorder, but business owners bitterly condemned state inaction. Furthermore, Russia's invasion of Ukraine in 2022 triggered a global oil shock that sparked fuel price hikes and increased costs for basic consumables. The year 2022 also saw the Phala Phala scandal, in which Ramaphosa himself was investigated after it emerged that a large sum of American dollars stashed on his Limpopo estate had been stolen in a robbery two years prior.[45] Meanwhile, Eskom could not keep the lights on. Rising levels of load shedding seemed to be the only way to prevent a system-wide grid collapse. Urban voters looked to other parties to address their concerns. The ANC received less than 50 percent of votes in the 2021 municipal elections and lost control of South Africa's major metropolitan areas.[46] Single-party dominance was on its way out.

The ANC might have retained a slim majority in the 2024 national elections had it not been for intraparty feuds. The center-right DA acted as an official opposition but was unable to shake off its image as a white party with a condescending attitude toward uneducated Black people. DA rule in the Western Cape did not threaten ANC rule at the national level. The rural poor remained dependent on social grants and refused to support DA calls for reductions in welfare expenditure.

Zuma's antagonism toward Ramaphosa's faction wrought far greater electoral damage. In December 2023, Zuma established the Umkhonto we Sizwe Party (MKP), an ethno-populist organization calling for radical economic reform and conservative social values. MKP ran on a separate ticket and Zuma refused to campaign for the ANC, although he was barred from parliament due to his prior prison sentence. MKP's pandering to Zulu nationalist sentiments and antiestablishment rhetoric resonated with poor voters, and the party siphoned off a significant portion of ANC support. DA talk of a purported doomsday coalition between the ANC and either the MKP or EFF did not appreciably grow its voter base. MKP received over 14 percent of the vote in 2024's general election. It gained the largest number of seats in KwaZulu-Natal's provincial legislature and became the third-largest party in parliament.[47] Coming out with just over 40 percent of votes, a chastened ANC negotiated to form a Government of National Unity (GNU). The ruling party had torn itself apart.

Maintaining Minority Privileges After Majority Rule

South Africa's purported GNU was, at best, an aspirational objective that required national-level negotiations between various stakeholders both inside and outside formal political institutions. Balancing the priorities of these various interests while reviving a sluggish economy required further hard bargaining and formulating a developmental strategy that prioritized industrial manufacturing. Political elites had to take cognizance of where they were if they wanted to facilitate inclusive economic growth.

South Africa's composite national political landscape bifurcated into a bipartisan core and multiparty periphery. Core members, comprising the ANC and DA, led the arrangement. Eight other small parties entering the GNU presented a picture of broad-based inclusivity; in reality, they occupied peripheral positions heavily dependent on ANC patronage.

The DA was certainly not above dispensing patronage to secure wider strategic interests. Leaders from the ANC and DA allocated the premiership of KwaZulu-Natal to the IFP to lock out Zuma's MKP from provincial governance.[48] Deprived of an administrative bailiwick from which to distribute sinecures and government tenders to cultivate its following, the MKP had a harder time increasing its support base. In addition, the appointment of IFP president Velenkosini Hlabisa as minister of cooperative governance and traditional affairs tilted many traditional Zulu leaders, eager to acquire greater politico-economic privileges, away from Zuma and toward a dispensation led by the ANC and DA.

However, the DA refused to enter a coalition arrangement in Gauteng, South Africa's main economic hub. Thus, ANC provincial premier Panyaza Lesufi, who had come to office in 2022, formed a minority government comprising the IFP, Patriotic Alliance, and RISE Mzansi. This configuration reduced DA leverage over national politics but made it more difficult to provide essential services to Black townships, plagued by high crime rates, power cuts, and water shortages. The ANC still relied on tenuous supply-and-confidence agreements with other parties to pass legislation. Such subnational multiparty governments are notoriously unstable entities prone to generating voter backlashes against incumbents.

If South Africa's municipal-level dysfunctions were cast upward to a national level, socioeconomic ructions would magnify accordingly. Policymakers at the Union Buildings, the official center of national government, were aware they were playing for higher stakes and could not afford very many missteps. Nonetheless, the DA made critical mistakes that the ANC took advantage of. At a basic level, DA leaders painted themselves into a corner. If they walked out of the GNU, they would court the very doomsday coalition, formed via an ANC alliance with the EFF or MKP, that they campaigned so vigorously against. Moreover, senior ANC officials selectively incorporated leaders from the multiparty periphery into secondary ministries of a thirty-two-member cabinet, bloated further by a panoply of largely ceremonial deputy ministers.[49] Beyond the obvious pressures this placed on an already constrained fiscus, DA representation was truncated under an aegis of inclusivity.

Critical briefs such as finance, police, and foreign affairs remained within the ANC's auspices. Global investors viewed finance minister Enoch Godongwana as a safe pair of hands, amenable to neoliberal macroeconomic policies espoused by ostensibly more conservative politicians. The police also stayed under ANC control.

It remains unlikely that the ANC would ever allow such a critical ministry to fall into the hands of another party while they hold the largest vote share. Presidents and their police ministers have come from the same party since 1994. No fundamental changes to foreign policy were expected under Ronald Lamola, the minister of international relations and cooperation. What little political capital the ANC has acquired during Ramaphosa's government has come from its stand against Israel's war in Gaza, though what impact this has had on the geopolitical balance in the Middle East is less clear. Moral authority aside, armed conflicts in that volatile region cannot be determined by South Africa's actions, and the DA has acquiesced to ANC control over foreign affairs for the foreseeable future.

Cabinet posts for peripheral parties can generate greater instability, as they might eat into the DA's electoral base in the Western Cape. The appointment of Patriotic Alliance president Gayton McKenzie as minister of sports, arts and culture gave him an entrée into a lucrative money spinner and had the potential to siphon Coloured voters from the DA.[50] The Western Cape's poor increasingly view the DA as a white party with little concern for Cape Town's impoverished nonwhite townships. McKenzie proved far more successful in mobilizing a mass base in the Western Cape than Patricia de Lille's ANC-aligned Good Party. Helen Zille's publicly voiced displeasure at the Patriotic Alliance's entry into the GNU may have scotched McKenzie's ambitions to obtain the home affairs portfolio, which went to the DA's Leon Schreiber instead. Yet McKenzie now had a national platform from which he could amplify his anti-immigrant, and to some extent anti-white-elite, populism. He posed no threat to his ANC patrons but could do considerable damage to his DA rivals.

In all, the ANC made the best of a bad situation. It has contained the impact of a DA entry into national government by drawing peripheral political elements into positions of executive power and privilege. Should DA leaders walk away from their subordinate position, the ANC might move to replace them with either the EFF or MKP. Although Zuma was expelled from the ANC shortly after the GNU was established, the MKP is hardly a coherent entity.[51] Zuma may intend to bequeath the party to his son Duduzane, yet the latter lacks his father's personal charisma and political heft. Opportunistic factions within MKP might break off and rejoin the ANC before or after Zuma exits the scene. Although the inherent danger of a leftward lurch allows the ANC to retain more than its fair share of executive power and rents, it provides little clarity regarding economic priorities. The ANC's main priority appears to be retaining power, and its associated privileges, for as long as possible.

ANC elites are still committed to policies that tax a stagnant economy for the sake of conspicuous consumption. Policymakers should instead put in place programs that will grow the economic pie and invest profits into fixed capital formation. Public sector salaries need to come down, and the ensuing savings must be channeled into social services for the unemployed and working poor. Without a viable basic education system and trade schools producing larger quantities of skilled labor, South Africa's economy will not take off. If the ANC does not prioritize economic development over political dominance and rent seeking, it will suffer further losses in future elections.

* * *

Throughout its thirty years in power, the ANC remained a conglomerate of elites and special interests. Factional feuds were not primarily driven by ideological differences. Rather, different political bosses backed by different business interests maneuvered for access to rents and status. Lower-ranking party officials backed one or another leader to secure access to government jobs. Administrative and public sector positions provided the salaries and perks necessary to enter the middle class, though the Black middle class accessed state salaries through political connections rather than professional qualifications. State functionaries and elected officials were thus extremely reluctant to investigate corruption. Predation on public assets fueled conspicuous consumption. Zuma's faction rapidly dissipated acquired wealth through extravagant expenditure and repeatedly revisited the feeding trough to plunder further resources. BEE oligarchs primarily obtained rents from private conglomerates and accrued more stable assets. However, they also engaged in lavish consumerism and added little economic value to the companies that bank-rolled them. BEE elites provided political protection without economic innovation.

Inclusive economic development remained an incidental concern across the political and corporate spectrum. Black politicians were primarily concerned with material acquisition and conspicuous consumption, while white corporate elites defended capital by co-opting ANC leaders able to defer downward distributions of wealth. Social services consequently deteriorated and drained electoral support away from the ruling party. It was, however, the inability of rival ANC elites to form workable partnerships that ultimately undermined single-party dominance. No single faction could fully subdue rival networks. Elite fragmentation precipitated political breakaways that eroded the ANC's parliamentary majority.

Conclusion

I contend that to think constructively and coherently about the massive challenges privileged minorities pose to inclusive development in South Africa today, it is necessary to understand how wealth was concentrated historically.

Within South Africa itself, informed commentators largely view current social problems through prisms of race. White professionals blame their country's present predicament on an inept African ruling elite, more interested in looting public resources than securing private property and providing basic services.[1] This is the underlying tone of South Africa's main media houses, podcasters, and talk show pundits. Railing against the ANC's lack of technocratic expertise, they deride patronage politics and long for the day when it will be fully removed from power. More extreme forms of criticism raise the menacing specter of imminent socialist revolution, with mass expropriation of private wealth and an inevitable slide into economic ruin, as experienced in Venezuela or Zimbabwe.[2] These arguments minimize a deep history of white corporate corruption, indigenous dispossession, and exclusive socioeconomic advantages. At base, most anti-ANC perspectives refuse to acknowledge that material affluence under white-minority rule was largely artificial. Such prosperity was premised on the subordination of an African majority to a white minority. As a small, shrinking minority, the white demographic was relatively easy to provide for, especially when African labor was yoked to serving its interests. This system proved untenable once a freedom struggle committed to nonracialism gained sufficient momentum to overturn it.

Black nationalists committed to radical economic transformation essentially make the same mistake in a different way. They contend that white prosperity depended on Black people tightening their belts. Africans coped with low wages, coercive labor systems, and squalid living conditions so a white settler minority could live in comfort and security. When majority rule came in 1994, many ANC elites felt it was at last their turn to partake in the bounty of the state. They would now indulge in the consumerism that typified white lives under colonialism, segregation, and apartheid. However, not all Black people could live like whites; there were simply too many of the former and too few of the latter. ANC elites have cultivated a Black middle class, which is committed to keeping the party in power, but this has done nothing to soak up terrifyingly high levels of unemployment in rural areas and urban townships. Suffering during the freedom struggle generated a culture of entitlement to the benefits of power. Extending white living standards to the African masses became an aspirational goal that justified ANC political dominance. Rhetorical pronouncements of broad-based Black economic empowerment masked the exclusive accumulation of private wealth by a narrow elite.

Broad publics within South Africa and beyond generally subscribe to narratives of racial injustice, particularly on university campuses. The transnational #RhodesMustFall movement has strongly condemned a formerly revered paladin of empire. The removal and defacement of imperial monuments across Britain generated a conservative backlash, or rather rehash, of tired arguments that however bad the British Empire may have been, it was better than other empires.[3] The University of Oxford's reliance on funding from the Rhodes Trust has, on occasion, resulted in ill-considered apologetics. Yet another whose-foot-stinks-least debate will not advance scholarly understandings of colonial domination. White rule in South Africa certainly cannot be seen as anything other than what it was: a project of dispossession and exploitation perpetuated by racial division. Nonetheless, critics of white rule must consider the memetic nature of African nationalism. Most Black political elites strove to emulate the material culture of their white oppressors. Acquisition of prestige goods, rather than structural economic reform, absorbed their energies. This exposed them to corporate capture and the repurposing of revolutionary parties toward schemes of illicit accumulation.

I do not take a middle ground between procolonial and anticolonial extremes. Rather, I argue that South Africa's corporate oligarchs and political elites have a deep history of mutual capture and exclusive accumulation. These practices persisted because they evolved. When the repression of hostile sociopolitical movements proved counterproductive, corporate capital shifted to the incorporation and envelopment of nationalist politicians into webs of patronage and dependency. If revolution could not be suppressed, its benefits could, at least, be so narrowly distributed as to be structurally meaningless.

In addition, race did not become the sole pathway to privilege in South Africa until the early twentieth century. Industrial mining and British imperial expansion certainly deepened indigenous impoverishment; however, white workers also experienced material dispossession through industrial conglomeration. South Africa's territorial union accelerated Black exclusion while heightening government hostility to white working-class demands for preferential treatment. The extension of economic privileges to white workers in the 1920s fully racialized minority privilege. Gradual socioeconomic convergence between Anglophone and Afrikaans-speaking whites was premised on heightened Black repression. This prompted the gradual consolidation of a Black protest elite no amount of state coercion could fully crush. When racial privilege was no longer conducive to corporate profits, white business elites delivered rents to Black politicians to demobilize social protests and secure company assets. Privilege persisted after 1994 because it was deracialized. Yet Black elites and their middle-class supporters primarily extracted rents from the private sector through share transfers and taxes to fund consumption. Divergent modes of private and public economic advantage consolidated a composite set of privileged minorities.

Various combinations of exclusive advantage fed into and reinforced a common path of minority privilege, thus solidifying majority exclusion. If South Africa is to change track and embark on a course of inclusive development, minorities must cease defending their privileges by privileging other minorities.

Notes

Introduction

1. Standard texts produced by the race/class debate are discussed in Christopher Saunders, *The Making of the South African Past: Major Historians on Race and Class* (David Philip, 1988). A more recent consideration of these arguments can be found in Steven Friedman and Judith Hudson, *Race, Class and Power: Harold Wolpe and the Radical Critique of Apartheid* (University of KwaZulu-Natal Press, 2015).

2. The major summation of liberal scholarship on pre-industrial South Africa from this period is Monica Wilson and Leonard Thompson, eds., *The Oxford History of South Africa,* 2 vols. (Oxford University Press, 1969–71).

3. Shula Marks and Richard Rathbone, eds., *Industrialisation and Social Change in South Africa: African Class Formation, Culture, and Consciousness, 1870–1930* (Longman, 1982); Belinda Bozzoli and Peter Delius, "Radical History and South African Society," *Radical History Review* 46, no. 7 (1990): 13–45; Ben Fine and Zavareh Rustomjee, *The Political Economy of South Africa: From Minerals-Energy Complex to Industrialisation* (Westview Press, 1996); Martin Legassick and Alexander C. Lichtenstein, "The Past and Present of Marxist Historiography in South Africa," *Radical History Review* 82, no. 1 (2002): 111–30.

4. S. J. Mosala et al., "The National Democratic Revolution (NDR) in South Africa: An Ideological Journey," *KOERS—Bulletin for Christian Scholarship* 84, no. 1 (2019): 1–16.

5. Merle Lipton, *Capitalism and Apartheid: South Africa, 1910–1986* (Wildwood House, 1986); Merle Lipton, *Liberals, Marxists, and Nationalists: Competing Interpretations of South African History* (Palgrave Macmillan, 2007).

6. Jeremy Seekings and Nicoli Nattrass, *Class, Race, and Inequality in South Africa* (Yale University Press, 2005); Moeletsi Mbeki, *Architects of Poverty: Why African Capitalism Needs Changing* (Picador Africa, 2009), 73–75.

7. Edward Webster and Karin Pampallis, eds., *The Unresolved National Question in South Africa: Left Thought Under Apartheid and Beyond* (Wits University Press, 2017).

8. For a recent expression of this view, see Anthea Jeffrey, *Countdown to Socialism: The National Democratic Revolution in South Africa Since 1994* (Jonathan Ball Publishers, 2023).

9. Ebrahim Harvey, *The Great Pretenders: Race and Class Under ANC Rule* (Jacana Media, 2021).

10. Steven Friedman, *Prisoners of the Past: South African Democracy and the Legacy of Minority Rule* (Wits University Press, 2021), 53. I have used this definition to formulate a preliminary analysis of oligarchy formation in Mesrob Vartavarian, "Entangled Oligarchies: Structure, Agency and Rent Seeking in South Africa," *Africa* 93, no. 4 (2023): 562–78. I wish to thank an anonymous manuscript reviewer for urging me to rethink my conceptualizations of rent seeking.

11. Friedman, *Prisoners of the Past,* passim. The locus classicus on path dependency theory remains Douglass

C. North, *Institutions, Institutional Change and Economic Performance* (Cambridge University Press, 1990). A concise formulation on economic path dependence can also be found in Douglass C. North, "Economic Performance Through Time," *American Economic Review* 84, no. 3 (1994): 359–68.

12. For definitions of monopoly profits and rent seeking, see Marshall Hargrave and Somer Anderson, "How Is Profit Maximized in a Monopoly Market?," *Investopedia,* May 18, 2024, https://www.investopedia.com/; and Christina Majaski, "What Is Rent Seeking in Economics, and What Are Some Examples?," *Investopedia,* August 26, 2024, https://www.investopedia.com/.

13. For South Africa's place on the settler/colonial spectrum, see Lorenzo Veracini, *Settler Colonialism: A Theoretical Overview* (Palgrave Macmillan, 2012), 5.

14. Measurements of income distribution are provided in Facundo Alvaredo and Anthony B. Atkinson, "Top Incomes in South Africa in the Twentieth Century," *Cliometrica* 16, no. 3 (2022): 477–546. For a macroeconomic history that gives equal consideration to discrimination and development, see Charles H. Feinstein, *An Economic History of South Africa: Conquest, Discrimination and Development* (Cambridge University Press, 2005).

15. Deborah Posel, *The Making of Apartheid, 1948–1961: Conflict and Compromise* (Clarendon Press, 1991).

16. Roger Southall, *Liberation Movements in Power: Party and State in Southern Africa* (James Currey, 2013) provides a regional perspective on party states.

17. Richard Sandbrook and Judith Barker, *The Politics of Africa's Economic Stagnation* (Cambridge University Press, 1985); Michael Bratton and Nicolas van de Walle, *Democratic Experiments in Africa: Regime Transitions in*

Comparative Perspective (Cambridge University Press, 1997); Patrick Chabal and Jean-Pascal Daloz, *Africa Works: Disorder as Political Instrument* (Indiana University Press, 1999); Nicolas van de Walle, *African Economies and the Politics of Permanent Crisis, 1979–1999* (Cambridge University Press, 2001); Jean-François Bayart, *The State in Africa: The Politics of the Belly* (Polity Press, 2009).

18. M. J. Masenya, "Neo-Patrimonialism, Corruption and Governance in South Africa," *African Journal of Public Affairs* 9, no. 9 (2017): 146–56; Jacques Pauw, *The President's Keepers: Those Keeping Zuma in Power and out of Prison* (Tafelberg, 2017); Mbongiseni Buthelezi and Peter Vale, eds., *State Capture in South Africa: How and Why It Happened* (Wits University Press, 2023).

19. Regulated and predatory forms of neopatrimonialism are considered in Daniel C. Bach, "Patrimonialism and Neopatrimonialism: Comparative Trajectories and Readings," *Commonwealth & Comparative Politics* 49, no. 3 (2011): 275–94. A case study covering the transition from relatively inclusive to predatory accumulation is provided by Peter Lewis, "From Prebendalism to Predation: The Political Economy of Decline in Nigeria," *Journal of Modern African Studies* 34, no. 1 (1996): 79–103.

20. Gero Erdmann and Ulf Engel, "Neopatrimonialism Reconsidered: Critical Review and Elaboration of an Elusive Concept," *Commonwealth & Comparative Politics* 45, no. 1 (2007): 95–119; Anne Pitcher et al., "Rethinking Patrimonialism and Neopatrimonialism in Africa," *African Studies Review* 52, no. 1 (2009): 125–56; Thandika Mkandawire, "Thinking About Developmental States in Africa," *Cambridge Journal of Economics* 25, no. 3 (2001): 289–314; Thandika Mkandawire, "Neopatrimonialism and the Political Economy of Economic

Performance in Africa: Critical Reflections," *World Politics* 67, no. 3 (2015): 563–612; Christian von Soest, "Neopatrimonialism: A Critical Assessment," in *Handbook on Governance and Development,* ed. Wil Hout and Jane Hutchison (Edward Elgar Publishing, 2022), 145–59.

21. For Botswana's developmental patrimonialism, see Kenneth Good, "Corruption and Mismanagement in Botswana: A Best-Case Example?," *Journal of Modern African Studies* 32, no. 3 (1994): 499–521. Mauritius is analyzed in Ganeshan Wignaraja and Sue O'Neil, *SME Exports and Public Policies in Mauritius* (Commonwealth Secretariat, 1999). Deromanticized portrayals of Rwanda's contemporary development can be found in Filip Reyntjens, *Political Governance in Post-Genocide Rwanda* (Cambridge University Press, 2013); and Michela Wrong, *Do Not Disturb: The Story of a Political Murder and an African Regime Gone Bad* (PublicAffairs, 2021).

22. Barry Driscoll, "Big Man or Boogey Man? The Concept of the Big Man in Political Science," *Journal of Modern African Studies* 58, no. 4 (2020): 521–50.

23. For a fascinating study of how a subaltern became a traditional Yoruba big man, see Wale Adebanwi, *How to Become a Big Man in Africa: Subalternity, Elites, and Ethnic Politics in Contemporary Nigeria* (Indiana University Press, 2024).

24. Michaela Collord, *Wealth, Power, and Authoritarian Institutions: Comparing Dominant Parties and Parliaments in Tanzania and Uganda* (Oxford University Press, 2024) makes an important contribution to debates on elite coalitions in postcolonial Africa.

25. Bruce Berman and John Lonsdale, *Unhappy Valley: Conflict in Kenya and Africa,* book 1, *State and Class* (James Currey, 1992), 13–90.

26. Susanne D. Mueller, "Government and Opposition in Kenya, 1966–9," *Journal of Modern African Studies* 22, no. 3 (1984): 399–427; Daniel Branch and Nicholas Cheeseman, "The Politics of Control in Kenya: Understanding the Bureaucratic-Executive State, 1952–78," *Review of African Political Economy* 33, no. 107 (2006): 11–31.

27. W. O. Maloba, "Toward the End: Corruption, the Family, and Struggles for Succession," chap. 5 in *The Anatomy of Neo-Colonialism in Kenya: British Imperialism and Kenyatta, 1963–1978* (Palgrave Macmillan, 2017).

28. Gabrielle Lynch, "*Harambee* to *Nyayo:* Control and Patronage in the President's Backyard," chap. 4 in *I Say to You: Ethnic Politics and the Kalenjin in Kenya* (University of Chicago Press, 2011).

29. David Throup and Charles Hornsby, "The Regime in Crisis, January 1990–December 1991," chap. 4 in *Multi-Party Politics in Kenya: The Kenyatta and Moi States and the Triumph of the System in the 1992 Election* (James Currey, 1998).

30. Michela Wrong, *It's Our Turn to Eat: The Story of a Kenyan Whistle-Blower* (HarperCollins, 2009), 73–74, 85, 172–73.

31. Basillioh Rukanga, "Kenya to Borrow More After New Taxes Withdrawn—President," *BBC,* July 1, 2024, www.bbc.com/.

32. Nic Cheeseman and Blessing-Miles Tendi, "Power-Sharing in Comparative Perspective: The Dynamics of 'Unity Government' in Kenya and Zimbabwe," *Journal of Modern African Studies* 48, no. 2 (2010): 207–10, 213–14, 223–25.

33. Julian Cobbing, "The Absent Priesthood: Another Look at the Rhodesian Risings of 1896–1897," *Journal of African History* 18, no. 1 (1977): 61–84; David N. Beach, "'Chimurenga': The Shona Rising of 1896–97," *Journal*

of African History 20, no. 3 (1979): 395–420; Arthur Keppel-Jones, *Rhodes and Rhodesia: The White Conquest of Zimbabwe, 1884–1902* (McGill-Queen's University Press, 1983).

34. Timothy Scarnecchia, *The Urban Roots of Democracy and Political Violence in Zimbabwe: Harare and Highfield, 1940–1964* (University of Rochester Press, 2008).

35. Norma Kriger, *Guerrilla Veterans in Post-War Zimbabwe: Symbolic and Violent Politics, 1980–1987* (Cambridge University Press, 2003), 33–39, 45–62.

36. Recent discussions on ZANU-PF's consolidation of power are provided by Stuart Doran, *Kingdom, Power, Glory: Mugabe, ZANU and the Quest for Supremacy, 1960–1987* (Sithatha, 2017); and Godfrey Kanyenze, *Leaving So Many Behind: The Link Between Politics and the Economy in Zimbabwe* (Weaver Press, 2021).

37. Cheeseman and Tendi, "Power-Sharing in Comparative Perspective," 217–18, 220–23.

38. David B. Moore, *Mugabe's Legacy: Coups, Conspiracies, and the Conceits of Power in Zimbabwe* (Hurst & Company, 2022).

39. Nicole Beardsworth et al., "Zimbabwe: The Coup That Never Was, and the Election That Could Have Been," *African Affairs* 118, no. 472 (2019): 580–96.

40. For an impactful, and highly controversial, analysis of African agency, see Olúfẹ́mi Táíwò, *Against Decolonisation: Taking African Agency Seriously* (Hurst & Company, 2022).

Chapter 1: White Gentries, Black Allies, and African Kings

1. A. Atmore and S. Marks, "The Imperial Factor in South Africa in the Nineteenth Century: Towards a

Reassessment," *Journal of Imperial and Commonwealth History* 3, no. 1 (1974): 105–39.

2. Richard Elphick, "Power and Wealth in Traditional Cape Khoikhoi Society," chap. 3 in *Kraal and Castle: Khoikhoi and the Founding of White South Africa* (Yale University Press, 1977).

3. Colin Bundy, *Poverty in South Africa: Past and Present* (Jacana Media, 2016), 23–26.

4. Elphick, "The Chainouqua and Hessequa: The Perils of Cooperation," chap. 7 in *Kraal and Castle*.

5. Shula Marks, "Khoisan Resistance to the Dutch in the Seventeenth and Eighteenth Centuries," *Journal of African History* 13, no. 1 (1972): 55–80.

6. Nigel Penn, *The Forgotten Frontier: Colonist and Khoisan on the Cape's Northern Frontier in the 18th Century* (Ohio University Press, 2006), 50–51; Susan Newton-King, *Masters and Servants on the Cape Eastern Frontier, 1760–1803* (Cambridge University Press, 1999), 66–91.

7. Nigel Penn, "Massacre on the Frontiers of the Cape Colony: Colonists, Khoisan and Xhosa," Lecture, University of Cape Town Summer School, YouTube, https://www.youtube.com/watch?v=6-6YpFgk0q4.

8. Mohamed Adhikari, *The Anatomy of a South African Genocide: The Extermination of the Cape San Peoples* (Ohio University Press, 2011).

9. Wayne Dooling, *Slavery, Emancipation and Colonial Rule in South Africa* (Ohio University Press, 2008), 26.

10. Johan Fourie, "The Remarkable Wealth of the Dutch Cape Colony: Measurements from Eighteenth-Century Probate Inventories," *Economic History Review* 66, no. 2 (2013): 419–48.

11. Nigel Worden, *Slavery in Dutch South Africa* (Cambridge University Press, 1985), 141.

12. Robert Ross, *Status and Respectability in the Cape Colony, 1750–1870: A Tragedy of Manners* (Cambridge University Press, 1999), 15.

13. Worden, *Slavery;* Newton-King, *Masters and Servants,* 188–209.

14. John L. Comaroff, "Images of Empire, Contests of Conscience: Models of Colonial Domination in South Africa," *American Ethnologist* 16, no. 4 (1989): 661–85; Alan Lester, *Imperial Networks: Creating Identities in Nineteenth-Century South Africa and Britian* (Routledge, 2001).

15. C. A. Bayly, *Imperial Meridian: The British Empire and the World, 1780–1830* (Longman, 1989); Timothy Keegan, "Imperial Renewal," chap. 3 in *Colonial South Africa and the Origins of the Racial Order* (University Press of Virginia, 1996).

16. Keegan, *Colonial South Africa,* 43–44.

17. Jean Comaroff and John Comaroff, *Of Revelation and Revolution: Christianity, Colonialism, and Consciousness in South Africa* (University of Chicago Press, 1991); Paul S. Landau, "Hegemony and History in Jean and John L. Comaroff's *Of Revelation and Revolution,*" *Africa* 70, no. 3 (2000): 501–19; Elizabeth Elbourne, *Blood Ground: Colonialism, Missions, and the Contest for Christianity in the Cape Colony and Britain, 1799–1853* (McGill-Queen's University Press, 2002).

18. Clifton C. Crais, *The Making of the Colonial Order: White Supremacy and Black Resistance in the Eastern Cape, 1770–1865* (Witwatersrand University Press, 1992), 82–84, 99–104.

19. This was particularly the case with the Coloured Kat River Settlement. See Robert Ross, *The Borders of Race in Colonial South Africa: The Kat River Settlement, 1829–1851* (Cambridge University Press, 2014).

20. Colin Bundy, "Lessons on the Frontier: Aspects of Eastern Cape History," *Kronos: Journal of Cape History* 30, no. 1 (2004): 9–21.

21. Crais, *The Making of the Colonial Order,* 135.

22. Crais, 136.

23. Keegan, *Colonial South Africa,* 147–48, 196–98.

24. Ross, *Status and Respectability,* 67, 169–72.

25. J. B. Peires, *The House of Phalo: A History of the Xhosa People in the Days of Their Independence* (Ravan Press, 1981).

26. Poppy Fry, "Siyamfenguza: The Creation of Fingoness in South Africa's Eastern Cape, 1800–1835," *Journal of Southern African Studies* 36, no. 1 (2010): 25–40.

27. I will refer to them as *Mfengu* from here on.

28. Timothy J. Stapleton, "Oral Evidence in a Pseudo-Ethnicity: The Fingo Debate," *History in Africa* 22 (1995): 359–68.

29. Fry, "Siyamfenguza," 36.

30. Not all rich Black farmers were Mfengu, but they made up a disproportionate number of this affluent category. In the late nineteenth-century Cape, prosperous African farmers amounted to no more than two thousand households out of a Black population of well over half a million. For these figures, see Clifton Crais, *Poverty, War, and Violence in South Africa* (Cambridge University Press, 2011), 121.

31. John Laband, *The Land Wars: The Dispossession of the Khoisan and AmaXhosa in the Cape Colony* (Penguin Books, 2020), 184–89, 209–12, 236–44, 246–50, 273–80.

32. J. B. Peires, *The Dead Will Arise: Nongqawuse and the Great Xhosa Cattle-Killing Movement of 1856-7* (Ravan Press, 1989).

33. Rodney Davenport and Christopher Saunders, *South Africa: A Modern History* (Macmillan Press, 2000), 116.

34. Carolyn Hamilton, *Terrific Majesty: The Powers of Shaka Zulu and the Limits of Historical Invention* (Harvard University Press, 1998), 72–129.

35. Thomas Spear, "Neo-Traditionalism and the Limits of Invention in British Colonial Africa," *Journal of African History* 44, no. 1 (2003): 12–13; Thomas V. McClendon, *White Chief, Black Lords: Shepstone and the Colonial State in Natal, South Africa, 1845–1878* (University of Rochester Press, 2010).

36. Jeff Guy, *The Heretic: A Study in the Life of John William Colenso, 1814–1883* (Ravan Press, 1983).

37. This paragraph relies on the empirical findings in Dooling, *Slavery*, 80–82.

38. Dooling, 119.

39. Dooling, 129–35, 159, 169.

40. Norman Etherington, *The Great Treks: The Transformation of Southern Africa, 1815–1854* (Longman, 2001); Nigel Worden, *The Making of Modern South Africa: Conquest, Apartheid, Democracy* (Blackwell Publishing, 2007), 14–15.

41. Philip Bonner, *Kings, Commoners and Concessionaries: The Evolution and Dissolution of the Nineteenth-Century Swazi State* (Cambridge University Press, 1983), 80–84; Peter Delius, *The Land Belongs to Us: The Pedi Polity, the Boers, and the British in the Nineteenth-Century Transvaal* (University of California Press, 1984); Davenport and Saunders, *South Africa,* 84–90.

42. Peter Delius et al., *Forgotten Worlds: The Stone-Walled Settlements of the Mpumalanga Escarpment* (Wits University Press, 2014).

43. Paul S. Landau, *Popular Politics in the History of South Africa, 1400–1948* (Cambridge University Press, 2010); Elizabeth A. Eldredge, *Kingdoms and Chiefdoms*

of Southeastern Africa: Oral Traditions and History, 1400–1830 (University of Rochester Press, 2015).

44. Critical interventions in a vast literature include J. D. Omer-Cooper, *The Zulu Aftermath: A Nineteenth-Century Revolution in Bantu Africa* (Northwestern University Press, 1966); Julian Cobbing, "The Mfecane as Alibi: Thoughts on Dithakong and Mbolompo," *Journal of African History* 29, no. 3 (1988): 487–519; Carolyn Hamilton, ed., *The Mfecane Aftermath: Reconstructive Debates in Southern African History* (Witwatersrand University Press, 1995); Etherington, *The Great Treks.*

45. For an example of this process, see Carolyn Hamilton and John Wright, "The Making of the Amalala: Ethnicity, Ideology and Relations of Subordination in a Precolonial Context," *South African Historical Journal* 22, no. 1 (1990): 3–23. A more recent reassessment that places greater emphasis on socioeconomic hierarchies than ethnic discrimination is provided in Carolyn Hamilton and John Wright, "Moving Beyond Ethnic Framing: Political Differentiation in the Chiefdoms of the KwaZulu-Natal Region Before 1830," *Journal of Southern African Studies* 43, no. 4 (2017): 663–79.

46. Brigette Lau, "Conflict and Power in Nineteenth-Century Namibia," *Journal of African History* 27, no. 1 (1986): 29–39.

47. Robert Ross, *Adam Kok's Griquas: A Study in the Development of Stratification in South Africa* (Cambridge University Press, 1976), 10, 79–80, 114.

48. Quoted in Elizabeth A. Eldredge, *The Creation of the Zulu Kingdom, 1815–1828: War, Shaka, and the Consolidation of Power* (Cambridge University Press, 2014), 231.

49. Malyn Newitt, *A History of Mozambique* (Indiana University Press, 1995), 256–62; R. Kent Rasmussen, *Migrant Kingdom: Mzilikazi's Ndebele in South Africa*

(Rex Collings, 1978); Alois S. Mlambo, *A History of Zimbabwe* (Cambridge University Press, 2014), 24–28.

50. Michael R. Mahoney, "The Zulu Kingdom as a Genocidal and Post-Genocidal Society, c. 1810 to the Present," *Journal of Genocide Research* 5, no. 2 (2003): 256–59.

51. Linell Chewins and Peter Delius, "The Northeastern Factor in South African History: Reevaluating the Volume of the Slave Trade out of Delagoa Bay and Its Impact on Its Hinterland in the Early Nineteenth Century," *Journal of African History* 61, no. 1 (2020): 89–110; Linell Chewins, "'Stealing Dingane's Title': The Fatal Significance of Saguate Gift-Giving in Zulu King Dingane's Killing of Governor Ribeiro (1833) and Piet Retief (1838)," *Journal of Southern African Studies* 48, no. 1 (2022): 119–38.

52. For a recent analysis of this conflict, see Michał Leśniewski, *The Zulu-Boer War, 1837–1840* (Brill, 2021).

53. Phillip A. Kennedy, "Mpande and the Zulu Kingship," *Journal of Natal and Zulu History* 4, no. 1 (1981): 21–38; Eldredge, *The Creation of the Zulu Kingdom*, 238, 279; John Laband, *The Eight Zulu Kings* (Jonathan Ball Publishers, 2018), 172–77, 190–91.

54. Leonard Thompson, *Survival in Two Worlds: Moshoeshoe of Lesotho, 1786–1870* (Clarendon Press, 1975); Elizabeth A. Eldredge, *A South African Kingdom: The Pursuit of Security in Nineteenth-Century Lesotho* (Cambridge University Press, 1993).

55. Davenport and Saunders, *South Africa,* 155–60.

Chapter 2: Wealth Concentration in an Age of Industrialization and Political Centralization

1. William H. Worger, *South Africa's City of Diamonds: Mine Workers and Monopoly Capitalism in Kimberley, 1867–1895* (Yale University Press, 1987), 10–23.

2. Robert Vicat Turrell, *Capital and Labour on the Kimberley Diamond Fields, 1871–1890* (Cambridge University Press, 1987), 19–25, 31.

3. Turrell, 34–59.

4. Colin Newbury, "Miners' Oligarchy," chap. 2 in *The Diamond Ring: Business, Politics, and Precious Stones in South Africa, 1867–1947* (Clarendon Press, 1989).

5. Rob Turrell, "Kimberley's Model Compounds," *Journal of African History* 25, no. 1 (1984): 59–75.

6. Newbury, *The Diamond Ring,* 73–74.

7. Worger, *South Africa's City of Diamonds,* 183.

8. William H. Worger, "Convict Labour, Industrialists and the State in the US South and South Africa, 1870–1930," *Journal of Southern African Studies* 30, no. 1 (2004): 71, 74–76.

9. Their careers are well covered in Stanley Jackson, *The Great Barnato* (Heinemann, 1970); Robert I. Rotberg and Miles F. Shore, *The Founder: Cecil Rhodes and the Pursuit of Power* (Oxford University Press, 1988); James Leasor, *Rhodes and Barnato: The Premier and the Prancer* (Leo Cooper, 1997).

10. Turrell, *Capital and Labour,* 195–98.

11. Turrell, 222–23, 227.

12. Worger, *South Africa's City of Diamonds,* 289–96; Worger, "Convict Labour," 71.

13. A. Atmore and S. Marks, "The Imperial Factor in South Africa in the Nineteenth Century: Towards a Reassessment," *Journal of Imperial and Commonwealth History* 3, no. 1 (1974): 105–39.

14. Abel Gwaindepi, "Serving God and Mammon: The 'Minerals-Railway Complex' and Its Effects on Colonial Public Finances in the British Cape Colony, 1810–1910," No. 44/2019 (African Economic History Working Paper Series, 2019), 27–28.

15. Britain's wars for confederation are covered in John Laband, *Zulu Warriors: The Battle for the South African Frontier* (Yale University Press, 2014).

16. Colin Bundy, *The Rise and Fall of the South African Peasantry* (University of California Press, 1979), 83–84, 86; Clifton Crais, *Poverty, War, and Violence in South Africa* (Cambridge University Press, 2011), 65, 118–19.

17. Michael R. Mahoney, *The Other Zulus: The Spread of Zulu Ethnicity in Colonial South Africa* (Duke University Press, 2012), 77–81; P. S. Thompson, *Black Soldiers of the Queen: The Natal Native Contingent in the Anglo-Zulu War* (The University of Alabama Press, 2006).

18. Peter Delius, *The Land Belongs to Us: The Pedi Polity, the Boers, and the British in the Nineteenth-Century Transvaal* (University of California Press, 1984), 243–46.

19. Heather Hughes, *First President: A Life of John L. Dube, Founding President of the ANC* (Jacana Media, 2011), 42.

20. André Odendaal, *The Founders: The Origins of the ANC and the Struggle for Democracy in South Africa* (Jacana Media, 2012).

21. Geoffrey Wheatcroft, *The Randlords: The Exploits and Exploitations of South Africa's Mining Magnates* (Atheneum, 1986).

22. Mendel Kaplan, *Jewish Roots in the South African Economy* (C. Struik Publishers, 1986).

23. Mariusz Lukasiewicz, "From Diamonds to Gold: The Making of the Johannesburg Stock Exchange, 1880–1890," *Journal of Southern African Studies* 43, no. 4 (2017): 715–32; Mariusz Lukasiewicz, "Early Regulation and Social Organisation on the Johannesburg Stock Exchange, 1887–1892," *Business History* 63, no. 4 (2021): 686–704.

24. Rotberg and Shore, *The Founder*, 197–98, 360–69, 467–77.

25. Wheatcroft, *The Randlords,* 159, 161; Richard Mendelsohn, *Sammy Marks: The Uncrowned King of the Transvaal* (David Philip, 1991), 87–101, 111–14.

26. Elizabeth Longford, *Jameson's Raid: The Prelude to the Boer War* (Weidenfeld and Nicolson, 1982).

27. Iain R. Smith, *The Origins of the South African War, 1899–1902* (Longman, 1996).

28. Thomas Pakenham, *The Boer War* (Random House, 1979); Bill Nasson, *The South African War, 1899–1902* (Arnold, 1999).

29. Nancy L. Clark and William H. Worger, *Voices of Sharpeville: The Long History of Racial Injustice* (Routledge, 2024), 14.

30. Peter Warwick, *Black People and the South African War, 1899–1902* (Cambridge University Press, 1983).

31. Stowell Kessler, *The Black Concentration Camps of the Anglo-Boer War, 1899–1902* (War Museum of the Boer Republics, 2012); Garth Benneyworth, "Land, Labour, War and Displacement: A History of Four Black Concentration Camps in the South African War (1899–1902)," *Historia* 64, no. 2 (2019): 1–20; Clark and Worger, *Voices of Sharpeville,* 11–14.

32. Shula Marks and Stanley Trapido, "Lord Milner and the South African State," *History Workshop* 8 (1979): 50–80.

33. A. A. Mawby, *Gold Mining and Politics: Johannesburg, 1900–1907,* vol. 1, *The Origins of the Old South Africa* (Edwin Mellen Press, 2000).

34. Martin Plaut, *Promise and Despair: The First Struggle for a Non-Racial South Africa* (Jacana Media, 2016).

Chapter 3: White Amalgamation, Corporate Integration, and Struggles for African Elite Inclusion

1. Tabulations of demographic data are provided in "South African Census 2022," p. 6, https://census.statssa

.gov.za/assets/documents/2022/P03014_Census_2022_Statistical_Release.pdf.

2. For comprehensive coverage of political events during this period, see W. K. Hancock, *Smuts: The Fields of Force* (Cambridge University Press, 1968).

3. The standard analysis of intra-Afrikaner sociopolitical tensions remains Dan O'Meara, *Volkskapitalisme: Class, Capital and Ideology in the Development of Afrikaner Nationalism, 1934–1948* (Cambridge University Press, 1983).

4. T. R. H. Davenport, "The South African Rebellion, 1914," *English Historical Review* 78, no. 306 (1963): 73–94.

5. Nancy L. Clark, *Manufacturing Apartheid: State Corporations in South Africa* (Yale University Press, 1994), 42; David Yudelman, *The Emergence of Modern South Africa: State, Capital, and the Incorporation of Organized Labour on the South African Gold Fields, 1902–1939* (Greenwood Press, 1983), 98–103.

6. Jeremy Krikler, *White Rising: The 1922 Insurrection and Racial Killing in South Africa* (Manchester University Press, 2005).

7. The following points are based on Colin Bundy, *Poverty in South Africa: Past and Present* (Jacana Media, 2016), 49–52.

8. Bundy, 50–51.

9. The company became known as Eskom in 1987.

10. Clark, *Manufacturing Apartheid,* 50–58, 86–106.

11. Theodore Gregory, *Ernest Oppenheimer and the Economic Development of Southern Africa* (Oxford University Press, 1962), 62–70, 73–74.

12. Jeff Guy, *The Maphumulo Uprising: War, Law and Ritual in the Zulu Rebellion* (University of KwaZulu-Natal Press, 2005); Robert R. Edgar, *The Finger of God: Enoch Mgijima, the Israelites, and the*

Bulhoek Massacre in South Africa (University of Virginia Press, 2018).

13. Charles Van Onselen, *The Seed Is Mine: The Life of Kas Maine, a South African Sharecropper, 1894–1985* (Hill and Wang, 1996).

14. Deborah Posel, *The Making of Apartheid, 1948–1961: Conflict and Compromise* (Clarendon Press, 1991).

15. Ebbe Dommisse and Willie Esterhuyse, *Anton Rupert: A Biography* (Tafelberg, 2005).

16. Pieter du Toit, *The Stellenbosch Mafia: Inside the Billionaires' Club* (Jonathan Ball Publishers, 2018), 62–63.

17. du Toit, 65.

18. For Remgro's company history, see "Company History," Remgro, https://www.remgro.com/about-remgro/history/.

19. David Pallister et al., *South Africa Inc.: The Oppenheimer Empire* (Simon and Schuster, 1987), 17–21.

20. Michael Cardo, *Harry Oppenheimer: Diamonds, Gold and Dynasty* (Jonathan Ball Publishers, 2023), 101–3.

21. Cardo, 195–99.

22. Clive Glaser, *The ANC Youth League* (Jacana Media, 2012); Ebrahim Harvey, *The Great Pretenders: Race and Class Under ANC Rule* (Jacana Media, 2021), 185–87.

23. Tom Lodge, "Neo-Patrimonial Politics in the ANC," *African Affairs* 113, no. 450 (2014): 9.

24. Tom Lodge, *Red Road to Freedom: A History of the South African Communist Party, 1921–2021* (James Currey, 2022).

25. Thula Simpson, *Umkhonto we Sizwe: The ANC's Armed Struggle* (Penguin Books, 2016), 57–93; Dale T.

McKinley, "Umkhonto We Sizwe: A Critical Analysis of the Armed Struggle of the African National Congress," *South African Historical Journal* 70, no. 1 (2018): 30–33.

26. Hugh Macmillan, *Chris Hani* (Ohio University Press, 2021), 48–60.

27. Alex Boraine, "The ANC in Exile: Early Years," chap. 1 in *What's Gone Wrong? South Africa on the Brink of Failed Statehood* (New York University Press, 2014).

28. Details of Zuma's struggle career can be found in Jeremy Gordin, "Silence, Exile and Cunning," chap. 4 in *Zuma: A Biography* (Jonathan Ball Publishers, 2010); Ronnie Kasrils, *A Simple Man: Kasrils and the Zuma Enigma* (Jacana Media, 2017), xx–xxiv.

29. Lodge, "Neo-Patrimonial Politics," 9–10.

30. Julian Brown, *The Road to Soweto: Resistance and the Uprising of 16 June 1976* (James Currey, 2016).

31. Baruch Hirson, *Year of Fire, Year of Ash: The Soweto Revolt, Roots of a Revolution?* (Zed Press, 1979); John D. Brewer, *After Soweto: An Unfinished Journey* (Clarendon Press, 1982); Noor Nieftagodien, *The Soweto Uprising* (Ohio University Press, 2014).

32. Roger Southall, *South Africa's Transkei: The Political Economy of an Independent Bantustan* (Monthly Review Press, 1983), 52–55, 140–42, 274–75; Michael Lawrence and Andrew Manson, "The 'Dog of the Boers': The Rise and Fall of Mangope in Bophuthatswana," *Journal of Southern African Studies* 20, no. 3 (1994): 447–61.

33. Anthony Butler, *Cyril Ramaphosa: The Road to Presidential Power* (James Currey, 2019), 90, 94–98.

34. Butler, 128–43.

35. Ray Hartley, *Ramaphosa: The Man Who Would Be King* (Jonathan Ball Publishers, 2017), 26–30.

36. Inkatha was rebranded the Inkatha Freedom Party (IFP) in 1990.

37. Gerhard Maré and Georgina Hamilton, *An Appetite for Power: Buthelezi's Inkatha and South Africa* (Ravan Press, 1987).

38. Jill E. Kelly, *To Swim with Crocodiles: Land, Violence, and Belonging in South Africa, 1800–1996* (Michigan State University Press, 2018), 167–71, 189–210; Gary Kynoch, *Township Violence and the End of Apartheid: War on the Reef* (James Currey, 2018); Anthea Jeffrey, *The Natal Story: 16 Years of Conflict* (South African Institute of Race Relations, 1997).

39. Jeremy Seekings, *The UDF: A History of the United Democratic Front in South Africa, 1983–1991* (David Philip, 2000).

40. Oppenheimer retired in late 1982 and handed off control to a cohort of personal assistants led by Gavin Relly.

41. Blaine Harden, "S. African Businessmen Meet with Exiled Guerrilla Leaders," *Washington Post*, September 13, 1985.

42. For various arguments on how a negotiated settlement came about, see Patti Waldmeir, *Anatomy of a Miracle: The End of Apartheid and the Birth of the New South Africa* (Viking, 1997); Patrick Bond, *Elite Transition: From Apartheid to Neoliberalism in South Africa* (Pluto Press, 2000); Hermann Giliomee, *The Last Afrikaner Leaders* (Tafelberg, 2012); Colin Bundy, *Short-Changed? South Africa Since Apartheid* (Ohio University Press, 2014), 21–31.

43. Butler, *Cyril Ramaphosa*, 226–30, 264–79.

44. Gordin, "The Talking Times," chap. 5 in *Zuma*.

45. The penury of African revolutionaries is covered in Pieter du Toit, *The ANC Billionaires: Big Capital's Gambit and the Rise of the Few* (Jonathan Ball Publishers, 2022).

46. Sampie Terreblanche, *A History of Inequality in South Africa, 1652–2002* (University of Natal Press, 2002), 102, 106, argues for the capture thesis.

47. Stefaans Brümmer and Sam Sole, "An UnShaikable Friendship," *Mail & Guardian,* December 6, 2002.

48. Moeletsi Mbeki, "A Tale of Two Nationalisms and How They Have Failed SA," *News24,* May 5, 2019, www .news24.com/.

Chapter 4: A Privileged, and Fractious, Political Minority

1. Local and regional politics retained a multiparty character, particularly in major metropolitan areas that saw a more diverse distribution of spoils, but this chapter's focus is on national-level politics and the exclusive advantages that flowed therefrom. Other political parties, that are not ANC splinter groups, have a minor role in my narrative until the advent of a multiparty national government in 2024.

2. Evan Lieberman, *Until We Have Won Our Liberty: South Africa After Apartheid* (Princeton University Press, 2022), provides a generally positive assessment of ANC rule.

3. William Mervin Gumede, *Thabo Mbeki and the Battle for the Soul of the ANC* (Zed Books, 2007), 42–46, 154, 159–60, 310–12; Tom Lodge, "Neo-Patrimonial Politics in the ANC," *African Affairs* 113, no. 450 (2014): 14.

4. John Weeks, "Stuck in Low GEAR? Macroeconomic Policy in South Africa, 1996–98," *Cambridge Journal of Economics* 23, no. 6 (1999): 795–811; Stephen Gelb, "The RDP, GEAR and All That: Reflections Ten Years Later," *Transformation: Critical Perspectives on Southern Africa* 62, no. 1 (2006): 1–8; Brian Pottinger, *The Mbeki Legacy* (Zebra Press, 2008), 69–71, 74–78.

5. Ebrahim Harvey, *The Great Pretenders: Race and Class Under ANC Rule* (Jacana Media, 2021), 223, 307–13; Nicoli Nattrass, *The Moral Economy of AIDS in South Africa* (Cambridge University Press, 2004).

6. Details on the arms deal can be found in Terry Crawford-Browne, "The Arms Deal Scandal," *Review of African Political Economy* 31, no. 100 (2004): 329–42; Andrew Feinstein, *After the Party: Corruption, the ANC and South Africa's Uncertain Future* (Verso, 2009); Paul Holden and Hennie Van Vuuren, *The Devil in the Detail: How the Arms Deal Changed Everything* (Jonathan Ball Publishers, 2011).

7. David Botha, "The Arms Deal Controversy," *African Security Review* 12, no. 3 (2003): 99–103.

8. Riaan Grobler, "NPA Finds Schabir Shaik Made Even More Payments to Jacob Zuma—Report," *News24,* May 13, 2020, www.news24.com/.

9. Michael Cardo, *Harry Oppenheimer: Diamonds, Gold and Dynasty* (Jonathan Ball Publishers, 2023), 417.

10. NAIL Company Statement, 2002, p. 2, https://www.sharedata.co.za/Data/000856/pdfs/NAIL_ar_02.pdf.

11. "JCI's Unbundling Gets Lacklustre Response," *Mail & Guardian,* March 3, 1995; "How Cyril Ramaphosa Obtained His Wealth," *News24,* July 13, 2015, www.news24.com/.

12. "Company Overview," Shanduka Group, https://www.phembani.com/index.php/history-of-shanduka/.

13. "Profile, Cyril Ramaphosa," *Forbes,* November 18, 2015.

14. Janet Smith, *Patrice Motsepe: An Appetite for Disruption* (Jonathan Ball Publishers, 2022), 122.

15. Cited in Smith, 124.

16. Allan Seccombe, "'Gold Sector Needs a Godsell,'" *News24,* August 11, 2008, www.news24.com/.

17. "Profile, Patrice Motsepe," *Forbes,* October 26, 2025.

18. Smith, *Patrice Motsepe,* 183–84, 210; Rebecca Davis, "The Big Eight Funders of South Africa's Major Political Parties," *Daily Maverick,* September 10, 2023.

19. Smith, *Patrice Motsepe,* 85–90.

20. David Smith, "Who Is Tokyo Sexwale, Subject of the Blatter-Ferdinand Twitter Row?," *The Guardian,* November 17, 2011.

21. Cardo, *Harry Oppenheimer,* 414–15; Laurence Sithole, "South Africa: Mark Willcox, Veteran Deal Maker and Mvelaphanda Holdings Architect Dies," *allAfrica,* September 29, 2022, https://allafrica.com/.

22. Steven Perlberg, "Tokyo Sexwale: Meet the Billionaire Diamond Magnate Who Went to Jail with Nelson Mandela," *Business Insider,* July 9, 2013; Lodge, "Neo-Patrimonial Politics," 13.

23. "Sakumzi 'Saki' Macozoma," Safika Holdings, https://www.safika.co.za/corporate-profile/sakumzi -macozoma/.

24. "Macozoma Buys 10% Stake in Safika," *IOL,* February 27, 2001, www.iol.co.za/; "Saki Macozoma Becomes New Head of Nail," *IOL,* July 18, 2001, www.iol.co.za/; "CEO Increases Safika Stake," *News24,* April 2, 2003, www.news24.com/.

25. "Bank Becomes a BEE Player," *Mail & Guardian,* July 8, 2005; "Top 10 Richest Black South Africans," Top Empowerment, accessed July 26, 2024, https://topempowerment.co.za/.

26. Nicky Oppenheimer shifted his focus to philanthropic pursuits after selling his stake in De Beers to Anglo in 2011 for over $5 billion. Johann Rupert, by contrast, remains heavily involved in domestic economic activities.

27. I owe this point to Anthony Butler, personal communication.

28. Chris McGreal, "ANC Veterans Accused of Plot to Harm Mbeki," *The Guardian,* April 25, 2001.

29. Mbongiseni Buthelezi and Peter Vale, eds., *State Capture in South Africa,* passim.

30. Pieter-Louis Myburgh, *The Republic of Gupta: A Story of State Capture* (Penguin Books, 2017); Adriaan Basson and Pieter du Toit, *Enemy of the People: How Jacob Zuma Stole South Africa and How the People Fought Back* (Jonathan Ball Publishers, 2017).

31. Mandy Wiener, *Ministry of Crime: An Underworld Explored* (Macmillan, 2018).

32. Ranjeni Munusamy, "ANC's Leadership Race: The Rise of the 'Premier League,'" *Daily Maverick,* September 7, 2015; Pieter-Louis Myburgh, *Gangster State: Unravelling Ace Magashule's Web of Capture* (Penguin Books, 2019); Rehana Rossouw, *Predator Politics: Mabuza, Fred Daniel and the Great Land Scam* (Jacana Media, 2020).

33. Greg Nicolson, "Ace Magashule's R255m Case 'Bears Hallmarks of Corruption,' Says Free State Prosecuting Authority," *Daily Maverick,* December 12, 2021.

34. Isaac Mahlangu, "'We All Know Supra Mahumapelo Is Corrupt'—Mahikeng Residents Have Had Enough," *Sowetan Live,* April 23, 2018, www.sowetanlive.co.za/.

35. Rossouw, *Predator Politics,* 105–15, 161–68.

36. Roger Southall, *Liberation Movements in Power: Party and State in Southern Africa* (James Currey, 2013), 273.

37. Julian Brown, *Marikana: A People's History* (James Currey, 2022), 95–98.

38. I again owe this point to Anthony Butler, personal communication.

39. Pauli van Wyk, "VBS Bank Heist: EFF's Family Ties and Moneyed Connections," *Daily Maverick,* November 21, 2018.

40. For a graph of the ANC's vote share over time, see "The African National Congress (ANC) General Election Results in South Africa from 1994 to 2024," Statista, accessed August 31, 2024, https://www.statista.com/statistics/1402238/anc-general-election-results-in-south-africa/.

41. Corinne Gretler and Dylan Griffiths, "Johann Rupert: Radical Economic Transformation Just a Code Word for Theft," *News24,* September 13, 2017, www.news24.com/.

42. Jason Burke, "South Africa Issues Arrest Warrant for ANC's Ace Magashule," *The Guardian,* November 10, 2020.

43. The Zondo Commission's report is available online at https://www.statecapture.org.za/site/information/reports; for a summation of its findings, see Paul Holden, *Zondo at Your Fingertips* (Jacana Media, 2023).

44. South African Human Rights Commission, "July's People: The National Investigative Hearing Report into the July 2021 Unrest in Gauteng and KwaZulu-Natal," January 29, 2024, https://www.sahrc.org.za/home/21/files/JULY%20UNREST%20REPORT%20FINAL_29%20JAN%202024.pdf.

45. Thabi Myeni, "What Is South Africa's Phala Phala Farm Robbery Scandal About?," *Al Jazeera,* June 9, 2022, www.aljazeera.com/.

46. Data from this election can be gleaned from the Electoral Commission of South Africa's website, https://www.elections.org.za/pw/Elections-and-results/Municipal-Elections-2021.

47. The 2024 election results can be found at https://results.elections.org.za/dashboards/npe/.

48. Paddy Harper, "ANC to Join DA, IFP and NFP to Form a Government in KwaZulu-Natal," *Mail & Guardian,* June 11, 2024.

49. Shingai Nyoka and Farouk Chothia, "The Winners and Losers in South Africa's Historic New Government," *BBC,* July 1, 2024, www.bbc.com/; "President Cyril Ramaphosa Unveils New Cabinet," event livestream, June 30, 2024, by *eNCA News,* YouTube, https://www.youtube.com/watch?v=Vo2qx9KWjOk. National government bloat is only the tip of the iceberg, as inflated public sector salaries at provincial and local levels have massively increased government wage bills and eaten into monetary resources available for investment.

50. Rafieka Williams, "The Ex-Gangster Who Has Become South Africa's Sports Minister," *BBC,* July 4, 2024, www.bbc.com/.

51. Rachel Savage, "South Africa's ANC Expels Ex-President Zuma for Leading Rival Party in Election," *The Guardian,* July 29, 2024.

Conclusion

1. André de Ruyter's *Truth to Power: My Three Years Inside Eskom* (Penguin Books, 2023) has made a particular impact among white suburban readers and commentators.

2. This perspective is best exemplified by Anthea Jeffrey, *Countdown to Socialism: The National Democratic Revolution in South Africa Since 1994* (Jonathan Ball Publishers, 2023).

3. See, for example, numerous public pronouncements on British imperial virtues by Niall Ferguson and, more recently, by Nigel Biggar.

Selected Bibliography

The following references are a selection of the main published works used to formulate the arguments in this book. A full list of sources is provided in the endnotes.

Bach, Daniel C. "Patrimonialism and Neopatrimonialism: Comparative Trajectories and Readings." *Commonwealth & Comparative Politics* 49, no. 3 (2011): 275–94.

Boraine, Alex. *What's Gone Wrong? South Africa on the Brink of Failed Statehood.* New York University Press, 2014.

Brown, Julian. *Marikana: A People's History.* James Currey, 2022.

Bundy, Colin. *Poverty in South Africa: Past and Present.* Jacana Media, 2016.

Butler, Anthony. *Cyril Ramaphosa: The Road to Presidential Power.* James Currey, 2019.

Cardo, Michael. *Harry Oppenheimer: Diamonds, Gold and Dynasty.* Jonathan Ball Publishers, 2023.

Clark, Nancy L. *Manufacturing Apartheid: State Corporations in South Africa.* Yale University Press, 1994.

Crais, Clifton C. *The Making of the Colonial Order: White Supremacy and Black Resistance in the Eastern Cape, 1770–1865.* Witwatersrand University Press, 1992.

Dooling, Wayne. *Slavery, Emancipation and Colonial Rule in South Africa.* Ohio University Press, 2008.

Driscoll, Barry. "Big Man or Boogey Man? The Concept of the Big Man in Political Science." *Journal of Modern African Studies* 58, no. 4 (2020): 521–50.

Eldredge, Elizabeth A. *The Creation of the Zulu Kingdom, 1815–1828: War, Shaka, and the Consolidation of Power.* Cambridge University Press, 2014.

Feinstein, Andrew. *After the Party: Corruption, the ANC and South Africa's Uncertain Future.* Verso, 2009.

Feinstein, Charles H. *An Economic History of South Africa: Conquest, Discrimination and Development.* Cambridge University Press, 2005.

Friedman, Steven. *Prisoners of the Past: South African Democracy and the Legacy of Minority Rule.* Wits University Press, 2021.

Fry, Poppy. "Siyamfenguza: The Creation of Fingo-ness in South Africa's Eastern Cape, 1800–1835." *Journal of Southern African Studies* 36, no. 1 (2010): 25–40.

Gumede, William Mervin. *Thabo Mbeki and the Battle for the Soul of the ANC.* Zed Books, 2007.

Harvey, Ebrahim. *The Great Pretenders: Race and Class Under ANC Rule.* Jacana Media, 2021.

Keegan, Timothy. *Colonial South Africa and the Origins of the Racial Order.* University Press of Virginia, 1996.

Laband, John. *Zulu Warriors: The Battle for the South African Frontier.* Yale University Press, 2014.

Lipton, Merle. *Liberals, Marxists, and Nationalists: Competing Interpretations of South African History.* Palgrave Macmillan, 2007.

Myburgh, Pieter-Louis. *The Republic of Gupta: A Story of State Capture.* Penguin Books, 2017.

North, Douglass C. *Institutions, Institutional Change and Economic Performance.* Cambridge University Press, 1990.

Odendaal, André. *The Founders: The Origins of the ANC and the Struggle for Democracy in South Africa.* Jacana Media, 2012.

Pauw, Jacques. *The President's Keepers: Those Keeping Zuma in Power and out of Prison.* Tafelberg, 2017.

Penn, Nigel. *The Forgotten Frontier: Colonist and Khoisan on the Cape's Northern Frontier in the 18th Century.* Ohio University Press, 2006.

Posel, Deborah. *The Making of Apartheid, 1948–1961: Conflict and Compromise.* Clarendon Press, 1991.

Ross, Robert. *Status and Respectability in the Cape Colony, 1750–1870: A Tragedy of Manners.* Cambridge University Press, 1999.

Saunders, Christopher. *The Making of the South African Past: Major Historians on Race and Class.* David Philip, 1988.

Smith, Iain R. *The Origins of the South African War, 1899–1902.* Longman, 1996.

Smith, Janet. *Patrice Motsepe: An Appetite for Disruption.* Jonathan Ball Publishers, 2022.

Southall, Roger. *Liberation Movements in Power: Party and State in Southern Africa.* James Currey, 2013.

Turrell, Robert Vicat. *Capital and Labour on the Kimberley Diamond Fields, 1871–1890.* Cambridge University Press, 1987.

Vartavarian, Mesrob. "Entangled Oligarchies: Structure, Agency and Rent Seeking in South Africa." *Africa* 93, no. 4 (2023): 562–78.

Veracini, Lorenzo. *Settler Colonialism: A Theoretical Overview.* Palgrave Macmillan, 2012.

Worger, William H. *South Africa's City of Diamonds: Mine Workers and Monopoly Capitalism in Kimberley, 1867–1895.* Yale University Press, 1987.

Index

missionaries and mission stations, 42, 44–45, 51, 58, 63, 78
Mnangagwa, Emmerson, 32–33
Modise, Joe, 104, 120–21
Moi, Daniel arap, 26–29
Moloi-Motsepe, Precious, 126
monopolies and monopoly profits, 14–15, 72–73, 103, 151n12
Morgan, J. P., 96
Moshoeshoe, King, 62–63
Motlana, Nthato, 123
Motsepe, Patrice, 124–26
Movement for Democratic Change, 31–32
Mozambique, 59, 92, 106, 108, 124
Mpande, 54, 61–62
Mpumalanga Province, 131, 132–33
Mthethwa confederacy, 58–59
Mugabe, Grace, 32
Mugabe, Robert, 30–33
Mvelaphanda Group, 126–27
Mzilikazi, 54, 59–60, 62

Namibia, 57, 83
Natal and Port Natal, 50–51, 60, 77, 78
National Empowerment Corporation, 124
nationalism / Black nationalism: and apartheid's decline and rise of protest elite and African empowerment, 107–12; apartheid's end and overthrowing white-minority rule by, 112–15; Black Consciousness movement and, 106–7, 126; economic and capitalist intentions of, 13–14, 90, 97, 111–15, 146; education of leaders of movement for, 78, 97; as fig leaf for state socialism, 14; mass protest tactics of, 19; political protection from threats of, 20; and Rupert's proposal for coexistence of Afrikaner and Black middle class, 101

National Party (NP), 94–95, 98–99, 101, 103, 105, 110–11, 112, 114, 115, 117, 120
National Union of Mineworkers (NUM), 109
Native Lands Act, 97
Native Trust and Land Act, 97
Ndwandwe, 59
neopatrimonialism, 20–24, 34, 152n19, 153n21
New African Investments Limited (NAIL), 123–24, 127–28
Nigeria, 124
Nkobi, Thomas, 114
Nkomo, Joshua, 30, 31
Northam Platinum, 127
North West Province, 131, 132
Nyanda, Siphiwe, 120–21

Odinga, Oginga, 26
Odinga, Raila, 27–28
Ohlange Institute, 78
Oppenheimer, Ernest, 96, 101, 108
Oppenheimer, Harry, 101–3, 128, 168n40
Oppenheimer, Nicky, 128, 171n26
Orange Free State republic, 54, 58, 63, 83–86, 102–3, 131–32

Paris Evangelical Missionary Society, 63
path dependency, 14, 150–51n11
Patriotic Alliance (PA), 140, 141–42
Pedi kingdom, 54–55, 74–75, 77
Phala Phala scandal, 138
Philippolis, 58
Phosa, Matthews, 129
Pietermaritzburg, 79
platinum mines, 127, 133
political violence and assassinations, 60, 107, 129, 132–33
politics: ANC dominance in unity government, 114, 116–17, 118; Black exclusion from political

wealth: access to through rent seeking, 117; concentration of for white minority, 88; diamond mining profits and, 68, 70–73; and global factors in inequality, 33; military mobilization and accumulation of, 16–18, 37; and mining profits and power of elites, 66; oligarchs and Black political elites and defense and accumulation of, 13–14, 19–20, 90, 113–14, 122–28, 143–44, 147–48; race and accumulation of, 9–10

wheat farms, 11, 40, 52

white minority: apartheid's end and overthrowing of rule of, 112–15; benefits of industrial production for, 88; concentration of wealth for, 88; exploitation by racial division under rule of, 146–48; and fight for white worker empowerment, 90–98; and intrawhite tension and consolidation of British imperial domination, 66; material affluence under rule of, 145–46; prosperity of, 146; subordination of African majority to, 145–46; violence and reform under Botha to preserve, 110–11; white welfare state for, 89–90

wine farms and wine making, 11, 40, 52–53

Wolseley, Garnet, 77

workers' revolution, 13

World Cup, 131, 132

Xhosa-speaking peoples/communities, 17, 42, 47–50, 53–54, 75, 77

Zambia, 106

Zille, Helen, 142

Zimbabwe, 21, 23, 29–33, 60, 145

Zimbabwe African National Union (ZANU), 30, 31

Zimbabwe African National Union-Patriotic Front (ZANU-PF), 24, 30–33, 155n36

Zimbabwe African People's Union (ZAPU), 30–31

Zondo Commission, 137, 173n43

Zulu-Boer War, 61, 161n52

Zulu kingdom and Zululand, 51, 58–62, 75, 77, 78, 110

Zuma, Duduzane, 142

Zuma, Jacob: ANC leadership role of, 106, 113, 167n28; arms deal role of, 120–21, 128–29; corruption and, 128–29; deputy presidency of, 120–21, 128–29; economic predation and elite fragmentation under presidency of, 20, 128–36, 143–44; exile of, 106; expulsion of from ANC, 142; graft and corruption under, 20, 120–21, 128–36, 143–44; Gupta family association with, 130–33, 134–36; imprisonment of, 106; jailing of, 137; management of finances of by Shaik, 114, 121; MKP established by, 138–41, 142; resignation of, 136